Coleridge and Kantian Ideas
in England, 1796–1817

Also Available From Bloomsbury

Coleridge and German Philosophy, Paul Hamilton
Coleridge, Revision and Romanticism, Ve-Yin Tee
Romanticism, Literature and Philosophy, Simon Swift
The Reception of S. T. Coleridge in Europe, Edited by Elinor Schaffer
and Edoardo Zuccato
Kant's Concept of Genius: Its Origin and Functon in the Third Critique, Paul W. Bruno
British Idealism: A Guide for the Perplexed, David Boucher and Andrew Vincent

Coleridge and Kantian Ideas in England, 1796–1817

Coleridge's Responses to German Philosophy

Monika Class

B L O O M S B U R Y

LONDON · NEW DELHI · NEW YORK · SYDNEY

Bloomsbury Academic

An imprint of Bloomsbury Publishing Plc

50 Bedford Square	175 Fifth Avenue
London	New York
WC1B 3DP	NY 10010
UK	USA

www.bloomsbury.com

First published 2012

British Library Cataloguing-in-Publication Data
A catalogue record for this book is available from the British Library.

ISBN: HB: 978-1-4411-8075-9

Library of Congress Cataloging-in-Publication Data
A catalog record for this book is available at the Library of Congress.

Typeset by Deanta Global Publishing Services, Chennai, India

To Raúl, Heidi und Walter

Contents

Acknowledgements

This book is based on the doctoral dissertation that I completed in 2008. I thank the funding bodies which have provided the financial support to conduct this research: the Daimler-Benz Foundation, the Arts and Humanities Research Council and, in the last stretch before the completion of this monograph, the European Union. Moreover, I am indebted to the institutions that have nurtured this work: Balliol College (University of Oxford), King's College London and Otto-Friedrich Universität, Bamberg.

The exchange of ideas described in this thesis also reflects my experience while working on this project. I am deeply grateful to all those people who supported my work. My doctoral supervisor Fiona Stafford and my college adviser Seamus Perry gave crucial advice and paid attention to minute details. Nicholas Halmi and Daniel N. Robinson provided additional guidance and support during a decisive stage of my work, as did in earlier stages Lucy Newlyn, Matthew Scott and Duncan Wu. The late Jonathan Wordsworth, Christoph Bode, and Nicholas Roe encouraged me, at a very early stage of my studies, to participate in conferences that turned out to be essential for the progress of my work. Felicity James, Jon Mee, Mark Crosby, David Fallon and David O'Shaughnessy helped to shape my ideas on British political and religious dissent. Angela Esterhammer shared her work about Joseph Johnson. Sally Bayley, William May and Andrew Blades were encouraging readers. Michael O'Neill and Fredrick Burwick have done much to lend support to my continued work on Coleridge and Kant after the completion of my doctoral degree. Over the past year, Daniel Carey, Neil Vickers, David Duff, Anthony Harding and Paul Hamilton helped to transform the project through their respective interest and recommendations. Countless other people have assisted and encouraged me to think about this book in different ways. My gratitude extends to all of them and is not limited to those named on this page.

I must also thank Helmut Rohlfing from the Niedersächsische Staats- und Universitätsbibliothek Göttingen, and the director of the Dr Williams's Library London, David Wykes, as well as the staffs of the Bodleian Library, the British Library, Senate House Library, the Fitzwilliam Museum and the Munich and Berlin Staatsbibliothek.

I have published some of the materials that Chapter 3 is based on before, in part under the title 'Coleridge and the Radical Roots of Critical Philosophy' in *Wordsworth Circle* 40 (2007), 51–55, and in part in the essay 'Coleridge, the Early Mediators of Kant and the Sensuous Departure from the Categorical Imperative', *Grasmere 2008: Selected papers from the Wordsworth Summer Conference,* ed. Richard Gravil, Penrith: Humanities-Ebooks, 2009, 22–37. In 2007, I published the article 'Dr J. A. O'Keeffe: Kantian Philosophy – Life, Work and Legacy' in *Eighteenth-Century Ireland* 22 (2007), 206–14, which informs my analysis of O'Keeffe and his connection with F. A. Nitsch in Chapter 1. I thank the editors and publishers, in particular Richard Gravil, Marilyn

Gaull and Eoin Magennis, for permission to redeploy the materials. I also thank Bloomsbury for all their support in producing this book.

This book is dedicated to my husband, Raúl Acosta, and my parents, Heidi and Walter Class, their sustaining energy, affection and inspiration.

London
15 March 2012   Monika Class

List of Abbreviated Titles

Coleridge's collected works

The Collected Works and the *Notebooks* are published by Routledge in London and elsewhere (with the exception of the first two volumes of the *Notebooks*, published by Pantheon Books), and by Princeton University Press. *The Collected Letters* are published by Clarendon Press in Oxford. In the text, volume numbers are indicated in capital Roman numbers.

Aids	*Aids to Reflection* ed. by John Beer, 1993.
Biographia	*Biographia Literaria or Biographical Sketches of My Literary Life and Opinions*, ed. by James Engell and W. Jackson Bate, 2 vols, 1983.
Church and State	*On the Constitution of Church and State,* ed. by John Colmer, 1976.
Essays	*Essays on His Times,* ed. by David V. Erdman, 3 vols, 1978.
Friend	*The Friend,* ed. by Barbara E. Rook, 2 vols, 1969.
Opus Maximum	*Opus Maximum*, ed. by Thomas McFarland with the assistance of Nicholas Halmi, 2002.
PW	*Poetical Works*, ed. by. J. C. C. Mays, 3 vols (in 2 parts each), 2001.
Shorter Works	*Shorter Works and Fragments,* ed. by H. J. Jackson and J. R. de J. Jackson, 2 vols, 1995.
Lay Sermons	*Lay Sermons,* ed. by R. J. White, 1972.
Lectures 1795	*Lectures 1795 on Politics and Religion,* ed. by Lewis Patton and Peter Mann, 1971.
Lectures 1808–19	*Lectures 1808–19 on Literature,* ed. by R. A. Foakes, 2 vols, 1987.
Lectures 1818–19	*Lectures 1818–19 on the History of Philosophy,* ed. by J. R. de Jackson, 2 vols, 2000.
Letters	*The Collected Letters of Samuel Taylor Coleridge,* ed. by Earl Leslie Griggs, 6 vols, 1956–71.

Logic	*Logic,* ed. by J. R. de J. Jackson, 1981.
Marginalia	*(a) Marginalia,* vols I–II, ed. by George Whalley, 1980–84; *(b) Marginalia,* vols III–VI, ed. by H. J. Jackson and George Whalley, 1992–2001.
Notebooks	*(a) Notebooks,* Vols I–III (each in 2 parts), ed. by Kathleen Coburn, 1957–73 (b) *Notebooks,* vol. IV (in 2 parts), ed. by Kathleen Coburn and Merton Christensen, 1990 (c) *Notebooks,* vol. V (in 2 parts), ed. by Kathleen Coburn and Anthony Harding, 2002.
Table Talk	*Table Talk,* ed. by Carl Woodring, 2 vols, 1990.
Watchman	*The Watchman,* ed. by Lewis Patton, 1970.

Kant's works

Short titles refer to Kant's works in the German Academy edition (1900 to date) followed by the short title for the respective English translation in the *Cambridge Edition of the Works of Immanuel Kant* published by Cambridge University Press in Cambridge.

Kant's *Kritik der reinen Vernunft* (*Critique of Pure Reason*) is cited by the page numbers of the first (1781) and the second (1787) edition as recorded on the margins of the German Academy edition, for example, *KrV* A 226 or *KrV* B 278, respectively. (Accordingly, *CpR* A 226 or *CpR* B 278 refers to the same title in translation. The numbers do not indicate page numbers in the Academy edition.) In all other works by Kant the numbers in quotations (preceded by 'p.' and 'pp.', respectively) refer to the page numbers in the German Academy edition *Kant's gesammelte Schriften* by the Royal Prussian (later German) Academy of Sciences. Thanks to the recent *Cambridge Edition of Kant's Work*, page numbers in the German Academy edition and the marginal numbers in the respective English translation are now congruent, for example, volume VI and page 190 in the Academy edition corresponds to the marginal number 6: 190 in the translation in the Cambridge edition.

Akk XI	*Kant's Briefwechsel, 1789–94, Kant's gesammelte Werke,* Band XI, ed. by Vereinigung wissenschaftlicher Verleger, Berlin und Leipzig: Walter de Gruyter, 1922.
Correspondence	*Correspondence,* ed. and trans. by Arnulf Zweig, 1999.
Akk XIII	*Kant's Briefwechsel, Anmerkungen und Register, Kant's gesammelte Werke,* Band XIII, ed. by Vereinigung wissenschaftlicher Verleger, Berlin und Leipzig: Walter de Gruyter, 1922.
Anthropologie	*Anthrologie in pragmatischer Hinsicht* in *Kant's gesammelte Werke,* Band VII, ed. by königlich preußischen Akademie der Wissenschaften, Berlin: Georg Reimer, 1917, pp. 117–335.

Anthropology	*Anthropology from a Pragmatic Point of View*, trans. and ed. by Robert B. Louden, intro. by Manfred Kühn, 2006.
Anthro Vorlesung	*Kant's Vorlesungen, Vorlesungen über Anthrologie, Kant's gesammelte Werke*, Band XXV (2 vols, 25.1 and 25.2), ed. by Akademie der Wissenschaften zu Göttingen, Berlin: Walter de Gruyter, 1997.
Aufklärung	'Beantwortung der Frage: Was heißt Aufklärung?' in *Kant's gesammelte Werke*, Band VIII, ed. by königlich preußischen Akademie der Wissenschaften, Berlin und Leipzig: Walter de Gruyter, 1923, pp. 33–42.
Enlightenment	'An answer to the question: What is enlightenment?' in *Practical Philosophy*, trans. and ed. by Mary J. Gregor, 1996, pp. 11–22.
Ewiger Frieden	*Zum Ewigen Frieden* in *Kant's gesammelte Werke*, Band VIII, ed. by königlich preußischen Akademie der Wissenschaften, Berlin und Leipzig: Walter de Gruyter, 1923, pp. 341–86.
Perpetual Peace	*Towards Perpetual Peace* in *Practical Philosophy*, trans. and ed. by Mary J. Gregor, 1996, pp. 311–51
Gemeinspruch	*Über den Gemeinspruch: Das mag in der Theorie richtig sein, taugt aber nicht für die Praxis* in *Kant's gesammelte Werke*, Band VIII, ed. by königlich preußischen Akademie der Wissenschaften, Berlin und Leipzig: Walter de Gruyter, 1923, pp. 273–313.
Common Saying	*On the Common Saying: That may be Correct in Theory, but it is of no Use in Practice* in *Practical Philosophy*, trans. and ed. by Mary J. Gregor, 1996, pp. 273–309.
Grundlegung	*Grundlegung zur Metaphysik der Sitten* in *Kant's gesammelte Werke*, Band IV, ed. by königlich preußischen Akademie der Wissenschaften, Berlin: Georg Reimer, 1911, pp. 385–463.
Groundwork	*Groundwork of the Metaphysics of Morals* in *Practical Philosophy*, trans. and ed. by Mary J. Gregor, 1996, pp. 37–108.
Idee	'Idee zu einer allgemeinen Geschichte in weltbürgerlicher Absicht' in *Kant's gesammelte Werke*, Band VIII, ed. by königlich preußischen Akademie der Wissenschaften, Berlin und Leipzig: Walter de Gruyter, 1923, pp. 15–31.
KdU	*Kritik der Urtheilskraft* in *Kant's gesammelt Werke*, Band V, ed. by königlich preußischen Akademie der Wissenschaften, Berlin: Georg Reimer, 1913, pp. 165–475.
CJ	*Critique of the Power of Judgment*, ed. by Paul Guyer, trans. by Paul Guyer and Eric Matthews, 2000.

KpV	*Kritik der Praktischen Vernunft* in *Kant's gesammelte Werke*, Band V, ed. by königlich preußischen Akademie der Wissenschaften, Berlin: Georg Reimer, 1913, pp. 1–163.
CpracR	*Critique of Practical Reason* in *Practical Philosophy*, trans. and ed. by Mary J. Gregor, 1996, pp. 137–271.
KrV	*Kritik der reinen Vernunft, Zweite Auflage 1787* [*KrV* B] in *Kant's gesammelt Werke*, Band III, ed. by königlich preußischen Akademie der Wissenschaften, Berlin: Georg Reimer, 1911.
	Kritik der reinen Vernunft, Erste Auflage 1781 [*KrV* A] in *Kant's gesammelt Werke*, Band IV, ed. by königlich preußischen Akademie der Wissenschaften, Berlin: Georg Reimer, 1911, pp. 1–238.
CpR	*Critique of Pure Reason*, trans. and ed. by Paul Guyer and Allen W. Wood, 1998.
Logik Vorlesung	*Kant's Vorlesungen, Vorlesungen über Logik, Kant's gesammelte Werke*, Band XXIV (2 vols, 24.1 and 24.2), ed. by Akademie der Wissenschaften zu Göttingen, Berlin: Walter de Gruyter, 1966.
Logic Lecture	*Lectures on Logic*, trans. and ed. by J. Michael Young, 1992.
Orientiren	*Was heißt: Sich im Denken orientiren?* in *Kant's gesammelte Werke*, Band VIII, ed. by königlich preußischen Akademie der Wissenschaften, Berlin und Leipzig: Walter de Gruyter, 1923, pp. 131–47.
Orient	*What Does it Mean to Orient Oneself in Thinking?* in *Religion and Rational Theology*, trans. and ed. by Allen W. Wood and George di Giovanni, 1996, pp. 1–18.
Reflexionen	*Reflexionen zur Anthropologie* in *Kant's gesammelte Werke*, Band XV, ed. by königlich preußischen Akademie der Wissenschaften, Berlin und Leipzig: Walter de Gruyter, 1923, pp. 55–654.
Religion	*Die Religion innerhalb der Grenzen der bloßen Vernunft* in *Kant's gesammelte Werke*, Band VI, ed. königlich preußischen Akademie der Wissenschaften, Berlin: Georg Reimer, 1914, pp. 1–190.
Religion 2	*Religion within the Boundaries of Mere Reason* in *Religion and Rational Theology*, trans. and ed. by Allen W. Wood and George di Giovanni, 1996, pp. 39–231.

Schiller's works

Schiller	Friedrich Schiller, *Schillers Werke Nationalausgabe*, ed. by Julius Petersen, Lieselotte Blumenthal, Benno von Wiese, Siegfried Seidel, 42 vols, Weimar: Hermann Böhlaus Nachfolger, 1940–2003.

Wordsworth's works

W Prose	William Wordsworth, *The Prose Works of William Wordsworth*, ed. by W. J. B. Owen and Jan Worthington Smyser, Oxford: Clarendon Press, 1974.
Prelude	William Wordsworth, *The Prelude: Four Texts (1798, 1799, 1805, 1850)*, ed. by Jonathan Wordsworth, London: Penguin, 1995.
Lyrical Ballads	William Wordsworth and Samuel Taylor Coleridge, *Lyrical Ballads*, ed. by R. L. Brett and A. R. Jones, London: Routledge, 1991.

Introduction

Coleridge and Kantian ideas in England, 1796–1817

This book reconsiders Samuel Taylor Coleridge's relationship with the philosophy of Immanuel Kant (1724–1804). It contends that when critical philosophy first arrived in England, it had a greater impact on the native culture than is commonly recognized; Coleridge's relation to Kant did not exist in a vacuum, nor was Coleridge a singular connoisseur followed only in the next generation by Thomas de Quincey and Thomas Carlyle, but he was a member of the radical and dissenting networks in which Kantian ideas had been circulating roughly since 1793. Immanuel Kant's philosophy is known to have initiated, among other philosophical and cultural phenomena, an entire movement that became known as early German Romanticism. Nineteenth-century writers and twentieth-century scholars have credited Coleridge with the role as the single most important mediator between German and British Romanticism. The biblical scholar and theologian Fenton John Anthony Hort (1818–92) observed that 'the popular impression about Coleridge's philosophy represents him almost solely in his relation to Kant . . . Here again a blind instinct has undoubtedly taken a right direction' (1856, p. 319). Thomas Carlyle noted poignantly that Coleridge 'was thought to hold, he alone in England, the key of German and other Transcendentalisms' (1851, p. 69). Coleridge contributed a great deal to the common image of Kant in British culture as a preserver of existing social order. The present study recovers the genealogy of early Kantianism in England and thus lays open Coleridge's ultimate reversal of Kant's political stance.

Some facts

Coleridge conceived of his plan to learn German in order to read and translate a number of German authors including 'Kant, the great german [sic] Metaphysician' in May 1796 (*Letters* I, p. 209). Although translations of Kant's writings had appeared in English since 1796, knowledge of German was necessary to read and study Immanuel Kant's three *critiques*, for the translations appeared only after Coleridge's death in 1834. The second of the three *critiques*, the *Critique of Practical Reason* (*Kritik der praktischen Vernunft*, 1788), appeared in an incomplete translation (*KpV* pp. 19–42, 71–107) by J. W. Semple as part of *Metaphysics of Ethics* in Edinburg and Hamburg in 1836 (Kant 1836a; Boswell 1991, pp. 235, 239). After that, the *Critique of Pure Reason* (*Kritik der reinen Vernunft*, 1781), or *first critique*, appeared anonymously in 1838 (Kant 1838) and later with the translator's name, Francis Haywood, in the second edition of 1848

(Kant 1848); J. M. D. Meiklejohn's translation of it appeared in 1845 (Boswell 1991, p. 236). The *Critique of the Power of Judgment (Kritik der Urteilskraft*, 1790), or *third critique*, was not published until the Irish scholar J. H. Bernard gave a full translation of the *Kritik of Judgment* more than a hundred years after the first publication (Kant 1892; Boswell 1991, p. 237). Yet, despite the absence of translations of the *three critiques* in 1790s Britain, one of Kant's shorter writings as well as expositions of his works were readily available in English for non-German speakers like Coleridge before 1798 (see Chapter 1).

It was in May 1796 that Coleridge informed Tom Poole about his plans for Jena. This date tellingly coincides with the time when Friedrich August Nitsch published his lectures about critical philosophy under the title *A General and Introductory View of Professor Kant concerning Man, the World and the Deity* (Nitsch 1796; Micheli 1990, p. 259). At the time, Coleridge was also corresponding regularly with a member of Nitsch's Kantian Society in London: John Thelwall (Roe 1990, p. 68).[1] This leading spokesman of the London Corresponding Society wrote on the margins of his copy of *Biographia Literaria* that he had several philosophical discussions with Nitsch (Pollin 1970, p. 92). Nitsch's pamphlet was advertised and reviewed favourably by the liberal press (Micheli 1990, pp. 266–73). The Unitarian minister William Enfield recommended Nitsch's work (*Monthly Review* 22 [1796], pp. 15–18). Another supporter of Nitsch's work was Coleridge's Bristol mentor, Dr Thomas Beddoes (1760–1808). He reviewed Nitsch's exposition in the *Monthly Magazine* and advocated the translation of Kant's works in a letter to the editor written on 28 March and published in May 1796 (*Monthly Magazine* 1 [1796], pp. 265–7). Beddoes had discussed Kant's epistemology three years earlier in his *Observations on the Nature of Demonstrative Evidence* (1793), and in August 1796, he reviewed Kant's *Zum Ewigen Frieden* (1795). The pamphlet was translated and published under the title *Perpetual Peace* by Vernor and Hood in London in October (Kant 1796; Micheli 1990, p. 232). Kant's pamphlet, which proposed a league of nations, was the first of Kant's texts to be translated into English. Its composition coincided with, and was possibly inspired by, the Treaty of Basel in 1795 – the Prussian peace treaty with Revolutionary France – and argued for opposition to the war. *Zum Ewigen Frieden* was an immediate success in Prussia as well as abroad; a second edition followed the first in brief succession, illegal print-offs circulated, and the work was translated into French, English and Danish a year after its first publication (Klemme 1992, p. lii; Malter 1984, p. 82). As England was still at war with Revolutionary France, however, the professed cosmopolitanism in Kant's *Perpetual Peace* smacked of treason in the eyes of many British counter-revolutionaries. For this and other reasons, which I will explain, Kant's works were generally subsumed under the label 'Jacobin'. Radicals and religious dissenters like Joseph Johnson did much for the Anglo-German exchange and especially for the transmission of the new German philosophy. Johnson's paper, the *Analytical Review*, regularly printed translated excerpts from the Jena *Allgemeine Literatur-Zeitung*.[2] Another committed advocate of Kant's philosophy was the Irish doctor J. A. O'Keeffe. He caused a minor scandal in late 1795 by publishing his pamphlet *An Essay on the Progress of Human Understanding* (O'Keeffe 1795). The Irish radical had appropriated Kantian philosophy as part of his attack on the monarchy.

This book concurs with scholars who have dated Coleridge's study of the *first critique* in German to 1800 and 1801, even as it disagrees with the standard view which conflates this date with the beginning of Coleridge's perusal of Kantian texts (Wellek 1931, p. 71; Orsini 1969, p. 47; Ashton 1980, pp. 36–48; Coleridge 2002, p. 163; Hamilton 2007, p. 13; Perry in Coleridge 2002, p. 163). Coleridge read Kant's *Kritik der reinen Vernunft* in German sometime after his return from Germany in June 1799. The textual evidence consists mainly of three pieces: two letters to Poole, one dated to 13 February 1801, when Coleridge mentioned in passing that '— I turn at times half reluctantly from Leibnitz or Kant even to read a smoking new newspaper/ such a purus putus Metaphysicus am I become' (*Letters* II, p. 676), and another letter dated to 'Monday Night [16 March 1801]' (*Letters* II, p. 706), and a notebook entry (*Notebooks* I, §887). Coburn has suggested that this notebook entry refers to Kant's Latin work *De Mundi Sensibilis* (*Notebooks [Notes]* I, §887), a publication that Coleridge recommended to Mr. Pryce in 1818 for containing 'the *Germs* of all the great works published by him [Kant] forty years afterwards – De formis Mundi intelligibilis et sensibilis' (*Letters* IV, p. 851). I agree, however, with Kathleen Wheeler and Raimonda Modiano that the source of Coleridge's Kantian studies in the winter of 1800 and 1801 was probably the *Critique of Pure Reason* (*Marginalia* III, p. 241). For Coleridge recorded a thought that refers to the ' "Transcendental Aesthetic" [in the *first critique*, which] concerns the *a priori* elements of sensible perceptions' (Guyer 2006, p. 53): 'Space – is it merely another word for the perception of a capability of additional magnitude – or does this very perception presuppose the idea of Space? – The latter is Kant's opinion' (*Notebooks* I, §887). In the 'Transcendental Aesthetic', Kant argued that the notion of space (besides that of time) constitutes a necessary condition of our sensibility. Coleridge's statement appears to refer to the passage that 'Der Raum ist eine nothwendige Vorstellung, *a priori*, die allen äußeren Anschauungen zum Grunde liegt' (*KrV* A 24; 'Space is a necessary representation, *a priori,* that is the ground of all outer intuitions' [*CpR* A 24]). Later on, in 1803, Coleridge read Kant's ethics, taking detailed notes from the *Grundlegung der Metaphysik der Sitten* (*Groundwork of the Metaphysics of Morals*, 1785*)* and *Metaphysik der Sitten* (*Metaphysics of Morals*, 1797) (*Notebooks* I, §1705, 1710–11, 1721 and 1723; Orsini 1969, pp. 149–52). Coleridge continued studying Kant. Copies of Kant's works with Coleridge's autograph commentary are preserved at the British Library and in University College, London, and published in the Bollingen Series of Coleridge's Collected Works. There we find Coleridge's annotations of *Anthropolog[ie] in pragmatischer Hinsicht, Critik der reinen Vernunft, Critik der Urtheilskraft, Grundlegung zur Metaphysik der Sitten, Logik, Die Metaphysik der Sitten, Metaphysische Anfangsgründe der Naturwissenschaft, Die Religion innerhalb der Grenzen der blossen Vernunft* and various shorter pieces published in *Sammlung einiger bisher unbekannt gebliebener Schriften* and in *Vermischte Schriften* (*Marginalia* III, pp. viii, 236–366). Coleridge's reading of works by and on Kant was extensive and exceeded the titles on this list. For instance, Coleridge studied Kant's moral philosophy in 1803 (Chapter 3) and started to assimilate the distinction between Reason and Understanding in 1806 (Chapter 7); in 1808, he used Kant's aesthetics for expounding the naïve in his lectures of the same year (Chapter 5), and subsequently in his *Essays on the Principles of Genial Criticism* (1814) and *Biographia Literaria* (1817) (Chapter 6).

Reappraisal of Coleridge's reception

By revising the assumption of Coleridge's singularity, this book further contends that the investigation of Coleridge's relation to Kant should no longer involve 'originality' as a criterion of intellectual merit. It proposes instead that the early reception of Kant in England is best understood when we appreciate the act of transmission as a form of intellectual interaction and as part of sociability despite the great importance of 'originality' during this particular period. Thus this book makes the controversial move to treat critical philosophy as a subject of serious study as well as of German and English fashionable conversation.

To date, there exists little scholarly awareness of how problematic value judgements on grounds of 'originality' have been for the study of Coleridge's reception of Kant, and of 'reception' studies more widely speaking. Wellek, for instance, regarded 'individuality' as the ultimate measure of a writer's achievement. For Wellek, Coleridge's philosophical thought was overrated because of 'a fundamental lack of real philosophical individuality in Coleridge' (Wellek 1931, p. 66). Since then, if not earlier, scholarship seems divided into two groups depending on the respective affirmation or rejection of Coleridge's 'originality'. John H. Muirhead (1930) and I. A. Richards (1934) disagreed fundamentally with Wellek's negative assessment of Coleridge. Entrenched in the Romantics' cult of genius, originality and individuality, Wellek saw the transmission of ideas as a minor achievement: 'Historically, of course, Coleridge is immensely important and can scarcely be overrated as a transmitter of ideas' (1931, p. 68). Indeed, an author's ultimate merit lies, according to Wellek's opinion, exclusively in individuality. Coleridge deserved, according to Wellek's first monograph, scholarly attention because of his seemingly exceptionally problematic personality: 'Individually as a person, he is so fascinating a problem that he well deserves closer study' (1931, p. 68). Wellek's stipulation of individuality provided also the ground for his dismissal of one of the major figures in this study: the long underestimated disciple of Kant and first Kantian lecturer in England, Friedrich August Nitsch. Assessing Nitsch's treatise superficially, Wellek came to the conclusion that 'the author [Nitsch] seems to have had the understanding of Kant which one can expect from a contemporary who was not himself an original mind and could not see the further implications and problems' (1931, p. 7). The stipulation of 'individuality' and 'originality' as a critical criterion is still palpable in the recent scholarship on Coleridge and Kant by internationally leading experts.[3] While 'individuality' and 'originality' are natural concerns for scholars of European Romanticism mainly because these concepts constitute two major legacies of the period, the concepts are, nonetheless, counterproductive for this type of investigation. From the perspective of 'individuality', Coleridge's reception of German philosophy appears always as a latent accusation of the lack of ingenuity. Elinor Shaffer has shown that Coleridge's engagement with Higher Biblical Criticism and the reinterpretation of major religious text of the West was a 'communal event' (1975, p. 6). The field of British Romanticism is moving beyond its traditional stipulation of individuality as Gillian Russell and Clara Tuite proclaim: '[i]t is our contention that the solitary self has stood for Romanticism for too long' (2002, p. 4). It is time for the studies of Coleridge's reception of German philosophy to relinquish 'individuality' and 'originality' not as a subject of investigation but as a criterion for our assessment of the writers' respective significance and merit.[4]

This book recovers the significance of interaction between the people who were involved in the process of mediating critical philosophy. It lays open that Nitsch wrote his pamphlet based on the conversations he had with the men and women in his audience. It traces Coleridge's conversations with Dr Beddoes. Beyond Coleridge's fear of his audiences and their reaction to German thought (Ashton 1980), this book recaptures an instance when a particular group of listeners in combination with a congenial setting elicited Coleridge's open endorsement of Kant and discussion of scepticism.

Elinor Shaffer, editor-in-chief of the open-ended and multi-volume series on the reception of British authors abroad published by Bloomsbury Books, observes that '[i]t is, of course, always possible, and indeed to be hoped and expected that further aspects of reception will later be uncovered' (2007b, p. x). Traditional reception studies run the danger of being limited to isolated comparisons of texts by canonical authors. Previous Coleridge studies, notably by René Wellek (1931) and Gian N. Orsini (1969), have examined Coleridge's reception of Kant as if it had been sealed off from his native culture. Paul Hamilton in *Coleridge's Poetics* (1983, p. 28) and Nigel Leask in *The Politics of the Imagination in Coleridge's Critical Thought* (1988, p. 83) have rightly criticized this tendency in comparative studies. Wellek's work was partly informed by the view that literature should overcome national boundaries. The influential Czech comparatist and literary historian (born in Vienna) became a proponent of departments of literature (rather than of English, German, etc.) after his emigration to the United States in 1939, having enrolled in a graduate programme in Princeton in 1927 (Procházka 2007, p. 267; Brown 2011, p. 7). He opposed together with Austin Warren in *Theory of Literature* (1949) the idea of national literatures (Brown 2011, p. 7): 'There is just literature' (Wellek and Warren cited in Brown 2011, p. 7). In his first book based on his *habilitation* dissertation of 1930 (at the Charles University, Prague), Wellek followed 'critical reflections of contemporary histories as master narratives of national identities' (Procházka 2007, p. 267); however, the chapter on Coleridge's reception of Kant is devoid of sociocultural analysis.[5] Contrary to this tendency, this book approaches Coleridge's reception of Kant from a position within English culture.

This reconsideration of 'reception' as a concept also entails a movement away from the long-dated linear history of ideas that presupposes a sequence of hitherto unprecedented ideas. The departure from linearity is one of the major reasons why this monograph draws on Michel Foucault. While this study employs a variety of critical approaches including close-reading and formal analyses of narrative and poetic structures, the book has an overall historicist framework. As an interdisciplinary study based on archival research, it applies the causal, diachronic mode of analysis which Foucault termed 'genealogy' in order to 'identify the accidents, the minute deviations – or conversely, the complete reversals – the errors, the false appraisals, and the faulty calculations that give birth to those things that continue to exist and have value for us [like Coleridge's distinction of 'Reason' and 'Understanding']' (Foucault cited in Gutting 2005, p. 49).

Accordingly, I mean by Coleridge's 'reception' of critical philosophy his encounter with, reaction to, and assimilation of Kantian themes (and not of stable, given concepts) either in speech (conversation or lecture) or in writing (printed and unprinted). My concern is not Coleridge's originality but his ability to adopt, to transform, to apply and above all to spread and disseminate.

Changes in Kant scholarship and their relevance for the study of Coleridge's reception

Furthermore, this study does not presuppose the stable meaning of Kant's respective texts, but tries to locate the respective editions alongside their then-current interpretations as specifically in time and place as possible. René Wellek's *Immanuel Kant in England 1793–1838* (1931) represents to date the central study in the field of British reception of critical philosophy. However, Wellek wrote from the perspective that he held the correct interpretation of Kant based on his training in German philosophy and literature by his teacher Otokar Fischer (1883–1938). As Shaffer notes, 'he spoke as an active and convinced Kantian in the present . . . his sense of the impossibility of combining that [British] empiricism with Kantian thought, were moulded in his student days' (2007a, p. 12). This trend in Coleridge reception studies continues in so far as Kant's works alone are thought to provide 'a point of reference that is stable and permanent enough to help locate and trace Samuel Taylor Coleridge's philosophical drift' (Bode 2009, p. 604). This approach is problematic.

To take as fixed points of reference a relatively small part of Kant's works, the Academy edition of which has taken almost a century and is still ongoing, means to disregard the variety of possible interpretations since their composition. In the late eighteenth century, for instance, Kant's account of the religion of practical reason, for which the concepts of supreme good and of evil are central, attracted a great deal of attention, also during the first wave of Kantian publications in England. The fact is critical that, as Otfried Höffe testifies, '[n]either concept [of supreme good and of evil] plays a significant role in present philosophy' (1994, p. 202). The perceived irrelevance of these concepts in the twentieth century (and less so in the twenty-first) appears as a major reason why Wellek's seminal study dismissed Karl Leonhard Reinhold so easily (see Chapter 1): '[n]o wonder that the confusion was transferred to England' (1931, p. 5). Over the past years, and depending on the fraction within Kant scholarship, the highest good is regaining recognition (Beiser 2006), as does the concept of evil (Muchnik 2009) or summum bonum in moral philosophy (Höffe 2010). The resurgence of scholarly interest in Reinhold's work since the 1970s (Lauth 1974) further adds to the revival in scholarly discussion of Kant's concept of practical reason. The problem is that these developments have barely been taken into consideration by studies of Coleridge's reception of Kant.

Structure of this book

The analysis of the historical documents of Kant's early transmission in England shows that the boundaries between disciplines and sub-disciplines were fluid at the time; my study reflects this interconnectedness through the combination of socio-political and hermeneutic-philosophical analyses.[6] The materials are too diverse to only suit one philosophically systematic argument; however, they all support the thesis that the early English materials on Kant exerted a significant influence on Coleridge and his native culture. Therefore, this book is concerned with several fundamental questions. It establishes close links between the Kantian-Reinholdian school and the English dissemination (Chapter 1), Coleridge's predisposition to rational morality and theology (Chapter 2), that, as F. A. Nitsch recognized, the demand for free will provided a niche for Kantian philosophy in mid-1790s England (Chapter 3), that Kant's concept of nature as the guarantee for peace offered Coleridge a possibility to legitimize his sympathies for the French Revolution even after the French expansionist turn in 1798 (Chapter 4), that anti-Kantian publications drove Coleridge into the closet for many years and ironically helped the recognition of the transformative power behind critical philosophy (Chapter 5), that Kant's early concept of genius is key to understanding Coleridge's self-construction as a philosopher of genius (Chapter 6), and that Nitsch primed Coleridge to assimilate the distinction between Reason and Understanding (Chapter 7). As this outline indicates, politics, religion and philosophy went hand in hand during the complex process in which Coleridge became acquainted with critical philosophy; so much so that they were, as I propose, inseparable. This contention challenges the widespread assumption in socio-historical and cultural studies of the late eighteenth and early nineteenth centuries that transcendentalism and politics mutually excluded each other. While there are good reasons for this view, I hope that this study will help not only to explain how this misunderstanding has prevailed for such a long time but also to convince readers to reconsider the relevance of Kant's sociopolitically transformative power in the eighteenth and nineteenth centuries.

Coleridge's reversal of Kant's radical sympathies

Lastly, the present study argues that the young Coleridge was initially attracted to Kant on the grounds of political reform and that the post-Jacobin Coleridge played a formative role in the obfuscation of the sociopolitically transformative power of Kantian principles and their appeal to Enlightenment and reform; indeed, each chapter is driven by desire to recapture the progressive dimension of Coleridge's engagement with Kant. Coleridge's first accidental encounters with Kant through fellow reformers and dissenters in the mid-1790s and ultimately Coleridge's complete reversal of Kant's radical Enlightenment principles into a form of Anglican conservatism constitute a case of what Foucault called a 'false appraisal' or 'faulty calculation' that 'gives birth to' an image that continues to exist and have value for us. I mean the image of Kant as the facilitator of (Coleridge's) conservatism.

We can see how especially Coleridge's critics latched on to the almost caricatural construction of Kant as a preserver of established order and Christian purpose almost from the moment that *Biographia Literaria* appeared. Late nineteenth- and early twentieth-century English responses to Kant spearheaded by the British Idealists have been studied (den Otter 1996, pp. 19–51; Sweet 2010; Boucher and Vincent 2012, pp. 15–29)[7]; my point here is to flag up indicators for one particular legacy of the Coleridgean construction of Kant. Infuriated by Coleridge's alleged apostasy, Hazlitt directed his outrage in his damning review of *Biographia Literaria* (1817) mainly against Coleridge's seemingly new conservative idol: 'As to the great German oracle Kant, we must take the liberty to say, that his system appears to us the most willful and monstrous absurdity that ever was invented' (Hazlitt 1933 XVI, p. 123). Coleridge's Kant was for Hazlitt 'an enormous heap of dogmatical and hardened assertions' (1933 XVI, p. 123). 'The whole theory' as delineated in *Biographia Literaria* consisted in Hazlitt's eyes out of authoritarian claims: 'He [Kant] has but one method of getting over difficulties: - when at a loss to account for any thing, . . . he turns short round upon the inquirer, and says that it is self-evident . . . His whole theory is machinery and scaffolding' (Hazlitt 1933 XVI, pp. 123–4). In the *Blackwood's Magazine* article 'The Last Days of Immanuel Kant', published in 1827, Thomas de Quincey painted a picture of Kant in old age as an easily annoyed, authoritarian and callous person who received the notice of a friend's death typically with such tranquillity that it appeared as hardened indifference (De Quincey 1863, pp. 99–166).[8] By dismissing Kant as a sclerotic conservative, Hazlitt unwittingly helped Coleridge to cover up his radical past. Thomas Carlyle, like De Quincey himself a major disseminator of German philosophy, pitied Coleridge for being trapped in 'the hazy infinitude of Kantean transcendentalism' (1851, p. 73). That Coleridge's Kant seemed utterly incompatible with political radicalism for Carlyle can be seen, for instance, in his belittling amusement over the cofounder of the *Athenaeum* John Sterling (1806–44) and his fascination with Coleridgean thought: 'Nor, with all the Coleridge fermentation, was [Sterling's] democratic Radicalism by any means given up; -though how it was to live if the Coleridgean moonshine took effect, might have been an abstruse question' (1851, p. 83). Although J. S. Mill valued the 'intellectual exertions', he considered 'the doctrines of Coleridge and the Germans . . . erroneous' (1967, p. 115). For him, the ultimate purpose of Coleridge and 'his masters the Germans' was to 'disguise and obscure'; indeed the philosophy was ultimately 'conservative' (Mill 1967, pp. 108, 115) and 'reactionary' (p. 129). Edward Caird (1835–1908) presented Kant in absolute idealist terms since the late 1860s and 1870s (den Otter 1996, p. 14). Caird belonged to the group of largely Oxford-based British Idealists including Thomas Hill Green (1836–82), Francis Herbert Bradley (1846–24), William Wallace (1843–97), Bernard Bosanquet (1848–1923), David George Richtie (1853–1903), John Henry Muirhead (1855–1940) and Sir Henry Jones (1852–1922) (den Otter 1996; Tyler 2012). They were favourably inclined to Coleridge, seeing him often as a significant precursor of their philosophical studies (Muirhead 1930, p. 65; den Otter 1996, p. 15). A similar anti-dualistic take on critical philosophy as that by Coleridge can be seen in Caird's comparison of Kant's philosophy to that of Spinoza, Fichte and Schelling. For Caird, they equally professed approaches to the absolute, '[n]ot only of Spinoza, but also of Kant, of Fichte, and even of Schelling, it might with some truth be said that their absolute is like the lion's den in the fable; for all the footsteps are directed towards it, but none seem to issue from it' (1892 II, p. 515). The British Idealists were experts on the topic and astute critics of late nineteenth-century society (Boucher 2001); as such they were not interested in Kantian caricatures. However, the stipulation of the absolute by Caird, Bardley, Bosanquet, Green and Ritchie perpetuated a concept that encouraged Kant's and Coleridge's critics. For Walter Pater, Coleridge and German transcendentalism, in particular Kant and Schelling, stood for the 'ancient' adherence to the 'absolute': 'Modern thought is distinguished from ancient by its cultivation of the "relative" spirit in place of the "absolute" ' (1922, p. 66). Coleridge's transcendental thought offended, in Pater's view, modern relativism: Coleridge's 'chief offence . . . is an excess of seriousness' (Pater 1922, p. 69). Pater perceptively noted that

> Coleridge's prose writings on philosophy, politics, religion, and criticism, were, in truth, but one element in a whole lifetime of endeavours to present the then recent metaphysics of Germany to English readers, as a legitimate expansion of what has been variously called the a priori, or absolute, or spiritual, or Platonic, view of things. (Pater 1922, p. 81)

Whether Pater was aware of Coleridge's deviations from Kant's dualism is unclear. What Pater criticized about Coleridge's *Aids to Reflection, The Friend, The Biographia* (1922, p. 72) is the underlying theory that struggles to find 'first principles . . . scheming to "apprehend the absolute," to affirm it effectively, to get it acknowledged' (1922, p. 68). According to Pater, Coleridge's German transcendentalism reinforced a system dangerously close to 'absolutism' (Wilson 2008, pp. 171–87). Charges of absolutist, totalizing and authoritarian tendencies by Coleridge critics continued in twentieth century and continue to date.

After the period of heightened interest in Coleridge studies in the 1930s (Lowes 1955 [first published 1927]), I. A. Richards (1962 [first published 1934]) and the ensuing growing appreciation of Coleridge as critic, poet and philosopher in the following decades, harsh critiques of Coleridge regained new prominence in the 1980s under the auspices of New Historicism. In his comparison of Coleridge to Hegel, Jerome McGann detected that Coleridge's 'fundamental weakness' consisted in 'his philosophic, totalizing grasp of cultural history' (1983, p. 44). The 'grasp' was 'totalizing', according to McGann, in so far as it was concerned with comprehending 'that central "idea" of them [historical facts] which balances and reconciles all opposite and discordant qualities' (1983, p. 44). The Coleridgean principle amounted to historical irresponsibility in New Historicist eyes.[9] This criticism seems reminiscent of Hazlitt's eloquent point in his 1817 review of *Biographia Literaria*:

> Mr Coleridge has ever since, from the combined forces of poetic levity and metaphysic bathos, been trying to fly, not in the air, but under ground – playing at hawk and buzzard between sense and nonsense, - floating or sinking in fine Kantean categories, in a state of suspended animation 'twixt dreaming and awake, - quitting the plain ground of 'history and particular facts' for the first butterfly theory, fancy-bred from the maggots of his brain. (Hazlitt 1933 XVI, p. 118)

While Hazlitt was mainly offended by Coleridge's attempt to hide his Jacobin past, his point is similar to McGann's, as both perceive Coleridge's interest in transcendentalism as an impediment to sociopolitical concern.

The charge of reactionary absolutism still informs current criticism of Coleridge and German idealism. Cairns Craig has recently drawn on Edward Caird's 1892 exposition of Kantian metaphysics in the first two volumes of *Essays on Literature and Philosophy* as part of his sociopolitical critique of German idealism (Craig 2007, p. 69). Based exclusively on Caird's absolute idealist exposition and an article by Hutchison Stirling (1884), Craig's chapter 'Kant has not answered Hume' (2007, pp. 41–84), in this context, comes to the unsurprising, but according to Kühn (1983 and 2005) unacceptable, conclusion that Kant, just like Coleridge, was allegedly unaware of the fallacy Hume exposed, namely the paradox of a first or final cause. Craig first proposes the thesis that (1) Coleridge's criticism of Hartley's materialism in the *Biographia* was a disguised attempt to refute Hume's scepticism (Craig 2007, p. 45), (2) Kant did not refute Hume (2007, p. 49) and (3) Coleridge's substitution of Hartley for Hume through Kant consequently amounted to Platonic disdain for human sensibility (2007, p. 55). This alleged disregard is then seen as a sure sign not only of Coleridge's but also of Kant's reactionary politics.

According to the above-cited views, the Germano-Coleridgean school was and is inherently conservative. J. S. Mill once said, 'Now the Germano-Coleridgean doctrine is, in our view of the matter, the result of such a reaction. It expresses the revolt of the human mind against the philosophy of the eighteenth century' (1967, p. 108). The present study complicates and challenges this notion of Coleridge's and Kant's conservative reaction against the Enlightenment by uncovering, for instance, the historical significance of the first Kantian translation *Zum Ewigen Frieden (Towards Perpetual Peace)*. British literary and cultural studies of the Romantic period have barely considered the fact that, although Kant no longer fully subscribed to the Enlightenment idea of progress, he professed that the latter would lead to political justice, including both national and international law. Critical philosophy is and was also concerned with outward events. As Höffe points out, 'it is not at all possible' in Kant's conception of history that the ultimate meaning of these events 'would lie in "inner" progress such as the development of man's moral attitude' (1994, pp. 197–8). This book concomitantly criticizes, as an oversimplification, the notion that a Romantic poet and writer like Coleridge turned completely against Enlightenment thought by taking up Kant's transcendentalism. Contrary to this common view, this book endeavours to recover the radical Enlightenment dimension of first principles in Kant's and Coleridge's early work during a period of profound crisis of human rationality around the turn of the eighteenth century; indeed, it aims to recapture the revolutionary impact of critical philosophy, not only of its radical break with traditional metaphysics but also of its characteristic confidence that the progress of human rationality despite its deficiencies entails sociopolitical reform. In doing so, this book proposes the argument that Coleridge's lasting and influential construction of the allegedly conservative Kant was preceded by his adoption of Kant's radicalism. The 'red thread' that runs through the entire study is the related and new view that the circulation of Kantian ideas, especially in the English democratic and dissenting milieu of the 1790s, had a profound impact not only on Coleridge's response to Kant but also on his thought on politics and religion. The argument of Coleridge's reversal of Kant's radical sympathies in this book builds on the link of Coleridge's reception of Kant with his political activism as a young man.

Developments in previous scholarship

It is important to remember that at the time of Wellek's publication, researchers had limited access to unpublished Coleridge manuscripts; although *Conciones ad Populum* was available in the nineteenth century (Hort 1856, p. 315), it took another 40 years and more until the testimonies of Coleridge's early career as radical lecturer and journalist – the editions of the *Lectures 1795* (1971) by Lewis Patton and Peter Mann, *The Watchman* (1970) by Patton and *Essays on Time* (1978) by David V. Erdman – became available (again) for the public. These publications (and republications) did a great deal to recover Coleridge's revolutionary past and the ways in which it had become obscured (Thompson 1971, p. 926). Coleridge's early political engagement in rational dissent and the movement for constitutional reform has been a matter of intensive research. Following E. P. Thompson's influential enquiry into the movement for constitutional reform in the late eighteenth century in *Making of the Working Class* (1963), Nicholas Roe in *Wordsworth and Coleridge: The Radical Years* (1988) and *The Politics of Nature* (2002) demonstrated Coleridge's adherence to republican principles through the poet's close friendship with William Frend and John Thelwall. Besides Roe, Michael Scrivener has analysed Thelwall's poetry and speeches in *Seditious Allegories: John Thelwall & Jacobin Writing* (2001). Judith Thompson has reconstructed the conversation between Coleridge and John Thelwall in order to expose the myth of domesticity and to 'inviolate imagination in "Frost at Midnight" by laying bare the circumstances of its composition, suggesting that it is a political poem precisely where it is most personal' (1997, p. 428). Nigel Leask's discussion of Coleridge in the 1790s in *The Politics of the Imagination* focused on Pantisocracy and the ideal of a communal, agrarian society in the spirit of Priestley's 'One Life' (1988, pp. 19–45). Ian Wylie's *Young Coleridge and the Philosophers of Nature* traced the connection to the Lunar Society that promoted social reform through scientific advance mainly in Coleridge's 'Religious Musings' (1989). While Jon Mee has examined Coleridge's lack of confidence to subscribe fully to rational enthusiasm (2003, pp. 132–72), he contrasts Coleridge's 'Religious Musings' with Blake's *Europe* in *Dangerous Enthusiasm* in order to gauge the unrestrained radicalism of the latter (1992, pp. 39–46). Stuart Andrews has uncovered even more evidence of how closely the forces of opposition and rational dissent cooperated (2003, pp. 105–46). However, Coleridge's interest in critical philosophy is barely mentioned in these studies, and if so, it appears as a matter independent of, or even opposed to, his early radicalism. As such, the investigation of Coleridge's acquaintance with critical philosophy lags behind the study of Coleridge's early work. This is mainly because *Biographia Literaria* misleadingly conflates Coleridge's philosophical enquiries, especially of German philosophy, with political retirement (Thompson 1969, pp. 149–81). Vice versa, studies of Kant's influence on

Coleridge have concentrated on his later period; justifiably so because Coleridge's time with the Morgans and the Gillmans, who kept his addiction in check, proved to be the most productive phase also for his Kantian enquiries.

Focus of this study

This book, as mentioned above, does not subscribe to a linear conception of history. It is true that the organization of chapters is chronological, but more importantly, it is thematic. Coleridge's acquaintance with Kant did not follow a model of linear progression; tracing this interrupted process has meant for me to select particular moments of engagement preserved in notebook entries and autograph commentaries on books, letters and lecture notes. I have found that sometimes such short or cryptic statements that remained unpublished during Coleridge's lifetime have, in many ways, been as insightful as Coleridge's major publications. Sara Coleridge once observed 'that "the fear of the press is not in them" ' (cited in Vigus 2009, p. 39). Accordingly, each chapter revolves around one central text by Coleridge but is not limited to the respective period of composition. While seventeenth-century authors such as Thomas Hobbes and Ralph Cudworth play a part in this book as do Coleridge's readers in the nineteenth century, this book covers a period of roughly 20 years between late 1795 and early 1796 and 1817, which corresponds to Coleridge's first extant Kantian notebook entry (*Notebooks* I, §249) and the publication of *Biographia Literaria*.

Chapter 1 establishes the significance of the early mediators departing from the first extant article on Kant in the English press in 1787, the year of the popular breakthrough of critical philosophy in Germany. Chapter 2 revisits Coleridge's political activism in Bristol, focusing on his conviction that politics should be based on a first principle in morality. Chapter 3 identifies a notebook entry dated to late 1795 and early 1796 as Coleridge's first extant attempt to capture Kant's categorical imperative. It argues that Kant's moral law as mediated by Nitsch supplemented Coleridge's political lectures at the time. Chapter 4 traces the conceptual affinities between 'France: An Ode' and Kant's *Perpetual Peace* (1796) arguing that Coleridge used Kant's concept of nature as the guarantee for peace and justice as a justification for the violent turn of the French Revolution at least until 1802, when he finally retracted his support for the French Republic. The chapter discloses the radical associations and notional content of Kant. Chapter 5 traces Coleridge's exposure to critical philosophy in Germany, the relentless persecution by the *Anti-Jacobin Review* and the persistent difficulty for Coleridge to speak or write about Kant in public. Chapter 6 discusses the only instance in Coleridge's writings published during his lifetime in which he publicly advocated critical philosophy without a shadow of doubt arguing that it was part of his self-construction as a philosopher of genius. Simultaneously, Chapter 6 uncovers Coleridge's omissions and alterations that suggest a deliberate misrepresentation of Kant as an intimidated aged philosopher. Chapter 7 closes with a circle and examines Coleridge's indebtedness to Nitsch and Reinhold and his appropriation of the distinction between Reason and Understanding not only in the context of his religious thought but also in the context of his endorsement of expedience in politics.

The young Coleridge did not engage directly with the vivid exchange of ideas Scottish philosophers entertained with Germany in the eighteenth century (Oz-Salzberger 1995). Therefore, the present analysis of the early mediators deals exclusively with the intellectual circles in Bristol and London to which Coleridge belonged in the 1790s. The Scottish interest in German literature preceded the English one (Stockley 1929, pp. 29–32). On 21 April 1788, Henry Mackenzie lectured on the merits of German literature in front of the audience of the Royal Society of Scotland, making 'much noise and produc[ing] a powerful effect' (Scott 1902, p. 40). Nor did the German-based translations by the Scottish John Richardson receive particular notice in Coleridge's intellectual circles. Richardson was resident in Germany; his translations were printed there at his own expense and met with utter silence from the press when they finally reached England (Micheli 1993, pp. xiv–xxi; Wellek 1931, pp. 15–20). Richardson's translation of Jakob Sigismund Beck's *The Principles of Critical Philosophy* appeared in 1797, followed by his *Essays and Treatises* (1798-9) and *Metaphysic of Moral* in 1799. In 1819, Richardson published a translation of the *Prolegomena* and *Logic* (Kant 1819). Guiseppe Micheli has shown that the Scotsman's translations of critical philosophy mark an important development in the history of Kant translations (1993, pp. xiv–xxix; 1990, pp. 280-1), but in the context of Coleridge's native background, they are only marginally important. After thorough investigation, another potential source of critical philosophy for Coleridge turned out to have barely any significance. Through Robert Southey, Coleridge was connected with William Taylor, whom he even mentioned in the *Biographia* (I, p. 86; Speck 2006, pp. 73-7). Contrary to John Boening's article (1982, pp. 65–87), I have found that Taylor, who brilliantly translated works by Bürger, Goethe, Lessing and Wieland (D. Chandler 1997b), contributed little constructive criticism for the debate of critical philosophy in 1790s England.[10] Although Taylor aided the cultural exchange with Germany (Maertz 1998, p. 212; Stockoe 1926, pp. 135, 285-7), he disapproved of Kant's speculative philosophy. For Taylor, Kant was the author of a 'very abstruse philosophy and pedantic phraseology' (*Monthly Review* 25 [1798], p. 584). Only in one review, namely on *Perpetual Peace*, did Taylor praise Kant as a 'bold philanthropist' (*Monthly Review* 22 [1797], p. 114). Besides that, he reviewed *Elements of Critical Philosophy* unfavourably expressing his regret about Kant's destructive approach to the rational evidence of God (*Monthly Review* 28 [1799], p. 69). Similar to Taylor, A. F. M. Willich had almost no bearing on Coleridge's acquaintance with critical philosophy. The Scottish mediator of Prussian origin moved to England in 1798 (Poschmann 1963, p. 476). Upon arrival there, he published his *Elements of Critical Philosophy* in the same year. The publication received mixed comments from the *Analytical Review*, by the *Critical Review* and by the *Monthly Review* (Micheli 1990, p. 280). As it mainly compiled English translations of German philosophers, ranging from K. L. Reinhold, J. E. Schulz to E. Schmid (Willich 1798, p. 9), it lacked coherent structure and contained so little instructive information that it most probably neither inspired Coleridge nor any of his friends to study Kant. Willich is nevertheless significant in this study because of his vehement defence of Kant's philosophy against the accusations by Abbé Barruel (Chapter 1).

Two of the most important contributions to the early transmission of critical philosophy in London and Bristol were the publications by Thomas Beddoes – the pamphlet and lectures by F. A. Nitsch and the first translation of *Perpetual Peace*. These materials reveal the popularity of Kantian concepts that have been highly controversial in the twentieth century, such as the highest good that Kant elaborated in *Critique of Practical Reason* or the postulates of empirical thinking in the *Critique of Pure Reason*. They also uncover the great significance of Kant's republican and cosmopolitan views as published in *Perpetual Peace*. None of these topics has received due attention either in the field of British Romanticism or in the study of the effective history ('Wirkungsgeschichte') of Kant in eighteenth- and nineteenth-century Britain.

Alongside the important, though hitherto neglected, works by Beddoes, Nitsch and the anonymous translator of *Perpetual Peace*, the authors of numerous contemporary reviews, articles and satires played a major role in the dissemination of Kant. Local English newspapers and magazines include Kantian materials ranging from mere title translations over brief abstracts to detailed articles. One of the periodicals deserves special attention in the context of the initial transmission of critical philosophy in England: the *Monthly Review*. The review paper is known as an important mediator of German literature and philosophy (D. Chandler 1997a, p. 359). Scholars, such as Derek Roper and Antonia Forster, have repeatedly stressed its significance in late eighteenth-century England, especially in relation to the later *Edinburgh Review* (Roper 1978; Forster 2003). Ralph Griffiths's paper contains occasional, but detailed, abstracts of German philosophy and literature from 1790 onwards (Micheli 1990, pp. 213–31). The *Monthly Review* published, for instance, Beddoes's distinguished reviews of Kant, Schiller and Goethe between 1796 and 1798.[11] The editor's copy of the paper is available at the Bodleian Library and makes it possible to identify the authors of the anonymous review articles without the help of Nangle's index of the paper (Nangle 1955 II).[12] Alongside the *Monthly Magazine* and *Analytical Review*, the *Monthly Review* is representative of the response to critical philosophy from the liberal side of the English readership, while the publications of the *Anti-Jacobin Review and Magazine* epitomize the counter-revolutionary reaction. The latter is an important focus for this study because it provided one of the reasons for Coleridge's retrospective dissociation from the early mediators of critical philosophy. As the examples of the *Monthly Review* and the *Anti-Jacobin Review* show, the significance of the individual articles and reviews depended largely on the practices and politics of respective periodicals at the time. My work is informed by a number of publications in this area. Alvin Sullivan's first two volumes of *British Literary Magazines* (1983a and b) have provided insights in the political orientation of various reviews ranging from the *Analytical, Critical, English, Monthly Review*, the *Monthly Magazine* and the *British Critic* to the *Anti-Jacobin Review and Magazine*. Kevin Gilmartin's *Print Politics* (1996), Jon Klancher's *The Making of the English Audiences 1790–1832* (1987) and Derek Roper's *Reviewing before the Edinburgh 1788–1802* (1978) have informed my understanding of the political climate, how the reviewing papers operated and how they positioned themselves in relation to each other and to the audience. These influential studies have shown that it is possible to segment journals and reviews into different sociopolitical groups. They have outlined wide-ranging networks and pinpointed political tensions that are integral to my analysis of the sociopolitical undertone of various 1790s reviews of Kantian philosophy. While these studies of networks and groups inform the present book, I have not attempted to give a sociological account of reading Kant in England between 1796 and 1817. The figure with whom this study is ultimately concerned in all its breath is Samuel Taylor Coleridge and his relationship with persons, religious or political groups as well as his contributions to, conversations about and reading of publications (books, pamphlet, articles) and unpublished manuscripts.

Coleridge's reception of Kant has traditionally been studied under the heading of 'Coleridge and German idealism'. The notion that Kant's philosophy opposes empiricism is still widespread in Coleridge studies despite the fact that Arthur Lovejoy already observed in 1940 that Kant's transcendental idealism was much too concerned with empiricism to account for Coleridge's emerging idealism, for which the 1802 poem 'Dejection: An Ode' usually serves as a marker (Lovejoy 1940, p. 347; Crisman 1991, p. 422). Seamus Perry observes that Coleridge's interest in German philosophy and his concomitant conviction that 'empiricism was . . . anti-philosophy' are two of the main reasons why 'Coleridge is seen as standing in opposition to everything that might be considered to form the mainstream of the contemporary British mind' (Perry 2007a, p. 14). The present recovery of the early English mediation of critical philosophy and its impact on Coleridge's works opens up the relevance of Coleridge's and Kant's work not to the mainstream of the nineteenth-century British mind but to a wider range of areas of scholarly investigation than has previously been recognized, including British associationism, social reform, religious dissent, journalism and sociability during the Romantic and Victorian age. It aims to invite further research on Coleridge, Nitsch and other English mediators of critical philosophy for the study of Kant's effective history and on the historical interconnectedness between philosophical schools across Europe and across the Atlantic.

1

The Early Mediators of Kant
in Bristol and London

That the system [of metaphysics] is capable of being converted into an irreligious
PANTHEISM, I well know. The ETHICS of SPINOZA, may, or may not, be
an instance. But at no time could I believe, that in itself and essentially it is
incompatible with religion, natural, or revealed: and now I am most thoroughly
persuaded of the contrary. The writings of the illustrious sage of Königsberg, the
founder of the Critical Philosophy, more than any other work, at once invigorated
and disciplined my understanding.

Samuel Taylor Coleridge, *Biographia* I, pp. 152–3

I first studied this system under Frederic Augustus Nitsch, who originally imported
the seeds of TRANSCENDENTAL PHILOSOPHY from its native country, to
plant them in our soil; and though, as is usually the case, many of these seeds were
scattered by the wind, I trust that a sufficient number have taken root to maintain
the growth of this vigorous and flourishing plant, till the time shall come when by its
general cultivation England may be enabled to enrich other nations with the most
perfect specimens of its produce.

Thomas Wirgman 1817, p. 783

So popular was critical philosophy when Coleridge arrived in Germany in 1798 that
the young Englishman had the (incorrect) impression that 'The Critique der r. V.
appeared -& the Universities of Germany *exploded*' (*Marginalia* III, p. 318).[1] Among
the philosophers who contributed to this explosion of Kantianism, Karl Leonhard
Reinhold was the most prominent.[2] After the publication of his 'Briefe über die
Kantische Philosophie' ('Letters about Kantian Philosophy') from 1786 until 1787,
Kant's philosophy became all the rage (Kühn 2006, p. 631). Coleridge was aware of
Reinhold and other early German disseminators, probably Erhard Schmid, Johann
Ernst Schulz (also spelt 'Schultz' or 'Schulze'),[3] Gottlob Ernst Schulze, Jakob Sigismund
Beck, and Johann Heinrich Tieftrunk, as we know from his marginal annotation '50
Vol. of Comments, from Reinhold, Schmidt, Schulz, Beck, Tieftrunk, &c &c &c'
(*Marginalia* III, p. 319). The '50 Vols of Comments' in the autograph commentary
suggests that Coleridge knew there had been plenty of Kant mediators. Reinhold
had before all others placed Kant's *first critique* strategically within the context of

the most heated philosophical debate in mid-1780s Germany: the 'Pantheismus Streit' ('pantheism controversy'; see Chapter 5). 'Reinhold's specific contribution to this popularization process was', according to George di Giovanni, 'the arguably very constructive move of injecting the Critique of Reason into the Spinoza-dispute that Jacobi had instigated in 1785, thereby altering both the tenor of the dispute and the course that the reception of Kant's critical work was to take' (2010, p. 1). Reinhold had made a 'momentous decision' by composing a series of eight letters expounding the neglected religiously affirmative dimension of the *Critique of Pure Reason* and by publishing them in Christoph Martin Wieland's *Teutscher Merkur* (Ameriks 2005, p. x). Reinhold recognized that by turning attention away from epistemological issues (e.g. the synthetic judgements a priori, the transcendental deduction) towards the practical use of Reason at the end of the *first critique*, he could win massive public interest, especially by those seeking an endorsement of rational religion.

The initial dissemination of Kant's philosophy in England began at the time of Reinhold's *Briefe* in 1787. The interest of the English public revolved around the religious and moral implications of the *first critique* that were implicitly political for them in much the same way as in Germany. This is the reason why the present historical reconstruction of the English transmission process cannot do without a prior explanation of the 'Transcendental Dialectic' in the *Critique of Pure Reason*. The 'Transcendental Dialectic' lies at the heart of the late eighteenth-century reception of Kant in England; readers disagreed about and still dispute today its ultimate meaning with regard to the possibility of metaphysics. As the debate about this represents an essential part of the rest of this study, a sketch of Kant's arguments is indispensible. Based on this outline, the chapter will then establish the pathways through which critical philosophy entered English culture in the mid-1790s. It will show that Kantianism spread thanks to less well-known, but historically important, figures like Friedrich August Nitsch, especially in the radical and dissenting milieu of England and that Kant's principles found a larger English audience and had a greater impact on English writers of the period such as William Godwin than has previously been thought.

Preliminary discussion of Kant's 'Transcendental Dialectic'

In *Prolegomena*, Kant speaks of 'having been awoken by Hume from his "dogmatic slumber" (*dogmatischer Schlummer*)' (Kühn 2005, p. 116). The 'Transcendental Dialectic' conveys strong affinities with the Scottish philosopher David Hume.[4] Kant knew 'Hume's philosophy very well from 1755 onwards and that similarity is indeed the result of influence' (Kühn 1983, p. 180; see also Tonelli 1966; Groos 1901). Traces of Hume's scepticism are palpable in the following extract from the 'Transcendental Dialectic':

> Die unbedingte Notwendigkeit, die wir, als den letzten Träger aller Dinge, so unentbehrlich bedürfen, ist der wahre Abgrund für die menschliche Vernunft. . . . Man kann sich des Gedankens nicht erwehren, man kann ihn aber auch nicht ertragen, daß ein Wesen, welches wir uns auch als ein höchstes unter

allen möglichen vorstellen, gleichsam zu sich selbst sage: Ich bin von Ewigkeit zu Ewigkeit, außer mir ist nichts ohne das, was bloß durch meinen Willen etwas ist; *aber woher bin ich denn*? Hier sinkt alles unter uns, und die größte Vollkommenheit, wie die kleinste, schwebt ohne Haltung bloß vor der spekulativen Vernunft, der es nichts kostet, die eine so wie die andere ohne die mindeste Hinderniß verschwinden zu lassen. (*KrV* B 641)

(The unconditioned necessity, which we need so indispensibly as the ultimate sustainer of all things, is for human reason the true abyss. . . . One cannot resist the thought of it, but one also cannot bear it that a being that we represent to ourselves as the highest among all possible beings might, as it were, say to itself: 'I am from eternity to eternity, outside me is nothing except what is something merely through my will; **but whence** then am I?' Here everything gives way beneath us, and the greatest perfection as well as the smallest, hovers without support before speculative reason, for which it would cost nothing to let the one as much as the other disappear without the least obstacle. [*CpR* B 641])

The thought of the absolutely necessary discussed here concerned not only the origin of self-consciousness but also the foundation of the entire metaphysical theory of the world and the cause of existence. The absolutely necessary was the axiom of Cartesian metaphysics – the metaphysics of a first principle, of an independent point of departure and a single identical thing not derived from anything else (Henrich 1960, pp. 3, 5, 127). The passage pointed to a profound ambivalence in the human attitude: unconditioned necessity was at once 'ultimate sustainer of all things' and 'true abyss . . . of human reason'. It indicates that Kant in his 'Transcendental Dialectic' supported, though somewhat reluctantly, Hume's analysis of causation. Like Hume's *Enquiry Concerning Human Understanding* (1748) and *A Treatise of Human Nature* (1739), Kant exposed in the *Critique of Pure Reason* (1781) the fundamental deficiency of traditional metaphysics. Nowhere else in his work would Kant's philosophy reach such a high degree of scepticism as in the *first critique* (Henrich 1960, p. 177).

In the *Prolegomena*, Kant explained retrospectively how Hume had influenced his thinking: 'Hume started in the main from a single concept in metaphysics, namely that of the connections between cause and effect' (cited in Kühn 2001, p. 256). The main inspiration Kant drew from Hume lay in the insight that 'Reason . . . pretends to have conceived this concept [of causality] in her womb' (cited in Kühn 2001, p. 256). Kant's metaphor of the womb of Reason for the method of logical deduction, which Hume and subsequently Kant criticized heavily, is revealing. On the one hand, 'womb' indicates the strong attachment to Reason as a mother figure and sustainer; on the other hand, it exposes the assumption in an almost misogynistic way that certain concepts were inherent in other concepts. Inference by way of deduction was vital for rational theology. Exposing the weaknesses of the latter, Hume's *Enquiry* stated that 'religious philosophers . . . indulge a rash curiosity, in trying how far they can establish religion upon the principles of reason; and they thereby excite, instead of satisfying, the doubts, which naturally arise from a diligent and scrutinous enquiry . . . the question is entirely speculative' (Hume 2000, p. 102; [section 11, paragraph 10]). Hume observed that the inference of a cause was meaningless if it were only known by the effect: '[i]f the cause be known only by the effect, we never ought to ascribe to it any qualities, beyond what are precisely requisite to produce the effect' (Hume 2000, p. 103 [section 11; paragraph 13]). Kant's *first critique* agreed with Hume's refutation of the method of joining or dissecting inherent concepts. Kant built on Hume's critique of metaphysics but ultimately reached very different conclusions (Henrich 1960, pp. 148–9). Yet before outlining Kant's attempt to obviate the deficits of Reason, it is necessary to indicate the profundity of Kant's relentless dissection of traditional metaphysics.

Sections Three to Seven of Chapter 3 of the 'Transcendental Dialectic' in the *Critique of Pure Reason* criticize the chief arguments of rational theology: the ontological argument of St Anselm and Descartes, the 'cosmological' argument found in Aquinas and favoured by Christian Wolff and the 'physico-theological' argument from design, especially popular among British divines including David Hartley and Joseph Priestley and influenced by John Locke. A major insight in the 'Transcendental Dialectic' was that existence is not a predicate, that is, existence is not inherent in, but superadded to, other concepts (Henrich 1960, pp. 140–2; Kühn 2001, pp. 248–9):

> Denn der Gegenstand ist bei der Wirklichkeit nicht bloß in meinem Begriffe analytisch enthalten, sondern kommt zu meinem Begriffe (der eine Bestimmung meines Zustandes ist) synthetisch hinzu. (*KrV* B 627)
>
> (For with actuality the object is not merely included in my concept analytically, but adds synthetically to my concept [which is a determination of my state]. [*CpR* B 627])

Kant employed this known argument to refute the ontological argument by St Anselm, who professed that the concept of existence could be unpacked from another concept as if it lay dormant within the concept of Deity or vice versa.[5] In order to expose the deficiency of the ontological argument, Kant drew on a now-famous example:

> Hundert wirkliche Taler enthalten nicht das Mindeste mehr, als hundert mögliche. Denn da diese den Begriff, jene aber den Gegenstand und dessen Position an sich selbst dedeuten, so würde, im Falle dieser mehr enthielte als jener, mein Begriff nicht den ganzen Gegenstand ausdrücken, und also auch nicht der angemessene Begriff von ihm sein. Aber in meinem Vormögenszustande ist mehr bei hundert wirklichen Talern, als bei dem bloßen Begriffe derselben (d. i. ihrer Möglichkeit) [enthalten]. (*KrV* B 627, my addition)
>
> (A hundred actual [pounds] do not contain the least bit more than a hundred possible ones. For since the latter signifies the concept and the former its object and its positing in itself, then, in case the former contained more than the latter, my concept would not express the entire object and thus would not be the suitable concept of it. But in my financial condition there is more with a hundred actual [pounds] than with the mere concept of them [i.e. their possibility]. [*CpR* B 627])

Kant compared the mere concept of a hundred pounds to the material amount of money. Both are equally perfect from a conceptual point of view, but this does not mean that the mere notion of a hundred pounds will purchase any goods. This example demonstrates, according to Kant, that existence is neither contained in perfection, nor can it be derived from perfection, but that it is something that needs to be added to a concept.

This insight exposed a paradox: as existence is not a predicate its determination requires external proof. Claims of existence can only be proven through determination by experience. This view had a devastating impact on anything unconditioned or autonomous, like God, but also on such concepts as freedom or the soul. The enquiry into the existence of the absolutely necessary thus posed a self-contradiction: if existence is not inferable but conditioned, the existence of the unconditioned amounts to a paradox. This paradox equally threatened the validity of the other two rational proofs of the existence of God which Kant discussed in the *Critique of Pure Reason*: the 'cosmological' and the 'physico-theological' argument. Kant 'makes clear in his subsequent separate criticism of the cosmological argument', as Paul Guyer observes, '[that] we never have any justification for assuming that the series of contingently existing things terminates in something absolutely necessary' (2006, p. 146).[6] The physico-theological argument of design is doomed, too, because 'we have no legitimate way to infer from anything we do experience to an unconditioned being, outside of the series of natural causes and effects, like the God of theology' (Guyer 2006, p. 150). If we attempt to infer the existence of God by including him within the chain of natural causes, like Hartley or Spinoza, then God too must be conditioned rather than unconditioned, limited rather than unlimited. Nothing unconditioned, nothing autonomous can therefore be proven to exist. All three attempts to find a rational proof for the existence of God have, as Kant pointed out, this paradox in common.

The theological implications of the 'Transcendental Dialectic' are contested to date.[7] Summing up the ambivalence, Guyer notes that 'it is possible to maintain that they [Kant's criticisms of the metaphysical arguments for the existence of God] are not knockdown criticisms. By the same token, however, Kant's criticisms have the weight of his whole theory of knowledge behind them: you cannot accept his basic distinction between concepts and intuitions, with our a priori intuition of the structure of space and time providing only the a priori form of our empirical intuitions of objects in space and time, and continue to accept the traditional arguments for the existence of God' (2006, p. 152). Nonetheless, after this rigorous criticism of rational theology, Kant did much to reinforce it in the remainder of the Chapter 3 of the 'Transcendental Dialectic':

> Das höchste Wesen bleibt also für den bloß spekulativen Gebrauch der Vernunft ein bloßes, aber doch *fehlerfreies Ideal*, ein Begriff, welcher die ganze menschliche Erkenntniß schließt und krönt, dessen objektive Realität auf diesem Wege zwar nicht bewiesen, aber auch nicht widerlegt werden kann. (*KrV* B 669)
>
> (Thus the highest being remains for the merely speculative use of reason a mere but nevertheless **faultless ideal**, a concept which concludes and crowns the whole of human cognition, whose objective reality cannot of course be proved on this path, but also cannot be refuted. [*CpR* B 669])

Kant abandoned the enquiry of whether God exists and asked instead whether God ought to exist. Thus he offered a philosophical basis for a belief in the existence of God founded in morality that is defiant of dogmatism. Kant added to the second edition (1787) a preface containing the following explanation:

> Ich mußte also das Wissen aufheben, um zum Glauben Platz zu bekommen, und der Dogmatism der Metaphysik, d. i. das Vorurteil, in ihr ohne Kritik der reinen Vernunft fortzukommen, ist die wahre Quelle alles der Moralität widerstreitenden Unglaubens, der jederzeit gar sehr dogmatisch ist. (*KrV* B XXX)
>
> (Thus I had to deny **knowledge** in order to make room for **faith**; and the dogmatism of metaphysics, i.e., the prejudice that without criticism reason can make progress in metaphysics, is the true source of all unbelief conflicting with morality, which unbelief is always very dogmatic. [*CpR* B XXX])

Kant supported Hume's position that knowledge must be based on experience. Contrary to the latter, Kant's system contained a possibility to maintain metaphysics but only within its boundaries. *The Critique of Pure Reason* introduced a strict dualism between the realm of knowledge and that of ethics, and distinguished sharply between their respective functions of Reason. Only in the realm of morality could (practical) Reason play a constitutive role. Some readers have taken this as a clear sign that 'Kant had left the door ajar for a troop of theological speculators' (Boulger 1961, p. 76).

In the twentieth century, Kant's commentators of 'scientific and logical positivist tendencies (such as Kemp Smith)' have deplored the reintroduction of this element of faith in the *Critique of Pure Reason* (Boulger 1961, p. 75). Yet towards the end of the eighteenth century, philosophers, theologians and poets had a natural interest in this section. The initial German 'Wirkungsgeschichte' (effective history) of the *Critique of Pure Reason* still requires, according to Kühn, further investigation (2006, p. 630), but one aspect in particular seems a matter of agreement between scholars: Kant struggled initially to have his philosophical views recognized as the 'most important contribution to the philosophy' since Locke, Leibniz, and Hume. It took Kant until 1787 to become 'convinced that his thoughts were taken seriously and that his ideas would be successful' (Kühn 2006, pp. 630–1; see Sassen 2000). And this was also the point where Reinhold came in. His interpretation entailed a blunting of the 'violence of Kant's' philosophical revolution (di Giovanni 2010, p. 2); some commentators also speak of Kant's 'fate' of having his ideas conflated with Reinhold's and Fichte's 'corrections or systematizations of these ideas' (Adams 2010, p. 28). Yet both philosophers paved the way for early German Romanticism (Frank 1987, 1989, 1997, 2004; Götze 2001).

Reinhold's contribution to the German dissemination of the *Critique of Pure Reason*

Throughout his life, Reinhold (1757–1823) was thoroughly committed to being an Enlightenment educator, that is, he sought a way 'to support social reform with a philosophy that met the double demand of being popular and systematic in the best sense' (Ameriks 2005, p. xiv). Starting out as a Jesuit novice until their dissolution, he was ordained as a priest in the Barnabite order. What Abbé Barruel would indiscriminately condemn all Kantians for applied to Reinhold: before having to seek refuge in Protestant Weimar, he was deeply involved in Vienna in the secret social-reform activities of the local Masonic lodge that, at the time, 'was dominated by the ideology of the Illuminati' (di Giovanni 2010, p. 3). After his arrival in Weimar, he married Wieland's daughter and eventually published his 'Briefe über die Kantische Philosophie' ('Letters on the Kantian Philosophy') in Wieland's *Der Teutsche Merkur* between August 1786 and September 1787 (Breazeale 2010, p. 90).

The pantheism controversy was a bitter, wide, and at times ferocious, public debate orchestrated by Friedrich Heinrich Jacobi who deliberately provoked Moses Mendelssohn, a leading German Enlightenment philosopher, by accusing his close friend Gotthold Ephraim Lessing of Spinozism. The controversy erupted publically in 1785 (di Giovanni 2005, p. 11), but started a few years earlier. After Lessing's death (in 1781), Jacobi reported at first privately that Lessing had been saying that the 'orthodox concepts of the deity are not for me any more. I cannot relish them. "Hen kai Pan!" I know of nothing else' (Jacobi cited in Hedley 2000, p. 67). This statement equalled the accusation of atheism at the time and had wide repercussions. 'For Jacobi', Karl Ameriks notes, 'not only Spinoza or Lessing but traditional theoretical philosophy in general encouraged pantheism because it appeared to be able to do little more than link dependent particulars together with one another as part of a necessarily connected all-inclusive whole' (2005, p. xvii). Jacobi's aim was to bring his readers back to a more God-centred Christian humanism or, to use Ameriks's phrase, to an ' "old-time" supernaturalism . . . the satisfying non-demonstrative beliefs that they had always held' (2005, p. xviii). For Jacobi, the immanent God proposed by rational theology was not an option; only forms of supernatural religion were viable.

Jacobi's insistence on a return to non-demonstrative beliefs combined with his perceptive polemic against rational philosophy was 'a huge embarrassment for most Enlightenment philosophers' (Ameriks 2005, p. xviii). The opposing parties in the pantheism controversy, Jacobi's fraction and Mendelssohn's one, both tried to gain the approval of Kant, who grew increasingly concerned about the anger and hostility involved in the controversy (Beiser 1987, pp. 109–15). Almost a year after the publication of Mendelssohn's *Morgenstunden* and Jacobi's *Briefe*,[8] and at a time when Kant was writing the *Critique of Practical Reason* (Breazeale 2010, p. 94), Kant finally published his contribution in the *Berlinische Monatsschrift* in October 1786: the short essay 'Was heißt: Sich im Denken orientiren [sic]?' ('What Does it Mean to Orient Oneself in Thinking?'), also called 'Orientation' essay. Against the weight of Kant's epistemology, the essay gives evidence of Kant's attempts to uphold rational faith. Kant did not fully subscribe to either of the two parties in the controversy. 'On the one hand, he agrees with Jacobi, that knowledge cannot justify faith; but he disagrees with his conclusion that reason cannot justify it [faith]. On the other hand, he concurs with Mendelssohn that it is necessary to justify faith through reason; but he does not accept the conclusion that to justify faith through reason demands knowledge' (Beiser 1987, pp. 115–16). What Kant contributed to the controversy was the 'new notion of *practical reason* outlined near the end of the *Critique of Pure Reason*' (Breazeale 2010, p. 94). Kant maintained the view in his essay that speculative or theoretical Reason was insufficient for any claims of existence. It was possible to make judgements about the first cause of everything, indeed it was a need of theoretical Reason to do so, but only as long as we knew that we made assumptions and never thought that this in any way proved that such a cause existed. For Reinhold, practical Reason reached the autonomy theoretical Reason could not have: 'the practical employment of reason – or rather, the pure employment of practical reason of the sort associated with recognition and legislation of the moral law – is conditioned by nothing whatsoever outside of itself' (Breazeale 2010, p. 95). Kant's 'Orientation' essay asserted that:

> Weit wichtiger ist das Bedürfniß der Vernunft in ihrem praktischen Gebrauche, weil es unbedingt ist, und wir die Existenz Gottes voraus zu setzen nicht bloß alsdann genöthigt werden, wenn wir *urtheilen wollen*, sondern weil wir *urtheilen müssen*. Denn der reine praktische Gebrauch der Vernunft besteht in der Vorschrift der moralischen Gesetze. Sie führen aber alle auf die Idee des *höchsten Gutes*, was in der Welt möglich ist, so fern es allein durch *Freiheit* möglich ist. (*Orientiren*, p. 139)
>
> (Far more important is the need of reason in its practical use, because it is unconditioned, and we are necessitated to presuppose the existence of God not only if we *want to judge*, but because we *have to judge*. For the pure practical use of reason consists in the precepts of moral laws. They all lead, however, to the idea of the *highest good* possible in the world insofar as it is possible only through *freedom*. [*Orient* 8: 139])

The only way to orientate oneself about the highest good is, according to Kant's essay, to heed to the inner voice of practical or moral Reason, 'a voice that announces itself not only as a need to act in a certain way but also as a need to think of certain objects and to posit or to postulate the reality of the same' (Breazeale 2010, p. 96). The way such a voice would announce itself would preoccupy Kant and his followers considerably. One possibility was excluded: it did so 'not by any kind of cognition' (Breazeale 2010, p. 96).

Around the same time, Reinhold had 'anticipated the position Kant was to elaborate' (Ameriks 2005, p. xi) in the 'Orientation' essay (1786), the preface of the second edition of the *Critique of Pure Reason* (cited above), more extensively in his treatment of the moral argument for God in the *Critique of Practical Reason* (1788), the *Critique of the Power of Judgment* (1790) and elsewhere. These were also the works in which Kant formulated his answer to Hume most fully, that is, his affirmation of rational faith under the consideration of the limits of Reason.[9] Reinhold wanted his readers to know that, contrary to Mendelssohn's reference to the 'all-crushing Kant' in his *Morgenstunden* (1785), Kant upheld rational faith.

> Man würde die *Kritik der Vernunft* sehr mißverstehen, wenn man im Ernste glaubte, sie *zermalme alles*, sie reiße ohne Unterschied ein, was unsere großen Denker bisher gebaut haben, und erkläre unsere bisherige Metaphysik ohne Einschränkung für unbrauchbar. (Reinhold 1923, p. 142)

(One would very much misunderstand the Critique of Reason if one were earnestly to believe that it crushes everything, indiscriminately tears down what our leading thinkers have previously built, and declares without reservation that our previous metaphysics is useless. [Reinhold 2005, p. 42])

And so it was that Reinhold contributed a great deal to the popularization of Kantianism by making Kant's *Critique of Pure Reason* widely known as the 'Evangelium der reinen Vernunft' ('gospel of Reason') (Reinhold 1923, p. 151). This does not mean that everyone was convinced by Reinhold's suppression of the sceptical dimension of the *Critique of Pure Reason*, but that he had brought the relevance of Kant's *first critique* for the pantheism controversy to public attention. At the same time, Reinhold's impact, however, meant that the early transmission revolved around a topic that modern Kant commentators used to see as peripheral, or as Kühn phrased it, 'at the very fringe of philosophical interest' (1985, p. 155). In the mid-1780s, however, the German reading public associated the name 'Kant' with the debate on rational theology, especially with the question regarding the religious or irreligious implications of the rational presupposition of unconditioned necessity or a first cause. News of Kant's philosophy reached England under the same banner.

Initial news of Kant in England

The effective history of Kant's philosophy during the period in England has been widely neglected. To date, René Wellek's and Giuseppe Micheli's studies (1931 and 1990, respectively) represent the only extensive sources of scholarly investigation. Both of these important studies fail to observe the full extent of the significance of the early English transmission of Kant's philosophy. It sheds a new light on the highly controversial debate of the highest good in Kant studies by illuminating an intriguing part of its effective history. The 'highest good' is the situation with an ideal coordination of virtue and happiness; it demands that we postulate the conditions that are necessary so that we can hope. This end becomes a rational possibility, namely our own immortality, and a God with the requisite power, wisdom and goodness (Ameriks 2005, p. xi). As such, the highest good also provides a historically momentous link between German Kantianism and English necessitarianism in the late eighteenth century (see also Chapter 3).[10] I use the term 'necessitarian' to designate those who think that free will alone has no constitutive power in human action. While the first English reviewers of Kant disagreed over the religious implications of critical philosophy, the religious dissenters were more thoroughly invested than other Kant commentators in England. They drew on the preface ('Vorrede') to the second edition of the *Critique of Pure Reason* and on the *Critique of Practical Reason* and thus built on two Kantian texts after 1781 suitable for affirmative answers to Hume's rejection of traditional metaphysics. In other words, the materials on Kant in late eighteenth-century England lay open that an idea which twentieth-century Kant scholars saw (and sometimes still see) as a matter of great contention or even of misconception was very important for the favourable reception in England.[11] By this I mean that during the earliest stage of transmission before 1800, the praise bestowed on Kant's philosophy depended in part on his notion of rational faith, which includes the highest good. Reinhold's *Briefe* played a significant role in this reception process. Although Wellek and particularly Micheli mention Reinhold in the context of the early English mediators (1931, p. 224; 1993, pp. 259–65), the assumption prevails until now that 'Anglophone countries ... did not experience the direct impact of Reinhold's *Letters* (Reinhold's work was not available in English until late in the twentieth century)' (Ameriks 2005, p. xii). While this statement adequately describes the development for the twentieth-century English-speaking world, this chapter will show that it is misleading for the late eighteenth and early nineteenth centuries. The majority of Kantian ideas to first reach England were those that both Reinhold and his opponents had filtered through the pantheism controversy.

Taking a look at the big picture, it is accurate that the Kantian impact on late eighteenth-century English culture remained relatively small (Wellek 1931, p. 4, Micheli 1990, p. 202); for the dissenting and radical circles in London and Bristol, however, the early dissemination of and response to Kant exerted a highly formative influence (see also Weber 1935). It is important to consider the interdependency of philosophical and sociopolitical factors in the English reception as well as the position of Kantianism outside the mainstream of English society. By the mid-eighteenth century, the tradition of English idealism spearheaded by Ralph Cudworth, Henry More and Benjamin Whichcote had, as Wellek observed, almost completely given way to the associationist principles proclaimed by Hartley and Priestley and to the thought of Scottish common sense philosophers, especially by Thomas Reid (1931, p. 4).[12] This development was accompanied by great sociopolitical change of the Continent and in Britain: the first serious reviews of Kant in England coincided with the outbreak of the war with France (1793). Protest and increasing repression in domestic affairs ensued. Furthermore, Edmund Burke's *Reflections on the Revolution in France* (1790) instigated a strong reaction against Enlightenment principles, which John Robison's *Proofs of a Conspiracy against all the Religions and Governments of Europe* (1797) and Abbé Barruel's *Memoirs: Illustrating the History of Jacobinism* (1799) expanded and transformed into a conspiracy theory (Simpson 1993, p. 87). Barruel equated Kant with Adam 'Spartacus' Weishaupt, the founder of the Illuminati and called them both the 'prototypes of German Jacobinism' (Barruel 1799 IV, p. 528); the influential *Anti-Jacobin Review* spread Barruel's views by launching an anti-German campaign in 1799 (see Chapter 5). As a result, Kant's name almost disappeared from English periodicals after 1806 (Micheli 1990, p. 307). The publication of angry letters about the significance of critical philosophy between Barruel and Anthony Florian Madinger Willich resulting from Willich's and Nitsch's meeting with Barruel in 1800 did nothing to improve the opinion of mainstream society. On the contrary the articles appear as a low point in the transmission of Kantian ideas (Willich: *Britannic Magazine* 7 [1800], p. 241). Prior to these events, Johann Christian Hüttner's report about the progress of Kantianism in England dating from May 1796 set out to sober all of Kant's adherents who might have hoped for the rapid spread of the new philosophy:

> Wie könnte auch, in diesem unermeßlichen Treiben und Drängen der alle Ländern und Zonen umfassenden Spekulationen, jetzt, wo die politische Krise von Monat zu Monat sichtbarer und bedenklicher wird, unter einem Volke, das nur noch

durch zwey große Hebel, Erwerbssucht und Genußbegierde, in Thätigkeit [sic] erhalten wird, [dass] das Reich der subtilen Abstraktion in einer fremden Sprache und Vorstellungsart, nur einige Ausbreitung erhalte? (*Neuer Teutscher Merkur* 2 [1796], p. 436)

(How could it also be, in this immeasurable hustle and bustle of speculations which comprise all nations and zones, now that the political crisis is becoming more visible and concerning every month, among a people that merely sustains action through the two levers acquisitiveness and avidity for pleasure, that the realm of subtle abstractions in a foreign tongue and way of thinking were expanded? [my translation])

Hüttner's consideration illustrates two major obstacles for critical philosophy in England. Concerns with trade and the political crisis prevailed among mainstream society and impeded the dissemination of metaphysical abstraction. Despite this gloomy prognosis, Hüttner's above-quoted article reported, nevertheless, that Kantianism found pathways into English culture leading off the beaten tracks of academic institutions and established societies into the radical and dissenting milieu in London and Bristol (Micheli 1990, p. 202).[13]

At the very time when Reinhold's *Briefe* were being published in the *Teutscher Merkur*, the epistolary article about the state of German literature and philosophy entitled 'German literature intelligence' in the *Political Magazine* included what is to my knowledge the first reference to Kant in the English press: 'The metaphysics of Prof. Kant, at Koenigsberg, gain ground. A parson in Bradenbrug [sic] has been suspended from his office for endeavouring to prove to his peasants that, upon Kant's principles, there exists no God' (*Political Magazine* 12 [1787], p. 94). The excerpt has been published twice (Morgan and Hohlfeld 1949, p. 40; Micheli 1990, p. 212), yet its significance has barely been scrutinized at all. A priest was said to have taught Kant's criticism of rational theology in his parish in an act that points to the reciprocity of social reform and philosophy. On the one hand, the article anticipated the period around 1800 when Kant's philosophy was condemned as a Jacobin conspiracy; on the other hand, it indicated that the debate on rational theology was a pathway for Kantianism to England.

Judging from two letters, dating from 15 April 1789 and 9 October 1789 (*Akk XI*, pp. 19ff., 92ff.; *Correspondence* 11: 21 [p. 295]), Kant's student Johann Benjamin Jachmann made attempts to spread Kantianism in England and Scotland, but apparently to little avail (Baum and Malter 1991, p. 462n).[14] In the following years until the mid-1790s, English periodicals largely disregarded Kant's philosophy with the exception of Ralph Griffiths's the *Monthly Review*, founded in 1749 (Micheli 1990, p. 213; Forster 2003, p. 171) and, later on, the *Monthly Magazine*. The *Monthly Review* and the younger *Monthly Magazine* (founded in 1796) were also the most successful periodicals at the time both maintaining a standard print-run of 5000. The *Monthly Review* had increased its sales steadily from 1000 in 1750–1 to 5000 in 1797, while the *Monthly Magazine* (1796), a paper to which Coleridge contributed regularly, achieved a startling success with 5000 sales within only one year of business (Roper 1978, p. 24). Kant's name appeared for the first time in the *Monthly Review* on page 483 of the third volume in 1790 in an article by Thomas Cogan with the telling title 'Prize Dissertation relative Natural and Revealed Religion' (*Monthly Review* 3 [1790], pp. 481–95).

It discussed the prize-winning essays in the competition of Teyler's Theological Society in Haarlem, Holland. The committee of the society had posed the following questions for the competition: are there 'satisfactory proofs of the immateriality of the soul of man? If such exist, what conclusions are to be made from them, with respect to the soul's duration, sensation, and employment in its state of separation from the body?' (*Monthly Review* 3 [1790], p. 481).[15] Cogan summarized the contribution by the future Dutch disseminator of Kant, the Mennonite pastor Allard Hulshoff, who emphasized similarities between Kant and Reid regarding the rejection of Locke's distinction between primary and secondary qualities (Micheli 1990, p. 216). Overall the article in the *Monthly Review* introduced Kant as a new important reference regarding questions of natural and revealed religion.

Three years later, Benjamin Sowden, the minister of the English Presbyterian Church in Rotterdam, published a review of the proceedings of the Dutch philosophical society: 'Verhandelingen uitgegeeven door de Hollandsche Maatschappye, &c.: Memoirs published by the Philosophical Society of Haarlem' (*Monthly Review* 10 [1793], pp. 523–31). It contained such a lucid introduction of Kantian philosophy that future articles on Kant in this paper referred to Sowden for further elucidation. It is significant for Kant scholarship that the first exposition of Kant in the London periodical was based, as Sowden explained in a footnote, on the second edition of the '*Kritik der Reinen Vernunft*' (1787) and on the '*Kritik der Praktischen Vernunft*' (1788) alongside an article by 'the ingenious Professor Van Hemert of Amsterdam' (*Monthly Review* 10 [1793], p. 524).[16] Sowden drew particular attention to the distinction between theoretical and practical Reason by asking: 'what is meant by practical reason, which is distinguished from that which is called speculative or theoretical?' (*Monthly Review* 10 [1793], p. 527). His article mentioned the constitutive function of practical Reason in the following words: 'our practical reason must determine us firmly to believe the existence of the Deity' (*Monthly Review* 10 [1793], p. 526). Furthermore, Sowden expounded that the highest good guaranteed happiness in proportion to our virtue: 'of a future state in which our happiness will be proportioned according to our internal worth' (*Monthly Review* 10 [1793], p. 526). He added correctly that faith 'is independent of all knowledge of its object; for the principles of religion can be neither demonstrated nor disproved by theoretical reason, but are mere postulates of practical reason' (*Monthly Review* 10 [1793], p. 526). In a way that is consistent with the *second critique*, the Presbyterian minister presented Kant as a proponent of rational faith, 'this is what our author [Kant] calls *rational faith*' (*Monthly Review* 10 [1793], p. 526). Sowden's insights into Kant's philosophy became a point of reference for the Unitarians William Enfield and William Taylor of Norwich, who quoted this article in their own reviews of critical philosophy in the *Monthly Review* (Enfield: 22 [1797], pp. 15–18; Taylor: 28 [1799], pp. 62–9 and 25 [1798], p. 584). Their articles show that Enfield and Taylor, too, were mainly interested in the affirmative dimension of Kant's innovation of metaphysics; Enfield was favourably inclined, Taylor less so. While Enfield and Taylor were looking for arguments that defended traditional metaphysics, Dr Thomas Beddoes opposed them (see Chapter 2).

Beddoes saw in Kant's *first critique* at first a confirmation of the traditional rationality he tended to oppose. He dismissed Kant's publication in his *Observations on the*

Nature of Demonstrative Evidence (1793) on grounds of the principle of induction: 'To observation and induction alone, whatever Mr Kant may imagine, it is easy to see that we owe our knowledge of the absolute necessity and strict universality of geometrical proofs' (Beddoes 1793, p. 101). Beddoes based his criticism on the introduction to the second edition of the *Critique of Pure Reason*, an excerpt from which he translated and inserted in his book (*KrV* B 2–6). Following the thrust of Hume's argument that 'the words, therefore, *necessary existence*, have no meaning; or, which is the same thing, none that is consistent' (Hume 1935, p. 233), Beddoes argued that the term 'cause' in Kant's *first critique* was an 'obliteration of that original signification, a remarkable abbreviation in language' (1793, pp. 96–7). He clarified that 'we see the term *cause* originating in the motion produced in living animals, by the application of a pointed body occasioning pain' (1793, p. 98). For Beddoes, causality consisted in an external stimulus in this world, and did not represent a universal and necessary condition of human cognition. Conflating Kant's concept a priori with innate ideas, Beddoes's *Observations* gave the impression that Kant opposed empiricism:

> *Ancient Metaphysics.* We know how studiously Plato deprecated the body, the senses, and the information of sense; how his excommunication of our perceptive powers was confirmed by the peripatetic *phantasms*, and how both were amalgamated with the fantastic religious opinions, that so long bewildered and brutalized mankind; as also what authority this monstrous mixture of heterogeneous reveries maintained during a long succession of ages. (Beddoes 1793, p. 119)

Over the course of the following years, Beddoes would study Kant's works more thoroughly and become one of the sharpest and most capable critics of Kant in England. His 1793 publication was, however, no great start as his discussion was rushed, and his criticism premature (Weber 1935, pp. 107–8). Beddoes admitted that he had inserted the passage about Kant after the manuscript of *Observations* had already been sent to Joseph Johnson's press: 'The great celebrity of a modern system of pneumatology, conspires with the opportunity I have had since the beginning of this essay was sent to the press, to induce me to alter the resolution I originally formed, to avoid the quotation and discussion of different opinions. The author of the system is Mr. Kant, Professor at Koenigsberg in Prussia' (1793, p. 89).[17] The fact remains that Beddoes at first placed Kant in the same category as Plato. By 1793, British writers had taken the first steps in the dissemination of Kant's philosophy in England; in these initial accounts Kant featured largely as a proponent of rational faith.

Breakthrough of critical philosophy in England

The year 1796 was something of an annus mirabilis for Kant's transmission in England. The 1790s were the decade with the highest number of references to German letters in British magazines between 1750 and 1850 (Morgan and Hohlfeld 1949, p. 125). In this light, Henry Beers's observation, though stemming from a different context, attains new relevance: 'the year 1796, then marks, the confluence, of English and German romantic movements' (1899, p. 398). While this statement disregards the huge popularity of earlier German works in England, such as Goethe's *Werther* in 1785 (Morgan and Hohlfeld 1949, p. 42), it adequately describes not only the boom in translations of Gottfried August Bürger's ballad 'Lenora', notably by William Taylor of Norwich and Walter Scott, but also in Kantian publications. J. A. O'Keeffe published a Kantian pamphlet in the final months of 1795,[18] Friedrich August Nitsch's introduction to Kantian philosophy appeared in May 1796 (Micheli 1990, p. 259), and the first English translation of Kant's *Zum Ewigen Frieden*, titled *Project for a Perpetual Peace*, became available in October (Micheli 1990, p. 277). By March 1796, Beddoes no longer opposed Kant's system, but publically supported the wish that 'this celebrated code of metaphysics were translated' (*Monthly Magazine* 2 [1796], p. 267; published in May). By this time Beddoes also reckoned that 'the majority of your [the *Monthly Magazine's*] readers are, doubtless, acquainted with the name of Emanuel Kant, professor at Koenigsburg [sic]' (*Monthly Magazine* 2 [1796], p. 265). After 1796, the window for Kantian philosophy in English culture was closing (Micheli 1990, pp. 280–3): John Richardson's *The Principles of Critical Philosophy* (1797) and Anthony Florian Madinger Willich's *Elements of the Critical Philosophy* (1798) received little attention. The books were compilations of various translations from Kantian and anti-Kantian commentators, which provided very little useful introductory material and accordingly met with mostly negative responses (e.g. William Taylor's review *Monthly Review* 28 [1799], pp. 62–9). Richardson's two-volume translation of various Kantian works in *Essays and Treatises,* including 'What is Enlightenment?' and other important essays, as well as his translation *Metaphysics of Moral*, though valuable by themselves, received hardly any attention (Micheli 1993, pp. xiv–xxi). The liveliest period of the discussion about Kant in late eighteenth-century England was around 1796. The publications of this year, Nitsch's book, *To Perpetual Peace* and Beddoes's articles on Kant left profound traces in Coleridge's thought and it remains for future studies to examine their traces on other Romantic writers.

The expositions of the early mediators of Kant, O'Keeffe, Nitsch, and Beddoes, drew on Reinhold's works. Their interests in Reinhold varied, but they all attested, in varying degrees, to Kant's support of rational belief. In an article dating from March 1796, Beddoes explained Kant's criticism of rational evidence for the existence of God with regard to the pantheism controversy and explicit reference to Reinhold. Beddoes distinguished between four categories of metaphysicians, (1) the dogmatic atheist, (2) dogmatic sceptic, (3) the supernaturalist, and (4) the dogmatic theist, which are reminiscent of Reinhold's *Briefe* ('Letter IV'; Reinhold *Briefe* [1923], pp. 114–23).[19] Building on these metaphysical groupings, Beddoes explained that the results of Kant's examination of our intellectual faculties depended on the sect of the reader. He added that Kant's arguments were purely negative in so far as they exposed misguided logic, but constituted no affirmative answer regarding the question of the demonstrability of the existence of God. Beddoes described the supernaturalist, for instance, with reference to Jacobi and the pantheism controversy as follows: '*According to the supernaturalist* (of which sect there are few eminent writers in England, but several in Germany, as Mr Jacobi, the adversary of Moses Mendelssohn) *the answer to that question* [concerning the existence of God] *lies beyond the boundary of reason, and is to be sought exclusively in revelation*' (*Monthly Magazine* 2 [1796], pp. 265–6). This sect would be dissatisfied with Kant's conclusion that God's existence cannot be '*answered from revelation*' (*Monthly Magazine* 2, p. 266). The dogmatic theists would be equally dissatisfied but for a different reason; indeed, they would object to Kant's argument that '*the existence of God does not admit of demonstrations*' (p. 266). The article through its reference to Jacobi and Mendelssohn and Kant's middle position between the two suggests that Beddoes knew one or several of Reinhold's works, probably *Briefe,* his *Versuch einer Theorie des menschlichen Vorstellungsvermögens (Attempt of a Theory of the Human Faculty of Representation)* as well as Kant's 'Orientation' essay. In this article in the *Monthly Magazine*, Beddoes drew on Reinhold to present Kant adequately as a philosopher who refuted the rational evidence for the existence of God and still resisted dogmatic atheism: '*The question of the existence of a God is not to be answered negatively*' (*Monthly Magazine* 2 [1796], p. 266). Beddoes refrained from further comments and thus left it open for the reader to decide what Kant's theological position was.

O'Keeffe's *On the Progress of Human Understanding* conveys interest in the historical and reformative element of the work of Reinhold and by extension of Kant. The pamphlet as a whole fervently supported revolutionary principles. O'Keeffe described it as 'a brief account of the religious, civil, and political intrigues, that gave rise to the prejudice and formed the principal impediments to the progress of human understanding and social happiness, compose the theme of the following pages, which terminate with a sketch of the literature of a new philosophy, especially that of Professor KANT, of Prussia' (1795, p. xvi). O'Keeffe echoed Reinhold's belief that the dissemination of Kant's philosophy would entail far-reaching social reform. Respectively, Kant's philosophy featured in O'Keeffe's work as the final sign of hope and progress in the otherwise impeded development of human understanding. In the short section on Kant at the end of the pamphlet, O'Keeffe referred explicitly to Reinhold's *Beyträge zur Berichtigung bisheriger Missverständnisse der Philosophen* (1790) (1795, p. 49; see Micheli 1990, pp. 236–40; Duddy 2004, p. 267). O'Keeffe's definition of philosophy echoed Reinhold's essay on 'Über den Begriff der Philosophie' ('On the Foundation of Philosophical Knowledge') published in the *Beyträge* (1790, pp. 56–7): 'Philosophy should have no other occupation or purport than to lay before our eyes the character of mankind, and make man acquainted, with his own destiny, by means of absolute and necessary facts which lie within the limits of his own mind' (O'Keeffe 1795, p. 45). This definition illustrates that O'Keeffe latched on to the emancipatory force of Reason in Reinhold's theory and on to the reinforcement of natural law. In the context of the French Revolution, 'Reinhold's conception of enlightenment' had become a conception of revolution (Bondeli 2010, p. 48, see pp. 48–50). Kant in his famous essay 'Beantwortung der Frage: Was heißt Aufklärung?' ('An answer to the question: What is Enlightenment?') proclaimed:

> Zu dieser Aufklärung aber wird nichts erfordert als *Freiheit*; und zwar die unschädliche unter allem, was nur Freiheit heißen mag, nämlich die: von seiner Vernunft in allen Stücken *öffentlich* Gebrauch zu machen. (*Aufklärung*, p. 36)
>
> (For this enlightenment, however, nothing is required but freedom, and indeed the least harmful of anything that could even be called *freedom*: namely, freedom to make *public use* of one's reason in all matters. [*Enlightenment* 8: 36])

In the first volume of *Beyträge*, Reinhold declared in the same spirit that 'die vornehmste Bestimmung der Philosophie sey diesen Charakter aus dem Chaos dunkler Gefühle, willkührlicher [sic] Voraussetzungen, und verworrener Begriffe zu entwikeln [sic]' (Reinhold 1790, p. 56) ('it should be the noblest destiny of philosophy to develop this character from the chaos of obscure feelings, random conditions, and confused concepts' [my translation]). However, the Irish doctor might also have used several other publications by Reinhold, such as the book version of the *Briefe* (1790–2), which contains Reinhold's political theory in Letter Six, or the article 'Gedanken über Aufklärung' ('Thoughts on Enlightenment') published in the *Teutscher Merkur* in 1784. Without mentioning any of these nor Kant's 'Enlightenment' essay, O'Keeffe stipulated like Reinhold that social reform depended on rational progress in the most basic sense and that Kant's 'gospel of Reason' had the power to resolve all previous problems of Reason (Ameriks 2010, p. 119; Breazeale 2010, p. 103). In short, Kant featured as O'Keeffe's idol of Enlightenment revolution.

The aggressive tone in O'Keeffe's pamphlet amplified the radical dimension of critical philosophy in such a way that the essay as a whole was widely seen as virulent attack[20]: a 'virulent attack on Religion and Morality in general, and on Christianity in particular' (*Gentleman's Magazine* 66 [1796], p. 137). The *Gentleman's Magazine* commented negatively on O'Keeffe's exposition of Kant's philosophy that 'all we learn from it [is] that like the French, all first principles are to be done away, and we are to being with a new set [of principles]' (*Gentleman's Magazine* 66 [1796], p. 137). John Aikin junior in the *Monthly Review* echoed the *Gentleman's Magazine* and expressed his concern about O'Keeffe's alleged abuse of Kantian philosophy:

> 'A Sketch on the Literature of New Philosophy', purporting to be an explanation of the outlines of a system of moral philosophy, by Professor Kant, which has excited considerable notice on the Continent. The mutilated state in which this new system is here presented to us precludes any remarks on the subject: nor would it be worthwhile, in such an abundance of greater faults, to descend to the more minute transgressions against grammar and idiomatic propriety. (*Monthly Review* 18 [1796], p. 477)

The Unitarian did not agree with O'Keeffe's interpretation of Kantian philosophy; for him the Kantian system had been mutilated. His pamphlet through its open attack on the monarchy and Christianity lent support to the counter-revolutionary opponents of Kant in England who gained prominence in 1799. Nitsch's introduction was by contrast a more sober account of critical philosophy, placing Kant within the history of philosophy and especially within the British empirical tradition.

A General and Introductory View of Professor Kant's Principles Concerning Man, the World and the Deity (London, 1796) was a substantial introductory work, over two hundred pages long. The aim of Nitsch's book was to familiarize his audience with Kantian thought, and was 'not at all intended to convince the reader of their truth' (1796, p. 70). Rather, Nitsch wanted to pave the way for future in-depth study: 'a translation of Kant's [major] works, however desirable, ought, for many reasons, not to appear without some proper introduction, I shall attempt in consequence . . . to lay before the reader in this Treatise . . . a preliminary consideration' (1796, p. 7). In addition, he had plans to further publications: 'I shall very soon submit them [the Principles of Kant] to the judgment of the public, in a work to be entitled "*An Analysis of Perceptive and Reasoning Faculties of the Human Mind, according to Kant's Principles*"' (1796, pp. 167–8; see pp. 70, 152). In contrast to Willich and Richardson, Nitsch did not merely compile translated fragments from Kant or other exponents, but composed a coherent volume.[21] Therefore, it is misleading to say that Nitsch 'expounded Kant's system in its two parts, the theoretical and the practical, according to Karl Leonhard REINHOLD's *Versuch einer neuen Theorie des menschlichen Vorstellungsvermögens* of 1789' (Micheli 2010, p. 858). It is true that Nitsch wrote to Kant in 1794 that he was composing an introduction according to Reinhold, 'nach Reinhold' (*Akk XI*, p. 518; *Correspondence* 11: 518 [p. 484]), but the finished pamphlet was the result of Nitsch's study as well as of his experience as an independent lecturer in London. As we learn from the biography of his mentor Professor Christian Jacob Kraus (1753–1807), Nitsch's book consisted of the publication of his lectures (Voigt 1819, p. 358). Nitsch knew that mere translations of various fragments of Reinhold's work would not do. The pamphlet was composed of an introduction (1796, pp. 1–18), followed by an introductory sketch of the history of philosophy (1796, pp. 19–71). The latter started with the 'antimonies of pure reason', that is, four sets of opposed demonstrations proving that pure Reason can arrive at contradictory conclusions from seemingly valid premises about the same problems (Boulger 1961, p. 74), and seems further indebted to Kant's 'history of pure reason' at the end of the *first critique*. To this historical sketch, Nitsch added a transition that carefully prepared the readers for the difficulty of Kant's specific principles. The next part consisted of an exposition of the theoretical philosophy based on the *first critique* with subsequent remarks (1796, pp. 72–152), an explanation of Kant's impact (1796, pp. 153–69), and an introduction to Kant's practical philosophy in two parts, that is, ethics (1796, pp. 170–218) and theology (1796, pp. 219–34). Nitsch's perhaps greatest achievement lies, as I explain below, in his independent demonstration of the relevance of Kant's principles for the English debate on philosophical necessity.

F. A. Nitsch represents an important figure for the effective history of critical philosophy as well as for British Romanticism. I contend that the established view of Nitsch and his exposition requires a complete revision. The treatise can hardly be seen as a 'faithful summary of the third book of Reinhold's *Versuch*' alone (Micheli 2010, p. 858) considering that it does not include the central principle of consciousness of the 'Elementarphilosophie' which Reinhold expounded in *Versuch* (1789), *Beyträge* (1790), *Über das Fundament des philosophischen Wissens* (1791), the second volume of the *Briefe* (1792), and the second volume of the *Beyträge* (1794) (Beiser 1987, pp. 238–65; di Giovanni 2005, pp. 91–104). Reinhold's theory overthrew Kant's dualism by positing consciousness as the first principle of philosophy. Book Three of the *Versuch* started with Reinhold's central principle: 'Das Bewusstsein [sic] überhaupt besteht aus dem Bezogenwerden der blossen [sic] Vorstellung auf das Objekt und Subjekt; und ist von jeder Vorstellung überhaupt unzertrennlich' (Reinhold 1789, p. 321) ('Consciousness in general consists of relating mere representations to object and subject; and is in general inseparable from any representation' [my translation]). Representations ('Vorstellungen') designated any cognitive state preceding cognition ('Erkenntnis') and lay at the heart of Reinhold's 'Elementarphilosophie' (Frank 1997, p. 237). Indeed representations were undetermined, non-cognized thoughts, but not all representations were purely mental; they could also be the intuitions of external objects. Accordingly, the concept of representations referred to both the stimuli from external objects as well as mental states (*KrV* B 376; Guyer 2006, p. 53). This two-fold nature matched the needs of Reinhold's monadic system because it comprised the external and the internal, subject and object, inside and outside, and unified both: 'das doppelte Bezogenwerden der Vorstellung auf Objekt und Subjekt' ('the double relation of presentation to object and subject' Reinhold cited in Frank 1997, p. 240 [my translation]). On the basis of this first principle, Reinhold reconstructed his unified metaphysical system despite the fact that it contradicted Kant's *Critique of Pure Reason*.

The blurry term 'representations' reintroduced the element into philosophy that Kant had exposed as a basic error, a so-called paralogism, namely that of idealism. The 'fourth paralogism' in the *first critique* showed that the certainty of external objects could only be proven by virtue of a dual system (Beiser 2002, pp. 113–14).

> Also ist das Dasein aller Gegenstände äußerer Sinne zweifelhaft. Diese Ungewißheit nenne ich die Idealität äußerer Erscheinungen, und die Lehre dieser Idealität heißt der *Idealism* [sic], in Vergleichung mit welchem die Behauptung einer möglichen Gewißheit von Gegenständen äußerer Sinne der *Dualism* [sic] genennt wird. (*KrV* A 367)
>
> (Thus the existence of all objects of outer sense is doubtful. This uncertainty I call the ideality of outer appearances, and the doctrine of this ideality is called **idealism,** in comparison with which the assertion of a possible certainty of objects of outer sense is called **dualism.** [*CpR* A 367])

Reinhold's proposition of consciousness disregarded this paralogism.

Nitsch gravitated towards idealism. Nevertheless, he did not abandon Kant's dualism in the very same fashion as Reinhold. Nitsch used, according to his own words, 'some hints contained in Professor Reinhold's excellent Theory of Human Representations' (1796, p. 7). Nitsch's theoretical exposition does not represent a copy of the function of representations in Reinhold's system. Like Reinhold and many of the early German Romantics including Fichte and Novalis, Nitsch was particularly interested in Kant's argument that spontaneity and not receptivity constituted the connection of the manifold necessary for experience (Götze 2001, p. 50; see *KrV* B 132–64). Nitsch's exposition of Kant's epistemology was nuanced and concluded with the observation:

> As reason neither by its ideas nor by its principles can know any thing; it follows that this faculty can give us no knowledge of immaterial existencies [sic]; . . . All ideas which it [Reason] produces, although they contain something that is not found in time and space, namely unconditioned totality; yet they contain no knowledge of objects distinct from the mind, and serve only to regulate our experience, and to promote our progress in experimental [empirical] knowledge. (1796, p. 140)

Nitsch made no claims of originality. One can tell, however, that he felt self-conscious due to his independent thought because he apologized for providing his readers merely with his own historical introduction. This circumstance further indicates that Nitsch's book, or at least parts of it, were the result of his own studies: 'To this historical sketch of philosophic opinions it may be objected – that it is unsupported by authority' (1796, p. 53). Nitsch apparently felt the need to disclaim his intellectual production; had he followed Reinhold slavishly he would hardly have expressed such concerns.

Similar to the German *Popularphilosophen*, who introduced a great deal of Scottish common sense and British empiricism into German culture (see Chapter 5), Nitsch was sensitive to his audience's interest in combining German rationality with, and not imposing it on, British philosophy. One of his main contributions lies in his attempt to place Kant within British empiricism or, as he called it, within

> Natural Philosophy I mean that Science, which enquires into the various properties and relations of the visible or sensible Phenomena in Nature, and which excludes from the compass of its contemplations all those things, properties, and relations whose existence is not attested by the incontrovertible evidence of the senses. (1796, p. 9)

Having said that, the similarities with Reinhold are important. Compared to Beddoes, Nitsch presented Kant, as Reinhold had done before him, as a decided adversary of atheism and clear alternative to Hume's scepticism.

> [T]he repeated attempts to demonstrate the existence of the Deity have already introduced into the world many doubts, opposite opinions, and demonstrations . . . a constant repugnance in sentiment respecting objects of great importance to mankind, must necessarily have a tendency, if not to erect the black standard of Atheism, yet to enlarge the empire of Scepticism, and to generate a kind of distrust in the decisions of reason, I shall proceed to exhibit those measures which Professor Kant thought proper to adopt in order to remove that evil. (1796, p. 23; see pp. 144–5)

While he admitted that it is possible to object that 'Kant's System leads into Scepticism' (1796, p. 144), Nitsch systematically supported the notion that Kant had rescued traditional metaphysics from perpetual doubt.

Nitsch, like Reinhold, introduced Kant's *first critique* in religious terms. Nitsch explained that the enquiry in 'Criticism of Pure Reason' (1796, p. 27) – '*What* can be known by man in general, or what is the nature and extent of human knowledge in general [?]' – developed out of the theological concern for what can be known about ideas outside the realm of experience 'Can any man have notions of real existencies [sic] which are imperceptible' (1796, p. 29). He possibly had in mind Kant's development since the 1763 publication of *Der einzig mögliche Beweis vom Daseyn Gottes (The Only Possible Basis for a Demonstration of the Existence of God),* which Nitsch listed as one of his references (1796, p. 3n). In this publication, Kant reiterated his charge that existence is not a predicate and further developed the argument that 'the existence of God can be proven as the necessary condition of any *possibility* whatever' (Guyer 2006, p. 22).

Kant himself had advised Nitsch in 1794 to use known metaphysical ideas as a point of departure for his lectures:

> Mir scheint es nützlich zu seyn [sic], wenn Sie zuvor die Endabsicht der Vernunft mit ihrer Metaphisick [sic] (die mehr oder weniger in allen Köpfen ist, und ewig

bleiben wird) anzeigten, welche in nichts anders besteht als von Sinnlichen zum Übersinnlichen (Gott Freyheit [sic], und Unsterblichkeit) aufzusteigen. (Kant cited in Baum and Malter 1991, p. 466)

(It seems for me useful for you to indicate beforehand the final intention [my alteration] of reason with respect to metaphysics [which is already more or less present in every mind and will forever remain]: it consists of nothing but the ascent from the sensible to the supersensible [God, freedom and immortality]. [Kant trans. by Zweig 2001, p. 286])

Kant's guideline shows that his opinion on the subject was not determined once and for all by publishing the *Critique of Pure Reason*; he had done much to expose the deficiency of this kind of thinking, but at the same time he encouraged it in his former student.[22] Nitsch followed the advice (1796, p. 32), while taking great care to differentiate carefully between Kant's system and that of other philosophers such as Berkeley (1796, p. 150). Nitsch himself had, as mentioned before, a tendency towards idealism. Occasionally, he gave a glimpse of his personal view:

nevertheless, I am bold enough to affirm, without being an advocate of Idealism, that his sect [the Idealists], when argument, and not custom or habit, shall decide, must necessarily gain additional strength ... It is, therefore, certain, that there being no external world, no sensitive faculty can exist, that, consequently, the world of ideas is the only world of realities, and that the endeavours of the Materialists, to convert the ideas and operations of our minds into external bodies and mechanical motions, will and can never succeed. (1796, pp. 45–7)

Despite Nitsch's idealist preference and occasional departures from Kant, his treatise did not fully obliterate Kant's dualism (see 1796, p. 110).[23]

The affirmative goal of critical philosophy was pivotal for the advocacy of Kant in England, as was atheism for its rejection. Two entries on critical philosophy dating from the early 1800s are representative of two opposing interpretations. What both entries further illustrate is the centrality of religion for the earliest phase of Kant's transmission in England. The Unitarians John Aikin junior and William Enfield published in volume six (1807) of *General Biography; or Lives, Critical and Historical, of the most Eminent Persons of All Ages, Countries, Conditions and Professions Arranged in Alphabetical Order* (1799–1815) a seven-page outline of Kant's life and work written by Revd Thomas Morgan.[24] The entry offers a typically Unitarian view of Kant. Morgan's natural concern as rational dissenter was the affirmation of metaphysics on rational grounds; accordingly he described Kant's philosophical enterprise as follows:

He [Kant] wished to establish all human knowledge on the basis of reason, and, therefore, rejected all principles as visionary, which did not admit of a fundamental explanation. He conceived, however, of religion as an inherent quality of our souls, which panted after some higher object than this transitory existence: it demanded no proof from without, it flowed of itself from within ourselves. From this view of the subject he [Kant] was accused by some of mysticism, while others thought that they saw in his doctrine what was inimical to divine truth. (Morgan 1807, p. 7)

Morgan saw Kant's denial of the possibility of demonstrating the existence of the Deity as an indication for his heartfelt belief that required no proof 'from without'. In order to remove any doubt about Kant's orthodoxy, the Unitarian added: 'Thus much, however, is certain, from the testimony of his best friends, and the whole tenor of his works, that he was a firm believer in the Deity, a future state, and Christianity' (1807, p. 7). Morgan's article of the early 1800s concurred with the message of Reinhold's 'gospel of pure reason' and harkened back to the first articles and publications on Kant in England in the mid-1790s. In doing so, it expressed almost the exact opposite of an earlier entry in the *Encyclopaedia Britannica*.

This entry in the 1801 *Supplement* to the third edition of *Encyclopaedia Britannica* exemplifies what its vehement opponents thought of critical philosophy. The text was the result of the collaboration between the *Anti-Jacobin Review*, the editor of the *Supplement* George Gleig and his co-editor John Robison the author of *Proofs of a Conspiracy*. It was based on the insightful article by Jean-Joseph Mounier (1758–1806), published in the *Anti-Jacobin Review*, and rewritten by James Walker and Robison. Similar to Abbé Barruel's *Memoirs illustrating the History of Jacobinism*, the printed text included marginal annotations, such as 'Impenetrability', 'Of which the fundamental principles are not new', 'Improper use of terms', 'Groundless or false assertions', 'Bad logic', 'Tendency of the system towards atheism', 'Kant confutes himself', 'His morality is extravagant'. According to the entry, critical philosophy was a 'mire of atheism'; its 'doctrines . . . detestable' (Gleig 1801 II, p. 359). The entry rejects critical philosophy on the grounds of its alleged atheism. The text did little else than to dissuade the reader from the study of this dangerous author. The entry is representative of a widespread opinion from 1799 onwards. The anti-Kantian campaign spearheaded by the *Anti-Jacobin Review* obliterated, with few exceptions, the budding public interest in Kant effectively and had a strong impact on potential disseminators like Coleridge, who remained reticent to publicize Kant studies for most of his life (see Chapter 5). The religious implications of critical philosophy alone were however not decisive for the English response. The political explosiveness of Kant, first revealed in England by O'Keeffe's pamphlet, became more fully known through the first English translation of Kant: *Zum Ewigen Frieden* (Micheli 1990, p. 277; Boswell 1991, p. 232).

The fact that *Perpetual Peace* was the first English translation of Kant is hugely important, albeit little known. Kant made his first public appearance in English print with a pamphlet that advocated action for the sake of a republican constitution for every nation state as well as of national and international peace. Kant's composition of the pamphlet coincided with, and was possibly even occasioned by the peace of Basel (between Prussia and Revolutionary France) with which Prussia quit the Alliance in spring 1795. *Perpetual Peace* set the tone for Kant's reception as a radical author (Höffe 2004, p. 5). The book appeared with the dissenting publisher Vernor and Hood.[25]

It contributed to the polarization of Kantian philosophy during the period: government supporters in principle rejected, and opponents of the war in principle approved of, the publication (Micheli 1990, pp. 273–7). For Barruel, *Perpetual Peace* was one of Kant's most dangerous publications (1799 IV, 526n). The series of publications on Kant in 1796 successively led deeper into the radical and dissenting milieu in England. One man in particular helped to cement the link in London. This person was Friedrich August Nitsch.[26]

The formation of the Kantian circle in 1790s London

Kant has been seen as one of the possible fathers of European Romanticisms in the Anglo-Saxon scholarship since the early twentieth century (Lovejoy 1924, p. 230). The extent of his influence on the British Romantic writers remains a matter of investigation. According to the accepted view, 'only Coleridge, De Quincey, – and Carlyle, if one considers him a Romantic (and he shares his birth-year with Keats) – were directly and deeply influenced by Kant and the post-Kantians' (Thorslev 1993, p. 81). Nitsch, his lectures, teachings and his publications expand the effective history of Kant in mid-1790s London circles considerably. Yet the significance of Nitsch for the Anglophone reception of Kant has barely been recognized. Nor has his informal Kantian Society in 1790s London received any scholarly attention since the 1930s, when August Weber in *Bristols Bedeutung* (1935, p. 110), and before him Leslie Stephen, referred to the group (1910, p. 54). This deficit matters because Nitsch's actions did much to spread Kantianism in late eighteenth-century England, and his work does much now to destabilize common views of transcendentalism in scholarship of British Romantic culture and literature. Since 2002, when the influential collection of essays *Romantic Sociability* by Gillian Russell and Clara Tuite was published, scholars of British Romanticism have started to deconstruct the Romantic myth of the solitary poet by exploring literary networks and circles of friends around public figures of the period like Leigh Hunt (Hay 2010) and Charles Lamb (James 2008). Kantian philosophy stands for traditional Romanticism, and his influential theory of genius in the *Critique of the Power of Judgment* and the ethics of autonomy have helped to sustain the myth of isolation in Romantic literature. Consequently Kant's philosophy stands for the facilitation of escapism and political disenchantment (McGann 1983, p. 98; Thompson 1969). According to Susan Manning, critical philosophy marked a new stage of specialization in philosophy because of its high demands on readers. Hence critical philosophy is seen as the beginning of an unprecedented era of philosophical impenetrability (Manning 1997, p. 587). The existence of Nitsch's Kantian Society, the content of Nitsch's lectures (published in the form of his introduction, 1796), and the names of the identified members challenge these assumptions and disclose that Nitsch's impact, and concomitantly that of Kant, was more important than previously thought.

Volume thirteen of the Academy edition of Kant's works (1922) dismissed Nitsch's treatise as insignificant: 'Das Buch hat keine Bedeutung' (*Akk XIII*, p. 370). Nitsch has received some minor credit for his introductory exposition (Wellek 1931, p. 8; Hall 1970; Baum and Malter 1991) and is mentioned by a few scholars as an intermediary figure between German and English Romanticism (Simpson 1993, p. 97; Leask 1988, p. 83; Rothenberg 1993, pp. 79–82). The entry on Nitsch in the *Dictionary of Eighteenth-Century German Philosophers* speaks of 'the failure of his book' (Micheli 2010, p. 858). Micheli's entry includes a biographical outline and a short summary of Nitsch's book and of the reviews it received. It tells a brief history of defeat, according to which, Nitsch was born in Gumbinnen, East Prussia, as the son of a military accountant (Poschmann 1963, p. 473). After studying theology at Königsberg, where he had matriculated in October 1785, Nitsch taught mathematics and Latin at the local Collegium Fridericianum. In 1793, he moved to London, lectured and published a book on Kant to little avail. According to Micheli, he returned 'possibly before the end of 1797' to Germany, where he died 'around 1813' (Micheli 2010, p. 858; Wilkes 1817, p. 783). This is the standard view of Nitsch's life and work.

Micheli's article omits several important circumstances, which change the picture of Nitsch's life, work and by extension of the circulation of Kantian ideas in mid-1790s London. First, it is surprising that Nitsch's book is still regarded as a 'failure' despite the fact that it made a very significant contribution to the English language by introducing a set of newly defined philosophical terms. Roland Hall listed in 1970 twenty-seven terms from Nitsch's book that either antedated entries in the *Oxford English Dictionary* for certain words or senses of words or represented the introduction of new words (1970, p. 315). Since the 1970s, the *Oxford English Dictionary* has updated, in most cases, Nitsch's contributions; they are now included. The *OED* records that Nitsch was the first to attribute specific philosophical meanings to at least thirteen English words (Nitsch has overall twenty-six entries). These terms include 'Empiricism' (Nitsch 1796, p. 218), 'ideal' ('which can only be approached, but never reached' 1796, p. 52n), 'Categorical Imperative' ('which represents an action which is necessary in itself, and imposes an obligation upon all those who would keep up their reason and not fall into contradiction with their own will' 1796, p. 195), 'intuition' ('may be called . . . sensations' because they are the result of 'changes . . . in our Receptivity' 1796, p. 84), 'Kantean' or 'Kantian', 'matter' ('the given matter in every perception, knowledge, &c. is a variety' 1796, p. 73), 'Noumenon' ('a world of Noumena or an intellectual world, or a world of substances' 1796, p. 118), 'schema' ('of a Category is no picture of any thing; but being a synthesis of time agreeably to a synthetical rule expressed in a Category' 1796, p. 103) and 'Schemata' ('are, therefore, determinations of time by the pure Intellect; their use is to bring a variety of intuitions under a few heads' 1796, p. 110), 'spiritualist' and 'spiritualism' ('mere inclination to the opinion of these sects' 1796, p. 52n), 'synthetical "judgment *á priori*"' ('where the objective unity is produced from an intuition *á priori*' 1796, p. 89); and 'unconditioned' ('no longer depending upon other limits' 1796, p. 127). The *OED* still omits, for instance, Nitsch's introduction of the term 'Category' (1796, p. 100), the first use of which is dated to 1829. I will discuss some of Nitsch's terminology in more detail (e.g. 'categorical imperative' in Chapter 3; 'intuition' in Chapter 7). At this point, they are mainly important to demonstrate Nitsch's philosophical and linguistic legacy.

Second, it is important to consider how his contemporaries saw Nitsch. The German press described Nitsch as a highly educated and hard-working young man with perfect English and expertise in classical literature, mathematics and philosophy

(*Berlinische Monatsschrift* [1794], p. 73). In 1804, his mentor Professor Kraus also spoke warmly of Nitsch, especially of his ambition and extraordinary intellectual energy despite his ill health (cited in Baum and Malter 1991, p. 461n).[27] If we trust the copy of a letter from Kant dating from October 1794, as Baum and Malter convincingly suggest we should, Kant approved of Nitsch. Not only did he praise Nitsch's decided and thorough way of thinking, he also supported his plans in England addressing him warmly as an esteemed and dear friend 'Geehrter and Geliebter Freund!' (Baum and Malter 1991, p. 466; see p. 467).

Third, new archival materials, an article in the *Berlinische Monatschrift (Berlin Monthly)* written in March 1794 and the biography of Nitsch's mentor Kraus (Voigt 1819, pp. 329, 340, 347, 354–6), disclose that, after teaching at the Fridericianum in Königsberg, Nitsch worked as a private tutor ('Hofmeister') for the children of the British envoy Ewart in Berlin. When Ewart died and his widow returned to England, Nitsch accompanied the family (*Berlinische Monatsschrift* [1794], pp. 72–7). This detail matters because his position helped Nitsch to enter London society smoothly. Nitsch stayed with a very wealthy medical doctor in No 88. St. Martin's Lane, near Charing Cross (*Berlinische Monatsschrift* [1794], p. 73; see *Akk XI*, p. 519; *Correspondence*, 11: 519 [p. 484]; Voigt 1819, p. 354).[28] During his first six months in London, Nitsch apparently made the acquaintance of several members of the Royal Society at the doctor's home as he reported in a letter to Kant (*Akk XI*, p. 518; *Correspondence* 11: 518 [p. 484]). Unhappy with his denigrating (unpaid) situation at Martin's Lane, Nitsch resolved to leave and confronted his need for an income by designing, planning and advertising a series of Kantian lectures (*Akk XI*, p. 518; *Correspondence* 11: 518 [p. 484]; Voigt 1819, p. 354–6). During the course of his stay in England, Nitsch managed to win the patronage of the son of the Danish emissary Count Wedel-Jarlsberg (Baum and Malter 1991, p. 461).[29] While the date of his departure from England is still unknown, an article in the *Britannic Magazine* suggests, contrary to Micheli's view, that he was still in London in 1800 (Willich 1800, p. 241).

Fourth, the fact that Nitsch's lectures met initially with great success has been completely neglected by previous scholarship (Voigt 1819, pp. 354–5; *Berlinische Monatsschrift* [1794], pp. 72–7). Nitsch told Kant in July 1794 about the great and unexpected applause he had earned (*Akk XI*, p. 518; *Correspondence* 11: 518 [p. 484]). Kraus gave the following description, which I quote from Ernest Belfort Bax's translation:

> On the evening of the 3rd of March [1794], the occasion of the first lecture, the street in which the lecturer room was situated was early lined with carriages, and Nitsch, on his appearance on the platform, found himself confronted by a large audience, composed of members of the nobility, the clergy, and the "learned" professions generally, and including, as we are informed, many "richly attired" ladies. The lecture lasted an hour and a half, and was received with applause, but Nitsch had no sooner concluded than he was forced to commence a disputation, lasting two hours, in the course of which he was required to answer every conceivable objection that could be raised in a running fire of questions. So successfully did he pass through this ordeal, and so much interest did the three introductory lectures

evoke, that a sufficiently large number of subscribers was got together to make it worth while for him to undertake a course of thirty-six lectures, at a fee of three guineas each person, expounding in detail the principles of the critical philosophy. He concluded them successfully [a few weeks ago] in August. But, meanwhile, the desire for further information had become so great, that a repetition of the lectures was commenced the following October. (Bax 1883, p. ixl)[30]

It is an extreme understatement to say that Nitsch 'began to give lessons there on KANT's philosophy' (Micheli 2010, p. 858). Nitsch gave several series of lectures, consisting of 36 lectures each, the first of which started in spring 1794. He advertised his subsequent series of lectures widely in the *True Briton* (5 March 1795) and the *Morning Chronicle* (21 March 1795) and elsewhere in *The Star* (27 June 1796) and the *Oracle and Public Advertiser* (12 May 1796).

The lectures took place between 1794 and 1797 in the West End area. The first lectures in 1794 were free of charge and attracted enough subscribers for the whole course. Nitsch charged three guineas for the subscription of the entire course of thirty-six lectures, one guinea per month, or two shillings and sixpence for a single lecture. A lecture by Nitsch thus cost double the amount of those by Coleridge or Thelwall held around the same time and equalled a fourth or a fifth of the average journeyman's weekly wages (Patton and Mann 1971, pp. xxxi, xxxix). While the location for his lectures might have changed several times, it is known that some, if not all, of Nitsch's lectures were held at No 23, King Street, Soho (*True Briton* [5 March 1795]) and No 16 Panton Square, Haymarket (*English Review* 27 [1796], p. 356). That means he lectured in close vicinity to the newspaper room in Compton Street, Soho, where John Thelwall began his lecturing career as a radical reformer (Russell 2002, p. 126), and nearby the venue where the Whigs and London Corresponding Society held their joint meeting in December 1795 (i.e. at 'Westminster Forum, Panton-street, in the Haymarket'). The number of lecture series that Nitsch gave in London is hard to determine. Wellek speaks of lectures in 1794, 1795, and 1796 (1931, p. 7), but announcements in the *Morning Chronicle* with a detailed prospectus (5 and 12 December 1796) indicate that Nitsch renewed his lectures in early 1797.

Fifthly, we know that Nitsch's exposition was based on his lectures (Voigt 1819, p. 356). Therefore, I contend that it is inaccurate to speak of the failure of Nitsch's book (Micheli 2010, p. 858). One of Nitsch's most important messages in support of Kant was the unwavering affirmation of free will that offered a needed alternative to the theories of Hartley and Thomas Hobbes (see Chapter 3).[31] Wellek once noted that Nitsch 'rarely succeeds in seeing the actual difficulties with which Kant's reception would have to cope in England' (1931, pp. 7–8). The statement suggests that Nitsch was unsuccessful in adapting Kant's philosophy to suit English tastes. Such a view is incorrect but perhaps understandable if we consider that Wellek wrote at a time when studies in British Romanticism still paid little attention to the radical and rational dissenting milieus in late eighteenth-century England. More than four decades after the publication of Wellek's seminal study, scholars of Coleridge's reception started to pay increasing attention to the affinity between Coleridge's Unitarianism and his German beliefs (see Shaffer 1975; Asthon 1980; Perry 1999). These circumstances explain to a certain extent why commentators have failed to realize that Nitsch was instrumental in the transmission of Kant's philosophy in England. Wellek, for instance, seems unaware of the great relevance of Nitsch's arguments for Coleridge and his contemporaries. These arguments were crucial in the context of 1790s religious dissent and reform.

A short article in *Telegraph* (21 February 1797) illustrates how Nitsch's advocacy of Kantian free will was circulated.[32] After a short introduction on the current philosophical debate about the term 'first cause', the article turned to the recent publication of Nitsch's *General and Introductory View* (published in May 1796) and gave an abstract. The article clearly demonstrates one of Nitsch's lasting legacies: the text focused on Kant's relevance for the debate on free will and designated those who opposed the doctrine as 'necessitarian'. By exposing the deficits of necessitarian views, Nitsch could relate critical philosophy to the philosophical interests of his audience:

> the Necessitarians confound in their argument the laws by which our intuition are arranged, with the laws by which the things themselves are arranged, of which we know nothing, and affords all the reasons necessary to prove that our notion of a free will is not contradictory nor imaginary. (1796, p. 197)

The philosophical interests of Nitsch's audience had been shaped by Locke's reaction against the reasoning of Descartes, Spinoza and Malebranche; philosophical determinism prevailed. For those unfamiliar with Kant's terminology, Nitsch paraphrased 'if . . . the active substance called man . . . is not in time, his will cannot be influenced by the laws of time, which are those of cause and effect; for these laws can be only where time is' (1796, pp. 197–8). Nitsch made clear that Kant offered a theory to escape laws of time and space without compromising the fidelity to experience. In doing so, he paid special attention to associationism. Associationists like Hartley and Priestley tended to be necessitarian, that is reject the constitutive power of will, because the determination of choice through physical and emotional needs fitted with 'the picture of the mind as a repetition-driven machine' (Harris 2005, p. 18). Accordingly, Nitsch related critical philosophy to the physiology of the brain:

> it has been attempted by many celebrated Philosophers to consider thought as a mere property of the nervous system, to take the capacity of reciprocal resistance in inert, solid, and incompressible bodies, for a mechanical species of perception, to account for all our sensations, ideas, and mental operations, from vibrations, vibratiuncles [sic], or miniature vibrations of the medullary substance of the nerves and brain. (1796, p. 44)

Almost twenty years later, Coleridge would use almost exactly the same words to condemn Hartley's philosophy in *Biographia Literaria*.

Here Nitsch put forward what all post-Kantian Idealists including Coleridge would, according to Hedley, regard as one of the major outcomes of Kant's philosophy: 'if the mind is synthetic, and not merely reading off information from the world, determinism cannot be correct. A true philosophy must be a philosophy of freedom' (2000, pp. 24–5). Simultaneously Nitsch's pamphlet transmitted, as I will explain in detail in Chapter 3, the concomitant Kantian idea that 'freedom is the *ratio essendi* of morality. Morality is not the acceptance of alien codes and precepts, but is derived from the proper exercise of autonomous reason' (Hedley 2000, p. 25). What distinguishes Nitsch from his German contemporaries is that he knew from experience, as a London lecturer, that freedom constituted a unique selling point of critical philosophy for his 1790s English audience. It remains one of Nitsch's lasting achievements that he inserted Kantian philosophy in the current debate on associationism and free will. It greatly aided the transmission Kant's philosophy within in the progressive milieu in London, in Bristol and elsewhere in England in the mid-1790s.

Nitsch's strategy was somewhat reminiscent of that of Reinhold, who had popularized Kant in German culture by introducing critical philosophy into the pantheism controversy. Similarly, Nitsch realized that there was a pathway for Kantianism into English culture through associationism (see 1796, pp. 17; 37–8; 61–4; 197–8; 172–4). He tried to make critical philosophy attractive to those who were interested in psychology and physiology of the brain but dissatisfied with the accompanying limitations on free will:

> Professor Kant observed, that in explaining the Power of Knowledge, which comprehends Reason, Understanding, and Sense, it would be erroneous to derive it from our pretended knowledge of the nerves, the brain, the visible and invisible worlds, and that we ought first of all to enquire into the true nature and constitution of this power. (1796, p. 61)

Yet the assimilation of Kant's transcendental enquiry to associationism was not enough. Scholars have credited Reinhold with developing the innovative argument of the historicity of Reason (Breazeale 2010, p. 90).[33] Reinhold's success exceeded that of Nitsch by far; nonetheless, Nitsch's efforts were not in vain but bore fruits. While Reinhold built on Kant to demonstrate the changes in the needs of Reason over time, one could say that Nitsch did so, too, but differently. He implicitly recognized the changes in the conditions of Reason across national boundaries. In 1794, he was studying the most popular English philosophers (*Akk XI*, p. 518; *Correspondence* 11: 518 [p. 484]). In 1796, Nitsch addressed the linguistic and cultural difficulties of introducing Kant's philosophy to an English audience. He discussed in great detail the grave problem of finding a stylistically satisfying way for communicating Kant's principles. In addition, he was aware of the importance of utilitarian inclination of his English audience: 'what use a science [Kant's philosophy] might be?' (*Monthly Magazine* 2 [1796], p. 703, see pp. 702–4). Concerning the former problem, Nitsch took great care to consistently paraphrase Kantian notions. Contrary to Wellek's dismissive comment ('verbose statements of trivialities', 1931, p. 7), I regard the accessible style of Nitsch's composition as a necessary and felicitous response to his English audience. Considering the applicability of critical philosophy, Nitsch declared, in a way that broadly accommodated British empiricism and alluded to Isaac Newton as well as to William Herschel, that Kant's philosophy represented essential reading for anyone interested in the mental faculties:

> every man of good education and learning, while he ranges about in the field of external objects, and learns to measure the sun and the stars, should reserve some little portion of his time to get acquainted with himself, and with the invariable laws of mental faculties. (*Monthly Magazine* 2 [1796], p. 703)

Here, Nitsch made a point that would prove crucial for Coleridge's intellectual development: it is known that the poet would gradually turn away from Hartley's philosophy to Kantian and post-Kantian philosophy, but it has remained unknown that Nitsch anticipated and prepared Coleridge for this gradual transition.

This study traces Nitsch's influence on Coleridge and analyses in Chapters 3 and 7 the ways in which Nitsch primed Coleridge to study Kant. The next section will therefore merely outline what would otherwise lead far beyond the scope of the present study. The following passage accounts for the sixth reason why Nitsch represents an important figure in Romantic culture. The German succeeded in gathering a group of people around himself who engaged with critical philosophy, some of them being influential members of society. The group included O'Keeffe, Thomas Wirgman, Henry James Richter and Thelwall (Wellek 1931, p. 205; Wheeler 1981, p. 81).[34] Wirgman published enthusiastic articles on Kant, his 'Logic' and 'Moral Philosophy' in the *Encyclopaedia Londinensis* respectively in 1812 (XI, pp. 603–29), 1815 (XIII, pp. 1–31) and 1817 (XV, pp. 198–240) (Wilkes and Jones 1810–29). Evidence in Mary Hays's *Correspondence* (2004, p. 447) and in Thomas Holcroft's diary, published by Hazlitt (1933 III, p. 192), suggests that one of Holcroft's daughters, Fanny Margretta Holcroft, belonged to the group, too. Her father, an expert in German translations, was less interested in critical philosophy, commenting in his entry on 28 June 1798 that 'the Doctor [chaplain of the Austrian Embassy] thinks with me, that Kant, who is at present so much admired in Germany, is little better than a jargonist' (Hazlitt 1933 III, p. 173; Wellek 1931, p. 70). Hays also noted in her letter to William Godwin dating from May 1796 that 'Dr O-Keefe and a Mr Nirch (if I spell their names right) professors of the Kantian philosophy . . . were very civil to me & endeavoured to teach me their principles but I confess they conveyed to me no clear ideas' (2004, p. 447). Hays's letter concurs with Kraus's account (Voigt 1819, p. 354) that Nitsch instructed a mixed group, men and women alike. It is unlikely that the circle formed a formal society, with regular meetings in a public venue. O'Keeffe called the circle 'Kantean society of Moral, Practical and Speculative Philosophy' and announced the publication of their 'transactions' (1795, p. 58), whereas Thelwall only remembered Nitsch to have 'attempted to establish a Kantean school or society here' (Pollin 1970, p. 92). What seems clear is that the group was known for its progressive politics. The conservative Hannah More still loathed the mere mention of the Kantian Society in 1814, supposedly on moral grounds (Weber 1935, p. 110). Yet what repulsed the conservative More attracted people like Godwin.

Godwin was familiar with Nitsch and his circle and by extension with Kant's philosophy. The English philosopher attended Nitsch's lecture on 23 March 1795 according to his diary (Myers et al. 2010).[35] Godwin's diary further contains entries with Kantians. It mentions 'Wirgman' on 29 April and 5 May 1812 as well as on 29 March and 6 May 1819.[36] The hitherto unidentified 'Wirgman' in Godwin's diary is the former member of the Kantian Society, Thomas Wirgman, whose first article on Kant appeared in the *Encyclopaedia Londinensis* in the same year (1812).[37] In addition, the diary records regular meetings with a further member of the Kantian Society, Henry J. Richter, during the period between 1795 and 1796.[38] The meeting with Wirgman on 5 May 1812 included Coleridge alongside Elton Hammond, Joseph Hume, and Francis

Place; the entry on 29 March 1819 contains three Kantians, Coleridge, Wirgman and Henry J. Richter, and must have been occasioned by Coleridge's last performance in his lecture series on philosophy in the 'Crown and Anchor' Tavern on the Strand. The meeting of Godwin, Coleridge, Wirgman and Henry Richter in the same place points to a reunion of the circle around Nitsch in the 1790s; by 1819, it was Coleridge who lectured on Kant (see Chapter 5).

In March 1795 when he attended Nitsch's lecture, Godwin was working on the second edition of *Political Justice*, published in November 1795 (Godwin 1993 III, p. 7). Godwin made great efforts to revise what he had come to see as three blemishes in *Political Justice* (1793): his stoicism and inattention to pleasure and pain; his inattention to the principles that feeling not judgement is the cause of human action; and the unqualified condemnation of private affections (Philp 1986, p. 142). In the first edition Godwin proclaimed that '[w]hen we do the most benevolent action, it is with a view only to our own advantage, and with the most sovereign and unreserved neglect of that of others' (1793 I, pp. 332–3). In the second edition, Godwin changed substantially sections of the key chapter on self-love and benevolence by giving a new account of ethical motivation in which Reason and sense content with each other (Philp 1986, p. 147). Mark Philp has shown that Godwin's alteration were concessions to a new social milieu, new experiences and new language of expression that he encountered between 1793 and 1795 in the company of Mary Hays, Thomas Holcroft and William Frend, as well as the result of his sporadic perusals of the 'sympathy school' of David Hume, Adam Smith and Edmund Burke (Philp 1986, pp. 143, 152, 166). Nitsch and his lectures formed part of this milieu. It is possible that Nitsch's treatment of Kantian ethics informed Godwin's thinking about voluntary action and our motivation for disinterested benevolence. Similar to Godwin's second edition and freely interpreting Kant, Nitsch agreed with Godwin that 'to motivate us to fulfil the requirements of disinterested benevolence there must be sufficient indirect motives to dispose us general towards the good of others' (Philp 1986, p. 153). Nitsch's take on Kant's ethics appealed to his English audience and is therefore central to the discussion of Coleridge's response in Chapter 3. At this point, it is important to note that contrary to Nitsch, Godwin proclaimed an atheistic system (Philp 1986, p. 161). This difference leads back to Reinhold's interpretation, Nitsch's embrace of religious faith, and its appeal for rational dissenters. Godwin's attendance of Nitsch's lectures raises questions of influence that would lead, as mentioned, beyond the framework of this study. Godwin is relevant because the affinities I have indicated give us an idea of the extent of Nitsch's and thus of Kant's effective circle in London.[39] Godwin must have been interested in critical philosophy for various reasons. His theory of evil, for instance, concurs with that of Kant. According to *Political Justice*, '[w]e bring into the world with us no innate principles: consequently we are neither virtuous nor vicious as we first come into existence' (1793 I, p. 12). Kant expounded similarly in the *second critique* that good and evil are determined by the compliance, or respectively the deviation from, the moral law and not by birth.[40] After moving out of St. Martin's Lane, Nitsch had to earn his living by lecturing and publishing and probably started to frequent then the radical and dissenting circles in London. It is true that critical philosophy marked a new level of specialization in philosophy (Manning 1997, p. 387), but thanks to Nitsch (and, later on, Willich) this development did not preclude critical philosophy from entering conversations, gatherings and lectures in 1790s London.[41] The roots of Coleridge's life-long preoccupation with critical philosophy lie in this sociopolitical environment in London and Bristol (Class 2009a).

1787, 1796 and the aftermath

1787 was the year in which Kant started to think that his contemporaries took critical philosophy seriously. It was the year when he published the second edition of the *Critique of Pure Reason* and the year when Reinhold completed the serial publication of eight articles on Kantian philosophy in the *Teutscher Merkur*. In 1787, Kantian philosophy became fashionable in Germany. It seems surprising that scholars have barely taken notice of, or dismissed, the significance of these events for the English transmission of critical philosophy. It can hardly be a coincidence that the first extant mention of critical philosophy in a British periodical appeared in 1787. It took a few years until the first expositions of critical philosophy followed. Reinhold shifted the public attentions to the 'Transcendental Dialectic' and the 'Transcendental Method' and emphasized the importance of practical Reason in Kant's system; he injected critical philosophy in the pantheism controversy. The first detailed review by Sowden in 1793 represented Kant in those constitutive terms, as did Beddoes in *Observations*. The first favourable English introductions to critical philosophy published in late 1795 and 1796 by Beddoes, O'Keeffe and Nitsch maintained Reinhold's focus on the affirmative dimension of the *Critique of Pure Reason*.

It seems difficult to maintain the view that the works of the early mediators were insignificant considering for instance the development of British theology in the nineteenth century. 'Kant's doctrine of the primacy of the practical reason remains', as Donald MacKinnon notes, 'the pivot of his influence on British theology' (1990, p. 348). The emphasis on practical Reason can be traced from Coleridge, via Thomas Arnold, Master of Rugby school, where T. H. Green was a student from 1850 to 1855, to Green's students and future high Anglicans of the school of *Lux Mundi* (1889) Charles Gore and Henry Scott-Holland (Sweet 2010, p. 2; MacKinnon 1990, p. 358). It is true that Reinhold's direct impact in the Anglophone world has been limited by the unavailability of translations – to date few works by him have been translated (di Giovanni and Harris 1985, Roehr 1995, Ameriks and Hebbeler 2005); indeed, the translation *Essay on a New Theory of the Human Capacity for Representation* by Tim Mehigan and Barry Empson appeared in 2011. However it is, historically speaking, inaccurate to think that he made no significant impact on English culture. This chapter has shown that through Beddoes, O'Keeffe and Nitsch Reinhold's theological and reformative approach to critical philosophy became formative in England. That is not to say that the advocacy of critical philosophy depended exclusively on Reinhold. Each of the disseminators drew on a variety of Kantian texts, preferably radical political texts and those that expanded on the function of practical Reason and the highest good, especially the *second critique*, and the *Critique of the Power of Judgment*. This focus can be also seen in the name of Nitsch's society: 'Kantean society of Moral,

Practical and Speculative Philosophy' (O'Keeffe 1795, p. 58). The first translation of *Perpetual Peace* (1796) played a particular role in making Kant known as a republican author. Previous commentators have failed to make these connections between the respective public transmission of critical philosophy in the German states and England during the last decade of the eighteenth century. The historical connections between Godwin and Kant via Nitsch have not been studied thoroughly yet. This circumstance seems linked with the low esteem in which the initial advocates of Kant in England (especially Nitsch) are commonly held. The remainder of this book will show how they (and the early opponents of Kant) exerted a formative impact on the thought of a young man who would eventually (and in part against his wish) become known as the most important mediator of German idealism in England of the nineteenth century: Samuel Taylor Coleridge, who wrote in a rather Reinholdian manner that through Kant he was 'most thoroughly persuaded' that metaphysics did not necessarily lead to 'irreligious PANTHEISM' *(Biographia Literaria* I, pp. 152–3).

2

Coleridge's Moral-Political Engagement in the mid-1790s

On Tuesday, 17 November, and Friday, 20 November 1795, the citizens of Bristol assembled at their local Guildhall. Everyone was agitated, though for different reasons. Some of them were alarmed by the news of an alleged attack on the king's life, and ready to follow the mayor's call for a meeting in celebration of the narrow escape of George III; others, however, were outraged over the ensuing new oppressive laws.[1] Lord Grenville (House of Lords) and William Pitt the Younger (House of Commons) had used the assault against the king as an opportunity to pass two bills, the Treasonable Practices Bill and the Seditious Meetings Bill, which became known as the 'Gagging Bills'. The first broadened the definition of treason to such an extent that any form of political dissent, private or public, could easily be charged with inciting the people to hatred or contempt of majesty. The second bill forbade public meetings of more than fifty people without the consent of a magistrate (Patton and Mann 1971, pp. xlvi–lii; Jay 2009, p. 125).

Nitsch recognized, as the previous chapter showed, that the debate on liberty and necessitarianism offered a pathway for critical philosophy into public debates in London and elsewhere in England, that he carved a niche for Kant by emphasizing the latter's stipulation of free will and that, furthermore, the dependence of virtue and happiness theorized in the concept of the highest good was highly important for the first appearance of Kant in English public life. This chapter establishes Coleridge's predisposition to critical philosophy as well as his political stance in the mid-1790s. Hence, the argument is twofold. First, the chapter contends that Coleridge harboured strong doubts concerning the necessitarian doctrine at the time and thus more than twenty years before his critique of Hartley in *Biographia Literaria*. Influential scholarship like that of Trevor Levere has tended to throw out the baby with the bathwater by presenting Coleridge's dissatisfaction with associationism in 'Destiny of Nations' as 'a revolt away from mere empiricism' (1981, p. 15). This chapter traces Coleridge's philosophical investment in the notion of free will in his poetry and prose around 1795 arguing that his disquiet notably with Priestley and Hartley as well as with Godwin is linked with Coleridge's awareness of their epistemological affinity with Thomas Hobbes's justification of despotism. In doing so, the chapter further proposes that Coleridge's doubts concerning associationism made him particularly responsive to the way that Nitsch marketed critical philosophy. Second, the chapter takes issue with the common view that Coleridge's concern with Christian morality was an impediment for his political radicalism. It is often thought that Coleridge was too concerned with God to endorse Godwin's progressive views consistently. I propose that, after his initial approval, Coleridge became too concerned with free will to subscribe to the first edition of Godwin's *Political Justice*. The chapter further aims to establish that Coleridge's desire to found politics on a first principle in morality is a distinctive sign of his progressive Enlightenment thinking as a young man and one that he came to abandon later on in his life (Chapters 4, 6 and 7). Simultaneously, this chapter emphasizes the importance of Coleridge's friendship with Thomas Beddoes and sheds a new light on a particular dimension of this relation that has been the subject of much-needed and excellent investigations: since Elinor Shaffer's *Kubla Khan and the Fall of Jerusalem* (1975), Beddoes has been credited with awakening Coleridge's interest in German Higher Bible Criticism. Neil Vickers's 'Coleridge, Thomas Beddoes, and Brunian Medicine' (1997, pp. 47–97), his monograph *Coleridge and the Doctors* (2004), Dorothy A. Stansfield's insightful book and article (1984; 1986) and Mike Jay's biography of Beddoes *The Atmosphere of Heaven* (2009) have further contributed to a better understanding of this historic friendship.

Political and philosophical collaborations: Coleridge and Beddoes's friendship

Samuel Taylor Coleridge and Dr Beddoes belonged to those in the assembly who condemned the limitation of free speech and public gatherings. Coleridge had come to Bristol early in 1795 with the intention of raising money for Pantisocracy through a series of political and religious lectures. Beddoes had moved to Bristol in 1793 with the long-term aim of establishing a pneumatic institute, part clinic, and part laboratory. He was known among the inhabitants of Bristol as a radical who had been 'forced to leave [his career as a reader in chemistry at the University of] Oxford on account of his political views' (Jay 2009, p. 72).[2] Both attended the Guildhall meeting in order to protest. The liberal newspaper *The Star* reported the speech by the democrat Edward Long Fox, at the beginning of the second meeting: 'One of those ancient and indubitable rights [in the Bill of Rights] was the peaceable assembling of the people together, to consider of the most proper methods of redress, when they laboured under, or were apprehensive of suffering, grievances, and to petition for their removal' (*Lectures 1795*, pp. 362–3). E. L. Fox warned the audience that the current government tried to preclude popular interference: 'these rights were attempted to be totally wrested from them' (*Lectures 1795*, p. 363). Under these conditions, the atmosphere at Bristol Guildhall assembly was tense. Some people in the audience were concerned that the magistrate might disperse the meeting unless it was conducted with extraordinary consideration. However, this fear did not hinder young Coleridge, who had just turned twenty-three. At the meeting on 17 November, he raised his voice against the mayor, who refused to hear suggestions for an amendment of the two bills, but 'was here authoritatively stopped' (*Lectures 1795*, p. 361). Despite the reluctance of 'some person on the Bench' (p. 361),

Coleridge 'did gain permission to be heard a few words . . . wherein he again declared that the whole war was a paradox' (*Lectures 1795*, p. 362). The meeting descended into chaos, but it had important consequences for the friendship of two men: Beddoes had seen Coleridge in action. The young poet had acted as one of the leading spokesmen for the liberal party who openly rejected of the war against Revolutionary France and demanded the preservation of the right to protest. By 17 November 1795, Beddoes must have been aware of, and perhaps even impressed by, Coleridge and his eloquence; the author of *The Star* report called the poet's speech 'the most sublime Address that was ever heard, perhaps, within the walls of that building' (*Lectures 1795*, p. 361).

Beddoes left the meeting and dashed off a vehement defence of British civil rights, which 'appeared in the bookshops of Joseph Cottle and John Rose, and on the stalls around the Corn Exchange . . . [t]he following morning' (Jay 2009, p. 128). The pamphlet *A Word in Defence of the Bill of Rights against the Gagging Bills* was first advertised in *Bristol Gazette* of 19 November. The controversy engendered by the pamphlet led to a meeting of opposing liberal forces on 20 November, where Beddoes advocated a petition to be signed by the citizens of Bristol and presented by two Members of Parliament for Bristol (*Lectures 1795*, p. 370). *The Star* reported that Coleridge publicly acceded to the doctor's proposal (*Lectures 1795,* p. 364). And so it was that, despite the mayor's attempt to suppress dissent – the military paraded outside the Guildhall to intimidate protesters – Beddoes, Coleridge and E. L. Fox succeeded in organizing a legal form of civil protest through a public petition. In this process, Beddoes and Coleridge had become political allies – the mayor's antagonism surely added to their sense of solidarity.[3]

Beddoes belonged to a celebrated group of experimental philosophers, rational dissenters and political radicals called the Lunar Society of Birmingham – a small, but nonetheless very influential group of optimists whose core members included Erasmus Darwin, Matthew Boulton, James Watt and Joseph Priestley (Schofield 1963, pp. 26–38; Uglow 2002, pp. 464–90). They intended to bring about social reform through scientific and technological innovation and were closely linked with the perhaps most progressive teaching institutions in England at the time, the dissenting Academies which, in contrast to older universities, encouraged modern disciplines such as mechanics, electrostatics and chemistry (Wykes 1996, pp. 124–35). Through the Lunar Society, Beddoes was in touch with Thomas Jefferson and Benjamin Franklin.[4] In 1758, Franklin met Matthew Boulton and Erasmus Darwin, with whom Beddoes corresponded. Franklin then became an honorary visitor of the group, especially later on when the rift between the American colonies and British government made the support of the discontented American States more difficult. By the time Coleridge met Beddoes in 1795, Franklin was dead and the confidence of the 'Lunatics' and other reform societies shaken. In July 1791, the Birmingham Riot had taken place when a mob burned down Priestley's house and laboratory in revenge for his revolutionary preaching (Wylie 1989, p. 51).[5] But new confidence in radical and rational dissenting circles began to widen again a couple of years later. Cambridge, for instance, survived as a centre for dissent with the foundation of the *Cambridge Intelligencer* in June 1793 and a new generation of reformers emerged in London led by John Thelwall and William Frend (Wylie 1989, p. 55). Beddoes was one of the major figures in Bristol to continue this trend; indeed, he 'was an inspiration' for Coleridge and Southey (Jay 2009, p. 117).

After November 1795, the two men made a joined effort to rebut the two bills. It seems as if they spurred each other on to further protest.[6] Coleridge subscribed to and defended Beddoes's opinions.[7] *The Plot Discovered* and *An Answer to 'A Letter to Edward Long Fox, M. D.'* either refer to Beddoes or are built on his ideas (*Lectures 1795*, p. 329). Coleridge's defence of the 'Liberty of Press' and 'of Speech' in *The Plot Discovered* echoes parts of the political thought in Beddoes's *A Word in Defence of the Bill of Rights against Gagging Bills*. Beddoes regarded the 'spirit of freedom' as the central value of society. Freedom was 'to the moral order of society', as Beddoes explained, 'what the vivifying sun himself is to the physical order of the universe' (*Lectures 1795*, p. 375). Here, freedom was the essence of society. In the face of the oppressive bills, Beddoes insisted on the article in the Bill of Rights that gave citizens the right to protest and to petition even against the will of ministers (*Lectures 1795*, p. 374). He exposed the self-interested use of power by government, the violation of the freedom of press, the increase of the power of the House of Lords as well as the sanguinary spirit of the recent legislation.

Coleridge found *A Word in Defence of the Bill of Rights* so erudite that he largely adopted Beddoes's points in *The Plot Discovered*. In a strikingly similar way to Beddoes, Coleridge diagnosed four causes of despotism. He explained, first, that the conflation of the legislative and executive branches of government allowed members of parliament to pass laws in their own interest; second, he condemned the 'attempt to assassinate the Liberty of the Press' (*Lectures 1795*, p. 286); third, he criticized the exclusion of all popular interference; and finally, he opposed heavy punishments. The echoes of Beddoes's *Defence* do not come as a surprise considering that *The Plot* was based on a lecture Coleridge gave only a week after Beddoes first published his protest against the two bills. The manifesto of his friend must still have been fresh in Coleridge's mind. He assimilated Beddoes's thought for *The Plot* and thus displayed his approval for, and conformity to, Beddoes publicly. For anyone who followed the local debate against the two bills in Bristol and elsewhere it was clear that Coleridge shared Beddoes's 'Jacobin' sentiments. Beyond politics, both men had a profound impact on each other's intellectual thought. But before discussing the philosophical fruits of this friendship, the next section examines Coleridge's political stance in more detail.

Coleridge's political and religious non-conformism

Coleridge found it difficult to identify his political conviction, let alone conform to the opinion of one political party. He defied any specific form of Realpolitik while search-ing for a moral ground for his early democratic views. The desire to found politics on first moral principles constitutes, as I contend, an essential part of Coleridge's political radicalism in the 1790s, and a stance that Coleridge would denounce as 'Jacobinism' in *The Friend* of 1809 (see Chapters 4, 6 and 7). Coleridge was, as Nicholas Roe points out, by no means '"insulated" from other reformists' (1988, p. 13), but he was deeply involved in the radical and dissenting milieu of the period. From his early undergraduate days at Jesus College, Coleridge's political activism was, as that of many of his fellow students, inseparable from his religious convictions. Religious dissenters from Cambridge, especially from Jesus College, were closely connected with the movement for parliamentary reform in London.[8] Under these circumstances Coleridge met the radical Unitarian William Frend (1757–1841) and became such a fervent supporter that he applauded him publicly in court when Frend was tried for seditious libel.[9] It was Frend who converted Coleridge to Unitarianism (Perry 1999, p. 70; Kitson 2002, p. 158). As R. K. Webb notes, 'in the dark days of the war and for long thereafter, the Unitarians seemed almost the sole open defenders of the legacy from Rational Dissent' (1996, p. 40). In agreement with his Unitarian friends and much to the regret of his older brother, Coleridge rejected the Church of England as the handmaid of a repressive state and affirmed the humanity of Christ even at the expense of being excluded from participating in the civic life of the state due to the Test and Corporation Acts against Catholics and Nonconformists including the Unitarians (1661, 1673, 1678) (Fruman 1992, p. 118). Coleridge devoured the works of the leading exponent of Unitarianism, the theologian, political writer and chemist Joseph Priestley, who emigrated to America in 1794 (Rivers and Wykes 2008). Then, after Cambridge, Coleridge together with Southey devised a scheme for emigration similar to that of Thomas Cooper and Priestley and called it Pantisocracy – a Utopian Christian community in Pennsylvania. In contrast to Priestley, Coleridge believed that the contamination of the original virtue of men was due to property: 'The real source of inconstancy, depravity, & prostitution, is Property, which mixes with & poisons every thing good' (*Letters* I, p. 214).[10] For Coleridge, property was the foremost evil he wished to remove: 'the leading Idea of Pantisocracy is to make men *necessarily* virtuous by removing all Motives to Evil – all possible Temptations' (*Letters* I, p. 114).[11] As a consequence, the young Coleridge renounced material values, which explains an important aspect of his philosophical inclination to immateriality, metaphysics and Platonism.

Coleridge had in common with various and fractured groups of radicals and reformers the wish of grounding his political ideas not necessarily on a purely religious basis, but on an ontological one. He continuously sought to reconcile moral and political freedom – a difficult position. On the one hand, his moral principles required his intellectual independence unrestrained by any party membership; on the other hand, it precluded his political intervention. In contrast to previous analysis (Colmer 1959, p. 175), I do not regard Coleridge's endeavour to combine moral and political freedom as an impediment but as a major force in his political activism, however hesitant it might have seemed. His decision to build politics on morality posed intellectual problems and consequently some degree of oscillation, but nonetheless, it was one of the ways in which Coleridge engaged with the Enlightenment belief of social and political progress. The Bristol lectures reveal that Coleridge was at great pains to define the nature of freedom and protect it from abuse. Coleridge saw himself as one of the 'zealous Advocates of Freedom' (*Lectures 1795*, p. 5), though one who no longer trusted the word 'freedom' himself any longer. He lamented the fact that the name 'freedom' had been tainted in prisons and by forced labour: 'At Genoa, the word, Liberty, is engraved on the chains of the galley-slaves, & the doors of Prisons' (*Notebooks* I, §206).

Appalled by such offences against true freedom, Coleridge attempted to specify, with considerable difficulty, which meanings of the term freedom he supported. The meaning of the term 'freedom' had become so arbitrary that Coleridge discerned four British groups who named themselves 'Friends of freedom' in 1795. In one of his earliest political statements, his lecture on morality and politics held in Bristol in late February, he singled out one of the four groups of the 'Friends of freedom' praising their critical independence and disinterested benevolence: 'that small but glorious band, whom we may truly distinguish by the name of thinking and disinterested Patriots' (*Lectures 1795*, p. 12). Due to their rational and moral skills, these men were deserving of the title 'Friends of freedom'. 'Thinking' and 'disinterested' are the key features of these role models, but what did these attributes mean for Coleridge?

Coleridge appealed to the rationality of his audience in an earlier passage that explains the connotation of 'thinking': 'It will be therefore our endeavour, not so much to excite the torpid, as to regulate the feelings of the ardent' (*Lectures 1795*, p. 5). Here, 'thinking' becomes synonymous with 'critical' as Coleridge calls for the ability of rational abstraction: 'let us not embattle our Feelings against our Reason. Let us not indulge our malignant Passions under the mask of Humanity' (*Lectures 1795*, p. 6). According to this syntax, Coleridge identified 'Reason' with 'Humanity' and gave it priority over feelings. Emotions thus rank at the lower end of the scale for they had an affinity with 'malignant Passions'. Coleridge's argument is clear. As part of his defence of Revolutionary France, he called for critical awareness of his English audience: 'In times of tumult firmness and consistency are peculiarly needful, because the passions and prejudice of mankind are then more powerfully excited' (*Lectures 1795*, p. 17). Emotional responses to the events in France seemed misleading to Coleridge. His appeal to people's rationality was motivated by his rejection of the war against Revolutionary France. Since the September Massacres in 1792, the British press had reported about the bloodshed in France; the sympathy with the victims of the revolution became consequently an instrument to win supporters for the war. Opponents like Coleridge, however, advised to humanize the French people; indeed, he wanted his audience to resist their emotional inclination, use their Reason and realize that the war against Revolutionary France was a repressive measure after all. By calling these exemplary patriots 'thinking', Coleridge emphasized this rational capability and appealed to people's independent thoughts and opinions. For the poet, the capacity to think rationally was bound up with the other main criterion to qualify as one of the true friends of freedom: disinterestedness.

'Disinterestedness' is a crucial, but complicated, notion in Coleridge's moral and political thought. It puzzled the poet in 1795 to such an extent that he found himself unable to explain it during his lecture in late February (mentioned above). Coleridge claimed hastily to have instructed his audience in disinterested behaviour, to 'have shewn the necessity of forming some fixed and determinate principles of action to which the familiarized mind may at all times advert' (*Lectures 1795*, p. 17). In contrast, the listeners felt that Coleridge had not offered any such moral guideline. A contemporary reviewer complained about the poet's failure to expound his principles: 'We also think that our young political lecturer leaves his auditors abruptly, and that he has not stated, in a form sufficiently scientific and determinate, those principles to which, as he expresses it, he now proceeds as the most *important point*' (*Lectures 1795*, p. 2). Indeed, all that Coleridge had asserted in his lecture was that 'those principles must be' (*Lectures 1795*, p. 17), which was not very instructive.

Coleridge's language started to blur when he tried to define disinterestedness in his speech. The closest expression of his moral ideal was a metaphor based on inward regression: 'Calmness and energy mark all their actions, benevolence is the silken thread that runs through the pearl chains of all their virtues' (*Lectures 1795*, p. 12). Incapable of finding a formula, Coleridge compared benevolence to the thin lace inside a pearl chain. This metaphor combines the renunciation of externality with an invocation of virtue and, above all, of benevolence as an immutable inner quality of humans which is independent of outward appearances. The glittering pearls of the necklace do not matter, but the hidden thread inside the chain. By way of analogy, this image suggests that benevolence is not determined by results or outward action, but by motivation, which remains interior. Coleridge's figurative use of language indicates his awareness of the paradoxes of disinterestedness; indeed, the contradictoriness of the concept seems to have pushed Coleridge towards the limits of his ability to express himself. His imagery is indicative of the oxymoronic nature of moral disinterestedness. The notion is ambivalent because the absence of interest is often seen to contradict the basic moral presupposition to serve the common Good. The implication for Coleridge is that morality was always already interested.

This dilemma was pivotal in Coleridge's attempt to decide on, and formulate, the first principle of his moral and political convictions. Coleridge's renunciation of specific ends is often seen as a feeble excuse for two personal flaws: passive complacency and stifling indecision. Concerning the former, Laurence S. Lockridge in *Coleridge the Moralist* states provokingly that the stipulation of inner moral principles in the 1790s bespeaks the weakness of 'a family deserter, pornographer (if one reads *Christabel* the way some contemporary critics did), dope addict, and plagiarist' (1977, p. 102, see pp. 105–15; Coleman 1988, pp. 68, 76). This criticism overlooks that disinterested ethics ultimately serve an end, namely the common Good. The fact that Coleridge disposed of specific ends in favour of inner motivation does not necessarily mean that he advocated complacency, but that he tried to limit self-interest. Coleridge's political thought is inseparable from his Christian belief. As L. S. H. Wright notes 'Coleridge's radicalism stemmed from his Christian beliefs' (2010, p. 58). It is clear from his lecture that he pursued sociopolitical ends. Coleridge wished to find and stipulate a set of principles that would help him to instruct his audience so that they were able to act and judge in an equally 'thinking' and 'disinterested' way as the 'small but glorious band'.[12] The poet intended to reinforce and safeguard the civil freedom in a peaceful manner, 'to place Liberty on her seat with bloodless hands' (*Lectures 1795*, p. 17).

Regarding the alleged second flaw, decision making, John Colmer has criticized Coleridge heavily. According to Colmer, the poet's metaphysics was an impediment to his political journalism; 'he failed to recognize the importance of political and legislative action. Consequently he wrote little that was immediately applicable to the contemporary scene' (1959, p. 175). It is true that this search for a metaphysical ground in politics proved so complicated that it tended to undermine Coleridge's ability to call for specific political actions. However, Coleridge's failure to make a decisive impact on contemporary politics should not be misunderstood as a lack of concern. On the contrary, his insight into the difficulty of combining morality and politics appears to be one of the major reasons which prevented Coleridge from committing to any manifestation of Realpolitik, one of the corresponding societies or a political party. From a hostile point of view, Coleridge's moral scruple can be interpreted as indecision, but from a sympathetic perspective, the poet's quest as a young man for a moral ground in politics was, I propose, a sign of his consistent dedication to social reform.

Coleridge's correspondence with John Thelwall

As his first lecture in Bristol shows, Coleridge's moral and political disquisition did not provide his audience with clear principles. But this shortcoming did not discourage the young thinker. He was determined to keep promoting disinterestedness for the sake of freedom and peace. It was by the combination of morality and politics that Coleridge intended to instruct his audience. The belief was such a powerful part of his political convictions that he spoke of the 'religion for Democrats' in his letter to John Thelwall in December 1796 (*Letters* I, p. 282).[13] For Coleridge, the 'religion for Democrats' was a principle which 'certainly teaches in the most explicit terms the rights of Man, his right to Wisdom, his right to an equal share in all the blessings of Nature; it commands it's disciples to go every where, & every where to preach these rights' (*Letters* I, p. 282).[14] With these passionate words, Coleridge tried to convince Thelwall that a position of belief was conducive and even integral to their mutual democratic ends. Coleridge regarded freedom as a quality humans had in common with God: 'I need not tell you, that Godliness is God*like*-ness, and is paraphrased by Peter – "that ye may be partakers of the divine nature." – i.e. act from a love of order, & happiness, & not from any self-respecting motive – from *excellency*, into which you have exalted your *nature*, not from the *keenness* of *mere prudence*' (*Letters* I, p. 284).[15] Coleridge knew that Thelwall opposed any attempts to be converted to God. The leading member of the London Corresponding Society had been frank with Coleridge by writing that 'there is near half of the poem [Religious Musings], that no poet in our language need have been ashamed to own; but this praise almost belongs exclusively to those parts that are not at all religious' (Thelwall cited in Gibbs 1930, p. 87). Religious conversion was out of question for Thelwall. Yet, as Coleridge's letters of June and December 1796 suggest, Thelwall's atheism was not the poet's major concern. For Coleridge, the validity of non-material, inner values – both of a religious and secular nature – was at stake.

Virtue represented an inner force for Coleridge and was integral for the process of moral amelioration. Coleridge 'read [Godwin's first edition of *Political Justice*] with greatest attention' in October 1794 (*Letters* I, p. 115) and published a sonnet 'To William Godwin' in the *Morning Post* on January 10, 1795, which is a testimony of his relatively short-lived admiration. At the time, Coleridge had read the first edition of *Political Justice* (1793).[16] He met Godwin on 21 January 1794 keeping a critical distance (Coleridge 2004, p. 284). Although Coleridge agreed with Godwin on human perfectibility when he wrote to Thelwall 'that if the Mind *is* good, that it *was* bad, imports nothing' (*Letters* I, p. 282), Coleridge's main disagreement with Godwin concerned the latter's disregard for private attachments in the name of abstract principles of justice, his licentious views on marriage, the intercourse of the sexes, religion and notably Godwin's determinist theory of mind as expounded in the first edition of *Political Justice*.[17] In the Appendix III 'Subject of Sincerity Resumed', Godwin argued regarding free will and necessity that '[v]olition is that state of an intellectual being, in which, the mind being affected in a certain manner by the apprehension of an end to be accomplished, a certain motion of organs and members of the animal frame is found to be produced' (1793 I, pp. 274–5). Free will is here reduced to the passive response of the mind to external stimulants: 'In volition, if the doctrine of necessity be true, the mind is altogether passive' (Godwin 1793 I, p. 299). Coleridge told Thelwell on 22 June 1796 that: 'it is not Atheism that has prejudiced me against Godwin; but Godwin who has perhaps *prejudiced* me against Atheism' (*Letters* I, p. 221).[18] By 1795, Godwin had become an atheist (Philp 1986, p. 161), but atheism was not Coleridge's major objection against Godwin's thought. I propose that Coleridge was largely dissatisfied with Godwin on the grounds of the latter's reduction of free will. In much the same way as Coleridge advocated disinterestedness on the basis of an image of interior regression (as discussed above), the poet opposed Godwin's political theory, according to his above-quoted letter of 22 June 1796, mainly because it limited what Coleridge perceived as the divine capacity of human freedom.

Coleridge's religious faith was strong, his reasoning subtle; so subtle indeed, that he distanced himself from Thelwall's and Godwin's politics partly on epistemological grounds. It is true that Coleridge's dissatisfaction with Godwin's materialism was not congruent with his persisting embrace of Joseph Priestley's mechanistic philosophy as professed in 'Religious Musing'.[19] Nevertheless, Coleridge's discontent was consistent with the poet's budding enthusiasm for Platonism at the time (Vigus 2007, p. 65). The poet wrote: 'I love Plato – his dear *gorgeous* nonsense' (*Letters* I, p. 295). The tone of the statement indicates that the poet felt self-conscious about his 'yet barely developed interest in Plato' and therefore joked about it defensively (Vigus 2009, p. 13). James Vigus points out that Coleridge 'sympathy for Plato was culturally eccentric' (2009, p. 13). If Coleridge saw Platonism as his singular interest among his political peers, he nevertheless found an equally radical companion who shared his thirst for knowledge across philosophical and political boundaries.

Coleridge and Beddoes's mutual borrowings from the Bristol library

With Dr Thomas Beddoes, Coleridge could discuss a wide range of epistemological, ethical and political questions despite their religious disagreement – Coleridge being at the time a zealous Unitarian, Beddoes harbouring a pronounced tendency to atheism.[20] Beddoes's home, at Rodney Place, was always open to visitors and offered the young bookworm a library containing 'well over a thousand of books, many in French and German' (Jay 2009, p. 117). In addition to the doctor's private collection, both men used the local public library. The latter has the advantage that we can learn more about

Coleridge and Beddoes's probable readings. The record of the Bristol library reveals a striking overlap between Coleridge and Beddoes's perusals, which shows that both men combined their political collaboration with their philosophical interests. According to Weber, Coleridge borrowed *Divine Benevolence Asserted* (1781) by Thomas Balguy (1716–95) from 18 May until June 1795 (Weber 1935, p. 130n). Beddoes consulted the same work a few months later. Furthermore, Coleridge borrowed the second volume of the works by Bishop George Berkeley (1685–1753) in March 1796 about three months after Beddoes (Weber 1935, p. 169 n).[21] This overlap was no coincidence. Coleridge and Beddoes borrowed together various works of Christian theologians in the mid- and late 1790s.

Balguy and Berkeley suited Coleridge's religious beliefs, but what aspects of these works attracted Beddoes's attention? A few years earlier, in 1793, Beddoes had still regarded Plato's metaphysics as the 'excommunication of our perceptive powers' (1793, p. 119). Beddoes had insisted that we owe our knowledge of absolute necessity to observation and induction alone. As regards Beddoes's strikingly sudden interest in immaterialism, Mike Jay perceptively notes that 'Beddoes was interested in the origins of religion and the forms it took in different societies, but he was never troubled by questions of faith' (2009, p. 119). But was the history of Christianity, as Jay suggests, the only reason for Beddoes's interest in these theological works?

The notional content of the works by Balguy and Berkeley that Beddoes and Coleridge borrowed indicates that their interest went beyond the historical dimension of theology. *Divine Benevolence Asserted; and Vindicated from the Objections of Ancient and Modern Sceptics* was the fruit of Balguy's interest in the question of how to obviate Hume's impiety in *Dialogues Concerning Natural Religion* (1779) – an issue which had preoccupied the Anglican clergyman since his days as an undergraduate at St. John's Cambridge in the early 1740s.[22] As Isabel Rivers notes, 'Hume's name is not mentioned [in *Divine Benevolence Asserted*], but the context can readily be inferred: in the preface Balguy describes it as a specimen of a larger work on natural religion, "why published at this time, will be too easily conjectured" (Balguy, *Divine Benevolence Asserted*, p. iii)' (Rivers 2012). Indeed Balguy's implicit response to Hume was so obvious that a contemporary reviewer wrote: Balguy's book 'seems to have been published with a view to obviate the objections advanced by Mr Hume in his Dialogues, published in 1779' (*The Critical Review, or, Annuals of Literature* 51 [1781], p. 455). Like Balguy's *Divine Benevolence Asserted*, volume II of Berkeley's works was not relevant for the history of Christianity alone as suggested by Jay but ranged from writings such as 'A Defence of Free-Thinking in Mathematics' to 'Maxims Concerning Patriotism' (1784 II). Coleridge drew upon the latter for his analysis of 'Modern Patriotism' in *The Watchman* of 17 March 1796 and would declare himself a '*Berkleian* [sic]' nine months later (*Letters* I, p. 278), 'enthused by the combination of theistic immediacy and Platonic transcendence he found in Berkeley's idealism' (Perry in Coleridge 2002a, p. 146). There is no extant evidence of Beddoes's and Coleridge's conversation about Balguy and Berkeley, but considering their sharpness, they must have probed as well as inspired each other's philosophical views. Similar to Coleridge's intellectual exchange with Thelwall, Coleridge shared with Beddoes a strong desire for political reform and a profound interest in philosophy. In this context, *Leviathan* appears as central reading for the philosophical pursuits of the two men.

Coleridge's defiance of Hobbes's justification of tyranny

It was during the time of the borrowings from May 1795 until March 1796 that Thomas Hobbes (1588–1679) featured in Coleridge's public speeches.[23] Hobbes's treatise was hugely influential. Isobel Rivers and Robert E. Norton agree that much of seventeenth- and eighteenth-century moral philosophy was motivated by the desire to oppose, and possibly refute, 'Hobbes's selfish ethics, his authoritarian political system and his repudiation of religious toleration and freedom of thought' (Rivers 2000, p. 20). Norton explains that '[a]lthough the publication in 1651 of Hobbes's disturbing masterpiece, *Leviathan*, does mark the inauguration of modern ethics, it was anything but a benevolent beginning' (1995, p. 11; see also Schneider 2000, pp. 92–115). In her investigation of British freethinking, Rivers states similarly that 'Shaftesbury's ethics are in part an answer to Hobbes' (2000, p. 20). According to Rivers, 'it seems fair to say that the freethinkers drew on aspects of Hobbes's treatment of religion and natural philosophy while discounting the uncongenial aspects of his moral and political thought' (2000, pp. 20–1). The attempt to refute Hobbes's sinister view of human society and virtue represents an important reason why seventeenth- and eighteenth-century philosophers and divines insisted on disinterestedness despite its often contradictory consequences.[24] The problem was an integral part of Coleridge's thought, as one can see in his writings of the early months of 1796.

On his promotion tour to the North for *The Watchman*, Coleridge gave a charity lecture on 31 January 1796 in Nottingham. The notes to the sermon anticipate his rebuttal of Thomas Hobbes in *The Friend* and reveal that Coleridge treated Hobbes already in 1796 with utter disdain: 'Hobbes was an unblushing Advocate for arbitrary Monarchy' (*Lectures 1795*, p. 353). Even though the notes lack further elucidation, it is likely that Coleridge extended his criticism of Hobbes's political theory orally, judging from the rough and fragmentary sketch in the respective passage. The fact that there is no transition to the subsequent point – a quotation from Thomas Hutton's *Investigation on the Principles of Knowledge* (1794) – suggests that Coleridge elaborated his notes *ad hoc* at the Nottingham service (*Lectures 1795*, pp. 353–4n).[25]

Hobbes has received little scholarly attention in the study of Coleridge's politics.[26] Yet the seventeenth-century philosopher is key to our understanding of the Coleridge's political philosophy of his early radical days until *The Friend* 1818 (*The Friend* I, pp. 31–2, 165–8, 172–3; Perry 2007b I, pp. 256–60). Hobbes's *Leviathan* repudiated not only the 'spirit of freedom' that had been one of Coleridge's and Beddoes's principal values, but the treatise rescinded inherent rights based on human rationality. According to Hobbes, human autonomy was futile, for the only way to create a commonwealth was for individuals to surrender all their power to a single leader:

> The only way to erect such a common power, as may be able to defend them [a people] from the invasion of foreigners, and the injuries of one another, and thereby to secure them in such sort, as that by their own industry, and by the fruits of the earth, they may nourish themselves and live contentedly; is, to confer all their power and strength upon one man, or upon one assembly of men, that may reduce all their wills, by plurality of voices, unto one will. (Hobbes 1839, p. 157 [Part II Ch. 17]).

Not only did Hobbes's 'Book on the Commonwealth' demand the submission of the free will, in the preceding 'Book of Man', the author also denied its very existence:

> And therefore if a man should talk to me of *a round quadrangle*; or, *accidents of bread in cheese*; or, *immaterial substances*; or of a *free subject; a free will*; or any *free*, but free from being hindered by opposition, I should not say he were in an error, but that his words were without meaning; that is to say, absurd. (Hobbes 1839, pp. 32–3 [Part I Ch. 5])

This sinister conclusion was based on the epistemological assumption that the mind is a passive receptacle. Hobbes thought that 'there is no conception in a man's mind, which hath not at first, totally, or by parts, been begotten upon the organs of sense' (Hobbes 1839, p. 1 [Part I Ch. 1]). Hobbes left no doubt that humans were determined by their surroundings and ruled out incorporeal qualities: 'they are every one a *representation* or *appearance*, of some quality, or other accident of a body without us' (Hobbes 1839, p. 1). Non-empirical qualities were obsolete for Hobbes.

Hobbes's negative view of human kind is evident in his definition of Reason. According to *Leviathan*, there existed no independence of thought, no impartiality, but only calculation towards one's own selfish end: 'For REASON, in this sense, is nothing but *reckoning*, that is, adding and subtracting, of the consequences' (Hobbes 1839, p. 30 [Part I, Ch. 5]). Jean Hampton notes that Hobbes 'argue[d] that it [Reason] is self-interested in nature' (1986, p. 272). Following Hobbes's view, Coleridge's 'glorious but small band' of 'thinking and disinterested Patriots' appeared as a mere illusion. In a relentlessly consistent way, Hobbes refuted the possibility of the moral integrity of humans: 'The notions of right and wrong, justice and injustice have there no place' (Hobbes 1839, p. 115 [Part 1 Ch. 15]). Humans were incapable of differentiating between right and wrong unless by reinforcement of law and punishment. Otherwise they were meaningless. Hobbes stated that all laws were arbitrary and, nevertheless, insisted that such arbitrariness was just as long as it constituted power, for '[w] here there is no common power, there is no law: where no law, no justice' (Hobbes 1839, p. 115). For this grim notion of justice, Hobbes offered an epistemological explanation.

This epistemological foundation appears particularly relevant to Coleridge's thought, for Hobbes based despotism on the theoretical assumption that humans are solely determined by external environment, have no resource for self-determination and that life in general is nothing but a sequence of reactions – a conglomeration of nerves and impulses: 'life itself is but motion, and can never be without desire, nor without fear, no more than without sense' (Hobbes 1839, p. 51 [Part I Ch. 6]). Hobbes's *Leviathan* viewed humans as weak beings with no determination other than their physical needs, impulse and greed for power. This mechanical determinist view of life served Hobbes as a justification for despotism. Coleridge knew the seventeenth-century philosopher and condemned his political theory in 1796; at a time when the poet grew increasingly sceptical of determinist principles, he did not doubt the principle of induction per se but identified its political and moral repercussions: the epistemological convergence of Hartley and Priestley with Hobbes's justification of despotism.

Coleridge's pursuit of free will in 'Destiny of Nations'

During the last decade of the eighteenth century, Coleridge still regarded himself as a disciple of Joseph Priestley's and David Hartley's associationism. His 'admiration at this time [in September 1796] of Hartley's Essay on Man' was 'so profound' that he 'gave his name to [his] first born' (*Biographia* I, p. 187). In the same year, Coleridge completed 'Religious Musings' in which he praised 'Priestley there, Patriot, and Saint, and Sage' (Coleridge 2004, p. 32, l. 387). Nevertheless, Coleridge's esteem of the polymath began to lessen; Priestley's necessitarianism, the view that free will alone has no constitutive power in human action, played a pivotal role in this development. 'Priestley had insisted', as Vigus notes, 'that "the will cannot properly determine *itself*, but is always determined by *motives*"' (2010, p. 2). According to Priestley's principle of necessity, 'God is the cause of everything, including evil; but since God is benevolent, evil is part of a chain of causes and effects that will necessarily result in greater good' (Vigus 2010, p. 2). Free will played no significant part in these chains of events. Coleridge's letters show that, from early on in his career, the poet doubted the determinist views professed by Priestley, Hartley, Locke and Newton. On 6 November 1794, Coleridge praises 'Locke, Hartley and others' for having 'written most wisely about the Nature of Man' (*Letters* I, p. 126). In December of the same year, however, Coleridge poked fun at Hartley by expressing his complete agreement with him and simultaneously reversing materialism to immaterialism: 'I am a compleat [sic] Necessitarian—understand the subject as well almost as Hartley himself—but I go further than Hartley and believe in the corporeality of *thought* – namely that it is motion' (*Letters* I, p. 137).[27] Then, in March 1796, the sorrow over his wife's miscarriage led him to doubt 'the thing which might have been a Newton or an Hartley' and to demand 'coercive . . . Immaterialism' instead (*Letters* I, p. 192). In such a despondent mood as that of Coleridge after the loss of his unborn child, associationism seemed cruel to the poet. Coleridge even charged Priestley with atheism: 'How is it that Dr Priestley is not an atheist?' (*Letters* I, p. 192). This suspicion does not mean that Coleridge abandoned this theory completely. But the letter of spring 1796 reveals his wariness of its determinist implications even at a time when he still adhered to Priestley's Unitarian creed.[28] 'Destiny of Nations' conveys signs of Coleridge's inner struggle with the ethical and political limitations of such a philosophy – a problem which would preoccupy Coleridge over a long time and eventually culminate in his open rejection of Hartley in the *Biographia*.

Not only did Coleridge repeat his objection, he also quoted the respective lines of 'Destiny of Nations' in *Biographia* (I, pp. 122–3). Coleridge struggled with Hartley for basically the same reasons in the mid-1790s as he rejected him in the late 1810s, though his later explanation appears doubtless more versatile. When he criticized Hartley in the *Biographia*, he lucidly exposed Hartley's preclusion of human agency and lamented the concomitant human deprivation and worthlessness: 'the poor worthless I!' (*Biographia* I, p. 119). He thought that Hartley's determinism prevented individuals from having any impact upon their own existence, 'I myself, and I alone, have nothing to do with it [my existence]' (*Biographia* I, p. 119), and added that men and women are, according to Hartley, mere receptacles: 'the causeless and *effectless* beholding of it [the whole universe]' (*Biographia* I, p. 119). This notion contradicted Coleridge's desire for human autonomy.

Coleridge's caricature of Hartley in the *Biographia* deploys epistemological similarities between Hobbes and Hartley against the latter. Summing up Hartley's theory, Coleridge remarked: 'It [the soul] is the mere motion of my muscles and nerves; and these again are set in motion from external causes equally passive, which external causes stand themselves in interdependent connection with every thing that exists or has existed' (*Biographia* I, pp. 118–19). The emphasis on motion, externality, passiveness and interdependency indicates Coleridge's anti-Hobbesian undertone. Even though Hartley's epistemological concurrence with Hobbes did not automatically entail further political parallels, it was a major point of criticism. Coleridge took issue with Hartley's associationism largely because it precluded free will. And this is the point where Nitsch's exposition of critical philosophy came in.

'Destiny of Nations', of which Carl Woodring once said that 'it takes an intrepid and hungry bookworm to eat through [this] romantico-politico-religious patch-work of 474 lines in blank verse' (1961, p. 169), dramatizes Coleridge's conflicting views of freedom and mechanical philosophy. Alluding to a number of philosophical schools, the poem's verse and retrospective annotations disclose Coleridge's wish to dissociate his philosophical convictions from the Hobbesian implications he perceived in the determinist views of Priestley, Hartley and Newton; as such it criticizes necessitarianism and stipulates free will. This can already be seen in the central figure Joan of Arc, who fought against English despotism. Indeed, the early version renounces usurpation in the very first line: 'No more of Usurpation's doom'd defeat' (*PW* I.1, p. 210, l. 1). When Coleridge assisted Southey in revising *Joan of Arc* in the summer of 1795, he contributed, besides some scattered lines, the major part of Book Two. About a year later, Coleridge started to rework and enlarge his contributions into an independent poem, which he published eventually in 1817 under the title 'Destiny of Nations'.[29] From the start, Coleridge conceived of the national heroine, Joan of Arc, as a preordained free spirit. By 'preordained' I mean that the heroine's power was completely independent from the circumstances under which she was born; indeed, Joan of Arc is Coleridge's personification of free will.[30] As Seamus Perry points out, 'the warrior maid of France, at the depth of her woes, feels that Impulse in the local form of her tutelary spirit, "an inevitable Presence"' (2001, p. 172). She is meant to draw the cause of her existence out of herself.

As in his Bristol lecture of 25 February 1795, Coleridge dedicated plenty of room in the poem to the moral premises of liberty; indeed, the first hundred and twenty lines or so illustrate Coleridge's attempt at tackling the problem of an ontological ground for freedom. My interpretation agrees with H. W. Piper's observation that Coleridge tried 'to prepare the ground for a belief' (1962, p. 38); however, I think that this belief is not limited to, as Piper suggests, 'a belief in divine activity of "matter"' (1962, p. 38). John Beer notes that the passage expresses the 'processes of thought' (1977, p. 61). What seems central to 'Destiny of Nations' is the search for the ground of the existence of freedom.

The poem identifies different types of freedom in ways similar to those in which Coleridge had tried to discern the true friends of freedom in his moral and political lecture. In contrast to the first lecture, the speaker does not discriminate between different groups of people but classifies different philosophical schools according to their predisposition to freedom. Coleridge's verse conveys the poet's uncertainty and shows that the existence of freedom is rationally indeterminable. Yet one group of philosophers meets the speaker's unequivocal disapproval:

> But some there are who deem themselves most free
> When they within this gross and visible sphere
> Chain down the winged thought, scoffing ascent
> Proud in their meanness: and themselves they cheat
> With noisy emptiness of learned phrase,
> Their subtle fluids, impacts, essences,
> Self-working Tools, uncaus'd Effects, and all
> Those blind Omniscients, those Almighty Slaves,
> Untenanting Creation of its God.
>
> (*PW* I.1, pp. 211–12, ll. 29–37)

These lines suggest that whoever makes claims of freedom on the basis of this particular philosophical school is a traitor: 'they cheat'. To the puzzlement of the reader, the lines leave open the names of the philosophers concerned and the nature of their respective offences against freedom. The reader can detect Coleridge's repulsion from the verse: these 'blind' philosophers and their 'subtle fluids, impacts, essences,/ self-working tools', are mentally constraining, 'chain down the winged thought', mean and arrogant, 'scoff ascent/ Proud in their meanness', and unsubstantiated, 'noisy emptiness'. These philosophers are then said to turn their converts into 'Almighty Slaves'. Oppression can barely be more pronounced.

While Coleridge's dissatisfaction is evident, it takes a footnote to identify the philosophers and Coleridge's objections against them.[31] Coleridge named as the target of his criticism the disciples of 'mechanic philosophy', explicitly referring to David Hartley and Isaac Newton. Coleridge opposed the philosophers principally because of their determinist preclusion of free will. This remark does not reject their empiricist philosophy as a whole as suggested by Levere, according to whom Coleridge's poem repudiates 'unthinking adherence to Locke's system of philosophy' (1981, p. 15). Perry has demonstrated that Coleridge's view of organicism, necessity and freedom sprang from the 'One Life' theory inspired largely by Priestley's *Matter and Spirit* (1777) and his edition of Hartley's *Theory of the Mind* (1775) (1999, pp. 68–85; see also Piper 1961, pp. 32–3). The name 'One Life' refers to the lines famously added to 'The Eolian Harp': 'O the one life within us and abroad' (*PW* I.1, p. 233, l. 26). The concepts originate in Coleridge's Unitarianism and offer an alternative to his Platonic notion of transcendent omnipotence through divine immanence: 'his religious language features an alternative, immanent, One Life vocabulary of divinity "diffused", "interfused", and so forth' (Perry 1999, p. 76). Within this 'One Life' framework, I propose that Coleridge's 'Destiny of Nations' entails a strong criticism that is not directed against empiricism per se but against necessitarian views that limit, or even deny the possibility of, free will. 'Destiny of Nations' marks Coleridge's increasing uncertainty of how to ground freedom ontologically and anticipates, thus, his engagement with critical philosophy via Nitsch.

Coleridge's criticism of the 'mechanic philosophy' was not ingenious, but reminiscent of the seventh-century accusations levelled against John Locke after the publication of *Essay Concerning Human Understanding* (1671–90). As Paul E. Sigmund points out, 'the Essay's frequent reference to pleasure and pain as the sources of our knowledge of good and evil led' Locke's contemporaries to accuse him of a hedonist and materialist approach to morality and to call it "Hobbism" ' (Sigmund 2005, p. 183). The charges were so significant that Locke added to the second edition, published in 1694, a description of divine law as a touchstone of moral rectitude as well as a new section to the chapter 'On Power' that argued for moral choice and free will (Sigmund 2005, p. 183). Coleridge's censure of 'mechanic philosophy' in 'Destiny of Nations' indicates that he harboured a similarly critical attitude as Locke's contemporaries as well as Nitsch. Coleridge wrote in a series of three philosophical letters to Josiah Wedgwood in February 1801 that 'in Locke there's a complete Whirl-dance of Confusion with the words *we, Soul, Mind, Consciousness, & Ideas*' (*Letters* II, p. 696; see also 676–85). Coleridge criticized his contemporaries who thought that Locke had succeeded in 'overthrowing the Doctrine of Innate Ideas' (*Letters* II, p. 686). Coleridge held the opinion that Locke had been anticipated by Descartes, 'Locke's *System* existed in the writings of Descartes' (*Letters* II, p. 686).[32] Book One of Locke's *Essay* failed to convince Coleridge sufficiently of the validity of autonomous concepts. Like Coleridge's letters to Wedgwood, his critique of 'mechanic philosophy' in 'Destiny of Nations' does not deprecate the bodily senses *per se*. Rather, the poem opposes determinism as an impediment to freedom.

In the same footnote, Coleridge censured, as mentioned, Newton and his disciple Hartley through a series of rhetorical questions. For Coleridge, their philosophy contradicted 'inherent right', 'the necessity of God' as well as 'Wisdom' and 'Benevolence':

> For if matter by any powers or properties *given* to it, can produce the order of the visible world, and even generate thought: why may it not have possessed such properties by *inherent* right? and where is the necessity of a God? matter is, according to the mechanic philosophy capable of acting most wisely and most beneficently without Wisdom or Benevolence; and what more does the Atheist assert? if matter possess those properties, why might it not have possessed them from all eternity? (*PW* I.1, p. 212 n ll. 41–7)

Here, Coleridge rejects what he calls the 'mechanic' notion that life is determined through a series of material reactions. The view that matter is the basis of our thinking was not only atheistic by implication; for Coleridge it also contradicted the notion of 'inherent right[s]'. In short, Coleridge doubted necessitarianism on political grounds; for him, it did not seem progressive enough. It was crucial for Coleridge's sense of justice that inherent right, wisdom and benevolence should retain a constitutive part in our actions. This view combined with his intellectual desire to find an adequate philosophical account for the existence of freedom gradually led to his disenchantment with Hartley and his school.

In the *Observations of Man* (1749), published in an abridged version by Joseph Priestley in 1775, Hartley reconciled the natural laws of Newton with ethics

(Wylie 1989, pp. 74–93). 'Hartley himself', as Perry points out, 'had admitted the determinism of his own scheme only with "the greatest reluctance"' (Perry 1999, p. 115). According to Hartley's theory, however, '[i]t is common to all Systems, to suppose some Motions attendant upon Sensation, since corporeal Objects must, by their Actions, impress some Motion upon our Bodies' (1749 I, p. 33). Coleridge felt both attracted to and repulsed by this theory. On the one hand, he poeticized Hartley's reactions of nerves in 'Religious Musings' praising the philosopher for having applied the Newtonian principles of natural philosophy to morality:

Adoring NEWTON his serener eye
Raises to heaven: and he of mortal kind
Wisest, he [David Hartley] first who mark'd the ideal tribes
Up the fine fibres thro' the sentient brain
Roll subtly-surging.

(PW I.1, 188–9, ll. 367–71)

On the other hand, Coleridge criticized Hartley's dependence on the motions of nerves in 'Destiny of Nations'. Here, Coleridge's annotations expose a disadvantage of Hartley's determinism: the deprecation of the qualities of wisdom and benevolence. Coleridge thought, according to the above-quoted footnote to 'Destiny of Nations', that 'Matter is, according to the mechanic philosophy, capable of acting most wisely and most beneficently *without* Wisdom or Benevolence' (my emphasis). Coleridge felt the need to safeguard human 'wisdom' and 'benevolence'. He wanted to defend human claims to autonomy and conceived of an immaterial ground of existence, according to which 'the visible world' as well as 'thought' are generated independently by way of '*inherent* right'. For Coleridge, existence was based on an autonomous ground, a first principle, which was synonymous for him with 'God'. But, as previously mentioned, Coleridge's criticism of 'mechanic philosophy' does not mean that the poet loathed necessitarian views to such an extent that he immediately gave up the theories professed by Hartley and Priestley.

At a time when the plan of Pantisocracy was failing – Southey abandoned any real intention by mid-1795 and departed to Portugal in December (Speck 2006, pp. 60–1) – Coleridge's intellectual preoccupations included his participation in peaceful protests to repeal the Gagging Bills, his opposition against the war with Revolutionary France, the revision of his political lectures as *Conciones,* a lecture tour to promote *The Watchman* and the composition of his contribution to *Joan of Arc* later published as 'Destiny of Nation' (Patton and Mann 1971, pp. xli–xliii). Coleridge's desire to base his political views on moral propositions can be seen in his attempts in prose and verse to ground freedom ontologically. Thus he hoped to find ways for safeguarding the true meaning of freedom and protecting it against abuse. In his moral and political lecture, Coleridge enthusiastically announced that he would instruct his audience how to act in accordance with moral freedom just like the 'small but glorious band, . . . of thinking and disinterested Patriots' (*Lectures* 1795, p. 12). However, as a commentator noticed, Coleridge failed to produce an adequate formulation of his guidelines. In 'Destiny of Nations', he questioned different philosophies regarding their predispositions to free will. Coleridge's pursuit of moral and political freedom manifests itself, furthermore, in his vehement repudiation of Hobbes's philosophy. Coleridge's stipulation of free will, the mind's constitutive power in determining action, played a major role in his disparagement of Godwin's *Political Justice*. Coleridge engaged in, and supported, Godwin's and Thelwall's democratic principles but differed from them – if we trust Coleridge's letter to Thelwall (*Letters* I, p. 221) – notably on the ground of free will. Coleridge shared his interest in politics and philosophy with his friend and mentor Dr Beddoes. The register of the Bristol library discloses that Coleridge and Beddoes almost simultaneously read the works of two theologians: Berkeley and Balguy. The engagement with Balguy's implicit criticism of Hume's repudiation of natural theology points to Coleridge's and Beddoes's preoccupation with a question that also formed a crucial part of the initial dissemination of Kant at the time, namely the controversy about the possibility of a rational evidence of the existence of God. Coleridge's activities during the years of 1795 and 1796 were in part driven by the desire to find a common philosophical ground, somewhat similar to an encompassing Enlightenment system, which suited his democratic and Unitarian pursuits. This aspiration spurred him on to devour an astonishing number of diverse books, pamphlets and periodicals. The next chapter will begin with Coleridge's retrospective observations about this very period in his life (1795–6). It draws on textual and circumstantial evidence that suggests that Coleridge became acquainted with Kantian principles during these years.

Coleridge and the Categorical Imperative in 1796

Around 1832, Coleridge described the year that followed the composition of his contribution to Southey's *Joan of Arc* (in summer 1795) in a brief comment to 'Destiny of Nations' on page 125 of the first of three volumes of *The Poetical Works of Samuel Taylor Coleridge, including the Dramas of Wallenstein, Remorse and Zapolya* published by William Pickering in London in 1828:

> N. B. within 12 months after the writing of this poem my bold Optimism, and Necessitarianism, together with the Infra, seu plusquam-Socinianism, down to which, step by step, I had *un*believed, gave way to the day-break of a more genial and less shallow System. But I contemplate with pleasure these Phases of my Transition. S. T. Coleridge[1]

These marginalia mark a special moment of self-meditation for Coleridge. When returning to his verse, Coleridge paused to cherish his remembrance of the first light of a new, profound philosophical system (the 'day-break'); indeed, Coleridge halted 'to contemplate with pleasure these Phases of my Transition'. The jotted lines specifically refer to the period of twelve months after Coleridge's composition of parts of *Joan of Arc* (the year starting in the summer of 1795, as discussed in the previous chapter). Musing on the verse of 'Destiny of Nations', the poet derived a deep sense of satisfaction from the philosophical transition he had made between 1795 and 1796. The comment is puzzling, for the indefinite article 'a' gives no answers as to whether Coleridge believed himself to have any part in the creation of this 'more genial' and 'less shallow system'. The only explicit ownership claimed by Coleridge is that of his philosophic transition towards this new system: 'these Phases of *my* Transition' (my emphasis). Considering this use of indefinite and possessive articles, Coleridge's autograph commentary seems to suggest that he participated in 'the day-break' of somebody else's system at the time – a system whose authorship remains open. Furthermore, we can infer from the pleasure and peace expressed by the poet that, despite the discrepancies in Coleridge's politico-philosophical views over the years, he still considered the system he referred to as a congenial and sophisticated one, even after almost forty years.

This sense of continuity matters. This chapter proposes that Kantian thought had been part of Coleridge's life for a longer time than has previously been thought, namely before the winter of 1800 and 1801, and that his encounter with the new philosophy was bound up with the pursuit of freedom. The solemn tone in the autograph commentary suggests that Coleridge followed a similar logic to Wilhelm Dilthey's criticism of historical Reason (1976, pp. 189–220), according to which the significance of past events is constituted by the present. The words imply Coleridge's distinctive need to attribute importance to his philosophical studies by picturing them as a journey with a certain destination; indeed they signal that in this instance Coleridge conceived of his intellectual development as having led towards critical philosophy. Writing as a mentor to James Gooden in 1814, Coleridge explained that Kant comprised everything his mentee needed to know about philosophy: 'I by no means recommend to you an extension of your philosophic researches beyond Kant. In him is contained all that can be *learnt*' (*Letters* V, p. 14). In 1817, Coleridge earnestly declared in a letter to J. H. Green that, despite Kant's stoicism and tendency to atheism, 'I reverence Immanuel Kant with my whole heart and soul; and believe him to be the only Philosopher, for all men who have the power of thinking. I can not conceive the liberal pursuit or profession, in which the service derived from a patient study of his works would not be incalculably great, both as cathartic, tonic and directly nutricious [sic]' (*Letters* IV, p. 792). Coleridge's brilliant daughter Sara was fully aware of the huge significance of Kant's writings for her father. She explained in her introduction to *Biographia Literaria* that 'to him [Coleridge] the philosophy of Kant was religion' (1847, p. cxxxviii). In *Biographia Literaria*, published in 1817, Coleridge openly advocated Kantian (and post-Kantian) philosophy.[2] By 1819, Coleridge based his philosophical writings on a principle derived from the *Critique of Pure Reason* (though J. H. Muirhead thought otherwise): the Kantian distinction between Reason and Understanding.[3] Other publications by Coleridge including *Essays on the Principles of Genial Criticism* (1814), *The Friend* (1809–10, 1812 and 1818), the Appendix to *Lay Sermons* (1816) (pp. 59–63), *Aids to Reflection* (1825) and *On the Constitution of State and Church* (1829) were imbued with Kantian thought, as were some of his unpublished works, such as the collated fragments presented under the title *Opus Maximum* and the fragmentary *Logic*, in which Coleridge attempted to write his own transcendental system between the early 1800s and 1829 (Jackson 1981, p. xxxix; Wellek 1931, p. 74; Orsini 1969, pp. 246–7).[4] F. J. A. Hort recalled that Coleridge 'frequently mentioned Kant's name with gratitude, as he did those of others, especially in this affair of the reason and understanding' (1856, p. 320). Hence the assumption that the mysterious 'day-break of a more genial and less shallow System' points to Kant makes good sense.[5]

The word 'genial' should not be overlooked, for it gestures towards one of Coleridge's favourite Kantian compositions (*Table Talk* I, p. 453), that is, his *Essays on the Principles of Genial Criticism*, first published in *Felix Farley's Bristol Journal* in August and September 1814 (*Shorter Works* I, p. 353). The attribute 'genial' is, according to Modiano, 'a tantalizing designation, used rather sparingly by Coleridge and insufficiently discussed by critics' (2009, p. 223). The *Oxford English Dictionary* lists Milton's *Paradise Lost* (IV 712) 'What day the genial Angel to our Sire Brought her in naked beauty' (*OED*), according to which 'genial' signifies 'pertaining to generation'. This meaning is congruent with those discerned by previous Coleridge commentators who have interpreted 'genial' as 'pertaining to genius' (Isaacs 1935, p. 101; Fogle 1962,

p. 175 n64; see Orsini 1969, p. 168; Modiano 2009, p. 224) in so far as all concur that 'genial' denotes an inner creative characteristic. The Latin root of 'genius' is, as delineated by Paul W. Bruno, *gen* (to be born, to beget, to come into being) and hence recognizable in English also as the root of 'generate', 'engender' and of 'generic' (2010, p. 9). The latter designates attributes of 'genre' and thus essential qualities of literary 'type', 'kind' and 'form' (Garber 1993, p. 456). Writing to his beloved son Derwent, Coleridge reassured him 'I know, that in a work of this kind a man must wait for genial hours' (*Letters* V, p. 143). What Coleridge referred to here was not a 'jovial', 'kindly' or 'sociable' moment (Coleridge 2004, p. 339), but the inspiration of genius. 'The most important influence on Coleridge's concept of "genial criticism" was', according to Modiano, 'Kant's *Critique of Judgment* . . . Coleridge derived from Kant several components of his philosophy of genial criticism, in particular the view that a critic can access the rules that guided an artist in their creation and like the artist, can even be elevated to the status of genius' (2009, p. 224). Coleridge's assimilation of Kant's aesthetics is central to the analysis of *Biographia Literaria* in Chapter 6 of the present study. Regarding Coleridge's cherished 'Phases of my Transition' all that is relevant at this point is our awareness of the particular meaning of 'genial' for Coleridge as an allusion to *Essays on the Principles of Genial Criticism* heavily influenced by Kant.

The period of the mid-1790s roughly matches Coleridge's account when he recalled in the above-quoted letter to Gooden that he had first become interested in Kant over twenty years ago: 'I will just tell you how I proceeded myself, 20 years & more ago when I first felt a curiosity about Kant, & was fully aware that to master his meaning, as a system, would be a work of great Labor & long Time —' (*Letters* V, p. 14). Coleridge dated the letter to 14 January 1814, yet the postmark states 'Highgate 15 Jan 1820' (*Letters* V, p. 13). The letter speaks of a 'medical Hercules' and a strict 'matrimonial Goddess' (*Letters* V, p. 13), which must be a teasing reference to Dr James Gillman and his wife Ann, with whom Coleridge had lived at Highgate since April 1816. The additional reference to 'my Literary Life' (*Letters* V, p. 14) leaves no doubt that Coleridge wrote the letter after 1817. The assumption put forward by René Wellek has been that Coleridge referred to the phase in winter 1800 and 1801 (1931, p. 72 f.).[6] However, this inference disregards not only the uncertainty of Coleridge's dating of his initial studies to '20 years & more ago', but another important detail.

Coleridge noted that he first read all the popular works of Kant before studying the three major *critiques*: 'I enquired after all the more popular writings of Kant—read them with delight—I then read the Prefaces to several of his systematic works, as the Prolegomena &c—here too every part, I understood, & that was nearly the whole, was replete with sound & plain tho' bold and novel truths to me' (*Letters* V, p. 14). Coleridge's 'more popular writings' point to *Perpetual Peace*, which is and was one of the most popular and widely read writings of Kant according to leading experts (Wood 1998, p. 62; Malter 1984, p. 72). The print-run for the first edition alone consisted of two thousand copies, a large amount even by today's standard (Kim 2007, pp. 203–26).[7] Furthermore, the letter makes clear that a period of delightful perusal, 'read them with delight', preceded the intensive study of the *first critique* in late 1800 and early 1801. Considering that Nitsch began lecturing on Kant in London in 1794 and published a detailed introduction in May 1796, which was followed by the publication of the highly topical translation *On Perpetual Peace* in October of the same year, I think that Coleridge's loosely dated first 'curiosity about Kant' – '20 years & more ago' – points to the same period as his philosophical 'day-break' in the mid-1790s.

Coleridge and seventeenth- and eighteenth-century British idealists

It is true, however, that Coleridge read several other philosophers to counterbalance his necessitarianism and Unitarianism between 1795 and 1796: Berkeley, Cudworth and Hutton are three authors of whom one can almost say with certainty that Coleridge studied them at the time (Whalley 1949, pp. 114–31). All three theologians share with Kant varying degrees of idealism.[8] As Coleridge's sentimental recollection is too imprecise to determine a single system, I contend that Coleridge's marginalia refer to different proponents of idealism including Kant. As mentioned in the previous chapter, Coleridge borrowed the works of Berkeley from the Bristol library in May 1796. It is unlikely that the 'more genial' system refers to the Irish bishop alone, since Coleridge, when he wrote the marginalia to 'Destiny of Nations', subsumed Berkeleyian idealism under Kantianism. To use Seamus Perry's words 'Coleridge's response to the post-Kantians, "Fichte versus Kant, Schelling versus Fichte" (*Notebooks* III, §4012), may also best be regarded as replaying the mixed feelings he had already experienced within the baggy empiricism of the 1790s' (Perry 1999, p. 137). Considering Kant's effective history, it would not come as a surprise if the lines between Berkeleyian and Kantian philosophy had blurred in Coleridge's retrospective meditation. Contemporary British reviews frequently echoed the early, extensive and very critical review of the *Critique of Pure Reason* by Christian Garve (1742–98) and Johann Georg Heinrich Feder (1740–1821) published in the *Göttingische Anzeigen von gelehrten Sachen* on 19 January 1782:[9] 'One basic pillar of the Kantian system rests on these concepts of sensations as mere modifications of ourselves (on which Berkeley, too, principally builds his idealism), and of space and time' (Sassen 2000, pp. 53–4).[10] Reviewers in mid-1790s England, including Nitsch, Mounier and Walker, addressed the similarity with Berkeley and thus aided its circulation in public.[11] In his later life, Coleridge tended to give pride of place to the 'German idiom' (Leask 1988, p. 22).[12] While Coleridge's uses of Berkeley as a means to fend off necessitarianism preceded that of Kant, the teleological weight insinuated by the poet's choice of the word 'day-break' suggests that Coleridge not only remembered the Irish philosopher, but also the much more refined idealism learnt from Kant. Berkeley's works surely formed part of the transition which the poet recalled, yet when speaking of a 'System', especially one that Coleridge lastingly esteemed as 'more genial and less shallow' than the works of Hartley and Priestley, Coleridge must have contemplated Kantianism, too.

Besides Berkeley, Coleridge's study of *Investigations of the Principles of Knowledge* also falls into the period of 1795/1796, still a marginal annotation by Coleridge accounts for his view of Hutton doubtlessly. A letter Coleridge wrote to Thelwall shows that Coleridge had perused Hutton's works prior to June 1796 (*Letters* I, p. 222).

In addition, he copied a passage from volume III of *Investigations of the Principles of Knowledge* into his notebooks (*Notebooks* I, §243) in late 1795 and early 1796 and quoted it in his sermon in Nottingham in January 1796.[13] On the title page of the first volume of Hutton's principles, Coleridge wrote down some years later the following autograph comment:

> There is a great Talent displayed in it [*Investigations of the Principles of Knowledge*]; and the Writer had made an important Step beyond Locke, Berkley & Hartley – **and was clearly on the precincts of the Critical Philosophy** – with which & the previous Treatises of Kant he appears to have had no acquaintance. (*Marginalia* II, pp. 1203–4; my emphasis)

Here, Coleridge sees Hutton's *Principles* as a threshold to Kantianism. *Investigations of the Principles of Knowledge* belonged to the 'phases of my transition' mentioned by Coleridge (above), however, the poet's jottings leave no question that Coleridge thought of Hutton not as the creator of the 'more genial . . . System', but merely as an anticipator of Kantianism: Hutton was 'on the precincts of the Critical Philosophy'. The fact that Coleridge associated Hutton retrospectively with Kant further supports the view that Coleridge's phases of transition in the mid-1790s contained critical philosophy.

Shortly after his first political lecture in May 1795, and again in November 1796, Coleridge borrowed from the Bristol library Cudworth's *The True Intellectual System of the Universe: wherein all the Reason and Philosophy of Atheism is confuted, and its Impossibility demonstrated, with a Treatise concerning Eternal and Immutable Morality* (1743) (Patton and Mann 1971, p. xxxvi). Coleridge included aspects of the treatise in his first lecture on revealed religion. Apart from Cudworth's influence on Coleridge's interpretation of the Old Testament,[14] his work was conducive to Coleridge's moral and political thought in the 1790s. Cudworth, and other Cambridge Platonists, reacted against the devastating message of Hobbes's *Leviathan*. According to Norton, they contested Hobbesian ideas by holding that 'Human virtue was . . . a separate, independent quality found in every man and woman, although often obscured by the blurring effect of circumstance or habit' (Norton 1995, p. 16). Cudworth's idealism can hence be seen as the attempt to disprove Hobbes on epistemological grounds and represented a question that preoccupied young Coleridge (see previous chapter). With regard to the absence of a detailed moral disquisition, Norton points out that 'instead of constructing an ethical theory per se, Cudworth devoted most of the *Treatise* to an elaboration of the epistemology designed to bolster' the independence of human virtue (1995, p. 16).[15] *The True and Intellectual System* gave Coleridge the Neo-platonic arguments to counteract the atheistic tendencies of Priestley and Hartley, but nonetheless the system still lacked the complexity of Kant's practical philosophy. Nitsch recognized, as mentioned, this niche in the English intellectual milieu.

By 1796, Nitsch was acquainted with the current philosophical trends in London and introduced Kant accordingly as a proponent of free will, that is, 'the existence of a certain power in man, which may act uninfluenced by other powers, and obey no other laws than those of its own constitution' (1796, p. 16). To illustrate this notion, Nitsch used an example that left no doubt about the revolutionary potential of his philosophy: it is man's volition that determines whether 'fire and sword, for instance, may, at one time, be the cause of flight and submission, and at another, of the strongest resolution to resist, even at the hazard of life itself' (1796, p. 16). The statement by Nitsch gives a revealing insight into Coleridge's initial encounter with Kantian philosophy as Nitsch addressed specifically the philosophic creed with which Coleridge identified at the time, 'I am a compleat [sic] Necessitarian' (*Letters* I, p. 137). 'For the Necessitarians', Nitsch explained, 'who, as is generally known, make a considerable party in the philosophic world, publicly protest against the arguments that have been brought forward in favour of such a power [human autonomy], and boldly affirm that they are not conclusive' (1796, p. 17). Nitsch's argument was directed towards the proponents of doctrine that all human action is necessarily determined by the law of causation including Hartley, who proclaimed in the second volume of *Observations on Man* 'that philosophical Liberty cannot take place in Man, but is an Impossibility' (1749 II, p. 56). One of the reasons why Hartley rejected the philosophical (not the religious) idea of free will was that 'to suppose that Man has a Power independent of God, is to suppose that God's Power, does not extend to all Things, i.e. is not infinite' (1749 II, p. 66). Nitsch exposed this deficit of human freedom and based his criticism of necessitarianism on the *Critique of Pure Reason* (*KrV* B 560–1). Nitsch claimed that, according to the necessitarian view, 'every human action are events in time' (1796, p. 173) and inferred that 'every human action must have a cause' (1796, p. 173). From this he concluded that 'on so long a series of causes and effects, human will can make no impression; it is totally impotent as to this; it is, therefore, not free' (1796, p. 173). Nitsch thus censured the very point that Coleridge had criticized, for instance, in his contribution to Southey's *Joan of Arc* (see previous chapter). Nitsch's pamphlet was clearly designed to appeal to Unitarians who were dissatisfied with Hartley's position on philosophical liberty and sought sophisticated affirmations of free will. Nitsch's strategy to place Kantian ethics within the native discourse on necessitarianism proved successful. The London *Telegraph* approved and quoted Nitsch's criticism (from page p. 173) in a detailed article about the public debate on a first cause in philosophy published on 21 February 1797. And so it was that Coleridge's commitment to free will and his resulting search for a concise formula to instruct his audience in disinterestedness was the point at which a Kantian reference came into Coleridge's early notebooks. It is this entry that strongly suggests that Coleridge's cherished phases of transition in the mid-1790s included Kantianism.

Kant's moral law in Coleridge's notebook
(late 1795/early 1796)

Coleridge entered a version of Kant's moral law in his notebook. The entry dated to late 1795 and early 1796 marks Coleridge's earliest acquaintance with Kantian philosophy:

> By obliging every one always to do that which to him shall seem in the then present time and circumstances conducive to the public good: or by enjoining the observation of some determinate Laws, which if universally obeyed would produce universal happiness. (*Notebooks* I, §249)[16]

After Coleridge's previous vain attempt to formulate a disinterested principle of morality in his lectures, he sketched this formula in his notebook. The self-reflexive phrase 'by obliging everyone always to do that which [is] conducive to the public good' obviates any specific end, such as aid for the poor or honour your parents. Instead, it demands the conformity of our actions to the highest moral principle. This formula is disinterested and renounces selfish objectives. As such, it captures a possible interpretation of the categorical imperative as expounded by Kant in the *Groundwork* (1785):

> Wenn ich mir einen *hypothetischen* Imperativ überhaupt denke, so weiß ich nicht zum voraus, was er enthalten werde: bis mir die Bedingung gegeben ist. Denke ich mir aber einen *kategorischen* Imperativ, so weiß ich sofort, was er enthalte. Denn da der Imperativ außer dem Gesetze nur die Notwendigkeit der Maxime enthält, diesem Gesetze gemäß zu sein, das Gesetz aber keine Bedingung enthält, auf die es eingeschränkt war, so bleibt nichts als die Allgemeinheit eines Gesetzes überhaupt übrig, welchem die Maxime der Handlung gemäß sein soll, und welche Gemäßheit allein der Imperativ eigentlich als notwendig vorstellt.
>
> Der kategorische Imperativ ist also nur ein einziger, und zwar dieser: *handle nur nach derjenigen Maxime, durch die du zugleich wollen kannst, daß sie ein allgemeines Gesetz werde. (Grundlegung* pp. 420–1)
>
> (When I think of a *hypothetical* imperative in general I do not know beforehand what it will contain; I do not know this until I am given the condition. But when I think of the *categorical* imperative I know at once what it contains. For, since the imperative contains, beyond the law, only the necessity that the maxim be in conformity with this law, while the law contains no condition to which it would be limited, nothing is left with which the maxim of action is to conform but the universality of a law as such; and this conformity alone is what the imperative properly represents as necessary.
>
> There is, therefore, only a single categorical imperative and it is this: *act only in accordance with that maxim through which you can at the same time will that it become a universal law.* [*Groundwork* 4: 420–1])

The categorical imperative epitomized disinterestedness by taking the defiance against Hobbesian calculation and self-interest to an extreme: it stipulated nothing but the conformity to the law irrespective of the consequences. Its command is not only independent from arbitrary self-interest but unconditioned as Henry J. Paton notes:

> the categorical imperative alone purports to be a practical law, while all the rest may be called principles of the will but not laws; for an action necessary merely in order to achieve an arbitrary purpose can be considered as in itself contingent, and we can always escape from the precept if we abandon the purpose; whereas an unconditioned command does not leave it open to the will to do the opposite at its discretion and therefore alone carries with it that necessity which we demand from the law. (Paton 1956, p. 87)

Kant's stipulation of the unconditioned moral law has nothing to do with uncritical obedience to the law (Schneewind 1992, p. 311). The moral stance behind Kant's emphasis on obligation opposed feudalism. While reading Rousseau early on in his career, Kant wrote on the margins of the *Social Contract* and *Emile* (around 1764): 'He who needs nothing from [these superiors called gracious lords] but justice and can hold them to their debts does not need this submissiveness' (Kant cited in Schneewind, p. 311, see pp. 334–5). The categorical imperative served as a means against the unjust limitation of individual freedom; indeed it aimed to protect people's lives from religious and political control. Beiser goes as far as to say that 'what disturbed Kant was not the problem of determinism but that of oppression. Tyranny and injustice are the threats to freedom, not the causality of the natural order' (1992, p. 30). Kant's new formulation of autonomy stipulated that every individual should act morally while accepting the possibility that their efforts were either unrewarded or 'in vain' (Beiser 2006, p. 616).[17] This should not be misunderstood as a sign of resignation, but be seen as an appeal for people's moral persistence despite tyrannical oppression. This primarily political context is absolutely crucial for Coleridge's initial encounter with Kant's philosophy and, in particular, for his engagement with the categorical imperative (see Chapter 7). I disagree with the view put forward by Deidre Coleman's influential study that 'Kant endorses only abstract version of Rousseau's political concepts, arguing that they are only valid as rational ideals' (1988, p. 159).

Coleridge's source was not the original passage in German in the *Groundwork* (cited above) as the poet's German skills were still too weak to comprehend Kant's formulation in 1796.[18] The literal translation of the categorical imperative in Kant's pamphlet *On Perpetual Peace (Zum Ewigen Frieden)* – '*act in such a manner, that thou mayest desire that the maxim according to which thou determinest may become a general law (let the end thou aimest at be whatever it may)*' (Kant 1796, p. 58)[19] – appeared in October 1796, probably after Coleridge had written his notebook entry (I, §249) and after the twelve-month period of Coleridge's philosophical 'day-break' (*PW* I.1, p. 280). However, the first detailed introduction to Kantianism in England falls into the very period of Coleridge's philosophical transition. As mentioned before, Friedrich August Nitsch published his lectures in London in May 1796.

Nitsch's ethical exposition within the field of Kant studies

Nitsch's exposition of Kant's practical philosophy is a neglected work. Nitsch's book was 'very rare' (Wellek 1931, p. 7) until Routledge Thoemmes Press republished the pamphlet in 1993 under the title *Kant's Thought in Britain: A General and Introductory View* (Malter 1995, p. 503). While little has been written on Nitsch's introduction as a whole (see Chapter 1), even less is known about his account of Kantian ethics. All that Wellek observed on the topic is that

> finally Nitsch gives a rather thin account of Kant's ideas on ethics. For the first time in English he quotes the universal law of morals, stresses the formal character of Kant's imperative, and sketches Kant's views on immortality, the deity and the moral law as the ground for belief in God. (1931, p. 9)

Wellek gave Nitsch credit for introducing the categorical imperative into the English language. Subsequent scholarship on Nitsch's introduction to Kant's ethics does not go much further than Wellek's acknowledgement: Micheli points out Nitsch's indebtedness to Reinhold's views on Kantian morals without clarifying what they entail (1990, p. 266).

Contrary to these established views, I propose that Nitsch's account of practical Reason merits new scholarly attention. It can hardly be called 'thin' (Wellek 1931, p. 9) considering that morals and religion compose a fifth of the entire volume, which Nitsch divided into two sections: 'Influence of Kant's Principles on the Science of Morals' (1796, pp. 169–218) and 'Influence of Kant's Principles on Religion' (1796, pp. 219–36). The alleged lack of substance does not account for the extant scarcity of commentary on Nitsch's moral introduction. Rather, it seems that the neglect of Nitsch's work is in part related to recent philosophical disputes.

Nitsch's emphasis on the reciprocity between morality and religion, in particular on the highest good, forms a subject that has become particularly controversial in Kant studies since the 1960s; even today 'no aspect of Kant's philosophy is more controversial than moral faith' (Beiser 2006, p. 589). Many philosophers in the twentieth and twenty-first centuries have wanted to establish moral philosophy that is independent of religion. 'Since the 1960s', Beiser notes, 'there has been a movement afoot in the Anglophone world to purge Kant's philosophy of all metaphysics, to make Kant scrubbed and sanitary for a more positivistic age' (2006, p. 589). In this context, Kant's concept of moral faith is highly disputed. One component of moral faith became the focus of the debate of the *Critique of Practical Reason* in the early 1960s: the ideal of the highest good (or *summum bonum*). Kant expounded the concept as follows:

> der Vernunft in ihrem praktischen Gebrauche geht es um nichts besser. Sie sucht als reine praktische Vernunft zu dem Praktisch Bedingten (was auf Neigungen und Naturbedürfniß beruht) ebenfalls das Unbedingte, und zwar nicht als Bestimmungsgrund des Willens, sondern, wenn dieser auch (im moralischen Gesetze) gegeben worden, die unbedingte Totalität des Gegenstandes der reinen praktischen Vernunft, unter dem Namen des *höchsten Guts*. (*KpV* p. 108)
>
> ([R]eason in its practical use is no better off. As pure practical reason it likewise seeks the unconditioned for the practically conditioned [which rests on inclinations and natural needs], not indeed as the determining ground of the will, but even when it is given [in the moral law], it seeks the unconditioned totality of the object of pure practical reason, under the name of the *highest good*. [*CpracR* 5: 108])

The highest good is the object that obliges and motivates us to fulfil our moral duty. It is the notion that combines virtue ('Tugend', 'Sittlichkeit') and happiness ('Glückseligkeit'):

> So fern nun Tugend und Glückseligkeit zusammen den Besitz des höchsten Guts in einer Person, ganz genau in Proportion der Sittlichkeit (als Werth der Person und deren Würdigkeit glücklich zu sein) ausgetheilt, das *höchste Gut* einer möglichen Welt ausmachen. (*KpV* p. 110)

(Now, in as much as virtue and happiness together constitute possession of the highest good in a person, and happiness distributed in exact proportion to morality [as the worth of a person and his worthiness to be happy] constitute the *highest good* of a possible world. [*CpracR* 5: 110])

It belongs to the conditions of our moral duty to believe in the highest good, and to assume the existence of God as part of it (Beiser 2006, p. 605). The scholarly debate about the concept of highest good revolved around the key issue whether its content is already contained within the moral law. In this debate, John Silber advocated the central importance of the highest good for Kant's Copernican Revolution in ethics (1963, p. 182; 1966, p. 55). The Kantian turn in ethics usually designates the notion that the good and evil do not pre-exist, but are determined by the moral law:

> *daß nämlich der Begriff des Guten und Bösen nicht vor dem moralischen Gesetze (dem es dem Anschein nach sogar zum Grunde gelegt werden müßte), sondern nur (wie hier auch geschieht) nach demselben und durch dasselbe bestimmt werden müsse.* (*KpV* pp. 62–3)
>
> (that the concept of good and evil must not be determined before the moral law [for which, as it would seem, this concept would have to be made the basis] but only [as was done here] after it and by means of it. [*CpracR* 5: 62–3])

In Silber's words, the Copernican Revolution in morality was 'the discovery that the object of moral volition – the good – is determined by the will of the moral agent and that the good does not determine the will of the moral agent' (Silber 1963, p. 182). He extended this definition later on by including the heterogeneous nature of the good: 'by searching the conditions of the possibility of this experience [of the obligation to the moral law] he [Kant] discovers that the good must be heterogeneous and that the moral concept of the good, instead of being defined prior to the moral law, must be determined by that law and posed by it as the object of the will' (Silber 1966, p. 101). In *A Commentary on Kant's Critique of Practical Reason*, Lewis White Beck challenged Silber's position insisting that the highest good is superfluous for our compliance with moral duty: 'For suppose I do all in my power – which is all any moral decree can demand of me – to promote the highest good, what am I to do? Simply act out of respect for the law, which I already knew' (1984, p. 244). According to Beck, the highest good added no new content to the moral law. All that the highest good accomplished was the contamination of Kant's rational purity. To use Jeffrie Murphy's words, 'if the moral good has the power to determine the will to action it thereby destroys the will [autonomy]' (Murphy 1966, p. 105). Drawing on Beck, Murphy held that Kant's introduction of the highest good was 'unnecessary and ill-advised, serving as it does extra-moral theological purposes by introducing confusions into the epistemology of his moral philosophy proper' (1966, p. 102). 'Confusions' is the very word used by Wellek for Reinhold's theory (1931, p. 5). Beiser tells us that the Silber-Beck dispute 'has now exhausted itself' (2006, p. 621).[20] Likewise, J. B. Schneewind in his 'standard introductory-level text' (Palmquist 1996, p. 373) notes that 'Kant is often thought to hold that happiness is not valuable, and even to have ignored it wholly in his ethics. This is a serious mistake' (1992, p. 333). Yet the disparagement of the highest good by previous scholarship is significant in the context of this chapter. While it provides a possible explanation for the neglect of Nitsch's work in Kant studies, it certainly had a palpable impact on the critical assessment of Coleridge's reception of Kantian ethics: commentators have failed to observe the importance of the highest good in Coleridge's initial understanding of Kant's ethics. The following analysis offers a sympathetic reading of Nitsch's work, which traces the heterogeneous concepts of virtue and happiness in the *second critique*.

Nitsch's exposition of Kantian moral principles

Nitsch's introduction of the categorical imperative tried to bridge between the strict formalism of the *Groundwork* (1785) and Kant's efforts to resolve the question regarding our motivation for moral duty in the *Critique of Practical Reason* (1788). Nitsch's understanding of Kantian ethics stemmed from a time when his teacher's thinking concerning the incentives for the moral law was still 'very much in flux' (Beiser 2006, p. 615). The German expatriate had started studying under Kant and his disciple Kraus in October 1785 (Baum and Malter 1991, p. 461). The *Groundwork* appeared in April 1785 and in the winter semester of 1784–5, Kant gave 'the first public presentation of [his] mature moral philosophy' (Schneewind 1997, p. xvii). Lecture notes by his former students disclose that Kant's teaching went beyond the *Groundwork* 'in remarks about the way in which morality needs God' (Schneewind 1997, p. xviii). Beiser notes that Kant had not yet written *Religion innerhalb der Grenzen der reinen Vernunft* (1793). In this work, Kant clarified that 'happiness of the highest good cannot be physical . . . but that it has to be moral. Moral happiness consists in the serenity of knowing that one's moral disposition will remain firm and not relapse into temptation' (Beiser 2006, p. 617). In the *second critique* of 1788, Kant's answer was not so clear-cut. The publication speaks of person worthiness of happiness in a 'möglichen Welt' (possible world) (*KpV* p. 110), not in another world. Nitsch probably left Königsberg between 1792 and 1793 as it is known that he taught at the Collegium Fridericianum until 1792 (Baum and Malter 1991, p. 461). Nitsch's list of his major Kantian reference at the beginning of his pamphlet included *Religion within the Boundaries of Reason* (1796, pp. 2–3 n). Nevertheless, he either learnt from Kant or thought himself that the highest good pertained to happiness in this world. In any case, his treatise acquainted readers with a version of Kant's moral theory that still included the physical dimension of happiness.

Nitsch's main source for his moral exposition was the *second critique*: 'the work wherein all this is treated more at large, is the Criticism of Practical Reason' (1796, p. 218). What complicated his explication was Nitsch's attempt to find a short transition from the categorical imperative to Kant's notion of the highest good. His moral exposition began with a discussion of Kant's concept of freedom and will (1796, pp. 169–206) followed by a recapitulation of moral principles from 'Socrates' to 'The Eclectics' (pp. 206–13). Nitsch added a translation of the categorical imperative, placing it within the text as if it was the ultimate innovation of the existing canon of moral principles: 'Act according to those principles only of which thou canst will that they ought to become the general laws on conduct among all reasonable beings' (1796, p. 214). The tension between the formalism of the moral law and the highest good entered Nitsch's exposition immediately after the introduction of the categorical imperative in a section that contrasted Kant's moral principle with those of his predecessors. Nitsch constructed an opposition between 'the first moral principle of Kant' and 'those of other philosophers' in analogy to which he added the following pairs: reason and non-reason; formal and material; universal and particular; independence from outcome and particular ends. Yet this opposition collapses when Nitsch came to speak of pleasing sensations. At this point, contrast turns into similarity as the syntax suddenly conflates the oppositional subjects (the 'latter' and the 'former'). As a consequence, the distinctions from Kantianism start to blur, and it is no longer clear for the reader which philosophers 'do not strive to realise the general laws of reason; but to acquire pleasing sensations, and reason must work as a servant to propose the best means of obtaining them . . . and make ourselves dependant upon things which change with the weather, and very often do not stand at our command' (Nitsch 1796, p. 215). Instead of renewing the contrast between the distinctions, the following sentence implied, without further explanation, a similarity.

The argument switched to Kant's notion of the highest good as expounded in the *second critique* by adding

> [i]t is perfectly right to strive after the pleasing sensations or happiness. . . . Every man has, therefore, two great ends in which all his exertions and desires ultimately centre, and these are happiness and independence, or virtue. Both ends taken together, form the great and complete object of all human desires or the highest good, and every man must necessarily desire both virtue and happiness as long as he retains the nature of his mind and body. (Nitsch 1796, pp. 215–16)

Here, bodily impulses were seen as part of the motivation for moral duty. Nitsch drew on Kant's comparison of the Stoics and the Epicureans specifying the human incentive (*KpV* p. 112): 'The highest good, therefore, consists not in mere virtue, as the Stoics believed, nor in mere happiness, as the Epicureans affirmed, but in the union of both' (Nitsch 1796, p. 216). Nitsch postponed for later Kant's qualification that virtue and happiness had no necessary connection in the sensuous world, 'diese Verbindung . . . nicht als aus der Erfahrung, abgeleitet wird' (*KpV* p. 113) ('this combination is cognized . . . not as derived from experience' [*CpracR* 5: 113]). According to Kant, the link between virtue and happiness could be guaranteed only through a higher authority:

> Die Lehre des Christentums, wenn man sie auch noch nicht als Religionslehre betrachtet, giebt in diesem Stücke einen Begriff des höchsten Guts (des Reichs Gottes), der allein der strengsten Forderung der praktischen Vernunft ein Gnüge thut (*KpV* pp. 127–8).
>
> (The doctrine of Christianity, even if it is not regarded as a religious doctrine, gives on this point a concept of the highest good [of kingdom of God] which alone satisfies the strictest demand of practical reason. [*CpracR* 5: 127–8])

Beiser explains that 'Our finite human will cannot be a sufficient cause for happiness to correspond with morality [virtue], and that the only such cause would be an infinite *moral* being, that is, one having an infinite will, power, and intelligence' (Beiser 2006, p. 605; see *KpV* 124–5; *CpracR* 5: 124–5). Nitsch did not discuss this aspect of Kant's morality until the second part of his moral exposition when he expounded, under the heading 'Influence of Kant's Principles on Religion', the Kantian notion that virtue and happiness are not necessarily linked within the physical world:

> As the moral law, which determines our will, is different from the determining grounds of the phenomena in nature; one being the law of freedom, and the others mechanical causes, it follows, that the moral law cannot contain the least ground for supposing a necessary connection between virtue and a proportionate happiness in a being belonging to the phenomena of nature, as a part, and which yet is directed in its actions by a law directly opposite to the mechanical course of nature. (1796, pp. 227–8)

Furthermore, he clarified that the presupposition of immortality is inherent in the highest good:

> as we are bound by reason to suppose our progress in virtue will be infinite, and as this progress cannot be made, unless the same person continues its existence, it follows that the highest good is practically possible only on the condition of man's immortality. (Nitsch 1796, p. 221)

Within the first moral chapter on 'Kant's Principles of the Science of Morals', however, Nitsch merely established the link between virtue and happiness and raised the issue of their respective priority. He explained the negative consequences of our exclusive pursuit of happiness: '[w]hen happiness is made the road to virtue, all virtue is destroyed, and disorder and confusion is the immediate consequence, which can neither be called happiness nor highest good' (Nitsch 1796, p. 217). And he reasoned accordingly: 'whereas if virtue be made the road to happiness, happiness will not be destroyed, but only confined to the general laws which preserve it against extravagance, and give it consistency' (Nitsch 1796, p. 217). Similar to Kant, Nitsch stipulated the primacy of virtue over happiness (*KpV* pp. 114–15). The German expatriate propounded that 'the highest good is practically possible, only upon the condition that VIRTUE BE THE CAUSE OF HAPPINESS' (Nitsch 1796, p. 217). In doing so, he considered the sensuous nature of humans carefully: 'and that man, before he strives after any particular set of pleasing sensations, should always reflect, first, whether the moral law would permit him the enjoyment of them or not' (1796, p. 217). Nitsch emphasized the role of the highest good and saw human desires as a significant part of it. It is possible that he echoed what he had learnt directly from his university teacher Kant. At the same time, he might have deliberately understated the significance of Kant's cautious addition that we can only assume the causal connection of virtue and proportionate happiness through our capacity of thinking about ourselves as part of the super-sensuous world (*KpV* p. 115). In any case, the outcome is clear. It was Nitsch's simplified and assertive proclamation that 'VIRTUE BE THE CAUSE OF HAPPINESS' that attracted the attention of his English readership.

The public response to Nitsch's pamphlet

Giuseppe Micheli has done a great deal to uncover the public response to Nitsch's pamphlet (1990, pp. 266–73). Like Coburn (*Notebooks [Notes]* I, §249), however, Micheli underestimates the significance of one of the earliest reviews of Nitsch's pamphlet: the article published in the *British Critic* in August 1796. Micheli explains that (1) the liberal *English Review* had anticipated the publication of Nitsch's work by giving an approximate outline (English Review 27 [1796], pp. 106–11);[21] that (2) in the same month (May 1796), the *Monthly Magazine* published a detailed recommendation of Kantianism by Coleridge's friend Dr Beddoes in the form of a letter to the editor, dated 28 March 1796 (*The Monthly Magazine and British Register* 1 [1796], pp. 265–7); and that (3) Beddoes reviewed Nitsch's introduction favourably and advocated a translation of Kant's critical works. However Micheli's assessment of the review in the *British Critic* – 'it was totally negative' (1990, p. 266) – is misleading. The review was unfavourable, but the history of the reception of Kant's *Critique of Pure Reason* shows that a detailed assessment albeit negative can still greatly aid publicity. I contend that it would be a mistake to brush the *British Critic* aside. The infamous review in the *Göttingische Anzeigen* by Garve and Feder 'upset Kant' (Kühn 2006, p. 636), but 'all in all, if only in retrospect, it was not a bad start. The review created a controversy, which attracted attention to the *Kritik*' (Beiser 1987, p. 172). There is good reason to think that the same was true for Nitsch in the case of the *British Critic*. Run by conservative English churchmen (Forster 2003, p. 179), the periodical was 'initially founded [in 1793] by a hundred pounds from William Pitt's Secret Service' (Sullivan 1983a, p. 58; see Roper 1978, p. 27). By 1797, the sales of the *British Critic* equalled those of the long-established *Critical Review*, that is, ca. 3500 sales (Forster 2003, p. 180; Roper 1978, p. 24). The review appeared in the *British Critic* in August 1796, three months after the publication of Nitsch's treatise *A General and Introductory View*. It offered an extensive account, quoting and summarizing the entire volume in about fourteen pages. The paper dedicated more space in a single article to the discussion of Nitsch's work than its liberal competitors did, namely the *Monthly Magazine* and the *Monthly Review*.[22] It is true that Beddoes's review included a recommendation of Nitsch (*Monthly Magazine* 1 [1796], pp. 265–7), yet the *British Critic* involuntarily did more for the public promotion of Kant than the favourable reviewers: the review was the first to assign a place within British thought to Nitsch's work.[23]

The article placed Nitsch in the context of the tradition of British freethinking that had taken shape in the 1690s (Rivers 2000, p. 13).[24] Although the *British Critic* did not use the term 'freethinking', the Anglican periodical insinuated that the Kantian system subverted Christian society. After a résumé of Nitsch's presentation of Kant's epistemology ('*Kant's theoretical Principles*'), the author stated that the whole review was driven by religious concerns: 'A motive yet more strong has more particularly induced us to give a well-connected chain of these propositions. They are intended to form a new base for religion' (*British Critic* 8, [1796], p. 143). The article noted that 'Kant does not admit Revelation' (*British Critic* 8, p. 144). Furthermore, it made clear that Kantian morality revolved around individual autonomy.[25] Addressing the central importance of free will within the Kantian system, the article raised the question, 'Has man a free will? – and wherein does free will consist?' (*British Critic* 8, p. 143). The reviewer concluded that

> knowing, from the existence of ages, how human reason contradicts itself upon such questions, it is sufficient for the christian [sic] philosopher to know that God, when he gave moral laws to men, declared to him also that his lot would depend upon his conduct. Whence he concludes, without a doubt, that man must have freedom of choice. (*British Critic* 8, p. 143)

As these quotations show, the article aimed at presenting Kant as an unbeliever in the eyes of orthodox Christians.

In doing so, the review categorized Nitsch's work as dangerous. According to Edmund Burke's *Reflections on the Revolution in France* (1790), the pursuit of morality came down to sacrilege: 'pert loquacity' (1790, p. 128). As Coleridge wrote, 'the writings of Burke exorcised from the higher and from the literary classes . . . the spirit of Jacobinism [sic]' (*Biographia* I, p. 192). Burke demanded in the *Reflections* that humans should not interfere with morality because the divine would be tempered by human insight:

> we know that *we* have made no discoveries; and we think that no discoveries are to be made, in morality; nor many in the great principles of government, nor in the idea of liberty, which were understood long before we were born, altogether as well as they will be after the grave has heaped its mould upon our presumption, and the silent tomb shall have imposed its law on our pert loquacity. (Burke 1790, pp. 127–8)

Simultaneously he belittled the importance of John Toland (1670–1722), Matthew Tindal (1657–1733), Anthony Collins (1676–1729), Thomas Chubb (1679–1747) and Abel Morgan (1673–1722) by asking the rhetorical question: 'Who, born within the last forty years, has read one word of Collins, and Toland, and Tindal, and Chubb, and Morgan, and that whole race who called themselves Freethinkers?' (Burke 1790, p. 133). The *British Critic* followed Burke's argument and applied it to Kant and his mediator in England by grouping them broadly with English deists like Anthony Collins and Tom Paine. For counterrevolutionaries, Nitsch's association with freethinking was a potential threat. Freethinkers tended to question revealed religion and divine law, and to dismiss the authority of the Bible, therefore necessarily opposing a monarchy like the British one that was closely connected to the Anglican Church. At the same time, this grouping attracted political reformist thinkers like Coleridge.[26] For the young poet the question of free will had become a kind of philosophical litmus test as 'Destiny of Nations' shows (see Chapter 2).

Coleridge perused the *British Critic* at the time, partly to look for reviews of his poetry and partly to gather information for his journalistic pursuits, be it for *The Watchman* or his future work for the *Morning Chronicle* in London. In July 1796, Coleridge quoted from the periodical in a letter to Poole, 'as to the British Critic [of May 1796, p. 549] they *durst not* condemn and they would not praise—so contented themselves with "commending me, as a *Poet*["]—and allowed me "tenderness of sentiment & elegance of diction"' (*Letters* I, p. 227). Even if Coleridge was primarily interested in reviews of his own work, he must have read the following issues of *British Critic* in August (1796), too. Coleridge was an extremely fast reader able to remember almost all the contents of his perusals albeit not in their respective order (Walker 1997, p. 325). The review of Nitsch in the *British Critic* treated a subject at the forefront of his mind: free will. The *British Critic* introduced Kant as the advocate of freedom and free will by quoting the explosive lines from Nitsch that 'every human will, therefore, as it is determined by practical principles, is free. As the human will is *free*, the formal practical principles are the true laws of *freedom*' (*British Critic* 8, p. 145; see Nitsch 1796, p. 202). A year after the poet's helpless insistence in his moral and political lecture that the principles of freedom 'must be' (without saying what they consisted in), Nitsch's introduction to Kant offered a possible formulation of the 'true laws' to the friends of freedom like Coleridge (*Lectures 1795*, p. 17): Kant's explicit formulation of the universal law in the *Groundwork* (4: 421) was even cited by the *British Critic*: '*Act according to those principles only of which thou canst will that they ought to become the general law on conduct among all reasonable beings.*' (8, p. 146; see Nitsch 1796, p. 214). The reviewer had selected from *A General and Introductory View* Nitsch's free translation of the categorical imperative.[27] Given Coleridge's strong interest in the periodical, it is nearly certain that Coleridge read this review. The *British Critic's* intended criticism (Nitsch's alleged freethinking) attracted Coleridge in the mid-1790s like a magnet. The fact that the conservative periodical accused Nitsch (and by extension Kant) indirectly of atheism may actually have encouraged Coleridge to read Nitsch. By way of reversed psychology, the conservatives' rejection made Nitsch even more attractive for Coleridge. His opponents' adversaries promised to be his allies in politics, which were inseparable from philosophy for Coleridge. Anthony Harding has shown that Coleridge sought atheist writers out, helped and influenced by Beddoes and other members of the radical circles in Bristol (2010, p. 138). In addition, many more materials by and on Nitsch were available to Coleridge at the time.

The *Morning Chronicle*, with which Coleridge was closely associated since the paper had published his poems in 1793 and 1794 (Engell and Bate 1983, p. xxx), publicized Nitsch's lectures several times between 1795 and 1796 (21 March 1795; 5 and 12 December 1796). In December 1796, the paper contained Nitsch's entire prospectus, according to which, Kant's philosophy was:

> novel and highly important to the Logician, the Metaphysician, the Natural Philosopher, the Moralist, the Theologian and to those who are involved in [matters] concerning our ideas of Matter, Cause and Effect, the Nature of Mind, and its influence on the Body, the Freedom of the Will, and the Origin of Moral and Religious Ideas. (*Morning Chronicle* 5 December 1796)

It was in Coleridge's professional interest as a lecturer and writer on these topics to attend or read Nitsch's exposition; one could say, he was obliged to do so. A close reading of Coleridge's notebook entry discloses that the German immigrant made a deep impression indeed.

Coleridge's conceptual affinity with Nitsch's concern for the sensuous nature of men and women

Although Coleridge's notebook entry conveys the self-reflexive formulation which distinguished Kant's moral law by placing the highest importance on motivation rather than outcome, it deviates slightly from the complete disinterestedness expressed in Kant's original, for Coleridge's two phrases, separated by a colon, link action with 'public good' and 'universal happiness' (*Notebooks* I, §249). This deviation supports the view that Coleridge was acquainted with Nitsch's work either in conversation or in print.[28] As shown above, Nitsch emphasized Kant's notion of the highest good and suggested a direct link between the moral law and universal happiness: 'the highest good is practically possible, only upon the condition that VIRTUE BE THE CAUSE OF HAPPINESS' (Nitsch 1796, p. 217). The German disciple of Kant stressed that 'it is perfectly right to strive after pleasing sensations and happiness' (1796, p. 215). This type of Kantianism appealed to the British audience embroiled in financial speculation and shaken by political crisis including Coleridge.

The *English Review* referred approvingly to Nitsch's association of moral virtue and universal happiness in 1796, as did an influential Unitarian preacher two years later.[29] Coleridge's acquaintance, the Unitarian minister William Enfield (1741–97), recommended *A General and Introductory View* to his readers in the *Monthly Review* (1798): 'we acknowledge him [Nitsch] to be an ingenious and able advocate; and we think this work entitled to an attentive perusal' (22 [1797], p. 18). Enfield based his approval on Nitsch's explication of the highest good and embraced the connection between the categorical imperative and happiness: 'Hence it follows, that the highest good is practically possible, only upon the condition that VIRTUE BE THE CAUSE OF HAPPINESS' (*Monthly Review* 22 [1797], p. 18). Nitsch's ethical delineation chimed with Enfield's views. For the Unitarian minister Hartley's *Observations on Man* was a staple part of his reading. Hartley's *Observations* conformed to the rational principles in so far as he declared: '*Religion presupposes . . . a voluntary power over our Affections and Actions*' (1749 II, p. 53). At the same time, *Observations on Man* frequently referred to happiness as the proper goal of moral self-discipline; 'By the Affections we are excited to pursue Happiness, and all its Means, fly from Misery, and all its apparent Causes' (Hartley 1749 I, p. iii). In the second volume, Hartley connected happiness with divine benevolence using a series of five logical possibilities that ended with the conclusion that 'I have now gone through with my Observations on the Frame, Duty, and Expectations of Man, finishing them with the doctrine of ultimate, unlimited Happiness to All' (1749 II, p. 438). By highlighting the connection of virtue and proportionate happiness in Nitsch's pamphlet, Enfield stressed a similarity with necessitarianism. Thus Enfield assimilated Nitsch's exposition of Kantian philosophy into the rational dissenting and radical milieu. It is important to note that Enfield's presentation implicitly associated Nitsch with Godwinian philosophy, too (see Chapter1). Although Godwin's moral position moved away from rational dissent during the period between 1790 and 1796 (Philp 1986, pp. 143, 161–6), happiness remained an integral part of his ethics as the titles of all three editions show (Godwin 1993 III, p. 7): *Enquiry Concerning Political Justice: and its Influence on General Virtue and Happiness* (1793) and respectively

Enquiry Concerning Political Justice: and its influence on Morals and Happiness (1796 and 1798). What Enfield's review communicated to Unitarians and democrats like young Coleridge was that Kant appeared to be guaranteeing the necessitarian promise of happiness through virtue while offering a more philosophically rigorous approach to the human mind, 'a more perfect discovery of the process of the human intellect in its operations' (*Monthly Review* 22 [1797], p. 16). As mentioned, this constitutes a historically momentous link between British freethinking and critical philosophy. Furthermore, it complicates our thinking about the conceptual boundaries between German and British thought in Coleridge's philosophy in terms of the rational versus the empirical.

The *British Critic* (1796) shared Enfield's moral interest, but bestowed less praise on Nitsch, to put it mildly. The reviewer of the *British Critic* raised the objection that the purity of practical Reason precluded sensibility from playing a constitutive part in Kant's morality. German scholars in the early 1790s raised similar objections, that is, that Kant's purity was undermined. Among these critics was the distinguished philosopher Christian Garve who published his view on the topic in his treatise *Versuche über verschiedene Gegenstände aus der Moral, Litteratur und dem gesellschaftlichen Leben* (1792; Beiser 2006, p. 627 n40). The critique of the *British Critic* started out by clarifying Nitsch's position. Taking Nitsch's insistence that 'Man is a compound of *reason* and *sense*' as a point of departure, the *British Critic* expounded Nitsch's explanation of moral principles a priori carefully:

> Any practical principle deriving from *experience*, extends so far as experience reaches, and is therefore not strictly universal; nor is it strictly necessary, because our experience may indeed show us that something is so and so, but never that it must be so. But it is a fact well established by consciousness that a practical principle is strictly necessary and universal. *For instance, Be [sic] virtuous at all times and under all circumstances of life; and let thy virtue ever be disinterested.* (*British Critic* 8 [1796], p. 144)

Subsequently, the reviewer pinpointed the flaw he perceived in Nitsch's elucidation by calling attention to the contradiction between the purely rational nature of practical Reason and the mixed nature of Man: 'we find as yet no notion of those desires determined by sense, which are the object of this moral doctrine' (*British Critic* 8, p. 145). The concession to the physical side of human life did not go far enough for the *British Critic*. What Coleridge appears to have gathered from the review is that the senses should play a constitutive role in Kant's laws of freedom, too.

Coleridge's notebook entry contains traces of Nitsch's exposition of Kant's ethics. Opposing the complete subjection of sensibility to Reason, Coleridge apparently endorsed Nitsch's interpretation of the highest good in much the same way as his contemporaries. '[T]he complete highest good of a rational and finite being', Nitsch declared, 'can never consist in only being virtuous; every being of this description has wants, desires, feelings, and necessarily must desire that the surrounding world should agree with his wants, desires and feelings, and not oppose them' (1796, p. 229). Ideally, both Reason and sensibility inclined us to act morally.[30] Therefore it does not come as a surprise that Coleridge's notebook entry did not capture Kant's strict formalism.

Although there is no proof in the extant sources to show that Coleridge had first-hand knowledge of Nitsch, the above-mentioned evidence strongly suggests that Coleridge was acquainted with Nitsch's work. He read the *British Critic* regularly and three of his intellectual role models, Beddoes, Thelwall and Godwin reviewed, read or attended the lectures of Nitsch (see Chapter 1). Moreover, the conceptual affinity between Nitsch's and Coleridge's modification of the categorical imperative is clear regardless of a proof of the extent of Coleridge's knowledge of Nitsch. His conflation of the categorical imperative with 'public good' and 'happiness' reveals that Coleridge espoused Nitsch's lessons of the highest good. 'Public good' and 'universal happiness' in the notebook entry indicate Coleridge's prevalent concern for physical and emotional needs in 1796: 'I judge of all things by their Utility' (*Letters* I, p. 279). Additionally they show his indebtedness to Nitsch, who went as far as to say 'to keep up the use of reason, and to preserve our natural freedom . . . we must necessarily suppose a proportionate happiness to be consequent upon virtue' (1796, p. 230). The conceptual affinities suggest that Nitsch's explanations helped Coleridge to make sense of Germany's 'profoundest [yet] most unintelligible [metaphysician] Emanuel Kant' (*Letters* I, p. 284); indeed the similarities are so strong that it seems hard to adequately understand Coleridge's reading experience of Kant without this initial primer.

Coleridge was a rapid reader (Walker 1997, p. 325), who enjoyed '*a proper Brain-cracker*' (*Marginalia* V, p. 173). Robert Southey's *The Life of Wesley* (1820) is one of the books that soothed the poet like a friend: 'I was used to resort whenever Sickness & Langour [sic] made me feel the want of an old friend, of whose company I could never be tired' (*Marginalia* V, pp. 120–1). As the volumes of this work were such intimate companions for Coleridge (roughly between 1820 and 1832), his annotations on the margins can be seen as earnest testimonies of the poet's thoughts and experiences. It is here that Coleridge pondered 'the spirit of authorship' and the experience of reading (*Marginalia* V, p. 173). Coleridge compared Southey's chapter on the writings of Wesley to *The Friend* and *Aids to Reflections* noting that in contrast to the former, 'the aim of every sentence is to solicit, nay, *tease* the Reader to ask himself, whether he *actually* does or does not understand *distinctly*? (*Marginalia* V, p. 174). In order to make readers understand 'distinctly' there should to be a text that 'has pointed out any passage of importance, which he [the author] having at length understood, he could propose other & more intelligible words that would have conveyed precisely the same meaning!' (*Marginalia* V, p. 173). Shifting the perspective from author to reader, Coleridge's remark discloses his own appreciation for aids to help his own understanding of '*Brain-crackers*' (*Marginalia* V, p. 173). Judging from his 1803 reading notes on the *Groundwork*, Coleridge appears to have used Nitsch's *General and Introductory View* as such an aid to reflection. The poet's response to the *Groundwork* is so consistent with the exposition that Coleridge must have been primed with Nitsch's lessons.

Reading the *Groundwork* by anticipation[31]

Coleridge read the *Grundlegung zur Metaphysik der Sitten* in 1803,[32] taking notes and writing on the margins of his copy while staying in Keswick. His handwriting on pages 54 and 55 of his now worn and shabby volume bear witness to a particular moment of disappointment: 'Strange Nonsense! . . . But Kant, & all his School, are miserable Reasoners, in Psychology & particular Morals- bad analysts of aught but Notions, equally clumsy in the illustrations & application of their Principles' (*Marginalia* III, p. 253). The autograph commentary, filled with adjectives and an exclamation mark, conveys how strong Coleridge's response was on an emotional level. Coleridge was displeased with the philosopher and even irritated by him. He sweepingly dismissed 'Kant, & all his School'. The initial 'But' followed by the emotionally charged attribute 'miserable' voices Coleridge's dissatisfaction with a particular passage in the *Groundwork*: Kant's argument against suicide, which is, according to Guyer, the fourth and admittedly 'weakest' illustration following the first formulation of the categorical imperative (2005, p. 170). Such disappointment is indicative of both frustrated expectations and an already existing bond. If Coleridge was familiar with Nitsch's pamphlet and knew the principle that virtue must be the cause of happiness, it is clear why the poet expected to find somewhat more convincing reasons to conform to the moral law than Kant's gloomy prospect that no matter how much 'Pain & Evil' (*Marginalia* III, p. 253) life entailed, Reason impels us to refrain from suicide. Kant reasoned that 'das Leben bey seiner längeren Frist mehr Übel droht' ('longer duration [of life] is likely to bring more evil than satisfaction') [Kant cited in *Marginalia* III, p. 252]). Appalled by this notion, the poet wrote on the top of page 55: 'Who could believe that these pages were written by the same man, who could produce the two [paragraphs] in pages 60 & 61?' (*Marginalia* III, p. 254, my addition). In the *Notebooks*, Coleridge wrote down the sober observation: 'So men preserve their Lives *conformably to Duty*, how seldom *out of Duty*. Kant instances it in men overwhelmed with their own misery' (I, §1705). Seemingly unprepared for such pessimism, Coleridge deplored 'Kant, and all his School': they 'shake my Faith in their general System. S.T.C. Decemb. 6. 1803. Keswick' (*Marginalia* III, p. 253). The marginal annotation states without a shadow of a doubt that Coleridge had already developed considerable 'Faith' in critical philosophy. Kant's illustrations of the categorical imperative in these passages of the *Groundwork* lacked the positive prospect of the highest good and happiness. This appears as a new, rather unexpected aspect for the poet; Coleridge was taken aback.

Nevertheless, Coleridge transcribed entire passages from the *Groundwork* into his notebook and included his own remarks. These study notes disclose Coleridge's awareness and approval of the highest good, although the latter is discussed in great detail in the *second critique* which Coleridge had probably not yet read. In the *Critique of Practical Reason* included Kant's attempt 'to reconstruct two of the most cherished doctrines of traditional metaphysics, the existence of God and the immortality of the soul' (Guyer 2006, p. 19). Coleridge's notes to the *Groundwork* allude to Kant's argument that practical Reason postulates the existence of God (*KpV* p. 124):

> It is not enough that we act in conformity to the Law of moral Reason – we must likewise FOR THE SAKE of that law/ **it must not only be our Guide, but likewise our Impulse - Like a strong current, it must make a visible Road on the Sea, & drive us along that road** gemäss – um desselben willen. God *der Wille* – Christ *Logos* – new exposition of the Text. Why callest thou me good? (*Notebooks* I, §1705)

Previous scholarship on Coleridge's reception of Kant's ethics has focused on the stoic dimension of *Groundwork* and the *second critique* to test the accuracy of the poet's reading. Coleridge experts largely agree that Kant's stoicism posed conceptual problems for the poet and led to scattered remarks of rejection. As Wellek has noted, 'Coleridge could not see why our emotional nature should be excluded from the essence of ethics' (1931, p. 88). Orsini has observed: 'In the notes of 1803 we can see Coleridge in this area of philosophy still enmeshed in empiricism, struggling to understand Kant's transcendentalism, and failing to do so at his first attempt, but succeeding later' (1969, p. 153). Anthony Harding has perceptively discerned Coleridge's attitude towards morality, 'Coleridge, for his part, had never been willing to leave the affections outside the sphere of ethical discussion' (1974, p. 167) and has proposed what recent scholarship notably by Douglas Hedley (2000) continues to explore, namely that the doctrines expounded in *Aids to Reflection* are 'in many important points similar to Plato's' (Harding 1974, p. 168).[33] Laurence S. Lockridge in *Coleridge: The Moralist* has focused on Coleridge's rejection of Kant's moral stoicism (1977, p. 139) arguing that Coleridge used the categorical imperative through its renunciation of particular ends as a convenient excuse for his sloth. Deirdre Coleman has discerned Coleridge's predisposition to the Kantian ethics in the Quaker belief of an inner light (1988, pp. 69–71). Christoph Bode, in his important essay, regards Kant's categorical imperative as 'his ethics in a nutshell' and 'the ideas of "God" and "immortality"' as mere by-products of free will' (2009, p. 601). It is true that Coleridge deviated (it is debatable whether consciously or not) from Kant's stoicism. Yet it is striking that since the 1960s, when the highest good was disparaged in Kantian studies, the major examinations of Coleridge's reception of Kantian ethics have attributed no particular importance to the highest good although it has the potential to account in part for Coleridge's insistence on moral inclination. Indeed Coleridge's initial reaction to the *Groundwork* contains clues that the highest good as delineated by Nitsch was pivotal to the poet's initial understanding of Kantian ethics.

In this notebook entry (*Notebooks* I, §1705), Coleridge emerges as a reader of Kant primed by Nitsch's lessons. Nitsch's emphasis on the highest good gives a major reason why Coleridge expressed his view so emphatically that the '*conformity to the Law of moral Reason*' is 'not enough'. Coleridge followed Nitsch's view that virtue alone was not sufficient but the prospect of proportionate happiness constituted a significant component in our moral behaviour. Building on Nitsch's lesson, Coleridge presupposed that we have a physical and a spiritual motivation to abide by the moral law: 'our Impulse'. The entry intensifies Nitsch's image of the 'road' of virtue to happiness (p. 217) by amplifying its power: the poet visualized the moral law as a 'visible Road' and compared it to one of the forces of nature, 'a strong current'. Moreover, it acknowledges that the mechanism of nature has no part in our obligation to act morally in much the same way as Nitsch explained that 'moral law cannot contain the least ground for supposing a necessary connection between virtue and a proportionate happiness in a being belonging to the phenomena of nature' (1796, p. 228); at the same time, Coleridge expanded Nitsch's statement by attributing such strength to the motivation to comply with the categorical imperative as if it were equally powerful as nature. It is the reference to the Bible ('Why callest thou me good?') and the omission of the respective answer, 'there is none good, but one, that is God' (*King James*, Mark 10), that completes Coleridge's entry. It brings the poet's meditation back to the highest good that was so central to Nitsch's exposition of Kantian ethics. Coleridge's interpretation corresponds with Kant in so far as the latter thought that Christianity alone satisfied the strictest demands of practical Reason through its concept of highest good (*KpV* pp. 127–8). And so it is that Coleridge's entry agrees with perfectly Nitsch and Kant: '**so men are really the happiest who take Virtue not Happiness for the ultimatum / - & must be so**' (*Notebooks* I, §1705).

The notebook entry (I, §1705) shows that Coleridge was also aware of a further critical disciple of Kant: Friedrich Schiller. Coleridge's admiration of the German poet, in whose honour Coleridge published the poem 'Effusion XX', started while reading *The Robbers* in Tytler's translation in 1794. Apart from his work as a playwright, Schiller studied Kant's *Critique of the Power of Judgment* in order to formulate his own treatises on aesthetics during the early 1790s. As part of these studies, Schiller composed 'Über die ästhetische Erziehung des Menschen in einer Reihe von Briefen' (*Schiller* XX, pp. 309–412) ('On the Aesthetic Education of Man'). Analysing Kant's concept of freedom, Schiller emphasized that it should not discredit the twofold nature of humans, 'gemischte Natur' ('mixed nature') (*Schiller* XX, p. 373 n, l. 33), which consists of both intellect and body. Schiller was fascinated by the possibility of physical or natural manifestation of freedom within time and space. Coleridge probably became familiar with this work while in Germany (Kooy 2002, pp. 33–44). The phrase '/Vide Schiller' in Coleridge's notebook entry refers to Schiller in the context of the question how nature brings to light human autonomy, 'to produce a pure will' (*Notebooks* I, §1705). Although Coleridge's remark does not mention the title of Schiller's work, the poet's association of Schiller with a particular scene '**sitting together in the Coach/ & forever are loving to look at Children/ Vide Schiller**' (§1705) points to a famous passage in 'Über naive und sentimentalische Dichtung' published in 1795 (*Schiller* XX, pp. 413–503) ('On Naïve and Sentimental Poetry' [Schiller 1988]):

> Was hätte auch eine unscheinbare Blume, eine Quelle, ein bemoßter Stein, das Gezwitscher der Vögel, das Summen der Bienen u.s.w. für sich selbst so gefälliges für uns? Was könnte ihm gar einen Anspruch auf unsere Liebe geben? Es sind nicht diese Gegenstände, es ist eine durch sie dargestellte Idee, was wir in ihnen lieben. Wir lieben in ihnen das stille schaffende Leben, das ruhige Wirken aus sich selbst, das Daseyn nach eignen Gesetzen, die innere Notwendigkeit, die ewige Einheit mit sich selbst. (*Schiller* XX, p. 414)
>
> (For what could a modest flower, a stream, a mossy stone, the chirping of birds, the humming of bees, etc., possess in themselves so pleasing to us? What could give them a claim even upon our love? It is not these objects, it is an idea represented by them which we love in them. We love in them the tacitly creative life, the serene spontaneity of their activity, the existence in accordance with their own laws, the inner necessity, the eternal unity with themselves. [Schiller 1988, p. 149])[34]

Here, Schiller expressed the view that the forms of nature, 'a modest flower, a stream, a mossy stone', or a similar scene, such as children at play, solicit in us the conformity with the moral law, which we experience as freedom; or, as Coleridge put it in his interpolation in the notebooks: a moral impulse.

It is possible that Coleridge knew 'On Naïve and Sentimental Poetry' by December 1803. Nevertheless, the reference to Schiller does not eclipse the influence of Nitsch. It is true that Julie Carlson has noted that 'Coleridge first thinks about Kant through Schiller' (Carlson 1994, pp. 68, 75). Even so, prior to May 1796, when Nitsch's pamphlet was published, Coleridge had only read Schiller's tempestuous Storm-and-Stress play in translation (1794). What is remarkable about Coleridge's studies of the moral law is that his notebook entry (*Notebooks* I, §1705) displays the poet's concurrence with the view that the moral law required an additional objective, the highest good besides mere conformity. Otherwise, the moral law would discredit the sensuous dimension of human existence. As Coleridge explained in 1817, 'I reject Kant's *stoic* principle, as false, unnatural, and even immoral, where in his Critik der Practischen Vernun[f]t he treats the affections as indifferent . . . in ethics' (*Letters* IV, p. 791). This point of criticism was not unique. Besides Nitsch and Schiller, Herder also took issue with Kant's strict formalism (Zammito 1992, pp. 1–16). By December 1803, Coleridge apparently knew, judging from the notebook entry, that Schiller advocated the laws of freedom while adhering to the twofold nature of man. The fact remains that Nitsch's exposition of Kantianism was the first work in English to impart the categorical imperative. The treatise did so while emphasizing the concept of the highest good and hence the human need for happiness besides virtue. The notebook entry (I, §249) indicates not only that the intricacies of Kant's practical philosophy fascinated Coleridge already before he studied the *Groundwork* in December 1803; it also conveys traces of Nitsch's lessons.

The 'Gothic cathedral' and the 'chapels of ease'

In *Biographia Literaria*, Coleridge compared his acquaintance with Kantianism to entering 'one of our largest Gothic cathedrals' (*Biographia* I, p. 301) for the first time. In the early nineteenth century, Coleridge retrospectively cultivated the sense of Kant's superiority over, and to some extent his incompatibility with, British philosophical schools. All native forms of philosophy, especially the works by Cambridge Platonist and other proponents of rational dissent, seemed like 'our light airy modern chapels of ease' in 1817. In the early 1790s, however, Nitsch adapted Kantian concepts to suit the debates of the native philosophers when he built up his Kantian school in London. By putting the link between virtue and happiness centre stage, which was compatible with the then dominant necessitarian thought in the freethinking milieu of 1790s England, he achieved a milestone in this Kantian enterprise. The concept of the highest good as mediated by Nitsch remained formative for Coleridge's ethical thought throughout his life. Coleridge's notebook entry, dated to late 1795 to early 1796, strongly supports the notion that Coleridge's philosophical transitions in the mid-1790s included critical philosophy. The poet's notebook entry further indicates the poet's familiarity with Kant's moral law more than five years prior to his in-depth study of the *Critique of Pure Reason* (1800/ 1801), which is traditionally seen as the beginning of Coleridge's reception of Kant. The entry also reveals that Coleridge latched on to one of the specific contributions that Kantian philosophy could make to English thought. Neither the British idealists he was studying – Berkeley, Hutton or Cudworth – nor associationism could offer a concise formula for disinterestedness – a formula that Coleridge was seeking urgently at the time in order to apply it to his moral and political work. While this chapter elucidates the ways in which Kant's laws of freedom became known as a distinctive trademark of the new philosophy in the late eighteenth-century British press, it aims also to lay open that, in accordance with the Enlightenment notion of the republic of letters (Goodman 1994; Jacob 1981), the boundaries between critical philosophy and native thought during the short period in the mid-1790s were fluid. Initially, critical philosophy in England did not appear as such a dark Gothic cathedral as in *Biographia*. The link in Coleridge's notebook entry between the moral law and 'public good' and 'universal happiness' conveys not only a striking conceptual affinity with Nitsch's exposition of practical philosophy but also represents a fruitful combination of formalism and reward.

The insights of this chapter thus shed a new light on Coleridge studies. We have seen that the Kantian philosophy became a part of the late eighteenth-century English public sphere from 1793 onwards. The dating of Coleridge's acquaintance with Kant to the mid-1790s has far-reaching implications. This undermines the association of Kantian philosophy with Coleridge's disenchantment from politics. In addition, commentators in the tradition of Wellek and Orsini have tended to limit their comparative analysis to four main Kantian texts, *Critique of Pure Reason, Critique of Practical Reason, Critique of the Power of Judgment* and the *Groundwork*, assuming that each of them was free from ambiguity. The present and the following chapters show that the investigation of Coleridge's response to critical philosophy needs to extend research to the interrelated areas of Kant's 'Wirkungsgeschichte' (effective history) and 'Entwicklungsgeschichte' (evolutionary history). Especially in the period following the publication of the *first critique* (1781), Kant's views were 'to a larger extent than is commonly realized determined by what his contemporaries in Königsberg and elsewhere thought, said, and wrote' (Kühn 2006, p. 630). For the analysis of Coleridge's response, it seems necessary to consider not only the immense body of Kantian texts but also late eighteenth-century intermediary publications, such as the first English translation of Kant or illegally printed lecture transcripts by some of Kant's students that were at Coleridge's disposal (see Chapters 4 and 5). Regarding Kantian ethics, Nitsch's work makes it necessary to revise the common view that Kantian ethics were and are stoic and Coleridge too much in favour of affections to fully grasp or subscribe to them. In the light of the early effective history of Kant in England, and contrary to Wellek's seminal study, Coleridge's interpretation of Kantian ethics deserves validity. Moreover, the notion of the highest good in critical philosophy has been neglected by studies of Coleridge's reception of Kant. Scholars of Coleridge's religious philosophy have emphasized his attraction to Plato. Hedley corrects the 'reasonable misapprehension' that 'Platonism is a theory about the good and happiness, whereas Kantian ethics is determined by duty and right' by stating that 'this apparent dichotomy becomes striking affinity' (Hedley 2000, p. 5). Vigus observes the importance of the highest good in the *third critique* in this context (Vigus 2009, p. 50). Joel Harter in *Coleridge's Philosophy of Faith* comments that Plato and Kant agree that philosophy 'is grounded in the practical . . . a cultivation of the soul in search of virtue' (2011, p. 87), but disregards one of the most central Kantian notions for this overlap. In short, the role of Kant's highest good in Coleridge's thought has been studied, yet still deserves further scholarly attention, particularly with regard to Coleridge's embrace of a notion closely resembling the Platonic concept of the Good.

For Coleridge, engagement with Kant's philosophy tended to be an intellectually and emotionally intense experience from early in his career, especially when he disagreed with the subject of his study. In his twenties and thirties, Coleridge understandably preferred the sensuous dimension of the highest good which he had probably first heard from Nitsch, who was roughly the same age as the poet. The next chapter shows that the sober views on the progress of freedom and peace expounded by the sage of Königsberg appear to have equally attracted the poet and to have sustained his republican hopes during a phase of profound political and personal crisis.

4

Coleridge's Poetic Response
to *Perpetual Peace*, 1796–1802

Edward Palmer Thompson, the author of the monumental *The Making of the Working Class* (1963), has had a profound impact on the way scholars and students view Coleridge's engagement with German culture and philosophy. In his seminal essay, Thompson did a great deal to establish Coleridge's and Wordsworth's political escapism in the 1790s before New Historicists spearheaded by Jerome McGann and his influential *Romantic Ideology* (1983) extended the charges against the poets' alleged indifference to politics and social plight. By Thompson's impact, I mean his association of Coleridge's and Wordsworth's trip to Germany with 'hopping the draft' (1969, p. 168) and with escape 'from armed conflict' (1969, p. 170): according to Thompson, Coleridge found in Germany 'a disenchantment profounder than his own' (1969, p. 170). The mark of Thompson can still be seen in standard biographies of Coleridge, such as Richard Holmes's *Coleridge: Early Visions* (1989) or Rosemary Ashton's *The Life of Samuel Taylor Coleridge* (1996, p. 143).[1] It is true that Coleridge's image of the apolitical Kant in *Biographia Literaria*, which I discuss in detail in Chapter 6, supports Thompson's equation of the stay in Germany with political retreat, yet it is time to uncover the myth created by Coleridge and perpetuated by numerous scholars.

It is the major aim of this chapter to contribute to the revision of Thompson's narrative of 'disenchantment or default' that Nicholas Roe and David Fairer have put forward in exemplary ways. Roe has uncovered that Wordsworth's and his friends' engagements with progressive natural sciences continued to 'address and answer the most pressing issues of the day' (Roe 2002, p. xi), which undermines Thompson's thesis of 'apostasy' (Thompson 1969, p. 172). Fairer has criticized Thompson on the grounds of a mistaken concept of organic unity, which Fairer traces back to its native, empiricist roots and which he understands 'not [as] a unifying power but [as] a process of making experience coherent, while registering and understanding change' (2009, p. 4). In the spirit of these revisions of Thompson's thesis, I propose a different and new argument that revolves around the central, but hitherto unnoticed, importance of the first Kantian translation: the radical text *Perpetual Peace*. By doing so, I challenge not only the narrative of disenchantment surrounding Coleridge's reception of Kant but also the common notion of the Germano-Coleridgean exclusive concern with a world beyond space and time. In other words, this chapter uncovers a formative moment in the history of the early transmission of Kant's ideas in England and analyses its impact on Coleridge's poetry and prose mainly during the period between 1796 and 1802. Transcending the boundaries between historicism, literary studies and German idealism, the following part of the discussion traces reactions to the French Revolution, demands for peace, and cosmopolitanism on notional and conceptual as well as formal and literary grounds.

According to the aim of tracing continuities during this period, my reading draws on the version of 'France: An Ode' published by Joseph Johnson in the quarto pamphlet *Fears in Solitude* (London, 1798). The version in *Poetical Works* in the Bollingen Series is based on the text Coleridge published in the *Morning Post* in 1802. Referring to the history of the first three publications of the ode, this chapter contends that the added prose 'Argument' of that year (1802) introduces a narrative of disenchantment that the verse of the earlier text does not completely support. J. C. C. Mays's comment is telling in this respect: the poem published in the Bollingen Series 'is not quite the text [Coleridge] wrote in Mar-Apr 1798, but it is the text he would have liked to have written then' (*PW* I.1, p. 463). What Mays means by this problematic remark becomes clear from the context in which he places the ode: 'The same period was also for WW and C a time of disengagement, and they had already decided to withdraw for a year or two to Germany, outside the zone of war' (*PW* I.1, p. 463). Apart from the fact that it is hard to maintain such a conflation of Coleridge's trip to Germany and political disenchantment – a point to which I shall return in the next chapter – I do not agree with Mays's treatment of 'France: An Ode' as Coleridge's departure from his radical politics. Recent scholarship has started to challenge this position (Fairer 2009, pp. 286–308; Stokes 2011, p. 43). Nevertheless, commentators have hardly paid attention to the discrepancy between Coleridge's ode of 1798 and the added outline of 1802, not to mention the poet's exposure to Kant's first English translation. With two exceptions, Coleridge criticism has barely taken notice of Kant's radical pamphlet (De Paolo 1985, pp. 130–4; Stansfield 1984, pp. 121–44). The inclusion of this fascinating text in the study of Coleridge's reception of Kant brings to light a concept of Nature that might seem surprising for students and scholars of British Romanticism. In this field, the *Kritik der Urteilskraft (Critique of the Power of Judgment*, 1790) has been the most common point of reference for Kant's concept of Nature; although Kant's concept of cosmopolitanism features in the *third critique* under section eighty-three which deals with nature as an end in itself (*KdU* p. 433), comparative analyses have concentrated on the Kantian sublime. Consequently, critics have analysed deviations in Coleridge's experience of the sublime in Nature from the supremacy of the human mind expounded in §28 of the *third critique*: the dynamic sublimity of Nature (Hamilton 1983, pp. 55–7; Perry 1999, p. 78; Modiano 1985, p. 137; Stokes 2011, p. 114). The analysis of Coleridge's probable familiarity with Kant's *Perpetual Peace* brings to light a less well-known Kantian concept, namely that of Nature as the guarantee for peace. My discussion of this concept is limited to Coleridge's poetic response to the French Revolution, yet its complexity merits further exploration. As mentioned before, this chapter is mainly driven by a dissatisfaction with two prevailing scholarly views in British Romanticism: first, that 'France: An Ode' marks the poet's retreat from politics; second, that Kant is one of the philosophers who facilitated the completion of this supposed disenchantment in Coleridge's later years. Contrary to these assumptions,

I argue in this chapter, which focuses on the period between 1796 and 1802, that the 1798 version of 'France: An Ode' conveys a resilient sympathy with republicanism and that *Perpetual Peace* offered a point of philosophical reference for intellectuals like Coleridge who had the courage to maintain democratic views in the repressive climate of the late 1790s. Kant's pamphlet requires a brief introduction.

Preliminary sketch of *Perpetual Peace* and its place within Kant's life and work

Since the 1770s, Kant was professor of logic and metaphysics at the University of Königsberg in Eastern Prussia (Kühn 2001, pp. xv–xxii). After the death of Frederick the Great in 1786, Friedrich Wilhelm II became King of Prussia. In contrast to his predecessor, Friedrich Wilhelm II regarded Enlightenment philosophy as a threat to orthodox Christianity. After the summer of 1789, he reacted against the French Revolution like all other European monarchs with a rain of oppressive measures. Critics of the existing order were stigmatized as 'Jacobin' on either side of the Channel. Leading scholars of Kant's philosophy, such as Lewis White Beck, Allen W. Wood, Manfred Kühn and Frederick Beiser agree that Kant remained 'a steadfast adherent of the Revolution' and 'openly republican' (Kühn 2001, pp. 342, 343).[2] His 'enthusiasm for the French Revolution, for the American Revolution and for the Irish efforts to throw off the English yoke' earned him the reputation of an 'old Jacobin' (Beck 1971, p. 411). Except for the public execution of Louis XVI, which he condemned severely, 'Kant's sympathy with the French Revolution remained firm' (Beiser 1992, p. 37). A letter to Moses Mendelssohn indicates that Kant's political views were too radical to express them openly. Kant wrote 'although I am absolutely convinced of many things that I shall never have the courage to say, I shall never say anything I do not believe' (8 April 1766, Kant cited in Beck 1971, p. 411). Despite the increasing threat of Friedrich Wilhelm's censorship, Kant kept publishing critical examinations of religious questions, such as the question of good and evil in *Religion innerhalb der Grenzen der bloßen Vernunft* (*Religion within the Boundaries of Mere Reason*), much to the dismay of the Prussian King. In 1794, Friedrich Wilhelm II had Kant reprimanded for his 'Socratic offenses of misleading the youth and showing disrespect for the Christian religion and the Holy Scriptures' (Wood 1998, p. 59). Faithful to his principle never to say anything that he did not believe, Kant responded with a letter to the king, which he later published in *Streit der Fakultäten* (*Conflict of the Faculties*), promising the king (and only him but not his successor) to neither lecture nor write on religious topics. He resumed his theological disquisitions, however, after the king's death in July 1797.

Kant wrote *Perpetual Peace* in 1795 at a time when he was still under pressure from Friedrich Wilhelm II. The pamphlet represents both Kant's endorsement of the peace of Basel between Prussia and France and his reaction against the king's repression by asserting 'that he had no intention of keeping silent on *other* matters of general public concern' (Wood 1998, p. 59). Kant believed that it was his duty to speak up and that he was fulfilling this duty. As Kühn notes, Kant 'saw himself as rising to the challenge, addressing the important issues resulting from the changes, and trying to nurture what was good in them' (2001, p. 385). It is true that Kant repudiated, as Deirdre Coleman observes (1988, pp. 136–55), the right to rebellion in his article *Über den Gemeinspruch (On the Common Saying)* in the *Berlinische Monatsschrift (Berlin Monthly)* published in 1793. Nonetheless, this did not preclude his sympathy with the French Revolution. In the '*Gemeinspruch*', Beck notes that 'Kant is making a point of boring obviousness, namely, that there can be no *legal* right of revolution. Revolution by its very nature is a denial that established legal and constitutional claims are indefeasible; and to tell a revolutionary that he should desist from revolutionary activity because he is breaking a law would be met with derision' (1971, p. 414).

Perpetual Peace is an attempt to establish a league of nations through a set of national, international and cosmopolitan laws. The text follows the structure of a treaty consisting first out of six preliminary articles, second of three definitive articles, third of two supplements and fourth of a detailed appendix. The preliminary articles represent a set of prohibitions, namely of secret reservations, of purchase or sale of territory, standing armies, debts between nation states, military interference in the constitution and administration of other nation states and of extreme measures in case of war. The three definitive articles stipulate that on a national level the constitution of every nation state be republican; second, a federal and non-coercive union of free nation states on an international level and third on a cosmopolitan level that visitors' rights are to be limited to hospitality and must not extend to exploitation, slavery or any other form of imperialism. The publication of the pamphlet was a success. The first edition of *Zum Ewigen Frieden* sold out quickly; the second edition followed in 1796, as did the translations into French, Danish and English. *Perpetual Peace* appeared in October in London published by the dissenting publishing house Vernor and Hood. British radical and dissenting periodicals sensed the transformative power of critical philosophy in general and *Perpetual Peace* in particular and welcomed both as a means for their course.

Coleridge, cosmopolitanism and pacifism in the mid-1790s

Kant's stipulation of non-interference in the preliminary articles supported the demands of peace by the Whig party led by Fox. Despite the reports of increasing violence in Revolutionary France, Coleridge remained on Fox's side until 1802 opposing the war against France and advising his audience to stay calm and rational in the pursuit of liberty. When Pitt showed no genuine interest in settling the conflict with France and increased his demands for the terms for peace after Charles Louis of Austria's victory on the Rhine, the young poet responded with the 'Ode on the Departing Year', written in late 1796 (*PW* I.1, p. 302; Coleridge 2004, pp. 34, 39). The Greek epigraph of the poem alluded to Cassandra's warning: 'Ha ha! Oh, oh, the agony! Once more the dreadful throes of true prophecy whirl and distract me with their ill-boding onset' (*PW* I.1, p. 303n). Coleridge loathed his nation and foretold its fall because Britain kept waging war against the country that personified his political ideals of equality and democracy. Years later, when Coleridge was rereading the poem published in *Sibylline Leaves*, he recorded on the margins of 'Ode on the Departing Year' that 'France: An Ode' was occasioned by the French invasion of Switzerland: 'the invasion of Switzerland by the French Republic, which occasioned the Ode that follows' (cited in Coleridge 2004, p. 117n). Coleridge wrote 'France: An Ode' between March and April 1798 around the time when the news of France's victory at Berne forced him to recognize that this nation posed a threat for other countries (*PW* I.1, pp. 462–3). Sensitive to accusations and prone to self-doubts, Coleridge was deeply affected by these events. 'France: An Ode' is the poetic manifestation of this painful realization. The poem's initial title 'Recantation' has been a major reason why eminent scholars have interpreted the ode of 1798 as a testimony for Coleridge's political disengagement.[3] Contrary to these readings, the present chapter explores the continuities in Coleridge's thinking by realigning it with the poet's exposure to Kant's *Perpetual Peace*.

Coleridge had been involved in other cosmopolitan and pacifist activities besides his Bristol lectures (see Chapter 2). In his periodical *The Watchman*, Coleridge supported Fox's non-interference policy in the first issue of 1 March 1796: 'REVIEW OF THE MOTIONS IN THE LEGISLATURE FOR A PEACE WITH FRANCE' (*Watchman*, p. 16, see pp. 16–29). Coleridge was so preoccupied with the advance of republican ideas in Europe that he decided to use his contributions to Southey's verse epic *Joan of Arc* (see Chapter 2) for an independent poem on 'the progress of European Liberty' (*Letters* I, p. 243). Joseph Cottle had called for a second edition of *Poems* (*PW* II.1, p. 382); European liberty had the potential to provide the focus the poet needed to finish the fragment. In November 1796, Coleridge informed Thomas Poole that 'I shall alter the lines of the Joan of Arc & make a *one* poem entitled the progress of European Liberty, a vision – the first line – Auspicious Reverence!' (*Letters* I, p. 243). Coleridge had an ambitious project of about 800 lines in mind but did not succeed in producing such a large poem. He published a fragment of about 150 lines in the *Morning Post* on 26 December 1797. In 1817, the poem appeared under an equally internationalist title in *Sibylline Leaves*: 'The Destiny of Nations'.[4] Two years later, he repeated this emphasis once more calling the poem 'the National Independence or the Vision of the . . . Maid of Orleans' (*Notebooks* III, §4202). Even if Coleridge neither reworked the poem substantially nor extended it to its anticipated size of 800 lines, his choice of titles reveals that he gave the poem a more distinctively cosmopolitan focus once he conceived of it as an independent piece in autumn 1796 (*PW* II.1, pp. 404–5), which is exactly the time when Kant's latest addition to the tradition of peace literature of Hugo Grotius, Samuel von Pufendorf and Emer de Vattel appeared in English (*Ewiger Frieden* p. 355; *Perpetual Peace* 8: 355).[5]

Reviews of *Perpetual Peace* and Coleridge

The liberal press received the pamphlet widely and favourably. The reviews of *Perpetual Peace* in England ranged from the *Monthly Review* and the *Analytical Review* to the *Critical Review* and the *Gentleman's Magazine* to the *Monthly Mirror*.[6] Coleridge's fellow Unitarian, William Taylor of Norwich, wrote a positive article for the *Monthly Review* that spoke of Kant as a 'deep thinker and bold philanthropist' and predicted that 'every reasoner will be gratified by studying this abstruse and excellent production' (*Monthly*

Review 22 [1797], pp. 114–15). The reviewer of the *Critical Review* lamented the repressive atmosphere in England but predicted that Kant would appeal to enlightened readers: 'though the temper of our country is not very favourable to political discussions, we are persuaded that there are still left among us men of candour and enlarged minds, who read, without flying into passion' (*Critical Review* 20 [1797], p. 89). As mentioned, English radical and dissenting periodicals clearly sensed the transformative power of critical philosophy and welcomed it as a means for their course.

In 1796, Joseph Johnson's paper, the *Analytical Review*, praised Kant's principle of publicity as 'an infallible criterion of unjust policy' and embraced the philosopher as a political radical in an anonymous article (*Analytical Review* 23 [1796], pp. 558–9). The abstract transmitted Kant's principle of publicity according to which my maxim is wrong, if I cannot announce my maxim of action aloud in public without thwarting my aims (Kim 2007, pp. 203–26): 'Every action which has reference to the rights of other men, if its principles do not admit of being made public, is my own purpose, which must be kept altogether secret for it to succeed, and which I cannot openly avow, without exciting the opposition of all people to my design, necessarily presupposes injustice to be essential to it; since I could on no other ground expect general opposition' (*Analytical Review* 23 [1796], p. 559).[7] This demand for transparency implied a criticism of the British government.[8]

At the time, Coleridge was immersed in the work on his periodical *The Watchman*. He published *The Watchman* under the motto: 'That All may know the TRUTH; And that the TRUTH may make us FREE!!' (*Watchman*, p. 3). Coleridge ardently opposed the manipulation of information by the government: 'The poor man is not only prevented from hearing the truth, but inflamed to a kind of political suicide by the false statements and calumnies, with which the creativeness of ministerial genius is accustomed to adorn its weekly or diurnal productions' (*Watchman*, p. 11). Coleridge had read Godwin's work in late 1794 (*Letters* I, p. 115; see Chapter 2). In *Enquiry Concerning Political Justice* (1793), Godwin had published 'his doctrine of sincerity and the cultivation of truth', which aimed in part at the 'transparency between self and other' (Scrivener 1978, p. 625). Under the heading 'sincerity', Godwin criticized 'state secrets' by raising the question of 'how ministers . . . came by their right to equivocate, to juggle and over-reach, while private men are obliged to be ingenuous, direct and sincere' (1793 I, p. 229). Godwin's thought must have helped to prepare English readers for Kant's similar arguments in *Perpetual Peace* including Coleridge. Coleridge's journalistic work and his knowledge of Godwin combined with his desire for peace and non-interference with France predisposed him to *Perpetual Peace*. Yet the probably closest link between Coleridge and Kant's republican pamphlet consisted in Coleridge's friend and mentor: Dr Thomas Beddoes. In Chapter 2, we have seen that Coleridge moved to Clevedon in August 1795 and soon became a frequent guest at Beddoes's Bristol home after the two men had met at a local protest meeting against the Gagging Bills in late 1795. This chapter traces the ways in which Beddoes inspired Coleridge's use of distinctive concepts in *Perpetual Peace*.

Beddoes did not only stand out as being the most discerning commentator among the reviewers of *Perpetual Peace*, he also was, besides the reviewer of the *Analytical*

Review, one of the first to assess the pamphlet publicly in England. Coleridge frequently visited, as I explained in Chapter 2, Rodney Place – Beddoes's home. Beddoes reviewed Kant's text based on the original German, *Zum Ewigen Frieden*, in August 1796, about two months prior to the publication of the English translation. The article included statements from Kant that Beddoes had translated into English. The review gives us a good idea of how Beddoes would have discussed Kant's radical text with Coleridge and what opinion he might have imparted to the younger poet.

Beddoes's translation of the German title with 'To Perpetual Peace, a philosophical Project' (*Monthly Review* 20 [1796], p. 486) indicates Beddoes's understanding of the sociopolitical dimension of the text. His use of the word 'perpetual' rather than 'eternal' for German 'ewig' demonstrates his awareness that the text did not aspire to eternal blessing in another world, but proclaimed a secular, perpetual struggle in this one. Kant's peace treatise was, according to Otfried Höffe, neither concerned with eternity after death as Augustine's *aeterna pax* (*De civitate Dei*) nor the Epicurean freedom from worldly worries (*Ataraxie*) or any other form of political retreat (Höffe 2004, p. 6). Beddoes's choice of the word 'perpetual' (instead of 'eternal') reflects his awareness of Kant's worldly concern with the legal terms for the protection of life and freedom in general, and of peace in particular.[9]

Beddoes welcomed the publication of *Perpetual Peace*, but was ultimately dissatisfied with it. Intrigued by and alert to its political challenges, Beddoes predicted that Kant's republican stipulation (*Ewiger Frieden* p. 350; *Perpetual Peace* 8: 350; Schneewind 1992, p. 310), 'the constitution of every state must be republican' (*Monthly Review* 20 [1796], p. 487), would be seen as a provocation: 'the reader will be startled at first' (*Monthly Review* 20 [1796], p. 487). Beddoes translated Kant's 'preliminary articles' including the principle that 'no state shall forcibly interfere in the constitution and administration of another state' (*Monthly Review* 20 [1796], p. 487). However, Beddoes disagreed with Kant's argument 'that peace is not a natural state, but must be "established"' (McLoughlin 2011, p. 190). He questioned Kant's seeming pessimism concerning man's capacity to secure peace: 'we are disappointed, because we allowed the title to raise expectations of a splendid project' (*Monthly Review* 20 [1796], p. 489). Beddoes mainly disapproved with what he perceived as the distrust in political institutions: 'the author [Kant] has been prudent in trusting in the operations of nature, rather than to positive institutions, for the accomplishment' of peace (*Monthly Review* 20 [1796], p. 489). By objecting to Kant's 'prudent' trust 'in the operations of nature', Beddoes took issue with the notion that not '*a sense of justice*', but war and '*the spirit of commerce*' (*Monthly Review* 20 [1796], p. 489) would eventually lead to alliances and peace agreements: 'We regret, however, that it [the peace process] should require an indefinite time, and the continuance of so dreadful a process as war' (*Monthly Review* 20 [1796], p. 489). In 1796, Beddoes apparently still thought the French Revolution would succeed in establishing peace and that the main obstacle in doing so was the coalition against France.

Beddoes's criticism attributed central importance to the concept of Nature in the section called: 'Erster Zusatz. Von der Garantie des ewigen Friedens' (*Ewiger Frieden* p. 360) ('First Supplement. About the Guarantee of perpetual Peace' [*Perpetual Peace* 8: 360]). In the pamphlet, Kant conceived of Nature as an underlying mechanism that operates outside of human control. This issue of the controllable and uncontrollable is also prevalent in Coleridge's 'France: An Ode'. Beddoes approved of Kant's ultimate goal but censured Kant for not giving humans enough credit for peace. As the first English translation of *Zum Ewigen Frieden* said:

> The guarantee of this treaty is nothing less than the great and ingenious artist nature (natura daedala rerum). Her mechanical march evidently announces the grand aim of producing among men, against their intention, harmony from the very bosom of their discords. Hence it is that we call it *destiny*, viewing it as a cause absolute in its effects, but unknown as to the laws of its operations. (Kant 1796, pp. 31–2)

Here, Nature solicits peace among humans even against their will.[10] Beddoes summarized Kant's argument sceptically: 'All this *may be* very right: but who is to guarantee the terms of perpetual amity? Our author replies, *Natura dædala rerum*' (*Monthly Review* 20 [1796], p. 488). As the above-quoted excerpt from the 1796 translation of *Perpetual Peace* shows, Kant's concept of nature as the guarantee for peace carried providential meaning (*Ewiger Frieden* pp. 360–2; *Perpetual Peace* 8: 360–2): 'we call it *destiny*' (Kant 1796, p. 32). Beddoes's review omitted this dimension probably deliberately.[11] Kant had adopted the Latin phrase *natura dædala rerum* from 'Lucretius's *De Rerum Natura*, a work much loved by Kant but one that resolutely denies that any teleological design is to be discerned in the working of nature' (Nussbaum 1997, p. 41). Beddoes followed the Lucretian line of argument in the first supplement of *Perpetual Peace* according to which 'more than half of the earth is simply uninhabitable because of climate, and that the rest is extremely inhospitable to humans on account of the presence of wild beasts' (Nussbaum 1997, p. 41), but disregarded the teleology of nature, which Kant maintained despite his Epicurean source: 'Kant [was] struggling against Lucretius's anti-teleological view of nature and allying himself with Stoic providential religion' (Nussbaum 1997, p. 41). Beddoes explained only the secular dimension of Kant's concept of Nature as a guarantee for peace, but he did so carefully.

As if responding to the persistent questions of a sharp young person like Coleridge, Beddoes continued his explanation in the review:

> The idea of a law of nations pre-supposes that separation of mankind into a number of independent nations; and, though such a state is in itself a state of warfare, it is better than their being confounded together and passing into an universal monarchy; because the laws are deprived of their force by over-grown extent of empire; and a lifeless despotism, after having extinguished the germ of every virtue, crumbles at last into anarchy. It is, however, the disposition of every state (or at least of every sovereign) to secure permanent peace by subjugating, if possible, the whole world: - *but Nature wills otherwise*. She employs two means to keep nations apart; a difference in speech and a difference in religion. These imply a disposition to mutual hatred, and a pretext for a war. By increase of culture, however, and by the gradual approximation of mankind, they lead to greater agreement in principle, and to acquiescence in peace; which is not brought about and secured. (*Monthly Review* 20 [1796], p. 488)

Beddoes translated the respective sentences from *Zum Ewigen Frieden* as literally as possible, clarifying that Nature in this excerpt was no place of prelapsarian harmony. On the contrary, it was a state of difference, and even hate: '*Nature wills otherwise.* She employs two means to keep nations apart; a difference in speech and a difference in religion. These imply a disposition to mutual hatred, and a pretext for a war'.[12] Albeit disapprovingly, Beddoes elucidated Kant's argument that hatred entailed a need for peace measures which, in turn, aided the formation of unions and hence of culture.[13] If the peace process were the product of the human will alone, then peace would merely be the result of the subjugation of other nations under a single nation or sovereign, 'to secure permanent peace by subjugating'. As Kant stated elsewhere in the text, it would take a nation of angels to establish a republican constitution:

> [E]s müsse ein Staat von Engeln sein, weil Menschen mit ihren selbstsüchtigen Neigungen einer Verfassung von so sublimer Form nicht fähig wären. (*Ewiger Frieden* p. 366)
>
> ([I]t would have to be a state of angels because human beings, with their self-seeking inclinations, would not be capable of such a sublime form of constitution. [*Perpetual Peace* 8: 366])[14]

In the face of this dilemma, Nature was the ultimate remedy against the human tendency to usurpation. She was said to counteract and ultimately correct the human ambition for power through the predisposition for difference particularly in languages and religions. Beddoes explained that the concept of difference, despite its association with conflict, is ultimately a good thing because it functions as an instrument of Nature, so to speak, by disrupting and correcting human hegemony. Difference does not only entail hatred and war, it also leads to new alliances and unions. Global justice is a perpetual process that requires a constant effort.

Changing significance of Kant's pamphlet, 1796 and 1798

Around 1796, Coleridge probably shared Beddoes's ultimate dissatisfaction with *Perpetual Peace* due to its sinister view of humanity. At the time, it still seemed possible that the French Revolution could confirm both men's political hopes of a peaceful republic. However, these hopes were shattered by France's invasion of Switzerland in early 1798.

I propose that it was at this moment that Coleridge turned to Kant and his precautionary measure of consigning the progress towards peace and freedom to the forces of Nature. A letter by Coleridge dating from March 1798 is often seen as a definite sign of the poet's political resignation. The letter contains Coleridge's attempt to regain his brother's favour by stating that 'equally with you I deprecate the moral & intellectual habits of those men both in England & France, who have modestly assumed to themselves the exclusive title of Philosophers & Friends of Freedom' (*Letters* I, p. 395). The same letter, however, expresses also Coleridge's 'consent to be deemed a Democrat & a Seditionist' (*Letters* I, p. 397).[15] I agree with Anthony Harding that Coleridge's communication with 'his brother George, who was concerned about young Samuel's unorthodox views and dangerously democratic leanings –"Talk not of Politics – Preach the Gospel!" – could be more than a little disingenuous' (2007, p. 19).[16] I contend that Coleridge remained sympathetic to republicanism and kept opposing the war after 1798. Philosophically speaking, *Perpetual Peace* provided Coleridge with a concept that allowed him to hold onto his republican views despite the fact that Revolutionary France had betrayed its principles through its imperialist turn. After all, *Perpetual Peace* was a radical text that supported the French Revolution in so far as it stipulated that every country should have a republican constitution and that conflict, even military conflict, was part of the process towards civil freedom and peace. Moreover, the pamphlet lent itself to Coleridge's previous demands for British non-interference. Psychologically and aesthetically speaking, *Perpetual Peace* cherished 'the great and ingenious artist' and thus suited Coleridge's inclination to turn to Nature in search for consolation and inspiration.

Reading 'France: An Ode' (1798)

The radical principles of Kant's *Perpetual Peace* are borne out in Coleridge's 'France: An Ode'. The verse is soul searching and ambivalent, which opens the poem up to countless interpretations. However, the standard interpretation that the poem marks Coleridge's disenchantment with political radicalism tends to overlook the fact that the liberal *Morning Post* classified one of Coleridge's stanzas in the ode on France as too scathing an attack on the government to have it published. Coleridge's first contribution to the *Morning Post* in January 1798 had demanded peace with France. The ode on France, among other pieces, followed on 16 April 1798. As Carl Woodring points out, the subeditor of the *Morning Post* took precautions and removed what was either the original fourth stanza, according to Woodring (1961, p. 183), or fifth stanza, according to the editor of Coleridge's *Complete Poetical Works* Ernest Hartley Coleridge (Coleridge 1962 I, p. 247).[17] In any case, the respective stanza opened by asking Africa, 'Shall I with *these* my patriot zeal combine?' and answered:

> No, Africa, no! they stand before my ken
> Loath'd as th' Hyaenas [sic], that in murky den
> Whine o'er their prey and mangle while they whine
> Divinest Liberty! with vain endeavour.
>
> (Coleridge 1962 I, p. 247)[18]

The lines leave open which side of the conflict the Hyenas represent, for both France and the Allegiance harboured imperialistic ambitions and abused the name of liberty. Yet the stanza announces that speaker's refusal to join, 'combine', his zeal with either party of war – a pledge for non-interference.

The poem in the form printed in 1798 resisted Pitt's pro-war position against France. The poem of 1798 expresses above all the speaker's personal crisis over the political dilemma. He seems distressed mainly because the word 'liberty' has become an empty signifier by way of frequent abuse; 'They break their manacles and wear the name/ Of Freedom graven on an heavier chain' (p. 17, ll. 87–8). Those chains were harsh reality; Coleridge knew that 'At Genoa, the word, Liberty, is engraved on the chains of the galley-slaves, & the doors of Prisons' (*Notebooks* I, §206). Nevertheless, the speaker beseeches the everlasting 'spirit of Liberty' to help him, 'Bear witness':

> Yea, every thing that is and will be free,
> Bear witness for me wheresoe'er ye be,
> With what deep worship I have still ador'd
> The spirit of divinest Liberty.
>
> (Coleridge 1798, p. 14, ll. 18–21)

The speaker appeals to liberty like a goddess reminding her of his 'deep' and unflinching 'worship'. The poem then evokes instances in the assault on freedom and the escalation of war. The French nation is allegorized as a savage creature and although this giant might be seen as a supernatural being, its primitive, natural side prevails mainly because it is described as acting in accordance with the natural right of defending one's own life, 'like a wounded dragon in his gore' (Coleridge 1798, p. 16, l. 57).

This animal imagery emerged from Coleridge's earliest poetic responses to the French Revolution. Coleridge's 'An Ode on the Destruction of the Bastille' (1789–91) personifies freedom: 'Yet Freedom rous'd by fierce Disdain/ Has wildly broke thy triple chain' (*PW* I.1, p. 20, ll. 7–8). In 'To a Young Lady, with a Poem on the French Revolution' (1794), freedom takes on giant fury: 'When slumb'ring FREEDOM rous'd by high DISDAIN/ With giant fury burst her triple chain!' (*PW* I.1, p. 137, ll. 17–18). By reiterating the line, 'France: An Ode' resuscitates this giant who is the embodiment of freedom. The animalist imagery continues in 'Address to a Young Jack-Ass' (1794), which exposes social injustice through the allegorized figure of a maltreated donkey, and 'Recantation: Illustrated in the Story of the Mad Ox' (July 1798), in which the liberated ox is goaded into madness (Chandler 1995, pp. 179–80).'France: An Ode' intimates a similar sympathy with the beast by justifying its actions that it has become aggressive because it is wounded and near defeat. Yet this giant is no domestic animal, but a savage creature standing on its hind legs and threatening its opponents. Its front is covered with scars and blood, 'her front deep-scar'd and gory' (Coleridge 1798, p. 16, l. 51); in agony, wrath and confusion, the dragon stamps and crushes its enemies in order to defend itself.[19] 'The principle of self-defence . . . justifie[d]', according to Coleridge's article 'On Peace I' published on 2 January 1798, the French delegates 'in their refusal to conclude a Treaty with us' (*Essays* I, p. 10). The imagery in the Stanza Three still suggests an act of self-defence, although France had breached this principle by the time Coleridge wrote the ode (March–April 1798). The poem bespeaks a subtle fascination for the natural spectacle performed by the savage creature and its instinctive force. Moreover, its animalist imagery echoes Coleridge's poetic salutations to the French Revolution; the resonances of the argument of self-defence point to a view shared by Kant: 'war in self-defence, in particular, is permissible' (Colclasure 2011, p. 241).

Whenever the speaker scorns France, the scorn extends to the Alliance. In Stanza Two, the speaker refers to France as the 'disenchanted nation' (Coleridge 1798, p. 14, l. 28), but it is 'the monarchs' and 'Britain' the speaker accuses of committing cruelties and blasphemy: 'to whelm the disenchanted nation,/ Like fiends embattled by a wizard's wand/ The monarchs march'd in evil day,/ And Britain join'd the dire array' (p. 14, ll. 28–31). In Stanza Four, the speaker calls out directly to France in the form of a rebuke: 'O France! that mockest heav'n, adult'rous, blind,/ And patriot only in pernicious toils!' (Coleridge 1798, p. 17, ll. 78–9). The tone is filled with agitation. Yet the speaker does not reject France alone; he exposes the expansionism on both sides. He condemns French expansionism as an act of participation: 'To mix with the kings in the low lust of sway' (p. 17, l. 81). Moreover, the figurative dimension of stanza supports the speaker's lasting sympathy. The venatorial imagery undermines the accusations, 'Yell in the hunt, and share the murd'rous prey' (Coleridge 1798, p. 16, l. 82), in so far as it simultaneously reminds the reader that France is identical with the chased savage creature (p. 16, ll. 51–7). The French nation is a force of nature in the poem; indeed she emerges as both the hunter and the prey. And so it is that even at the moment when the speaker comes close to renouncing the French Revolution in the poem, the verse conveys his reluctance to see only one side of the conflict. 'France: An Ode' exposes the injustice, tyranny and usurpation on the one hand, and on the other hand, it clings to the possibility of freedom in this world. France stands for both, but in contrast to the Alliance, she belongs to nature; whereas the troops of the Allied monarchs appear 'dire' and 'swoln'.

Indeed, the speaker's lasting sympathy depends on the classification of Revolutionary France under the state of nature. The ode insinuates that the Alliance behaved unnaturally. The verse contradistinguishes between France as characterized by animal and savage forces and the artificiality of the Allied monarchs. The ode calls the Alliance the 'dire array' (Coleridge 1798, p. 14, l. 31). Its troops are, as mentioned, summoned by a 'wizard's wand' and 'march'd in evil day' (p. 14, ll. 29–30). British patriotism is depicted as a bloating of earnest feelings, 'many friendships, many youthful loves/ Had swoln the patriot emotion' (p. 15, ll. 33–4).[20] The speaker is not in favour of the anti-French Alliance; on the contrary, the depiction of the Allied troops still seems to imply that the declaration of war against Revolutionary French was unnatural in the first place and that the natural thing would have been to refrain from interfering with the internal affairs of a foreign country in much the same way as the preliminary article in *Perpetual Peace* demands. What is more is that the speaker seems curiously mesmerized by the outraged and dangerous creature that is France. Even though the speaker in 'France: An Ode' accuses the beast in the final couplet of Stanza IV of destroying the 'bloodless freedom of the mountaineer' (Coleridge 1798, p. 17, ll. 77), the poem does not determine the point at which France betrayed its revolutionary ideals. Was it the invasion of Switzerland or were there earlier warnings? Coleridge glossed the final couplet of Stanza Four in Sir George Beaumont's copy, clarifying that they 'allud[ed] to Venice, and Holland' (Evans 1935, p. 255), and not France's invasion of Switzerland (Woodring 1961, p. 183). The poem itself resists a precise judgement on the guilt of France. It seems as if the speaker has deferred his final detachment from the now tyrannical nation, as if the hope existed that the usurpation might be part of the process towards peace as *Perpetual Peace* suggested.

Instead of determining the guilt of France, the speaker accuses above all himself. His sense of personal failure seems stronger than his disdain for France. Why did he not recognize the betrayal before? He freely confesses his inability to distinguish the divine spirit of liberty from misleading illusions, 'O Liberty! with profitless endeavour/ Have I pursued thee many a weary hour' (Coleridge 1798, p. 18, ll. 89–90). His belief appears in hindsight obsessive to the speaker: he seemed to have been blind (p.17, l. 86). The speaker confesses his lack of discrimination and admits French imperialism simultaneously. 'France: An Ode' re-enacts the insufficiency of human Reason and the human need for Nature as a corrective exposed by *Perpetual Peace*. Both texts acknowledge the impossibility of objective and impartial judgements while aspiring towards them. The first supplement of *Perpetual Peace* and the last stanza of the ode both call out for Nature suggesting that it is the only way to compensate for man's incapability. Coleridge's ode performs this dilemma on a personal level by disclosing feelings of guilt and embarrassment that spring from the painful awareness of one's own inadequacy. Where Kant's pamphlet is sober and restrained, Coleridge's ode is frustrated and impulsive. In line with *Perpetual Peace*, 'France: An Ode' never extends its frustration to a full disavowal of revolutionary ideals.

On the contrary, the conclusion of the poem abandons any forms of lament. The ode transforms into an enthusiastic affirmation of the existence of freedom through the forces of nature:

> And then I felt thee on that sea-cliff's verge,
> Whose pines, scarce travell'd by the breeze above,
> Had made one murmur with the distant surge!
> Yes! while I stood and gaz'd, my temples bare,
> And shot my being thro' earth, sea, and air,
> Possessing all things with intensest love –
> O Liberty, my spirit felt thee there!
>
> (Coleridge 1798, p. 18, ll. 99–105)

Here, we can see that the bellicose imagery does not entail a disavowal of democratic ideals. In much the same way as *Perpetual Peace* endorses conflict (Höffe 2004, p. 15), these lines embrace combat as part of the process towards freedom. True freedom in this verse is not a gentle revelation of Nature. The speaker is standing on the edge of a cliff high above the sea; his tone in the poem is assertive to the extent that it is unyielding.[21] The speaker experiences no harmony, but passion, 'intensest love' and even usurpation, 'possessing all things'. Indeed the sudden epiphany takes hold of the speaker with such force that his being is literally 'shot . . . thro' earth, sea, and air'. The extraordinary use of the verb 'shot', with its combative implications, links the speaker's epiphany with Kant's concept of Nature, according to which, the disposition to war in Nature will ultimately lead to peace (*Ewiger Frieden* p. 367; *Perpetual Peace* 8: 367). Coleridge rarely ever confirmed freedom in this world more enthusiastically.

The contemporary audience in the late 1790s understood Coleridge's ode as such and not as a renunciation of republican ideas. The liberal *Monthly Review* praised the 'beautiful address to Liberty [that] constitutes the last stanza' (Reiman 1972 II, p. 712). The *Critical Review* made it very plain: 'but those who conceive that Mr. Coleridge has, in these poems [*Fears in Solitude*], recanted his former principles, should consider the general tenor of them' (Reiman 1972 I, p. 311). The anonymous author of this review was Southey (Paley 1999, p. 137), who suggested that Coleridge's *Fears in Solitude* in general, and 'France: An Ode' in particular, contained one of his friend's allegedly outlandish political ideas. Southey's suspicion further confirms the suggestion that Coleridge drew on one of those 'obscure' Jacobin principles of Kant. The similarities between both texts are far-reaching and extend to formal aspects of structure and design.

Formal similarities between 'France: An Ode' and *Perpetual Peace*

A formal comparison of *Perpetual Peace* and 'France: An Ode' is complicated by the question of the genre of Kant's text. During the resurgence of publications on *Perpetual Peace* occasioned by the two-hundredth anniversary of its appearance in 1995 (Ruffing 1997, pp. 473–511), Wood pointed out that the literary genre of this text is one of the bristling problems that 'have scarcely been noticed, let alone resolved. To what literary genre does *Perpetual Peace* belong?' (Wood 1998, p. 66). Kant called the text 'ein philosopher Entwurf': 'a philosophical Project' as Beddoes translated Kant's description (*Monthly Review* 20 [1796], p. 486). 'Entwurf' also means 'outline', 'draft' or 'sketch'. While the translation 'project' retains special significance due to its 'allusion to Abbé de Saint-Pierre's *Projet*' (Wood 1998, p. 66), all of these translations confirm the notion that this text formally conveys tentativeness and open-endedness in much the same way as it conceptually proclaims a perpetual struggle towards peace. The text appears as if it were a draft of an international peace treaty, a document of great importance for the nation states involved. Yet, in contrast to Saint-Pierre's *Projet* (1713), the composition of *Perpetual Peace* was independent from any immediate political negotiation.[22] Despite this hypothetical dimension, *Perpetual Peace* is 'clearly not a philosophical treatise of any ordinary kind' (Wood 1998, p. 66). A close analysis of Kant's project within literary history would lead far beyond Coleridge's response to the pamphlet. John N. Kim has recently examined the text as an 'ironic and performative critique of the political censorship of philosophical texts' (2007, pp. 203–26), while Andreas Gailus has analysed the language of emotional affect behind the insistence on rationality in a range of Kantian texts (2006, pp. 28–73). Due to the focus of the present study, the following comparison focuses on the insights into the textually self-referential qualities of Kant's *Perpetual Peace* that are relevant for Coleridge's response in 'France: An Ode'.

At first glance, it may seem that Coleridge's Pindaric ode through its lyric mode and variety of metaphorical particulars has little in common with Kant's universals in *Perpetual Peace*. Yet both texts display a heightened awareness of the problem of controlling textual meaning. In Stanza One, the speaker of 'France: An Ode' evokes 'Ye clouds . . . no mortal may control!' (Coleridge 1798, p. 13, ll. 1–2). According to Michael O'Neill, 'the [entire] poem is a latent contest between the controlling and the uncontrollable' (1997, p. 63). David Duff explains that Edward Young in his 'Essay on Lyrick Poetry' (1728) revised contemporary misconceptions of the Pindaric ode (2009,

p. 88). 'Coleridge had taken notes from Young's essay in 1795 and refers to it again in a letter of 1802' (Duff 2009, p. 88n). In this essay, Young established the importance of an underlying control for the genre: 'the secret of the ode . . . being its ability to appear imaginatively chaotic while in fact retaining an underlying order and control' (Duff 2009, p. 88). This dynamic of apparent ambiguity and ultimate control is in part reversed in *Perpetual Peace*. Through its prose, and above all its structure, Kant's text discusses the possibility of establishing peace between free, republican nation states systematically; it is clear that the text treats social peace (Höffe 2004, p. 18).[23] This surface may seem deceivingly straightforward. But when reading the text closely, it relinquishes the full control of meaning; for instance, it challenges the reader right at beginning through an anecdote about the title 'Perpetual Peace'. What does it mean that it is taken from a Dutch sign representing a churchyard?[24] Beddoes was sensitive to this aspect of the text. He explained in his review that 'Kant . . . leaves it undecided' (*Monthly Review* 20 [1796], p. 486). The doctor was aware that the uncontrollable was part of the design of *Perpetual Peace*, too. Besides the textual awareness of the uncontrollable, Kant's project and Coleridge's ode have a further formal dynamic in common.

'France: An Ode' voices the experience of political crisis at the intersection between private and public utterance. It is the ode's 'double orientation' that Duff identifies as a distinctive mode of the great odes of the Romantic period (2009, p. 209). Aspects of genre strongly support the revision of the established view of 'France: An Ode' as political disengagement. Scholars have interpreted the speaker's epiphany in the last stanza of 'France: An Ode' as the speaker's withdrawal from the public sphere of politics on notional grounds (Butler 1981, p. 80; Cronin 2000, p. 73; Morrow 1990, p. 73; Roe 1988, pp. 262–8). Fairer takes genre into consideration but sees the Pindaric character as a limitation of Coleridge's poem. According to him, the Pindaric form precludes 'elements of introspective questioning that might have complicated its topic of second thoughts' (Fairer 2009, p. 293). I propose an interpretation that combines aspects of philosophy and genre to challenge these interpretations. Duff notes in agreement with Stuart Curran that the Romantic ode did not introduce but intensified the psychological function of the English ode. The speaker's introspection in the last stanza, 'I felt thee there', can therefore be attributed to the development of the genre which manifested itself, according to Duff and Curran, in a heightened degree of internalization (Duff 2009, p. 208; Curran 1986, p. 66). Collins's 'Ode to Liberty', for instance, turns inward when questioning the speaker's expressive adequacy: 'How may the poet now unfold/ What never tongue or numbers told?' (Fairer and Gerrard 2004, pp. 374–6). Such introspection does not necessarily entail a retreat from political principle. 'France: An Ode' belongs, according to Duff, to the great Romantic odes (besides Byron's 'Ode to Napoleon Bonaparte', Wordsworth's 'Thanksgiving Ode' and Shelley's 'Ode to Naples') that unleash 'the full declamatory power of the ode at just the point in its history when it was being used to explore the internal world of private emotion' (Duff 2009, p. 209). As part of the intensified subjective experience that distinguishes the ode as a literary genre, the apostrophes in Coleridge's ode vary, alternating between the elements of Nature, freedom, and – only in one single instance – France. Although Kant's prose is measured, even restrained and calls out to no person or concept, on a formal level, both *Perpetual Peace* and 'France: An Ode' constitute utterances that are directed at a public audience. As a Pindaric ode, Coleridge's 'France: An Ode' is bound up with the tradition of ancient Greek oratory (Preminger and Brogan 1993, p. 856).[25] *Perpetual Peace* mirrors the form of an international peace treaty consisting of six preliminary articles, three definitive articles, two supplements and an addendum in two parts.[26] Both forms of texts played a historically central role in public life, national and international politics. Both appear to operate specifically on legal grounds (Esterhammer 2000, p. 149; 2002b, pp. 143–62): legalistic terminology, 'eternal laws' (Coleridge 1798, p. 13, l. 4) and 'bear witness for me' (p. 14, l. 19), show the poem's public pitch whereas *Perpetual Peace* aims to elicit the readers' commitment to peace by employing the very terms and structure of a peace treaty.

Coleridge's ode contains a unique variation of the Pindaric form that links it closely to Kant's project ('Entwurf'). While Coleridge's 'Ode on the Departing Year' is a more completely regular Pindaric ode containing the poet's fullest definition of the genre, 'France: An Ode' ends irregularly by falling short of one stanza to complete the sequence of strophe, anti-strophe and epode (Class 2004, pp. 51–8). This irregularity is probably the result of the above-mentioned deletion of the governmentally offensive stanza criticizing British imperialism in Africa. Nevertheless, this change is formally highly significant. It renders the Pindaric ode fragmentary and thus lends it the same unfinished status that is so characteristic of the form of Kant's 'project'. Through this alteration Coleridge's ode acknowledges by virtue of its fragmentary shape the conceptual dilemma that the peace offered by Kant was no eternal blessing but an incessant approach. At the same time, Coleridge's ode re-enacts the infinite process performed by Kant's deliberate draft.

The state of nature

The imperialist turn of Revolutionary France entailed a profound political crisis. We have seen in Chapter 3 that Coleridge's insistence on human disinterestedness and his opposition to Hobbes's *Leviathan* predisposed him to critical philosophy. The events in France, especially in spring 1798, however, cast doubt on man's capability to act disinterestedly when it came to political power; indeed they seemed to confirm Hobbes's sinister view of humankind (see Chapter 3). The state of nature was a hypothetical condition characterized by a complete absence of governmental authority (Bobbio 1993, p. 2). For Hobbes, this state was merely warlike and as such an evil which had to be overcome by a single despot. While Coleridge continued to reject Hobbes's justification of tyranny, it must have become impossible for Coleridge in spring 1798 to build his republican hopes on the state of nature proposed by John Locke and Jean-Jacques Rousseau. Like Kant, Locke and Rousseau belonged to those proponents of political philosophy who tried to refute Hobbes's legitimization of despotism. Both Locke and Rousseau characterized the state of nature as one of freedom and deemed it as something worthwhile preserving. Accordingly, they formulated theories about the significance of nature in the political process towards social justice. Locke in *Two Treatises of Government* (1690) and Rousseau in *Du Contrat Social* (1762) intended to safeguard the individual from oppression by an all-too-powerful ruler. Both texts ground social justice in the state of nature. According to Locke's 'Second Treatise of Government' §19, the state of nature was synonymous with peace:

> And here we have the plain *difference between the State of Nature and the State of War,* which however some Men have confounded, are as distant, as a State of Peace, Good Will, Mutual Assistance, and Preservation, and a State of Enmity, Malice, Violence, and Mutual Destruction are one from another. (Locke 1988, p. 280)

Here, the state of nature is incompatible with war.[27] Similar to Locke, the state of nature was unwarlike for Rousseau.[28] The latter regarded it as a realm of natural freedom. Its loss entailed a painful, though necessary sacrifice, '[w]hat man loses by the social contract is his natural freedom and an unlimited right to anything by which he is tempted and can obtain' (Rousseau 1994, p. 59).[29] Even if natural freedom included selfishness, 'anything by which he is tempted', Rousseau still regarded the passions of Nature as the source of morality. According to Book II, Chapter XII, natural feeling was more conducive to civic rights for Rousseau than the regulations imposed by the subsequent stages of civilization: 'In addition to these three categories of law there is a fourth, which is the most important of all; it is not graven in marble or bronze, but in citizens' hearts; in it lies the true constitution of the state' (Rousseau 1994, p. 89). Rousseau shared with Locke the notion that the state of nature was a hypothetical condition of unalienable human rights and harmony. Yet for Coleridge, this position seemed no longer sustainable in early 1798. The French Revolution had shaken his view that humans in their primary condition were peaceful beings. Thus, the state of nature lost its persuasiveness as a consequence for him as for many contemporaries of the French Revolution. The Reign of Terror in France must have appeared as a confirmation of Hobbes's 'savage and lawless liberty' (Bohman and Lutz-Bachmann 1997, p. 4).[30] Kant offered Coleridge a solution that largely agreed with Locke's and Rousseau's defence of unalienable natural rights but differed from them by accommodating human aggressions, which were undeniable during these times of war.[31]

Kant shared with Locke and Rousseau the proposition of concepts of political obligation which distinguished themselves from other doctrines through their attempts to ground political authority on individual self-determination and rational consent. What Coleridge's ode resonates with so intriguingly is Kant's distinctive restraint of our trust in human rationality. *Perpetual Peace* and 'France: an Ode' concede to Hobbes's position that man has a natural predisposition to war; both acknowledge the danger of usurpation in any form of human government. Kant's pamphlet warns against the corrupting effect of power; indeed *Perpetual Peace* cautioned, as English readers knew from the 1796 translation that 'It will then be said, he who has the power in his own hands will not suffer the people to prescribe laws for him' (1796, p. 49).[32] Just like Kant, Coleridge's poem exposes the selfishness of revolutionaries. The last stanza of 'France: An Ode' denounces the revolutionaries' lust for power: 'The sensual and the dark rebel in vain,/ Slaves by their own compulsion!' (Coleridge 1798, p. 17, ll. 85–6). On the one hand, these lines point to Coleridge's psychological profile of French revolutionaries like Robespierre, who 'to prevent tyranny he became a Tyrant'

(*Lectures 1795*, p. 35). As Coleridge explained, 'if we clearly perceive any one thing to be of vast and infinite importance to ourselves and all mankind, our first feelings impel us to turn with angry contempt from those, who doubt and oppose it' (*Lectures 1795*, p. 35). On the other hand, Coleridge's censure in the ode does not lay the blame for the violent excesses of the French Revolution on political figures in France alone but extends to the British government. The removed stanza, in which the term 'Hyaenas' points to the British government, implied harsh criticism. According to Woodring, the omitted stanza now lost, 'made the French share with the Ministry [the speaker's] full contempt' (1961, p. 183). In an article published in the *Morning Post*, Coleridge condemned selfishness as an obstacle to freedom, 'Every man seems to be impelled by the desire of acquiring wealth, and a sordid and selfish principle has introduced itself among us, which has been fatal to the cause of freedom' (*Essays* I, p. 27). In the ode, this selfish compulsion leads to madness: the revolutionaries 'in mad game/ They burst their manacles' (Coleridge 1798, p. 17, ll. 86–7). This madness is what makes Nature as a corrective indispensable for the pursuit of highest political good.

The notion of Nature as a corrective in 'France: An Ode' has been noted before (Esterhammer 2000, p. 149). Despite this and the important critical discussions of Kant's impact on Coleridge's thinking on peace and war (De Paolo 1985, pp. 3–13; Stansfield 1984, pp. 121–44; 1986, pp. 130–4), commentators have failed to observe that Nature as the corrective against human selfishness in combination with the (in Coleridge's case indirect) support of republican ideals marks a striking affinity between 'France: An Ode' and *Perpetual Peace*. In the ideological battle against the Hobbesian denial of human morality, Coleridge and Kant adopted a remarkably similar defence strategy: they admitted the human predisposition to war but refuted Hobbes with the argument that mankind moved towards peace and freedom nevertheless largely because of the beneficial effect of Nature which regulated human vice. Through the predisposition of difference, Nature solicits the advance of culture indirectly. As difference constituted by Nature entails conflict and war, it ultimately leads to an amelioration of sociopolitical conditions through the formation of unions in a slow and never-ending process. In the late 1790s, this concept of Nature lent itself to the French Revolution not as a justification but as an optimistic interpretation: it gave hope.

As such, modern critics continue to struggle with the notion. Martha Nussbaum notes that Kant's concept of Nature as a guarantee is an inessential part of his theory of international law: 'a kind of reassurance to the faint-hearted' (1997, p. 43). Paul Guyer suggests that Kant argues 'that a guarantee of the *possibility* of perpetual peace is a necessary condition for the morally mandatory effort to bring it about' (2006, p. 407). Many commentators today treat the argument as part of Kant's anthropology and philosophy of history (Wood 1998, pp. 66–7; Beck 1957, pp. ix–xiv) or alternatively as a parallel to Kant's moral theory of international justice (Kersting 2004, pp. 163–8). For the earliest English readers of *Perpetual Peace* in the late eighteenth century, the first supplement was certainly not inconsequential either. It offered a philosophical concept that allowed them to see imperialist France in a more positive light, namely not as the end but as a part of the perpetual progress towards freedom. Views like this provoked accusations of Jacobinism while critics of the established order in Britain embraced them tentatively.

The first place of publication of Coleridge's ode on France

One might object to the present reading that Coleridge gave the ode the title 'Recantation'. However, 'recantation' in the poet's use of language had little to do with 'renunciation', 'disavowal' or 'retraction' (*Oxford English Dictionary*). 'Recantation' also signifies the 'action of signing again', when used as in R. Wilson's *Coblers Prophesie* 1594 (*OED*). David V. Erdman has pointed out that Coleridge employed the term 'Recantation' for himself but used the term 'oscillation' to designate the same frame of mind in others (1978, p. lxv). The title 'Recantation' in its common meaning suited the change in the paper's editorial policy that had been imposed by government pressure (to condemn French imperialism), while its less well-known significance undermined the very action of alleged disavowal. The head-note following the title and printed in the *Morning Post* appears somewhat forced: '[i]t is very satisfactory to find so zealous and steady an advocate for Freedom as Mr COLERIDGE concur with us in condemning the conduct of France towards the Swiss Cantons' (Coleridge 1962 I, p. 243). It is possible that Coleridge chose the title 'Recantation' merely as a result of the government pressure on his editor. If so, the title still retained an element of dissent. Coleridge abandoned the title once he republished the poem in the same year in a less widely distributed medium than the *Morning Post*, namely as part of the pamphlet *Fears in Solitude* printed and sold by the rational dissenter Joseph Johnson, which I discuss below.

The first place of publication of 'France: An Ode' was overall pacifist and anti-ministerial. The poem formed part of the 'verses and political Essays' that Coleridge had agreed to write for Daniel Stuart, editor of the *London Morning Post and Gazetteer*, in exchange for 'a very small stipend' (*Letters* I, p. 360). Beddoes had arranged the deal to help alleviate Coleridge's fraught financial situation in November 1797. As Coleridge's mentor, Beddoes was looking for an employment where his like-minded friend did not have to compromise his radical views. In early 1798, the *Morning Post* initially welcomed even the French invasion of Switzerland as the defeat of the Swiss oligarchy and the frustration of English interests in Switzerland. One might suspect that a paper with such a Jacobin inclination imposed no limits on the opinion of their contributors. Yet government pressure led the editor to revise his cosmopolitan views and criticize French imperialism. Nevertheless, neither Coleridge nor the editors of the *Morning Post* actively demanded war against France until the Peace of Amiens. This fact was clear for F. J. A. Hort in the second half of the nineteenth century:

> On his return from Germany, he [Coleridge] renewed his interest in politics with the first whiff of English air, and wrote vigorously for the *Morning Post* for some months. He still opposed the war, and indignantly assailed the ministry for rejecting Napoleon's overtures of peace; but at the same time condemned the internal policy of imperialism then being established in France. (Hort 1856, p. 314)

As Erdmann notes, Stuart 'kept . . . the paper flexibly anti-ministerial until the fall of Pitt in 1801, and anti-war until the autumn of 1802, when the swing of circulation figures and the arguments of Coleridge persuaded him to attack Fox and the peace' (1978, p. lxx).

Within the limits of seditious libel, the *Morning Post* was a forum that challenged the government and its foreign policy.

Context of the second publication

Coleridge's ode first appeared under the title 'France: An Ode' in late August or early September 1798 as part of the pamphlet *Fears in Solitude*. In *Reading Public Romanticism*, Paul Magnuson has uncovered the relevance of the Anti-Jacobin propaganda for Coleridge's quarto in an exemplary way. He points out the circumvention of censorship through duplicity: '*Fears in Solitude* wants to have it both ways [revolutionary and counter-revolutionary] and is a public utterance crafted for widely different audiences. Its author is a public figure who is both a friend of liberty and a loyal patriot, someone who enters a public dispute that is far more rhetorical than reasonable, far more duplicitous than disinterested' (Magnuson 1998, p. 79). According to Magnuson, *Fears in Solitude* was 'designed to answer criticism of himself and Johnson' (1998, p. 77), which had culminated in the 'New Morality' (July 1798) and a slandering footnote published in the *Beauties of the Anti-Jacobin* (1799). Canning and his co-authors included a brief, derogatory outline of Coleridge's life that concluded with the words: 'he has since married, had children, and has now quitted the country, become a citizen of the world, left his little ones fatherless, and his wife destitute' (Anonymous 1799, p. 306). Magnuson's argument is complicated by the fact that Coleridge had written all three poems of *Fears in Solitude* prior to publication of the 'New Morality' in July 1798. How could he have defended himself against the charges before they had even arisen? According to Magnuson, the accusations were already apparent prior to their publication. I contend that it was unlikely that Coleridge anticipated, as Magnuson suggests, the full extent of the humiliation. After all, they affected him so strongly that he wrote to Southey that he intended to take legal action in December 1799 (*Letters* I, p. 552). Magnuson presupposes, moreover, that the tenor of *Fears in Solitude* was defensive, or, to use his words, the pamphlet was 'dominated by the threat of legal action against seditious writing' (1998, p. 79). Although Magnuson points out ambivalences in *Fears in Solitude,* he resolves the ambiguity in such a way that the pamphlet is said to ultimately repress revolutionary ideas – 'defensive duplicity stands guard over dissent' (1998, p. 79). Contrary to Magnuson, I propose that due to the pamphlet's resilient dissent, especially its cosmopolitanism, Coleridge began to see *Fears in Solitude* temporarily as a matter of concern after the publication of a defamatory 'New Morality'.

Coleridge's retrospective defensiveness around 1800 can be seen from the above-mentioned letter to Southey written in late 1799. It shows Coleridge's apprehensive attitude towards *Fears in Solitude* after having been confronted with the denigrating footnote in the *Beauties of the Anti-Jacobin*:

> I have bought the Beauties of the Anti-jacobin [sic] – & Attorneys & Counsellors
> advise me to prosecute – offer to undertake it, so as that I shall have neither trouble

or expence [sic]. They say, it is a clear Case. – I will speak to Johnson about the Fears in Solitude [sic] – if he give them up, they are your's [sic]. That dull ode has been printed often enough; & may now be allowed to 'sink with dead swoop, & to the bottom *go*' – to quote an admired Author; – but the two others will do with a little Trimming. (*Letters* I, p. 552)

Here, 'France: An Ode' is 'dull' – the reference is clear because it is the only ode. Coleridge was reluctant to reprint and wished it to 'sink with dead swoop, & to the bottom *go*'. 'Fears in Solitude' and 'Frost at Midnight' allegedly required revision 'a little Trimming'. Without these forms of self-censorship, Coleridge was unwilling to republish the poems even in such a small, local publication as Southey's *Annual Anthology* (Bristol, 1800). Coleridge's self-esteem in the letter seemed low, his words sounded wary.

Coleridge had good reasons to be concerned about the reaction to *Fears in Solitude*. After all, the three poems criticized the current government. The counter-revolutionaries were anxious to strengthen public support for the war and to increase a sense of British nationalism. The most patriotic of the three poems, 'Fears in Solitude', received more attention in contemporary reviews than the other two poems (Roper 1978, p. 93). Nonetheless, Coleridge must have been aware that 'Fears in Solitude' only praised 'native Britain' (Coleridge 1798, p. 8, l. 179) after subjecting Britons to fierce criticism, 'O Britons! O my brethren!' (p. 8, l. 151). Coleridge's lines resonate with Cassandra's warning in 'Ode on the Departing Year', when the speaker addresses his readers, 'We have offended, O my countrymen' and draws their attention to the 'carnage' of warfare (Coleridge 1798, p. 3, ll. 41–2) and 'bitter truth' (p. 8, l. 152). As Roper put it, '"Fears in Solitude" expresses once more Coleridge's fear that divine retribution may overtake Britain for her crimes in Europe and Africa' (1978, p. 92). Clearly, such criticism of the current war was neither the sort of publicity that won Pitt more subscriptions; nor did it flatter the editors of the Anti-Jacobin press.

The reviews of *Fears in Solitude*, which Coleridge followed eagerly, made clear that readers were conscious of the young poet's political defiance. The *British Critic* lamented '[Coleridge's] absurd and preposterous prejudices against his country' (Roper 1978, p. 92). The *Analytical Review* felt the need to defend Coleridge's publication in December 1798: 'Mr C., in common with many others of the purest patriotism, has been slandered with the appellation of an enemy to his country' (Reinman 1972 I, p. 11). Southey followed the tone of the *British Critic* when he published his commentary in the *Critical Review* of August 1799 commenting that Coleridge's anxiety for an imminent invasion in 'Fears in Solitude' was exaggerated: 'Mr Coleridge has become an alarmist' (Reiman 1972 I, p. 311). Referring to Coleridge's exposure of British colonialism in 'Fears in Solitude', Southey concluded 'the following passage surely is not written in conformity with the fashionable opinions of the day' (Reinman 1972 I, p. 311).

Even the most universally agreeable poem in Coleridge's pamphlet, 'Frost at Midnight', included a notion that had the potential to offend the Anglican clergy. According to their orthodox standards, the pantheist echoes of Coleridge's 'eternal language [of Nature], which thy God/ Utters in all, and all things in himself' (Coleridge 1798, p. 22, ll. 65–7) signified a form of atheism. It is true though that the *British*

Critic approved of the conversation poem in June 1799: 'The Poem called Frost at Midnight, not being defaced by any of these absurdities, is entitled to much praise' (Reiman 1972 I, p. 127). Yet the *British Critic* praised 'Frost at Midnight' on grounds of its 'expressive tenderness' not of politics (Reiman 1972 I, p. 663). Neither 'Fears in Solitude' nor 'France: An Ode' nor 'Frost at Midnight' appear as a strategic defence against Jacobinism. On the contrary, in retrospect Coleridge seemed concerned that pamphlet might lead to further accusations of Jacobinism. After all *Fears in Solitude* linked him with Joseph Johnson, who had been arrested in July 1798 on charges of seditious libel for having sold a pamphlet by Gilbert Wakefield.[33]

The importance of this link with Johnson goes beyond reasons of 'metropolitan radicalism' (Roe 2002, p. 25).[34] Coleridge held the influential publisher Joseph Johnson in high esteem (Tyson 1979; White 2005, pp. 39–40). Shortly after his arrival in Germany, in October 1798, Coleridge recalled in a letter to his wife 'I had introduced myself to Johnson, the Bookseller, who received me civilly the first time, cordially the second, and affectionately the third - & and finally took leave of me with tears in his eyes' (*Letters* I, p. 420). Coleridge was pleased with his encounter with Johnson. Not only had the reserved man shown affection towards him, he had also agreed to give him a generous allowance of '30 pound' (*Letters* I, p. 417). Coleridge wrote that the payment was an advance for future projects, 'part of any thing I *might* do for him' (*Letters* I, p. 417). Coleridge was about to start his education at a German University. This academic interest qualified him in the eyes of Johnson for prospective, most likely Anglo-German, projects.[35] Johnson collaborated with a publishing house in Hamburg and published translations of German reviews in his own paper, the *Analytical Review*; he had pioneered the transmission of critical philosophy in England by publishing Beddoes's *Observations on the Nature of Demonstrative Evidence* (1793) and by commissioning an English translation of J. S. Beck's popularization of critical philosophy (1797). These ventures made the Unitarian publisher one of the leading promoters of critical philosophy in England. In this context, *Fears in Solitude* gives us a glimpse not only of Coleridge's involvement in metropolitan radicalism but also of his connection with the Germanophile dissenting circles in London that pioneered the dissemination of critical philosophy. It is telling that Johnson tried to secure future collaboration with Coleridge when the poet was about to embark on his journey to Göttingen. The fact that Coleridge did not renew his collaboration with Johnson after the publication of *Fears in Solitude* appears as a further indication of the poet's retrospective apprehension. A continued connection with Johnson might have exposed Coleridge to more vicious attacks by the Anti-Jacobins.

The third place of publication of 'France: An Ode'

When Coleridge republished 'France: An Ode' in the *Morning Post* and the *Courier* in 1802, he prefaced the ode with a prose 'Argument' that limited the freedom of interpretation (*PW* I.1, p. 463–4). In contrast to Mays, who notes the prose Argument 'strengthened' the design of the poem (*PW* I.1, p. 463), I propose that the added outline tamed the passionate tenor of the ode and smoothed over the defiant sympathy with

France. According to Esterhammer, 'the argument of "France: An Ode" belongs in the context of the 1790s debate over natural rights, of which the right to liberty is the prime example' (2000, p. 150). Esterhammer links the semantics of 'France: An Ode' with Edmund Burke's *Philosophical Enquiry into the Origins of Our Ideas of the Sublime and Beautiful* (1757). It would be possible to extend the point made in this chapter by including a comparison with Burke, that is, that the retrospective disavowal of republican ideals in the 'Argument' is closer to *Reflections on the French Revolution* than to *Perpetual Peace*. The discrepancy in the poem's 1802 version between verse and prose, poem and outline emerges, for instance, in Stanza Four. Whereas the latter conveys that even peace is no longer attached to harmony: 'Where Peace her jealous home had built' (Coleridge 1798, p. 17, l. 73), the 'Argument' merely gives an elliptic statement 'Switzerland, and the Poet's recantation' (*PW* I.1, p. 464, l. -1. 14–15). Likewise, the first stanza is said to be 'an invocation of these objects in Nature' that insinuate a state of harmony: Nature is seen as a direct source of peace and tranquillity. This docile depiction has little to do with the force of freedom the speaker conjures up, as mentioned, in Stanza One: 'Ye clouds . . . no mortal may control' (Coleridge 1798, p. 13, ll. 1–2). The expression at the beginning of the 'Argument', 'devotional love of Liberty' (*PW* I.1, p. 463, l. -1.3), is repeated in the last line: 'love and adoration of God in Nature' (*PW* I.1, p. 464, ll. – 1.22–3). Yet the final lines of Stanza Five elicit feelings of passion and violent death when the speaker's being is 'shot' through earth, sea and air. Nature in the verse, is, as explained above, a perilous place; however, one that the speaker embraces fully. By describing Nature as essentially peaceful and unwarlike, the 1802 'Argument' simplifies and tames the poem; indeed it did much to transform the ode into a complete renunciation of the French Revolution. Whereas the verse condemns the human tendency to hegemony and usurpation 'nor ever/ Didst though breathe thy soul in forms of human pow'r' (Coleridge 1798, p. 18, ll. 91–2), the 'Argument' relinquishes the compatibility of freedom and human government:

> [T]hat grand *ideal*, of freedom, which the mind attains by its contemplation of its individual nature, and of the sublime surrounding objects (see Stanza the First), do not belong to men, as a society, nor can possibly be either gratified, or realised [sic], under any form of human government. (*PW* I.1, p. 464, ll. -1.16–21)

As such, the 'Argument' reflects Coleridge's imminent transition 'from warm interest in the cause of the French nation to decided Anti-Gallicanism, from earnest demands for peace to vigorous defence of renewed and continued war' (Sara Coleridge cited in Erdman 1978, p. lxiv). I agree with Michael J. Kooy (2000, pp. 929–300) and John Morrow (1990, p. 73) that it was Napoleon's conduct during and after the Peace of Amiens that caused Coleridge to take a reluctant and tentative pro-war position.

Contrary to Mays's view that 'C's reference to the poem are few, slighting, and without affection' (*PW* I.1, p. 463), I think that 'France: An Ode' was not a dull poem for Coleridge, and if so, it was only a passing whim. As Michael O'Neill observed, it is a 'richly orchestrated poem' (2009, p. 388). Percy B. Shelley even 'told Byron that the best modern ode was Coleridge's *France: An Ode*' (Bloom 1971, p. 220).[36] The Victorians particularly valued Coleridge's ode alongside 'Ode on the Departing Year': they 'will not easily be forgotten' (Hort 1856, p. 312). When Coleridge revisited the poem in later years he approved of it consistently while he repeatedly appropriated it for his retrospective defence against Jacobinism. In 1807, Coleridge wrote assertive comments on the margins of *Fears in Solitude*; in 1817, he published an excerpt in *Biographia Literaria* (I, 199–200) and in 1828 he compared his ode to the *Anthropologie* by Heinrich Steffens, whom he admired (*Marginalia* V, p. 242; Halmi 2007, p. 81; Perkins 1994, pp. 122–4).[37] In later years, he sometimes dwelled on the last stanza despite, and independent from, the fact that his political views had changed profoundly by then. Similarly, scattered comments indicate that Coleridge returned to *Perpetual Peace* and remembered Beddoes's assessment of it.

Perpetual Peace and Coleridge's permanent silence

Throughout his lifetime, Coleridge remained silent about *Perpetual Peace*. The text was so profoundly connected to radical politics and its notional content so explicitly democratic that it would have been impossible to represent the pamphlet in any less radical light if Coleridge had wished to do so. In other words, an explicit reference to *Perpetual Peace* would have immediately exposed Coleridge's (former) Jacobinism – and this was exactly what the poet tried to conceal when he was growing older and more anxious about his political past. Nevertheless, he appears to have continued pursuing *Perpetual Peace* as similarities between Coleridge's writing and Kant's pamphlet recur after 1798 in the notebooks (De Paolo 1985, pp. 3–13), in the *Morning Post* articles, 'Our Future Prospects', 6 January 1803 (*Essays* I, pp. 419–22) and 'Letters on the Spaniards I', 7 December 1809 (*Essays* II, pp. 37–43) and in essay 'On the Law of Nations', 15 February 1809 (*Friend* II, pp. 321–33).

A particular notebook entry, dated to the time between March and July 1803, contains a statement that further supports the assumption that Coleridge read Beddoes's review of Kant's *Perpetual Peace*. The entry sets out as follows:

> In Natural Objects we feel ourselves, or think of ourselves, *only by Likenesses* – among men too often by *Differences*. Hence the soothing love-kindling effect of rural Nature/ the bad passions of human societies. – And why is Difference linked with Hatred? (*Notebooks* I, §1376)

The last line 'why is Difference linked with Hatred' seems to refer directly to the Beddoes's criticism (*Monthly Review* 20 [1796], p. 488) of the following passage in Kant's text:

> Aber die Natur will es anders. – Sie bedient sich zweier Mittel, um Völker von der Vermischung abzuhalten und sie abzusondern, der Verschiedenheit der Sprachen und der Religionen, die zwar den Hang zum wechselseitigen Hasse und Vorward zum Kriege bei sich führt (*Ewiger Frieden* p. 367)
>
> (But *nature wills* otherwise. It makes use of two means to prevent people from intermingling and to separate them: difference of language and of religion, which do bring with them the propensity to mutual hatred and pretexts for war. [*Perpetual Peace* 8: 367])

Like Beddoes, Coleridge questioned the presupposition in Kant's concept of Nature as the guarantee for peace. The entry casts doubt on the notion that Man's natural inclination to war is based on religious and linguistic difference. It appears as a fundamental disagreement with Kant's argument that nature will lead to peace by way of conflict and resulting unions. By 1803, Coleridge was, judging from this notebook entry, less inclined to accept Kant's first supplement than in 1798. Coleridge's rhetorical question 'And why is Difference linked with Hatred?' suggests that there is no necessary link and agrees with Beddoes's rejection of the concept in his review of 1796. In the 1802 'Argument' Coleridge omitted the inherently violent state of nature in 'France: An Ode'. The gloss declared the impossibility of freedom in society: the 'ideal of Freedom' does 'not belong to men, as a society, nor can possibly be either gratified or realized, under any form of human government' (*PW* I.1, p. 464, ll. -1.20–1). In much the same way, the notebook entry of 1803 professes an image of nature that is tame and synonymous with harmony. It resonates with Friedrich Schiller's dialectics of the naïve and the sentimental that Coleridge appears to have known by then: '*Vide Schiller*' (*Notebooks* I, §1705; Chapter 3). Coleridge's binary opposition, 'the soothing love-kindling effect of rural Nature/ the bad passions of human societies', (*Notebook* I, §1376) calls to mind Schiller's identification of nature with harmony and love, and his definition of culture as the loss of the former

> Ist der Mensch in den Stand der Kultur getreten, und hat die Kunst ihre Hand an ihn gelegt, so ist jene *sinnliche* Harmonie in ihm aufgehoben, und er kann nur noch als *moralische* Einheit, d. h. als nach Einheit strebend, sich äußern (*Schiller* XX, p. 437)
>
> (Once man has passed into the state of civilisation and art has laid her hand upon him, the sensuous harmony in him is withdrawn, and he can now express himself only as a *moral* unity, i.e., as striving after *unity*. [*Schiller* 1988, p. 159])

While Schiller's aesthetics retains the ambivalence between the state of nature and that of culture – both have advantages – Coleridge's oppositional pair in the notebook entry is fixed: the state of culture is clearly inferior to that of nature, the 'passions' of 'human society' are 'bad' (*Notebook* I, §1376). Coleridge's short notebook entry gives us a glimpse of what Coleridge's studies of German philosophy might have been like in 1803. Leaning over two texts, he contemplated Kant's concept of Nature in *Perpetual Peace* on the one hand, and Schiller's state of nature on the other hand. Weighing one theory against the other, he adopted Schiller's naïve and picked holes in Kant's association of nature with difference and hatred.

Coleridge's annotations to Sir Beaumont's copy of *Fears in Solitude*

Years later, Coleridge found out that Southey was the author of the above-mentioned review of *Fears in Solitude* in the *Critical Review*. It is impossible to know whether he ever addressed this issue in a conversation with Southey, yet Coleridge's annotations to

Sir Beaumont's copy of *Fears in Solitude* give us insights to Coleridge's imagined reply to his friend and brother-in-law.

> Southey in a review made some (me judice) unfounded objections to this last Stanza – as if I had confounded moral with political Freedom – but surely the Object of the Stanza is to show that true political Freedom can only arise out of moral Freedom – what indeed is it but a *Dilatation* of those *golden* Lines of Milton. (Coleridge cited in Evans 1935, p. 255)

This response is remarkable. It seems as if the confined space on the margins to Sir Beaumont's copy made Coleridge feel at ease to unleash the radical significance of the last stanza of 'France: An Ode'. The annotation captures a moment when Coleridge clearly stated that the purpose of the last stanza was 'to show that true political Freedom can only arise out of moral Freedom'. Within the corpus of Coleridge's writings this statement amounts to an indirect confession of Jacobinism at a late stage in the poet's career. In two instances, in 'Once A Jacobin always a Jacobin' (1802) and in 'On the Principles of Political Philosophy' (1809), Coleridge stated that he regarded the dependence of political on moral freedom as Jacobinism. In the 1809 *Friend*, Coleridge declared that 'the essence of JACOBINISM, as far as Jacobinism is any thing but a term of abuse' (*Friend* II, p. 105) consists in the theory that governments be derived from moral principles: 'all rightful origin to Governments . . . are derivable from Principles contained in the REASON of Man' (*Friend* II, p. 105). The essay 'On the Grounds of Government' denounced any form of the politics of first principles and advocated instead the notion of expedience: 'every Institution of national origin needs no other Justification than a proof, that under the particular circumstances it is EXPEDIENT' (II, pp. 103–4). Coleridge championed 'expedience' in *The Friend* and used the notion as a justification for his rejection of universal male suffrage (*Friend* II, p. 133). Coleridge's stipulation of expedience entailed the condemnation of the politics of first principles, notably by Rousseau, and thus of a form of politics that he had advocated passionately in his Bristol lectures. Expedience marked Coleridge's growing conservatism in 1800s and 1810s. This is the reason why Coleridge's autograph commentary, that the last stanza of 'France: An Ode' shows that political freedom can only arise from moral freedom, is so profoundly radical within the context of *The Friend*. The statement harks back to the Bristol lectures, his political activism against government oppression and his first encounter with the categorical imperative in the 1790s radical and dissenting environment in London and Bristol. Within the safety of the marginal space on the page, Coleridge retracted the retreat from his political past by admitting that 'France: An Ode' retained a pro-revolutionary element. Publically Coleridge professed a different version in 1818, one that severed the categorical imperative from any legislative or executive form of government, but this is a topic I discuss in more detail in Chapters 6 and 7 of this study.

From moral law to international peace

In Chapter 3, we have seen Coleridge's engagement with Kant's categorical imperative. The notion of a moral law inside of us appealed to Coleridge. It offered a formulation to instruct his audience how they, as individuals, could realize their potential for disinterested behaviour. This chapter has dealt with Coleridge's exposure to and affinity with Kant on a level that leads beyond personal motivation. The definite articles in *Perpetual Peace* cover three categories of public law: national, international and cosmopolitan (Höffe 2004, pp. 6–7, 9). The affinities between Coleridge's 'France: An Ode' and Kant's pamphlet mainly extend to national law and the question of how to solve the problem that even devils can accomplish the foundation of a nation state with a republican constitution. In contrast to the previous chapter, the view of mankind taken by Kant and Coleridge was cautious, even gloomy; it took into consideration the violent nature of man that had emerged during the Reign of Terror in France. As Beddoes shrewdly observed, the idea of sociopolitical progress in the pamphlet built on Nature, not human institutions. In 1796, numerous reviews contained abstracts of *Perpetual Peace*, the pamphlet appeared in October, and Coleridge's mentor studied Kant's radical treatise with much enthusiasm, though ultimate disappointment. For a journalist like Coleridge who demanded non-interference against France, *Perpetual Peace* represented an absolutely crucial reference. Although no extant evidence exists that he had read the pamphlet in 1796, internal evidence strongly suggests that Coleridge turned to *Perpetual Peace* in 1798. By that time, the weakness that Beddoes had perceived in *Perpetual Peace* must have appeared as strength: human disinterestedness alone could not be trusted in questions of government. At this time of political turmoil caused by the increasing expansionism of France, *Perpetual Peace* still helped Coleridge to anchor his democratic ideals of freedom. For Kant, a peaceful state was a state with a republican constitution. It offered concepts that could be applied to a positive interpretation of the events in France. Nature, the great artist, through its disposition to war would force humans in the long term and against their will to do what they 'ought to do' in terms of national governance, that is, to found a nation state based on the division between legislative and executive power to secure freedom for all.[38] The concept of Nature as a guarantee allowed Coleridge to accommodate his abhorrence for France's military aggression as well as his feelings of personal failure for having misjudged the course of the French Revolution. Through the allegorized figure of the savage creature, 'France: An Ode' attributes France to the forces of Nature which ultimately lead to freedom and peace. The poem's last stanza anticipates this event by performing the subjective experience in Nature, an epiphany in which freedom in this world is actualized by the speaker's violent union with earth, sea and air. This epiphany is no political renunciation yet but a powerful conclusion in the struggle to obtain freedom in this world. The high degree of internalization especially in the last stanza of 'France: an Ode' marks no disavowal of public issues. On the contrary, the ode unleashes the speaker's innermost desire to actualize freedom in an act of public proclamation. Drawing on the first three places of publication, the chapter has proposed that it was only in 1802 that Coleridge's addition of the 'Argument' constituted his retraction of revolutionary sympathies. The original place of publication in the *Morning Post* underpinned the ode's aspiration towards freedom and republicanism. The paper had initially greeted France's invasion as the defeat of Swiss oligarchy and frustration of English aspiration; it only started to condemn French expansionism after Stuart had been 'closely questioned by the Privy Council on his Jacobin associations'

(Erdman 1978, p. lxxiv). Following the subeditor's warning, Coleridge removed one of the original Stanzas, which alluded to British imperialism on the African continent. The original title 'Recantation' might have been a similar measure of precaution in response to government pressure. The publication in *Fears in Solitude* by Joseph Johnson gives us insights in Coleridge's connection with metropolitan Kant disseminators. Johnson's stipend indicates that Coleridge's training plans in a German university qualified him as an asset for future projects in the publisher's eyes. The affinities between 'France: An Ode' and *Perpetual Peace* match these publishing interests. Moreover, they account in part for Coleridge's retrospective reluctance to republish the poem in 1799. Shortly after the personal assault by the Anti-Jacobin press, Coleridge appears to have feared that further publications of 'Fears in Solitude', 'Frost at Midnight' and especially 'France: An Ode' could potentially lead to further defamation. When Coleridge decided to republish the ode again in 1802, he ensured that its subversive implications were subdued by the prefacing outline. The 'Argument' marks Coleridge's slow turn away from his radical ideals and the beginning of a transition to a nuanced pro-war position.

5

The Closet Kantian

Before Coleridge left Göttingen on 24 June 1799 (Holmes 1989, pp. 219–21; Breitkreuz 1973, p. 56; Sisman 2007, p. 269), he sent a letter to his sponsor Josiah Wedgwood summarizing his activities. Justifying his expenses, Coleridge wrote: 'I shall have bought 30 pounds worth of books (chiefly metaphysics/ & with a view to the one work, to which I hope to dedicate in silence the prime of my life)' (*Letters* I, p. 519). Coleridge was bringing books from Germany. The letter is remarkable not only because it expresses Coleridge's wish to dedicate 'the prime of my life' to these books but also because he saw a need to do so 'in silence'. Building on Rosemary Ashton's argument that Coleridge's public reticence about German, and in particular Kantian, philosophy was largely motivated by his awareness of the public hostility towards them (1980, p. 44), this chapter lays open the, at times, drastic changes in the public attitude towards Kantianism before, during and after Coleridge's trip to Germany. It specifically aims to establish the nature of the perceived threats posed by Kantian philosophy for the existing order in England, the vicious personal attacks on Coleridge on ideological grounds and the poet's experience of the sociable dimension of critical philosophy in Germany and England.

The above-quoted letter betrays some insecurity on Coleridge's part as to whether Wedgwood would approve of this plan and especially the purchases. Such doubts can be explained in part by Coleridge's confession in 1822 that he had bought a pirate copy of Kantian lectures during his first stay in Germany: 'Before I left Germany in 1799, I procured from the Nachdrücker or privileged Book-pirates a thin Octavo of two or at most 3 Sheets, under the name of Kant's Logic – doubtless, published by, or from the Notes of, one of his Lecture-pupils' (*Marginalia* III, p. 256; Wellek 1931, p. 71).[1] This admission belongs to a memory that Coleridge confided to the unprinted spaces in Gottlieb Benjamin Jäsche's manual of Kant's lectures on logic, entitled *Immanuel Kants Logik ein Handbuch zu Vorlesungen* (1800) (*Marginalia* III, p. 256). Coleridge's autograph commentary greets readers on the first pages of the book, neatly written on exactly one sheet. The opposite page is empty except for a tiny doodle. Coleridge used ink, which indicates his intention to capture these thoughts for posterity; indeed the handwritten note appears as an informal preface. This intimate introduction functions mainly as a vignette for the precursor of the present copy of Jäsche's *Logik*: a 'little volume' of Kant (*Marginalia* III, p. 257) that Coleridge had lost by 1822. 'I highly approved of it', Coleridge wrote nostalgically (*Marginialia* III, p. 257). The marginalia disclose a special example of Coleridge's bibliophilia. So dear had the lost booklet been to Coleridge that it appeared to him like an old acquaintance: 'I was at first surprized [sic] at beholding my old acquaintance transformed or fatted up into a goodly Octavo of 232 pages!' (*Marginalia* III, p. 257). Jäsche's manual was considerably thicker than Coleridge's first unidentified copy,[2] an illegally printed pamphlet of Kant's lectures on logic. Coleridge's warm attachment to it suggests that he read it closely in much the same way as he had anticipated in 1799 in the above-quoted letter to Josiah Wedgwood (*Letters* I, p. 519). The significance of this letter has been recognized before. Holmes has observed that it contains 'an oblique reference to the world of Kantian metaphysics, which he had first seen beckoning him in his notebooks of 1796' (1989, p. 221). Yet a particular detail in Coleridge's letter (*Letters* I, p. 519) has escaped previous scholarly attention: if the one work, to which Coleridge wished to dedicate the prime of his life was Kant's philosophy, why did he envision himself at the turn of the century to do so 'in silence'?

Coleridge's and Wordsworth's trip coincided with a period when British prejudices against the new German school of Kantian philosophy intensified in England roughly between '1798 until 1802' (Micheli 1990, p. 306). During Coleridge's time in Germany, a dispute between Willich and Abbé Barruel (see Chapter 1) erupted over Kant's alleged atheism and Jacobinism. So bitter was the dispute that it attracted the attention of numerous journalists and reviewers and amplified the existing aversion to Kantian principles (Micheli 1990, p. 290). Coleridge's statements in notebooks, marginalia and letters alongside contemporary periodicals disclose the profound impact of the anti-German campaign spearheaded by British counter-revolutionaries. In short, the philosophy that Coleridge sought in and exported from Germany was profoundly political at the time, even if some of the notional content was purely philosophical. E. P. Thompson's thesis (1969) overlooks these facts and thus fails to acknowledge the threat posed by German, particularly Kantian, thought. Against the background of the public campaign against Kant, Coleridge's intention to study Kant 'in silence' in 1799 can hardly be understood as an exchange of political principles for non-political Kantian metaphysics. So self-conscious felt Coleridge during the time of his initial immersion in Kant's *first critique* in 1801 that he promised Poole to keep his new philosophical discoveries secret: 'I assure you, solemnly assure you, that you & Wordsworth are the only men on Earth to whom I would have uttered a word on this subject' (*Letters* II, p. 709). For Coleridge, Kant's Copernican Revolution, to which I shall return further on in this chapter, was at first a matter that demanded secrecy.

While Coleridge's phrase 'in silence' might simply have referred to the practicalities of a quiet place of study for Kantian metaphysics, it seems more likely that, within the context of Coleridge's projected 'prime of . . . life', 'in silence' points to his envisioned uses of Kantian philosophy. Indeed it appears as if Coleridge, in a moment when he had to account for his 'main business at Göttingen' (*Letter* I, p. 519), felt compelled to obscure and refrain from publicizing his Kantian interests.[3] Not only did Coleridge omit the name of the author of his most precious book purchase in Germany in this letter to Josiah Wedgwood, he would refrain from openly advocating Kant's philosophy, despite his fascination for it, until 1817 when he came out of the closet, for the first time, and professed publically that he was a devoted disciple of Kant in

Biographia Literaria (I, p. 153) (see Chapter 6). Even then, Coleridge did not admit the politically radical dimension of his engagement with Kant. Independent of that, it is true that he continued to use Kant's (and others') ideas without acknowledging his sources. While scholars have hotly debated Coleridge's plagiarisms (Modiano 2009, pp. 207–8; Keanie 2009, pp. 435–6; McFarland 1974; Fruman 1971), I write from a similar viewpoint as M. F. Schulz, who gives the question of Coleridge's place within a larger 'European intellectual community' priority over the detection of plagiarism (1985, p. 411).

In Coleridge scholarship, it is a well-known fact that, after his return to Stowey at the end of July 1799 (Holmes 1989, p. 238), Coleridge found himself confronted with a profound marital crisis largely caused by his failure to come home when he received the news of the death of his son Berkeley (Vickers 2009, p. 76). To the poet's great dismay in 1799, George Canning, 'then a junior minister in the Pitt government' (Vardy 2010, p. 10) and the co-authors of the 'New Morality', George Ellis and John Hookman Frere, had used information about his private life to pummel Coleridge in public (*Letters* I, p. 552; Stones 1999 I, pp. 268–85; see Chapter 4).[4] A number of articles in the *Anti-Jacobin Review and Magazine*, the successor to William Gifford's *Anti-Jacobin, or Weekly Examiner,* continued defaming Coleridge's reputation. What has remained hitherto unnoticed is that James Walker and his colleagues condemned Coleridge partly on the grounds of a perceived affinity with Kantian philosophy and that they did so at a time when the poet's serious study of the *first critique* had barely begun. While previous commentators have largely focused on the 'New Morality', Guiseppe Micheli has excavated important details in further articles dating from 1799 and 1800 (1993, p. 294). Alan D. Vardy's recent monograph draws on one of these articles (without reference to Micheli). Vardy places the epistle 'German Literati and Literature' of the *Anti-Jacobin Review* (1800) in the context of Coleridge's attempt to obviate accusations of Jacobinism (2010, p. 13). However, Vardy does not mention James Walker as the author of this and several other articles in *Anti-Jacobin Review,* although this information helps to situate the attack on Coleridge in this historical context. Walker wrote five articles for the *Anti-Jacobin Review,* all of which appeared in 1800 (Montluzin 1988, pp. 157–8). His debut consisted of a polemical attack on Karl August Böttiger (1760–1835) for having criticized a work by his colleague John Robison: *Proofs of a Conspiracy* (1797) (*Anti-Jacobin Review* 6 [1800], pp. 342–9). At the time, Walker was a tutor to Sir John Hope during his travels on the Continent, which took him to Weimar. The young cleric published a sweeping rebuke of German thought in the form of two epistolary articles entitled 'The Literati and Literature of Germany', which appear as some of the most extreme manifestations of Germanophobia in the *Anti-Jacobin Review.*

Anti-Jacobin attacks against Coleridge, 1798, 1799 and 1800

The fourth volume of the *Anti-Jacobin Review and Magazine* (1799), edited by John Gifford, who was no relative of William Gifford – his real name being John Richard

Green (Montluzin 1988, p. 26)⁵– deprecated Coleridge in its preface for the explicit reason of proselytizing German philosophy:

> we are led to depreciate the importation of German philosophy in this country. One of the associates of the twin bards, whose patriotic efforts received just applause in the admirable poem the 'New Morality', was, not long since, at the University of Gottingen [sic] where he passed a considerable time with another Englishman . . . for the express purpose of becoming an adept in the mysteries of philosophism and for qualifying himself for the task of translating such of the favourite productions of the German school as are best calculated to facilitate the eradication of the British prejudice. (*Anti-Jacobin Review* 4 [1799], p. xiii)

Although the preface does not mention the name, the reference to one of 'the twin bards' of the 'New Morality' was sufficient to identify Coleridge. On 9 July 1798, around the time when Coleridge had been preparing for his trip to Germany together with William and Dorothy Wordsworth (see *Letters* I, pp. 402, 414), William Gifford had published the 'New Morality' in the last issue of the *Anti-Jacobin, or Weekly Examiner*. The political satire had targeted Coleridge and his friends, Robert Southey, Charles Lloyd and Charles Lamb, and ridiculed their cosmopolitan views. Allegedly indifferent to the domestic needs of Britain at the time of war, 'a steady patriot of the world alone,/ the friend of every country – but his own' (Anonymous 1799, p. 297, ll. 113–14), Coleridge and his friends were accused of betraying their country through their cosmopolitanism.⁶ This example further indicates how opposite the publication of Kant's *Perpetual Peace* was to counter-revolutionary tastes. While the 'New Morality' focused on the French republican and 'philosophe' Louis-Marie de Révellière-Lepeaux in Coleridge's writings, the attack in the preface of the *Anti-Jacobin Review* (4 [1799]) hinged on Coleridge's pursuit of Germany philosophy. Three articles in the *Anti-Jacobin Review* built on the 'New Morality' and perpetuated the vicious slander on Coleridge's name by implicating that he was involved in spreading the poisonous German philosophy in British society. Subsequently, in the third of the three vilifications of the poet, the Anti-Jacobin press narrowed down Coleridge's moral and political offence to accusations of Kantianism.

In the second of his two-part epistle on 'The Literati and Literature of Germany' (1800), Walker renewed the Anti-Jacobin defamation of Coleridge's reputation:

> two of these gentlemen, who were . . . the projectors of this admirable colony for America, and who are writers for The Morning Chronicle, and other publications of Jacobinal notoriety, came afterwards to Germany, to enable themselves, by acquiring the language and philosophy of this favoured country, to enlighten more completely the ignorant people of England. (*Anti-Jacobin Review* 6 [1800], p. 574)

Here, Coleridge featured again as a Germanophile conspirator; Walker's link with Kantianism was indirect yet unequivocal. In a previous passage, Walker established through a sweeping generalization that nearly every German professor taught the metaphysical jargon of Kant:

> In all the German universities, the chief study is the new system of philosophy, or what may be called the German metaphysics . . . . There are many Professors, who

go much greater lengths than Kant, who make no difficulty of exploding Deity from the universe as an idle prejudice . . . all of them [German Professors] teach a metaphysical jargon, which neither they nor their scholars comprehend, as they are almost all partizans [sic] of the incomprehensible system of Kant, and warmly attached to the doctrine of the unlimited improvement and perfection of human nature their labours abundantly pave the way for the sublimest flights of the *newly deified intellect of man*. (*Anti-Jacobin Review* 6 [1800], pp. 569–70)

According to Walker, 'in all German universities, the chief study is the new system of philosophy'. By publicizing the fact that Coleridge had gone to Germany to learn the language and study philosophy, Walker implicitly accused Coleridge of advocating Kantianism. Coleridge posed a dangerous threat in Walker's eyes because of his German university education. It is possible that Walker's view was partly informed by the German debates on Kant. Especially the defenders of Wolff's system in Germany attacked Kant, according to Beiser, on political grounds and associated him with the French Revolution (1987, pp. 193–8). Walker inflated the existing charges of Jacobinism against Kant and went beyond them by accusing him of dissolving the entire social order. Walker appears to have understood the great sociopolitically transformative power behind critical philosophy and was utterly repulsed by it. Kantians taught, according to Walker, 'that civil society is progressively improving; that each of us contributes to its improvement; and that therefore every government is carrying on its own dissolution, since a time will certainly arrive, when man and nature will be so perfect, as to be able to go on without government, laws, or submission' (*Anti-Jacobin Review* 6 [1800], p. 570). Walker feared that these were the disastrous consequences of Kantianism and his mediators. Despite the fact that a number of Englishmen had spread Kantian philosophy in their home country, Walker singled out Coleridge mainly because the poet studied at a German university. Walker's two articles on the literature and literati of Germany warned readers against Coleridge's spreading of Kantianism, or to use his sarcastic words, they tried to prevent Coleridge from 'enlighten[ing] more completely the ignorant people of England' (*Anti-Jacobin Review* 6 [1800], p. 574).

The 'New Morality' (1798), the preface of volume four for the *Anti-Jacobin Review* (1799) in combination with Walker's vicious articles (1800) can be visualized as a series of accusations that were ultimately centred in Kantianism. At first the Anti-Jacobin press took issue with Coleridge's interest in Continental philosophy ('New Morality'), then it condemned Coleridge's engagement with German philosophy (Preface of the *Anti-Jacobin Review* 4 [1799], pp. i–xiii) and lastly it took offence with the poet's allegedly Kantian education (*Anti-Jacobin Review* 6 [1800], pp. 562–76). Canning's, Gifford's and Walker's slanderous remarks give us an idea of the scenario that Coleridge would have faced if he had decided to publicize his interest in Kantian philosophy at the turn of the century. They simultaneously show us the widespread awareness of Kant's profound Enlightenment radicalism in Germany as well as England. The Anti-Jacobins exploited the few pieces of information they had managed to obtain about Coleridge to bully him. The above-quoted conflation of Robert Southey with William Wordsworth, 'two . . . gentlemen . . . the projectors of this admirable colony for America [Pantisocracy]' indicates that the articles were mostly based on speculation. Moreover, the excerpts above show that the Anti-Jacobin press saw Coleridge as one of the 'Germanized Englishm[e]n' (*Anti-Jacobin Review* 5 [1799], p. 569) as early as in 1799, of whom they suspected 'a systematic design to extend such depravity of a regular importation of exotic poison from the envenomed crucibles of the literary and political alchymists [sic] of the New German school' (*Anti-Jacobin Review* 4 [1799], p. vii).

Since Coleridge contemplated legal action after his discovery of the slanderous footnote in the *Beauties of the Anti-Jacobin*, he was very sensitive to further accusations from this political camp. Coleridge probably followed the publications of the Anti-Jacobin press and took the continued defamations to heart. The poet tended to be easily affected by unfair treatment from his political opponents and expressed his fears regarding this matter at an early stage in his career: 'I begin to fear, that the Good I do is not proportionate to the Evil I occasion—Mobs and Mayors, Blockheads and Brickbats, Placards and Press gangs have leagued in horrible Conspiracy against me –' (*Letters* I, p. 152). The particular problem with Walker's texts was that some of his speculations actually applied to Coleridge.

A couple of examples taken from Walker's allegations, one against Germanophiles in general and another against Kant disciples in particular, demonstrate their remarkable suitability to target specific political and philosophical views harboured by Coleridge in his late twenties. One of the principles which Walker believed to originate from the Kantian school was that which had attracted Coleridge's attention in the first place in 1796 (*Notebooks* I, §249 discussed in Chapter 3):

> With respect to morality, they teach that duty is the only rule of conduct, that there is no other law than the sense of duty which exists in the mind of every individual, that each man stands single in the universe, and must act from his particular sense of duty, without thinking of his fellow men, or expecting any reward, which would be meanness in the extreme. (*Anti-Jacobin Review* 6 [1800], p. 570)

Walker paraphrased the categorical imperative somewhat ironically, 'meanness to the extreme', but after all recognizably. If Coleridge read the article, it probably struck him how closely Walker's summary of Kantian principles resembled his own fascination with the philosophy. The categorical imperative exemplifies that the ideas condemned by Walker under the auspices of the *Anti-Jacobin Review* coalesced with the notions that enticed Coleridge to study Kant's philosophy more thoroughly.

A further aspect of Walker's letters to the editor of the *Anti-Jacobin Review* is relevant for the political implications of Coleridge's decision to travel to Germany. Contrary to the view of political disengagement, Walker's article suggests that the demand for peace was the most compelling reason for Britons to visit Germany:

> When I asked [Germanized Englishmen] in what respect the Germans were so very superior to our countrymen; where were their useful discoveries; and what were the effects of their most useful improvements? The reply, without attending to any of my questions, was generally transformed into a violent declamation against the present war and its baneful effects in repressing genius, and in rendering difficult or impossible, all useful and scientific enquiry, with *a nota bene*

at the end, asserting in spite of all contradiction, that Germany is at present the only country in Europe distinguished for literary pursuits. (*Anti-Jacobin Review* 5 [1800], p. 569)

Coleridge, Wordsworth and Dorothy probably had similar views in mind when they decided to stay in Lower Saxony. By 1800, Prussian neutrality in the war had become a matter of concern and even of scandal from the counter-revolutionary point of view.[7] In early 1795, Prussia had withdrawn under Friedrich Wilhelm II from the First Coalition by concluding a separate peace in Switzerland. The Peace of Basel marked, as Philip Dwyer points out, 'the beginning of a neutrality policy that was to last in one form or another for over a decade and was to end by Prussia resuming war against France in 1806' (Dwyer 1994, p. 351). The *Anti-Jacobin Review* supported Pitt's demands for military assistance against France and condemned not only the refusal of continued support by Friedrich Wilhelm II but also that by other German states: 'All the poisoners of the public mind, from the source of the Danube to Jutland, agree on enforcing the necessity of peace' (*Anti-Jacobin Review* 1 [1798], p. 731). Judging from the *Anti-Jacobin Review,* there was a fear among counter-revolutionaries that Prussian neutrality entailed repercussions for the native support of the war. The *Anti-Jacobin Review* saw a future Prussian renewal of war as a pivotal measure to suppress the venomous impact of German thought at home: the periodical predicted that 'literary poison . . . will ultimately deluge from Germany, unless a renewal of the war [of Prussia with France], a strict police, and an exemplary punishment of the guilty, impose a speedy check' (*Anti-Jacobin Review* 1 [1798], p. 732). These words indicate the counter-revolutionary concern that British war opponents might use the Peace of Basel as an argument to support their demands. Against this background, Coleridge's decision to study in Germany seems consistent with his opposition against the war until the Peace of Amiens. One of the major political reasons for his dislike of 'Each petty German Princeling, nurs'd in gore!' (Coleridge 2004, p. 27, l. 193) had become obsolete through the Peace of Basel. For the British Anti-Jacobin press, the German states spearheaded by Prussia stood for peace with Revolutionary France, and not for disenchantment from the principle.

Walker's criticism applied to Coleridge in the late 1790s when the poet, despite increasing doubts, still opposed the war and sketched the categorical imperative in his notebook in 1796. Like Vardy (2010, p. 13), I think that the harsh attacks by the Anti-Jacobins must have elicited a response from Coleridge. This reaction consisted, I propose, partly in Coleridge's precaution to study Kant 'in silence'. Had Coleridge chosen to publicize his Kantian interest after the return from Germany he would have raised even stronger charges of Jacobinism.

Coleridge at Göttingen

A departure from English culture is necessary not only to put the views purported by the *Anti-Jacobin Review* into perspective but also to uncover how much Coleridge appears to have learnt about Kant while in Germany. It is generally thought that Coleridge did not read critical philosophy as part of his formal studies at Göttingen. Coleridge arrived in Lower Saxony via Hamburg and Ratzeburg, matriculating at the Georg-August University on 16 February 1799 in *studia humaniora* (Breitkreuz 1973, p. 56). He left Göttingen on 24 June 1799 (*Letters* I, 520; Holmes 1989, p. 219). Professor Christian Gottlieb Heyne generously extended the special borrowing privilege to Coleridge, which normally only applied to professors. Coleridge's borrowings are documented in the library records ('Ausleihregister') of two semesters: Michealmas 1798 until Easter 1799 and Easter 1799 until Michealmas 1799. Alice D. Snyder first transcribed and published the records (1928).[8] Coleridge worked perhaps uncharacteristically hard at the university library: 'I have worked harder than, I trust in God Almighty, I shall ever have occasion to work again—this endless Transcription is such a body-and-soul-wearying Purgatory!' (*Letters* I, p. 519). The probable absence of Kant from his formal studies, however, does not preclude any reading of Kantianism. At a party described in Charles Lamb's obituary, Coleridge is said to have reminisced about his first trip to Germany: 'in the Hartz [sic] forest . . . I was reading the "Limits of the Knowable and the Unknowable," the profoundest of all his [Kant's] works with great attention' (*The Annual Biography and Obituary* 20 [1835], pp. 1–16; Wellek 1931, p. 7). Coleridge's walking tour through the Harz in May 1799 was spectacularly strenuous. Towards the end of the trip, the poet spoke of 'inexpressible Fatigue' (*Letters* I, p. 503) due to 'such in[tense] bodily exercise' (*Letters* I, p. 504). Even if the poet read Kant 'with great attention' then, as he claimed, he must have been exhausted while doing so.

At the beginning of the letter to Josiah Wedgwood, Coleridge enumerated five of his accomplishments while in Germany but omitted others:

> What have I done in Germany? — I have learnt the language, both high & low German / I can read both, & speak the former so fluently, that it must be a *torture* for a German to be in my company — that is, I have words enough & phrases enough, & I arrange them tolerably; but my pronunciation is hideous. — 2ndly, I can read the oldest German, the Frankish and the Swabian. 3dly — I have attended the lectures on Physiology, Anatomy, & Natural History with regularity, & have endeavoured to understand these subjects. — 4th — I have read & made collections for an history of the Belles Lettres in Germany before the time of Lessing — & 5thly — very large collections for a Life of Lessing; — to which I was led by the miserably bald &unsatisf[act]ory Biographies that have been hitherto given, & by my personal acquaintance with two of Lessing's Friends. (*Letters* I, p. 518)

Coleridge had not only acquired fluency in the German language, he had also learnt Old and Middle German ('2ndly'). Coleridge's letter mentions Blumenbach's physiology and natural history ('3dly') but omits the fact that the poet also attended Johann Gottfried Eichhorn's lectures on Higher Biblical Criticism and Heyne's philology seminar (Shaffer 2009, p. 560). Schiller is equally absent from Coleridge's brief summary, although recent scholarship has uncovered Schiller's significance for Coleridge's studies abroad (Kooy 2002, pp. 33–44). As the letter stated under '-4th-', Coleridge researched the history of German literature until the time of Gottfried Ephiram Lessing (1729–81). Not only did he gather 'very large collections' of material on Lessing ('5thly'), he also 'read all the numerous Controversies in which

L. was engaged' (*Letters* I, p. 519). These 'numerous Controversies' included the interpretation of the Bible and the 'Pantheismusstreit'.

The pantheism controversy received an enormous amount of publicity. Therefore Coleridge's seemingly casual remark that he 'read all the controversies in which L. engaged' (*Letters* I, 519) points also to a great number of Kantian texts including Kant's 'Was heißt: Sich im Denken orientiren [sic]?' ('What Does it Mean to Orient Oneself in Thinking?') (Zammito 1992, p. 230; see Chapter 1). The pantheism controversy began in the summer of 1783 'as a private quarrel' (Beiser 1987, p. 44) between Friedrich Heinrich Jacobi (1743–1819) and Moses Mendelssohn (1729–86) over the 'alleged Spinozism of [the late] Lessing' (di Giovanni 1998, p. 44; Altmann 1973). 'Two years later, the dispute became public and engaged almost all the best minds of late eighteenth century Germany' including the 'celebrities Kant, Herder, Goethe, and Hamann' (Beiser 1987, p. 44). Thomas McFarland has regarded Coleridge's interest in Spinoza's pantheism as a lifelong preoccupation (1969, p. 112). It is known that the question of Coleridge's engagement with pantheism is intricately bound up with his adherence to Socinian beliefs in the 1790s. Pantheism overlapped with Priestley's 'necessitarian, mechanical world-view' in so far as it threatened to leave 'no place for a personal God who would provide miraculous events or revelation; the Unitarian God would be entirely indistinguishable from his creation, and his traditional roles thus effectively redundant' (Vigus 2010, p. 3). Since McFarland's influential study (1969), scholars have continued to examine Coleridge's pantheism, his 'doctrine of the One Life' and the added lines to 'The Eolian Harp' (Perry 1999, p. 70; Berkeley 2004, p. 59). Perry's seminal *Coleridge and the Uses of Division* has done a great deal to clarify Coleridge's lasting fascination with Unitarian principles, but the impact of Lessing and the pantheism controversy around him has, according to Shaffer, not yet been fully accounted for (Shaffer 2010, p. 115).[9] What is important in the context of this chapter is that Coleridge's explicit reference to the controversies surrounding Lessing implies his awareness of the historical fact, discussed in Chapter 1, that the pantheism controversy played an important role for the dissemination of Kantianism.[10] Due to Reinhold's role in the controversy surrounding Lessing's alleged Spinozism, Coleridge's claim of having read all about Lessing's controversies hence contains a possible hint that he was already exposed to some of Reinhold's work while at Göttingen.[11] It is Reinhold's work and his reformative agenda that suited young Coleridge at the time more than Jacobi's conservative outlook, to which McFarland has attributed such high importance in Coleridge's thought (1969).

It is true, nevertheless, that in comparison to Jena, the place where Coleridge had initially intended to study in 1796 (*Letters* I, p. 209),[12] the intellectual milieu in Göttingen was relatively unresponsive to critical philosophy.[13] Anglo-Saxon influences in Göttingen were historically very strong. Belonging to Hanover, Göttingen was part of the British Empire; Hanover being by personal union the family seat of the Kings of Great Britain (see Kühn 1987, p. 70).[14] George II, Elector of Hanover, had founded the local university in 1734 leaving it in charge of Gerlach Adolph von Münchhausen.[15] By the 1770s, the Georg-August University had become 'one of the most modern, most successful and most respected institutions of higher learning in Germany' (Kühn 1987, p. 70). Beiser explains that Münchhausen's liberal policies enhanced the progress of philosophy at Göttingen. Particularly there, and also in Berlin, under the enlightened despotism of Frederick II, a new philosophical movement dedicated to the popular philosophy of the German Enlightenment formed, 'and accordingly went by the name *Popularphilosophie*' (Beiser 1987, p. 165).[16] Modelled on the French and British Enlightenment, the movement was immensely diverse and manifested itself in a vast amount of materials (pamphlets, articles and reviews). Emphasizing the response of the *Popularphilosophen* to trends within Germany, Beiser considers their discussions of the authority of Reason in the late eighteenth century, in particular their criticism of Kant, their most important contribution. 'They often raised acute objections that questioned Kant's claim to uphold the authority of reason' (Beiser 1987, p. 168).[17] In contrast, Manfred Kühn regards the Göttinger philosophers Johann Georg Heinrich Feder, Christian Meiner and Georg Christoph Lichtenberg as a separate group of thinkers who turned to Scottish common sense philosophy mainly because they felt that 'philosophy has to become more modest' (1987, p. 44; see also pp. 70–85).

The English correspondent of the *Neuer Teutscher Merkur (New German Mercury)*, Johann Christian Hüttner, interpreted the resistance to critical philosophy at Göttingen as a lack of interest. According to him, Kant experts were rare in Göttingen. He observed in May 1796 that the University had so far 'stayed clean of the Kantian sourdough': 'vor dem Kantischen Sauerteig rein erhalten hat' (*Neuer Teutscher Merkur* 2 [1796], p. 437). However, Hüttner mentioned exceptions. In fact, local scholars included at least three published Kant connoisseurs, two in Göttingen and one in Helmstadt. It was their work that Coleridge might have come into contact with, be it in conversation or in print. One of the local authorities on Kant, albeit an antagonistic one, was J. G. H. Feder. He was the editor of the infamous first review of the *Critique of Pure Reason* in the influential periodical *Göttingische Anzeigen* (see Chapter 3). Feder published a general polemic against the *first critique* entitled *Über Raum und Caussalität [sic]: zur Prüfung der Kantischen Philosophie (On Space and Causality: an Examination of the Kantian Philosophy)* in Göttingen in 1787 (Sassen 2004, p. 320). Loyal to the tradition of Locke (Beiser 1987, p. 169), Feder founded the journal *Philosophische Bibliothek* with the aim to 'stem the swelling tide of Kantianism' (Beiser 1987, p. 181; see p. 167).[18] After the miserable failure of his campaign against Kant, he ceased teaching at the Georg-August University prior to Coleridge's arrival.[19]

Yet Johann Gottlieb Buhle (1763–1821), a supporter of Kant (Röttgers 1984, p. 431), held a full professorship from 1794 until 1804 publishing an introduction to logic and to the *Critique of Pure Reason (Einleitung in die Allgemeine Logik und die Kritik der reinen Vernunft)* in Göttingen in 1795 (Klemme and Kühn 2010 I, p. 169). De Quincey referred to the German professor Buhle in a different context, namely De Quincey's 'Historico-critical Inquiry into the Origin of the Rosicrucian and the Free masons' (1824) (Roberts 2000, p. 154). Roberts points out that 'Coleridge's influence on De Quincey is nowhere more evident than in the latter's reading of Kant and of German literature and philosophy in general' (Roberts 2000, p. 153). Hence Buhle might have been significant for Coleridge.

A stop in Coleridge's itinerary back to England in 1799 points to Gottlob Ernst Schulze (1761–1833), whose publication *Aenesidemus* (1792) was widely seen as one of the most brilliant analyses of Kant's *first critique* and Reinhold's theory of representations. Schulze was closely connected to Feder's circle in Göttingen as his son-in-law (Beiser 1987, p. 267). Coleridge and Chester stayed in Helmstadt in July 1799. After their arrival in the small university town, 'Hofrath Bruns' invited Coleridge to his home, where an academic couple joined them: 'another professor & his wife came' (*Letters* I, p. 521). Apparently Coleridge did not keep a record of the professor's name. Many years later the poet mentioned in his annotations to Kant's *Vermischte Schriften* a Kant commentator named 'Schulz', which might be a misspelling of the name (*Marginalia* III, pp. 318–19).[20] If so, Schulze features literally on the margins of *Vermischte Schriften*, and figuratively on those of Coleridge's trip.

Shaffer notes that Coleridge 'did not while in Germany undertake his full study of Kant's own difficult texts, but he sent them home' (Shaffer 2009, p. 558). This was probably the case for Coleridge's in-depth study of the *first critique* in German (below), but it is necessary to add that Coleridge's acquaintance with and study of Kant in general predates his return from Germany. Coleridge was exposed to a number of Kantian sources while studying in Göttingen. One aspect of his stay is certain in this regard: among the books he brought from Germany was the little pirate copy of Kant's logic to which Coleridge grew so attached that it became an 'old acquaintance' (*Marginalia* III, p. 256). This copy will carry great importance in the following chapter. It remains, however, uncertain whether Coleridge met the published Kant experts in Göttingen and in Helmstadt and if so what he learnt from them. All we know about his encounters from his letters written at the time is that he met (non-professional) Kantians during his year abroad in 1798 and 1799 and that he felt both inspired and repulsed by them.

Kantianism had in fact become 'all the rage in Germany' since the first publication of Reinhold's *Letters* in 1786 (Zammito 1992, p. 241; Di Giovanni 2005, pp. 36–65; Kühn 2001, pp. 351–3). Benjamin Sowden reported in the *Monthly Review* of 1794 that 'we find that, from its becoming [of Critical Philosophy] a fashionable topic of conversation, it has engaged the attention of the ladies, many of whom are zealous adherents to it' (14, p. 542). Walker in the *Anti-Jacobin Review* observed rightly in 1800 that Kantianism was seen as a badge of intellectual exclusivity:

> What I have found often remarked among the *Kantists* in Germany, I have not unfrequently [sic] observed among the partisans of German literature whatever Frenchmen or Englishmen . . . The philosophy of Kant is the most valuable production of human beings – why? Because his partisans *assert* it; because, they who are not in the secret, cannot *comprehend* it. (*Anti-Jacobin Review* 5 [1800], p. 568)

According to Walker, Kantianism instilled a sense of secrecy through its jargon and worked like coded language. He suspected all Kantians used these clandestine messages for the ultimate purpose of advancing the grand republican conspiracy.

Coleridge himself remembered the immense popularity of Kantianism in Germany: 'The Critique der r. V. appeared -& the Universities of Germany *exploded!*' (*Marginalia* III, p. 318). One of his letters to Poole gives us a glimpse of the poet's encounter with fashionable Kantians. Recalling the conversation between Wordsworth and Klopstock in November 1798, Coleridge wrote:

> Of Kant he [Klopstock] said, that he was a Mountebank & the Disgrace of Germany — an unintelligible Jargonist. — And that his New Lights were going out very fast in Germany. (N.B. / *I* meet every wheretho', with some SNUFFS that have a live spark in them — & fume under your nose in every company. — All are Kantians whom I have met with.) (*Letters* I, p. 444)

Coleridge's comment in parenthesis indicates his disagreement with Klopstock's unfavourable opinion of Kant and his disciples. Coleridge thought that Kantians were almost ubiquitous 'every where' (at least in Holstein). They attracted his attention through their intellectual energy, 'a live spark in them', but also through their bad manners 'fum[ing] under your nose in very company'. By calling them 'SNUFFS', Coleridge invoked a picture of being placed among these Kantians having to inhale their burnt tobacco while feeling excluded and not yet able to fully participate in their conversation in German. Henry Crabb Robinson's experience was not entirely dissimilar although the Kantians he encountered were inclusive and more polite than these 'SNUFFS'. The fashionable status of Kant's philosophy and the sociability among his disciples also impressed Robinson considerably. As Vigus has shown in more detail than Wellek (1931, p. 139–59), Robinson's resolution to study Kant's philosophy was motivated by his friendship with the admirer and scholar of Kant Christian Brentano (Vigus 2010, pp. 4–5). James Walker exaggerated when he called almost all German professors Kantians, but Kant enthusiasts were common and included women as was known in England through Sowden's article in the *Monthly Review*. Even if Coleridge belittled a female attempt at reading Kant, he was at least aware that women were familiar with critical philosophy, too: 'a sweet pretty German girl, about fifteen, came behind my chair, and, leaning over, said, "What you read Kant? Why, I that am German born don't understand him"' (*The Annual Biography and Obituary* 20 [1835], p. 8). The unusually flirtatious dimension of this Kantian conversation points to a host of other social situations during which Coleridge might have heard or learnt more about Kant while in Germany.[21]

Walker and the other authors of the *Anti-Jacobin Review* knew little about Coleridge's activities in Germany, as their confusion of Wordsworth with Southey shows. For them, the fact alone that Coleridge travelled there to study was a matter of alarm and even scandal. German Universities were heretic institutions for British counter-revolutionaries: '*In some of the Universities not a single professor is to be found who dares to admit the existence of a God*' (*Anti-Jacobin Review* 1 [1798], p. 729). Coleridge's letter to Poole, written in October 1798, sounds like a defence against such Germanophobia. According to the *Anti-Jacobin Review* published in late summer to fall 1798, the majority of literary men in Germany were corrupted by the French Revolution:

> Ninety-nine in every hundred of literary men in Germany, or of men who assume that appellation, either are, or have been, professors at Universities. Electrified, at first by French principles, afterwards tempted by the success which many writers

had obtained, either in the revolution, or by means of it, they espoused all its extravagant doctrines, and propagate them, with the zeal or converts and the fury of bigots. (*Anti-Jacobin Review* 1 [1798], pp. 728–9)

As if trying to disprove the news from Britain that Poole might have communicated, Coleridge wrote back home: 'It is absolutely false that the literary Men are Democrats in Germany' (*Letters* I, p. 435). Coleridge apparently knew the counter-revolutionary prejudices against German writers. Arriving home in England, it seemed sensible for him to conduct his Kantian studies at first in the closet (*Letters* I, p. 519).

Coleridge's silent study of Kant in 1800 and 1801

Once Coleridge had arrived in England, he soon began to long for the company of the Wordsworths and, after half-hearted attempts to find lodgings in the West Country, decided to move to the Lakes (Holmes 1989, p. 275; Vickers 2009, p. 760). The relocation of his family allowed him to be near the Wordsworths but further strained his relationship with his wife. It is known that in the months following his arrival in the Lake District, he studied Kant's *first critique* thoroughly (see Introduction). While experts largely agree that the letters to Tom Poole in February and March 1801 and the notebook entry (*Notebooks* I, §887) mark the beginning of Coleridge's thorough study of Kantian philosophy, commentators have overlooked the excited, but also anxious tone, in Coleridge's written communication with Poole.

Two letters to Poole dating from March 1801 convey Coleridge's nervous excitement while studying the *Critique of Pure Reason.* The letter of 16 March starts immediately by mentioning 'the most intense Study' over the past month. Coleridge's health had collapsed in January, and since then the poet had retreated to the upper rooms of Greta Hall, a former astronomical observatory he rented in Keswick (Holmes 1989, p. 278). In these rooms, he devoured the German texts by Kant, 'I have not only completely extricated the notions of Time, and Space; but have overthrown the doctrine of Association, as taught by Hartley' (*Letters* II, p. 706). Writing almost breathlessly, Coleridge paused 'This I have *done*' and continued proudly, 'but I trust, that I am about to do more' (*Letters* II, p. 706). This sense of excitement subsided, however, in the next letter. On 23 March, Coleridge expressed not only his regret that Locke was more interesting for Poole than the new German school—'I was agreeably disappointed in finding you had been interested in the Letters respecting Locke' (*Letters* II, p. 708)—he also intimated his awareness that his fascination with Kant might expose him to ridicule: 'I need not observe, My dear Friend, how unutterably silly & contemptible these Opinions would be if written to any but to another Self' (*Letters* II, p. 709). 'These Opinions' do not seem so silly after all. Kant proposed in the *first critique* a procedure analogous to the basic thought behind Copernicus's theory (*KrV* B XVI; *CpR* B XVI). Kant's so-called Copernican Revolution consists, according to Silber,

in the recognition of the knower's contribution to the knowledge of objects. Instead of vainly striving to assure the conformity of our ideas to objects, Kant argued that we should rather concern ourselves with the necessary conditions of experience to which objects must conform if they are to be known. (1963, p. 182)[22]

Taking the clue from Kant, Coleridge speculated that

> if the mind be not passive, if it be indeed made in God's Image, & that too in the sublimest sense – the Image of the Creator – there is ground for suspicion, that any system built on the passiveness of the mind must be false, as a system. (*Letters* II, p. 709)

So revolutionary seemed this thought to Coleridge that he, as mentioned, promised to only speak about his new discoveries with Poole and Wordsworth: 'I assure you, solemnly assure you' (*Letters* II, p. 709). On the one hand, this remark points to Coleridge's philosophical conversations with Wordsworth and the project of the 'Recluse'. On the other hand, as mentioned at the outset of this chapter, the letter unfolds the sociopolitical implications of Coleridge's philosophical studies: Kant's Copernican Revolution seemed such a radical innovation at the turn of the century that Coleridge felt the need to hide his views. Possibly Poole's previous reply (namely to his letter from 18 March) had included a warning which in turn elicited this 'solemn' vow of silence. As the interlocutor between Coleridge and his wife, Poole kept an eye on the family's interests (Sisman 2007, pp. 270–5).

Coleridge's exploration of Kant formed part of a larger project in the winter of 1800 and 1801. He composed a series of letters to Josiah Wedgwood, partly to show that he deserved the Wedgwood annuity and partly to prove his expertise in comparison to another member of the Wedgwood circle, that is, James, later Sir James, Mackintosh (Jackson 2000, pp. xlix, li). As Jackson observes, there is no extant evidence that Coleridge 'shared his new enthusiasm with his patron' (2000, p. li). Considering Coleridge's solemn promise to Poole, it seems indeed likely that Coleridge hid his new discovery from Wedgwood. Coleridge's latest study of a German Jacobin was a potentially dangerous enterprise, which confirmed some of the worst suspicions of the *Anti-Jacobin Review*: Kant and his disciples might 'pave the way for the sublimest flights of the *newly deified intellect of man*' (*Anti-Jacobin Review* 6 [1800], pp. 569–70). While statements like this explain in part Coleridge's pervasive caution to acknowledge his indebtedness to Kant (*Letters* I, p. 519), they also lay open a growing perceived cultural difference between England and the German states around 1800. While Kantianism was fashionable, for instance, in Lower Saxony, Saxony, Prussia and Holstein in the late 1790s, it became increasingly difficult and almost impossible to have an open public debate or even professional conversations about Kant in England.

Coleridge's lasting reticence

From the early 1800s until his death, Coleridge obscured his references to Kant in published work in different ways, doing so even at time when the philosopher's name was no longer the focus of accusations of Jacobinism. Kant's name disappeared temporarily from English periodicals after 1806. This can be seen, as Micheli suggests as, 'a sign of a lack of interest which was by now general and of the distance of German philosophy from the cultural debate of the time' (Micheli 1990, p. 307). Neither the English translation of Mme de Staël's *De l' Allemagne* (trans. *Germany*, 1813) nor Thomas Wirgman's articles on Kant in the *Encyclopaedia Londinensis* (Wilkes and Jones 1810–29; see Introduction) led to a wide-spread resurgence of public interest (Wellek 1931, pp. 165, 214; Micheli 1990, p. 307). Throughout those years, Coleridge remained somewhat afraid of his English audience, and their either indifferent or potentially hostile reaction to German philosophy in general and Kant in particular. This attitude played a significant role in Coleridge's assimilation throughout the rest of his career.[23]

Coleridge tended to apologize for his Kantianism. Even when sharing his admiration for Kant with a close friend like J. H. Green (*Letters* IV, p. 792), he felt obliged to send a retrospective disclaimer within ten days clarifying that 'I am no Zealot or Bigot for German Philosophy' (*Letters* IV, p. 793). After the publication of *Biographia Literaria*, Coleridge was hoping to institutionalize his academic interests in form of a 'German Library in London':

> I write now to say, that there has been long brooding a sort of Plan for bringing together the Teutonics, Germans & English, in some sort of Club or Society: so as to have the German Periodical Papers &c, and at the same time to lay the foundation of a German Library in London. (*Letters* IV, p. 794)

Characteristically, Coleridge thought that his Germanophile enterprise required some sort of disguise: '— If the name "German" should have any thing objectionable, it might easily be entitled, The Friends of Northern Literature, Swedish, Danish, and German' (*Letters* IV, p. 794). Anticipating that 'German' was 'objectionable' for Londoners, Coleridge called the library 'Northern' and placed 'German' at the end of the list of nationalities. Coleridge accordingly settled for the non-offensive name 'Library of Northern Literature' in 1820 (*Letters* V, p. 13) explaining that 'our most sensible men look at the German Muses thro' a film of prejudice & utter misconception' (*Letters* V, p. 13). The Anti-Jacobin authors –William Gifford, James Walker and their colleagues – played a significant part in convincing Coleridge that his investment in German metaphysics was a liability. Gifford remained an influential public figure becoming the editor of Murray's *Quarterly Review*. Coleridge complained to Robert Southey in 1820 that the periodical might as well be named the 'Anti-german': 'the Quarterly Review & the prejudices respecting my supposed German Metaphysics (tho' Anti-german would be the more appropriate epithet)' (*Letters* V, p. 51). Hence it is unsurprising that Coleridge omitted Kant's name from his publications. In the *Friend*, Coleridge included, without mentioning Kant's name, the ideality of space and time, 'we perceive and imagine all things under the forms of Space and Time' (*Friend* II, p. 104n), and a few pages further on he assimilated Kantian morality (*Friend* II, p. 125) (Wellek 1931, p. 162).[24] Likewise, Coleridge drew, as we will see in the next chapter, heavily on Kant's *Critique of the Power of Judgment* in his *Essays on the Principles of Genial Criticism* (1814) without acknowledgement. There are further cases when Coleridge used Kantian ideas, but gave biblical, native, or ancient authors most of the credit for them. In Chapter 10 of *Biographia Literaria*, Coleridge claimed that

St. Paul and the Book of Job lead him to doubt the possibility of a rational proof of the existence of God 'before I had met with the Critique of Pure Reason' (*Biographia* I, p. 201) although, as Wellek has pointed out rightly, 'the particular terms of this solution must have been derived from Kant' (1931, p. 115). Coleridge was only ready to address Kant's scepticism openly later on, that is, in his lectures of philosophy starting in December 1818. Shaffer points out Coleridge's strategic deflection from Kant in *Aids to Reflection*. 'The book is a prime example of Coleridge's misleading use of his sources: it is strung as a series of long quotations from Archbishop Leighton, it follows the thread of the argument of Kant's *Religion* through a series of Anglican controversies; it lays Schelling's *On Human Freedom (Über die menschliche Freiheit,*1809) under contribution; and it employs wherever possible traditional religious language' (Shaffer 1970, p. 200; see Shaffer 2004, p. 42). One can add that Coleridge applied a similar strategy in *The Friend* and the *Statesman's Manual*. In *The Friend*, he introduced the Kantian distinction between 'Vernunft' and 'Verstand' as fundamental principle of his thought (see Chapter 7). Instead of acknowledging Kant, Coleridge prefaced his essay with an epitaph by Harrington (*Friend* I, p. 154) and declared in the first sentence of the article: 'If the Reader will substitute the word "Understanding" for "Reason," and the word "Reason" for "*Religion*," Harrington has here completely expressed the Truth for which the Friend is contending' (*Friend* I, p. 154). Previously, in the *Statesman's Manual (Appendix E)* published in 1816, Coleridge drew on the Kantian principle of the merely regulative function of speculative Reason. He mentioned Kant but credited Aristotle before mentioning the German philosopher although the formulation came straight from the *Critique of Reason* (*KrV* B 537), 'whether Ideas are regulative, according to Aristotle and Kant' (*Lay Sermons,* pp. 113–14). The references to Leighton (*Aids*), Harrington (*The Friend*), Aristotle (*Lay Sermons*) and St Paul (*Biographia*) indicate that Coleridge was willing to name his native or ancient sources but refrained from doing so with his Kantian ones. A piece of scrap paper taped into Coleridge's copy of Kant's *Religion* between pages 210 and 211 contains the poet's confession: 'I may be innocently silent but could not innocently disguise' (*Marginalia* III, p. 308).

The reticence about his use of Kant's texts can be further traced in his sketches for his respective projects to teach, lecture and publish on philosophy. The impact of *Anti-Jacobin* seems palpable when comparing Coleridge's career plans in 1796 and in 1803. In 1796, Coleridge still reckoned that a German education including Kant's philosophy would increase his economic prospects. In a letter to Poole, he anticipated:

> If I could realize this scheme, I should there study Chemistry & Anatomy, [and] bring over with me all the works of Semler&Michaelis, the German Theologians, & of Kant, the great german Metaphysician. On my return I would commence a School for 8 young men at 100 guineas each — proposing to perfect them in the following studies in order as follows. (*Letters* I, p. 209)

Kant featured next to Locke and Hartley in the syllabus: 'Man as an Intellectual Being: including the ancient Metaphysics, the systems of Locke & Hartley,—of the Scotch Philosophers—& the new Kantian S[ystem—]' (*Letters* I, p. 209). By the early 1800s, however, German thought, and Kantianism in particular, appeared less lucrative to Coleridge. While continuing his efforts to earn an additional income from his philosophical enquiries, he sought advice from Godwin in 1803 sending him a draft for a book proposal on the history of philosophy. In this letter the name Kant was conspicuously absent from the long list of philosophers ranging from Plato and Aristotle, over Reid, Bacon, Descartes, Condillac, to Hartley (*Letters* II, pp. 947–8). This absence is striking because, as discussed in Chapter 3, Coleridge was studying Kantian ethics around the same time.

Judging from the fragmentary accounts of Coleridge's lectures in later years, now available in the excellent editions by Foakes (*Lectures 1808–19*) and Jackson (*Lectures 1818–19*), Coleridge acknowledged Kant publically by name after 1817 albeit rarely and tentatively.[25] Coleridge appears to have omitted Kant's name in the first 'Lectures on the Principles of Poetry'. Robinson, who started to attend them regularly in 1808 (Holmes 1989, pp. 113–17), observed in his letter to Mrs Clarkson dated to 15 May 1808 that 'Coleridge contrived to work into his speech Kant's admirably profound definition of the naïf, that is *nature putting art to shame*' (*Lectures 1808–19* I, p. 115). It has been noted that '[i]t is not surprising if HCR caught Kantian echoes' (*Lectures 1808–19* I, p. 487). However, Robinson's awareness of the Kantian reference can be explained by his own exceptional expertise in Kantian philosophy rather than Coleridge's open acknowledgement. Coleridge's auditors in 1808 were unaware of his reference unless they were familiar with Kant's or Schiller's work through their own perusal. This changed after the publication of *Biographia Literaria*. In the lectures held between January and March 1819 at the 'Crown and Anchor' Tavern on Arundel Street to the south of the Strand (Jackson 2000, p. xxxvi; *Lectures 1818–19* II, p. 506), Coleridge not only used Kantian concepts, but he explicitly referred to Kant's contribution to the debates on scepticism.

It is telling that he did so while standing on a table in the 'Crown and Anchor', addressing his audience: 'What! We have been told that a truly great man, Professor Kant, has justified this scepticism. Now that requires an answer' (*Lectures 1818–19* II, pp. 536–7; see also I, p. 151; II, p. 503; II, pp. 584–8). Coleridge's tone is assertive and almost teasing. As Jackson observes, 'the very specific introduction of Kant at this point [in Lecture Twelve] is unusual' (2000, p. cxxxiv). Indeed, I propose that Coleridge's open acknowledgement had to do with the setting of his lecture as well as with his audience. The venue for the lectures on philosophy, including Lectures Twelve and Thirteen, in which Coleridge finally spoke of Kant openly, was a place associated with political radicalism (Jackson 2000, p. xxxvi). Not long before his death, Coleridge still remembered the rough crowd of the 'Crown & Anchor Patriots' (*Marginalia* III, p. 146). Godwin's diary reveals, in the entry of 29 March 1819, that two former members of Nitsch's Kantian Society, Thomas Wirgman and Henry Richter, attended the lecture alongside Godwin (Myers et al. 2010). Wirgman and Richter might have attended the lectures regularly. No wonder that Coleridge felt at ease to leave the Kantian closet. The 'Crown and Anchor' and the people in the audience appeared congenial to the open expression of Kantian philosophy to Coleridge. The attendants and the setting might also have reminded Coleridge of his early Kantian days. Indeed, these two performances that name Kant appear as a liberating experience when Coleridge temporarily forgot about the stigma of being a German 'Zealot' or 'Bigot' (*Letters* IV, p. 793).

Coleridge mentioned Kant's sceptical stance briefly in the lecture without elaborating this dimension of Kant's *Critique of Pure Reason* and *Religion* (*Lectures 1818–19* II, pp. 536–7). Owen Barfield observed in the introduction and notes to the lectures that Coleridge's 'treatment of German philosophy in general in the same lecture [lecture 13]' was 'sketchy' (*Lectures 1818–19* II, p. 874). Barfield explained:

> The subject, as announced, was to have been 'the GERMAN PHILOSOPHY with its bearings on the System of Locke, comprising the systems of Leibniz, Kant and Schelling'. In fact, though something is indeed said about Leibniz's critique of Locke, there is no mention of Fichte, nor of any other of the German school except Kant, who is accorded less space than had been allowed in earlier lectures to St. Theresa and Agrippa, and except Schelling, who is dismissed for lack of time and because the lecturer 'should be puzzled to give you a true account'. (*Lectures 1818–19* II, p. 874)

Like Barfield, I think that we cannot take this brevity solely as the effect of Coleridge's ill health and fatigue and therefore suggest that such sketchiness was also a sign of his remaining inhibition to speak in public about German philosophy. What Coleridge said about Kant in the lecture, however, can be seen as a public embrace. Following his own inclination, Coleridge drew the attention of his audience to Kantian ethics, the constitutive function of Reason and the categorical imperative. He proclaimed in Lecture Thirteen that

> [Kant] disclosed what I may call the [proof] of his Christianity which rendered him truly deserving the name of philosopher and not the analysis of mind. He says, in my . . . into the whole human being. There is yet another, and not only another, but a far higher and nobler, constituent of his being, his will, the 'practical reason'. (*Lectures 1818–19* II, pp. 585–6)

In agreement with his Christian interpretation, and the view taken by the dissenter Morgan (1807, p. 7), Coleridge paraphrased the categorical imperative in terms of 'Christ's "golden rule" in Matt 7.12' (*Lectures 1818–19* II, p. 586n):

> this [practical Reason] does not announce itself by arguing but by direct command and precept: thou shalt do to others as thou wouldst be done by, thou shalt act so that there shall be no contradiction in thy being. And from this he deduced a direct moral necessity for the belief or the faith of reason. (*Lectures 1818–19* II, p. 586)

On the one hand, one can see in Lecture Thirteen a glimpse of Coleridge's first encounter with the categorical imperative in the radical milieu of the 1790s and sense the liberating atmosphere Coleridge enjoyed when proclaiming that Kant was 'truly deserving the name of philosopher' (*Lectures 1818–19* II, p. 874). On the other hand, the brevity of Coleridge's account, for instance, the omission of the atheistic Fichte, signals that Coleridge's reluctance to reveal the extent of his knowledge of German metaphysics continued even after 1815 when Jacobinism had lost its threat for Britain and radicalism experienced a revival.

In the 1810s and 1820s, Kantian metaphysics continued to be a source of public humiliation for Coleridge. William Hazlitt ridiculed his former mentor in his notorious review of *Biographia Literaria* in the *Edinburgh Review* on the grounds of Coleridge's profound adherence to Kantian metaphysics: 'floating or sinking in fine Kantean categories [taking] the first butterfly theory, fancy-bred from the maggots of his brain' (Hazlitt 1933 XVI, p. 118). In Hazlitt's eyes, Kant epitomized the failure of Coleridge's *Biographia* (Hazlitt 1933 XVI, p. 123). It is true that in earlier articles Hazlitt expressed his interest in certain basic elements of Kant's philosophy that matched Hazlitt's own opposition to the Lockean tradition (Wellek 1931, p. 171; see Natarajan 1998, pp. 154–9), yet he firmly rejected Coleridge's use of critical philosophy in *Biographia*. The *Blackwood's Magazine* and the *New Monthly Magazine* largely agreed with Hazlitt's assessment in 1817. The former noted that the 'greatest piece of Quackery in the Book, is his pretended account of the Metaphysical System of Kant' (Jackson 1970, p. 348). Likewise, the *New Monthly Magazine* criticized that 'such a cloudiness of metaphysical jargon in the mystical language of the Platonists and schoolmen, of Kant and Jacob Behmen' (Jackson 1970, p. 322). While the third edition of *The Friend* elicited positive reviews in the years following its publication in 1818, the reviews kept censuring Coleridge for his Germanophilia. 'But what shall we say of Mr. Coleridge . . . ?', wrote the *London Magazine* in April 1820, 'he is of the transcendental German school' (Jackson 1970, p. 452). Sadly, even Henry Nelson Coleridge shared this negative view. He wrote a supposed defence of his father-in-law and published it in the *Etonian* in 1821. In the article, Henry Nelson Coleridge praised British common sense philosophy; 'Lord Bacon and Sir Isaac Newton both made as great advances in knowledge of Mind and Nature as any two men that ever lived' (Jackson 1970, p. 462), but he dismissed idealist philosophy in a sweeping fashion: 'I do not affirm that this whole system of commingled Platonism, Kantianism, and Christianity may not be true; but I do affirm, and I fear not contradiction, that it will never be useful' (Jackson 1970, p. 462). A close family member like his son-in-law regarded Coleridge's investment in idealism as useless. This hostile atmosphere towards Kantianism did not change significantly until after Coleridge's death.

People and places

While it is generally thought that Coleridge learnt little about Kant while in Germany, statements by Coleridge, such as his having read all about the controversies surrounding Lessing, point to his knowledge of publications like Reinhold's *Briefe*, Kant's 'Orientation' essay and other materials on critical philosophy that contributed to the pantheism controversy. Coleridge possibly also profited from the expertise of the German *Popularphilosophen*, Feder, Buhle and Schulze or their publications. Due to its fashionable status by 1786, Kantianism was part of Coleridge's social life while travelling through Holstein and Lower Saxony. By the time Coleridge returned to England, the public attitude towards German thought had changed from tentative Germanophilia in the mid-1790s to growing Germanophobia spearheaded by counter-revolutionaries. Coleridge's conflicted attitude towards Kantianism was largely shaped by these early developments and reinforced by the hostility with which Coleridge's metaphysics were met in the press in the 1810s and 1820s. Evidence from Godwin's diary and the setting of Coleridge's lectures in the 'Crown and Anchor' Tavern in early 1819 further support the argument that Coleridge's public endorsement of Kant depended largely on the friendly predisposition of his audience and venue. The only place that Coleridge deemed congenial enough to address Kant's scepticism publically in the late 1810s was associated with political radicalism (Jackson 2000, p. xxxvi). Coleridge's public endorsements of Kant in lectures or in print were exceptions. Therefore his most enthusiastic advocacy of Kant published in *Biographia Literaria* (1817) requires detailed analysis.

6

Kant's Giant Hand: Repression and Genial Self-Construction in *Biographia Literaria*

During the period between Coleridge's study of Kant in 1801 and the time of composition of *Biographia Literaria*, Coleridge's health declined mainly as a result of his opium addiction. Due to his ill health, he travelled to Malta in April 1804, served as secretary to Alexander Ball, returned via Italy and arrived back in England in August 1806, where he separated from his wife (Engell and Bate 1983, p. xliv). His self-esteem suffered above all from the loss of the immediate company of the two people he loved and admired most, Wordsworth and Sara Hutchinson: 'Wordsworth has given me up' (cited in Engell and Bate 1983, p. xliv). These painful events were accompanied by changes in Coleridge's religious and political thought.

Chapter 4 has shown that Coleridge gradually adopted a pro-war and counter-revolutionary position from 1802 onwards and condemned the politics of first principles as a form of Jacobinism, turning instead to the principle of expedience. These drastic changes were bound up with Coleridge's religious reorientation. During the first decade of the nineteenth century, Coleridge stopped identifying with Unitarianism. 'Even during the years', John Beer notes, 'when Coleridge was a Unitarian, his religious thinking was disturbed by intellectual conflict' (1993, p. xliii). And one might add that even when he was no longer a Unitarian, the sceptical dimension of Unitarianism 'remained with him to the last' (S. Coleridge 1847, p. lxvii). The way he scrutinized natural theology predisposed and attracted him to Kant's *critique*. While his interest in Kant persisted throughout his life, his Unitarian period 'lasted at least until his journey to Malta in 1804' (Beer 1993, p. xliii). Some roots of Coleridge's Unitarianism were preserved, for instance, in his thought of the 'One Life', manifest in the famous lines added to 'The Eolian Harp', 'O! the one Life within us and abroad', which appear on the errata sheets of *Sybilline Leaves* in 1817 (Perry 1999, p. 69). Yet we can see his disenchantment with Unitarianism distinctively in his notebook entry on February 1805 (Ulmer 2006, pp. 526–44): 'Unitarianism in all its Forms is Idolatry' (*Notebooks* II, §2448). Coleridge felt the need to find a position which would allow him to accommodate the thinking of St Paul and St John. To the latter he looked for doctrines on 'the conviction of man's sin and unworthiness before God; to St John for the doctrine (unfolded in the fourth Gospel) that showed the workings of the Creative Word as an essential part of the whole divine process' (Beer 1993, p. xlii). A series of letters to George Fricker and Thomas Clarkson dating from the autumn of 1806 include Coleridge's religious confession (Tee 2009, p. 36): 'I have experienced a similar alteration. I was for many years a Socinian; and at times almost a Naturalist, but sorrow, and ill health, and disappointment in the only deep wish I had ever cherished, forced me to look into myself; . . . I became fully convinced, that Socinianism . . . scarcely deserved the name of a religion in any sense' (*Letters* II, p. 1189). By 1806, it is clear that Coleridge no longer regarded himself as a follower of Priestley's Unitarianism. Despite these fundamental changes in Coleridge's intellectual positions, I propose that his interest in the philosophy of Kant remained an example of his constancy.

Before announcing the principles of transcendentalism in Chapter 12 of *Biographia Literaria*, Coleridge admitted that 'it requires some courage to avow it [transcendental philosophy] in an age and country, in which disquisitions on all subjects, not privileged to adopt technical terms or scientific symbols, must be addressed to the PUBLIC' (*Biographia* I, p. 236). Coleridge was still concerned about the response of the public to his transmission of German philosophy partly because of his fear of being charged with the importation of the 'exotic poison from the envenomed crucibles . . . of the New German school' (*Anti-Jacobin Review* 4 [1799], p. vii) and partly because he was aware of Kant's Christian unorthodoxy and republicanism. Coleridge added with forced determination that 'it is time to tell the truth' (*Biographia* I, p. 236) as if he had not dared to make the stipulations in chapter 12 public any earlier. It is likely that it took Coleridge equal courage to publicize his fascination with critical philosophy in *Biographia Literaria*:

> The writings of the illustrious sage of Königsberg, the founder of the Critical Philosophy, more than any other work, at once invigorated and disciplined my understanding. The originality, the depth, and the compression of the thoughts; the novelty and subtlety, yet the solidity and importance, of the distinctions; the adamantine chain of the logic; and I will venture to add (paradox as it will appear to those who have taken their notion of IMMANUEL KANT, from Reviewers and Frenchmen) the *clearness* and *evidence*, of the 'CRITIQUE OF THE PURE REASON;' of the JUDGMENT; of the 'METAPHYSICAL ELEMENTS OF NATURAL PHILOSOPHY,' and of his 'RELIGION WITHIN THE BOUNDS OF PURE REASON,' took possession of me as with a giant's hand. (*Biographia* I, p. 153)

This passage constitutes a highly crafted piece of myth-making and has wide ramifications.

'Reviewers' and 'Frenchmen'

In the first place, Coleridge affirmed the philosophy's '*clearness*'. He thus contradicted the common charge against Kant's obscurity (e.g. *Monthly Magazine* 1 [1796], p. 266). At the same time, however, the statement also belittled those who admitted the difficulties in understanding the theory. Scholars have observed that Coleridge tried to distinguish himself from 'Reviewers and Frenchmen' (Morrison 1995, p. 180; Vigus 2009, p. 39; Class 2009, p. 51). Wellek attached great importance to a damning review in the January issue of *Edinburgh Review* (1931, p. 32): 'Review of "Philosophie de Kant, ou Principes Fondamentaux de la Philosophie Transcendentale, &c. The Philosophy of Kant, or, The Fundamental Principles of Transcendental Metaphysics. By Charles de Villers, Fellow of the Royal Society of Sciences of Göttingen"' (*Edinburgh Review* 1 [1802–3], pp. 253–80). Building on Wellek, Robert Morrison identifies Thomas Brown, Professor of Moral Philosophy at Edinburgh (1810–20), as the 'Reviewer' and Charles de Villers, author of *Philosophie de Kant*, as the Frenchman (1995, p. 180). James Vigus argues more convincingly that Coleridge aimed at Mme de Staël, whose work on German aesthetics appeared in English in 1813: 'he would have considered that Staël made too many concessions to popular readability' (2009, p. 39). Considering the plural employed by Coleridge, his censorship of 'Frenchmen' referred to several writers and probably included Jean-Joseph Mounier, the author of a concise article on Kant (see Chapters 1 and 5). Similarly, the mention of 'Reviewers' comprised a number of critics ranging from Beddoes, Enfield and Taylor to Walker (see Chapter 1; Micheli 1990, pp. 202–314). Rather than attacking specific individuals, it seems more likely that Coleridge had an interest in belittling every mediator of critical philosophy. Coleridge's private comments on the Germans who helped popularize Kant's philosophy were similarly hostile: '50 Vol. of Comments' followed by '&c &c &c' (*Marginalia* III, p. 319) suggests that Coleridge thought there had been too much additional commentary on Kant.

Coleridge's repression of Kant's association with Jacobinism

In the second place, the absence of *Perpetual Peace* from Coleridge's list of his cherished Kantian works is noticeable. Coleridge built his praise exclusively on non-political merit: 'originality', 'depth' and 'compression of the through'. David Simpson and David Baulch have done much to reintroduce Coleridge's response to Kant into the debate of Coleridge's politics. Departing from Peacock's satire in *Nightmare Abby*, Simpson has discerned that Coleridge played an active role, besides Mme de Staël, in transforming German philosophy into a conservative creed for English society (1993, p. 102).[1] Baulch, in his thought-provoking analysis of *Biographia Literaria*, has also commented on the apolitical nature of this construction of Kant. Without further historical investigation, Baulch has proposed, on the basis of two biographies, that 'Coleridge does not seem to make a significant association of Kant without radical politics' (Baulch 2004, p. 568). I hope that readers of the previous three chapters of the present book agree with me that this assumption is wrong. Coleridge's apolitical description of Kant makes perfect sense if we consider that Kant had been rejected by the British mainstream around 1800 on the grounds of his alleged conflation of atheism and revolutionary ideas (Chapter 1). However, Kant's essential link with Jacobinism leads to a controversy in Coleridge studies: the question of apostasy.

Norman Fruman has pointed out that James Engell, the editor of the first volume of the Bollingen edition of the *Biographia*, thoroughly traced Coleridge's philosophical sources but failed to record the charges by William Hazlitt and John Thelwall (1985, pp. 152–4). Thelwall wrote his objections against Coleridge's anti-Jacobin statements on the margins of his copy of the *Biographia* rebuking his former friend as a turncoat (Burwick 1989, p. xvi):

> [T]hat Mr C. was indeed far from Democracy, because he was far beyond it, I well remember – for he was a down right zealous leveller & indeed in one of the worst sense of the word he was a Jacobin, a man of blood. (Pollin 1970, p. 81)

Hazlitt, too, had scoffed at Coleridge's disclaimer from his Jacobin sympathies: 'we are quite safe in asserting, that [Coleridge's principles in the *Watchman* and *Conciones ad Populum*] were still more opposite to those of the Anti-Jacobins, and the party to which he admits he has gone over' (Hazlitt 1933 XVI, p. 129).[2] For Hazlitt, *Biographia Literaria* was an example of the 'true history of our reformed Antijacobin poets; the life of one whom is here recorded' (Hazlitt 1933 XVI, p. 138). Based on the charges against the *Biographia*, Fruman accused Coleridge of having deliberately and consistently misrepresented his past and declared that 'there cannot at this late date any longer be a legitimate controversy over whether or not the early Coleridge was a Jacobin and a believer of democracy' (1985, p. 152; see also 1989, pp. 1–19; 1992, pp. 115–33). Contrary to this statement, the controversy has continued. Thomas McFarland, Fruman's chief opponent in this matter, argued that Coleridge's conservatism was consistent with his past (McFarland 1989, pp. 191–232; 1995, pp. 75–139). The controversy, however, only scratches the surface as long as it still subscribes to Coleridge's claim that his interest in metaphysics was non-political: 'For the young English politician belief was a necessity of life, not of speculation' (Hort 1856, p. 323).

Where does Kant come into this? Coleridge was capable of what he called 'half contradictions' (*Friend* II, p. 124). By 'half-contradictions', Coleridge meant that philosophical positions could be made subservient to certain political objectives. The first instance, I shall discuss in some detail is taken from Coleridge's *The Friend* (1809). Coleridge did not perceive his own capacity for 'half contradictions'; on the contrary, he claimed that *The Friend* was 'the best antidote to Falsehoods' (*Friend* II, p. 124). Accordingly, Coleridge detected the capability for 'half contradictions' in others:

> I do not mean, that this great man Man [Edmund Burke] supported different Principles at different æreas [sic] of his political Life. On the contrary, no man was ever more like himself! . . . . The inconsistency to which I allude, is of a different kind: it is the want of congruity in the Principles appealed to in different parts of the same Work, it is apparent versatility of the Principle with the Occasion. If his Opponents are Theorists, then every thing is to be founded on PRUDENCE, on mere calculations of EXPEDIENCY . . . . Are his Opponents Calculators? *Then* Calculation itself is represented as a sort of crime. God has given us FEELINGS . . . I have not forgotten, that Burke defended these half contradictions. (*Friend* II, pp. 123–4)

Coleridge exposed the fact that Burke became a proponent of expedience when it served Burke to oppose theorists, or vice versa. However, Coleridge's use of philosophy was not entirely dissimilar from that of Burke. He was also capable of 'half contradictions' when it came to applying Kantian philosophy to politics. Chapter 4 has elucidated that Coleridge equated Jacobinism with the politics that are based on first principles. Although Coleridge still wrote privately that 'political Freedom can only arise from moral Freedom' (cited in Evans 1935, p. 255), he publically recanted the notion that politics should be based on 'archetypal IDEAS co-essential with the Reason, and the consciousness of which is the sign and necessary product of its full development' (*Friend* II, p. 105). Scholars have examined the conservative implications of Coleridge's rejection of rationality in politics (Simpson 1993, pp. 57–63). Coleridge even anticipated that his essay 'On the Principles of Political Philosophy' would be met with 'charge[s] of inconsistency' (*Friend* II, p. 104). Commentators have disagreed about the nature of the inconsistency. I contend that it consisted in Coleridge's use of Kantian principles to establish a complete separation between morality and politics. Although Coleridge apparently succeeded in convincing generations of scholars of British Romanticism that his engagement with Kant's philosophy had always been 'purely' philosophical (moral, aesthetic, metaphysical) and utterly divorced from politics, the investigation of his early encounter with critical philosophy in the previous three chapters shows that, although Coleridge might have been able to convince himself otherwise, it could not have escaped any reader of the 1790s English Kantian materials that Kant's writings included republican content and was wholly identified with radical politics. After all, the very first (extant) notice in 1787 warned Britons already that Kant had been used to inflame peasants in Brandenburg (*Political Magazine* 12 [1787], p. 94). It is time to establish a scholarly awareness that much of Coleridge's defence against the charges of Jacobinism rests on the wedge between Kantian moral theology and politics that Coleridge created.

I agree with Deirdre Coleman's erudite study that Coleridge's *The Friend* (1809) 'fails to do justice to Rousseau's *Du Contrat Social* (1988, p. 147) and that Coleridge is deeply indebted to Kant's thought. However, I disagree, as we have seen in Chapters 3 and 4, with her assessment of Kant's political position: his alleged 'pragmatic conservatism – his tendency to endorse the prevailing system of government' (1988, p. 155). According to Coleman, Coleridge's conservative *The Friend* 'is echoing Kant's own acknowledgement of the formal nature of his moral philosophy, the fact that it is confined to the enunciation of an ideal only' (1988, p. 159). Coleman disregards the republican stance behind Kant's morality. Contrary to her thesis, I propose that Coleridge appropriated Kant's principle for his conservative outlook despite the radical and transformative power of critical philosophy. It is known that *The Friend* is replete with Kant's moral principles (Wellek 1931, pp. 107–8). Yet the tensions between Coleridge's lasting admiration for Kant's philosophy and his conservative reorientation have been overlooked.

Coleridge wholeheartedly endorsed as 'undeniable Truth[s]' (*Friend* II, p. 125) the moral merits of Reason derived from Kant that 'the distinction between Person and Things consists herein, that the latter may rightfully be used, altogether and merely, as a *Means*; but the former must always be included in the *End*, and form a part of the final Cause' (*Friend* II, p. 125) and that 'Man must be *free*' (*Friend* II, p. 126). This argument seems incongruent with the subsequent declaration that the 'Application of these Principles to the social State' was a form of Jacobinism. Considering that he fervently supported these principles, why should they not inform public policies?

We have seen in Chapter 3 that Coleridge encountered the categorical imperative for the first time as part of his activism as a radical and Unitarian. Kant's categorical imperative opposed feudalism and was in part the result of Rousseau's formative impact; as Kant said, Rousseau taught him 'democratic respect for the common person' early in his career (Lawler 2005, p. 459). Contrary to all these historical factors, *The Friend* introduced the categorical imperative in such a way that it deprived it of any political potential: 'So act that thou mayest be able without involving any contradiction to will that the Maxim of thy Conduct should be the Law of all intelligent Beings' (*Friend* II, p. 128). Not only did Coleridge omit the Jacobin name Kant, he also made sure to tame the categorical imperative and to disconnect it explicitly from any form of political activism: the categorical imperative is 'the one universal and sufficient Principle and Guide of Morality. Any why? Because the *object* of Morality is not the outward act, but the internal Maxims of our Actions' (*Friend* II, p. 128). The stipulation of disinterestedness can be found in the *Groundwork*; however, the strict separation of morality from outward action in such vehement terms as 'And [only] so far it is infallible' (*Friend* II, p. 128) is Coleridge's addition. In comparison to Coleridge's first sketch of the categorical imperative in his notebook between late 1795 and early 1796, this version seems completely impotent. *The Friend* contains further aspects that enhance our understanding of Coleridge's engagement with the moral law over a period of about two decades.

For those who take a closer look at *The Friend*, it will be evident that the paper was far from relinquishing the constitutive power of Reason in its Kantian version completely. Even if Coleridge banned it from the political arena and suggested indirectly that this separation was Kantian, we can see the remnants of his radical and Unitarian past in the striking affinities with Nitsch's treatise. These traces emerge for instance from Coleridge's description of the awful and invisible power of law inside of us. Although Coleridge severed Reason from the laws of government, he emphasized its importance for the individual within the state: 'This [spirit of the law] is the true necessity, which compels man into the social State, now and always, by a still-beginning, never-ceasing force of moral Cohesion' (*Friend* II, p. 101). Coleridge probably drew on his own experiences in Malta when he witnessed the extraordinary achievement of a captain to dissuade the crew from committing mutiny (Holmes 1998, pp. 27–9). The story tried to explain how ordinary men arrive at the knowledge of the moral principles inside of them. Coleridge recalled how the captain's discipline regarding himself and others, his sense of justice, empathy with pain and disdain of pride solicited in his men a new sense of self-worth and willingness to abide by rules. Coleridge described this new sense as follows:

> An invisible Power it was, that quelled them [offender within the crew], a Power, which was therefore irresistible, because it took away the very Will of resisting? It was the aweful [sic] power of LAW, acting on natures pre-configured to its influences. A Faculty was appealed to in the Offender's own being; a Faculty and a Presence, of which he had not been previously made aware- but that answered to the appeal! its real Existence therefore could not be doubted, or its reply rendered inaudible! (*Friend* II, pp. 100–1)

The captain managed to oblige an offender within the crew to heed the voice of a hitherto unnoticed faculty within him. Coleridge described the offenders as an 'uneducated' or convicted man (*Friend* II, p. 99). He stressed the universality of the moral faculty by describing it as one that had been 'preconfigured', while he also pointed out that the men 'had not been made previously aware' of it. Through the example and guidance of the captain the men of the crew start to hear the voice of the 'invisible Power' of 'LAW' and abide by it. It is an act that has to be learnt despite the human predisposition for it. For Coleridge the sense of the law was identical with the sense of self. This identity was possible because free-will and the moral law coalesced: '*for me* its power is the same with that of my own permanent Self, and that all the Choice, which is permitted to me, consists in having it form my Guardian Angel or my avenging Fiend! This is the Spirit of LAW!' (*Friend* II, p. 101). Although Coleridge praised the captain's power to stimulate the moral law in his crew, the 'Ancient Mariner' suggests that Coleridge had the tendency to rather identify with the offenders on board the ship; the protagonist of this ballad shoots an albatross and thus brings misery over the whole crew (Perry 1999, p. 282). Consequently, the identification of self and the moral law can be understood as an appeal to others as much as to Coleridge himself.

Coleridge's illustrations closely resemble those of Nitsch. The 1796 treatise established the identity of human will, practical Reason and the laws of freedom:

> The HUMAN WILL is determined by PRACTICAL REASON, therefore it is FREE . . . . As the human will is free, the formal Practical Principles of Reason are the true laws of freedom, for it is by keeping to them only that man can elevate himself above the influence of the surrounding world, and follow the natural laws of his reason. (Nitsch 1796, pp. 198–202)

Nitsch carefully related this abstract principle to people's lives as closely as possible. In doing so, he addressed the question of 'Who can, however, strictly execute such rigorous laws?' (1796, p. 204). For the future author of the 'Ancient Mariner', it must have been consoling to read that Nitsch conceded that 'no mortal will ever be able to execute them completely' (1796, p. 204). Furthermore, Nitsch discussed the same topic as Coleridge's tale of the brave captain in *The Friend*: 'How can man arrive at an accurate knowledge of the moral laws?' (1796, p. 202). Like Coleridge, Nitsch was aware that to 'obey any law supposes knowledge of it' (1796, p. 202). Like the English poet, Nitsch explained that people might not be conscious of the moral law inside of them despite humans' universal predisposition to it. He gave the following explanation:

> Man arrives at the knowledge of the Moral Law, or the law of his natural freedom, by the consciousness of the operations of his reason, although he is often a loss to express them by words, or does not clearly understand them. Let him only ask himself when conversing with his friends and the world, Is my mode of action such as to be fit for an universal law of conduct among reasonable beings? (Nitsch 1796, pp. 202–3)

Becoming aware of the moral law inside of us is a communal act for Nitsch as well as Coleridge. Coleridge accounted for it through the captain's interaction with his crew,

Nitsch through the conversation with friends and the observation of our environment. Neither Coleridge nor Nitsch excluded emotions from the moral law. According to *The Friend* (1809), the moral law is something that affects us powerfully, as it involves both feeling and thought in much the same way as Coleridge described the moral law in 1803 (see Chapter 3). So too does Nitsch note explicitly that we become aware of the moral law 'by paying due attention to the natural emotions of the heart and conscience' (1796, p. 202). Coleridge observed a similar point and recorded it in his notebook in 1810: 'I possess Reason, or a Law of Right and Wrong, which uniting with my sense of moral responsibility constitutes the voice of Conscience' (*Notebooks* III, §4005). Nitsch was aware that certain aspects in Kant's exposition of the categorical imperative in the *Groundwork* required fleshing out. He admitted that Kant's notion of duty was unusually demanding, that the moral law required an awareness that cannot necessarily be presupposed and that the impulse of the heart and conscience were acceptable as forms of moral inspiration until people reached a higher level of rationality. Nitsch's introduction to Kantian ethics appears to have struck a chord with Coleridge.

Despite these affinities, Coleridge's 1809 illustration of the moral law and Nitsch's explanation differ crucially in terms of their sociopolitical implications: Coleridge's tale is set in a fierce hierarchical environment on board a military ship and involves the infliction of physical punishment. The voice of conscience ultimately serves to reinforce military orders. This appropriation of Kantian ethics is neither supported by Kant's examples in the *Groundwork* nor elsewhere nor by Nitsch's explanation. In stark contrast to Coleridge, Nitsch aimed to open up the moral law in egalitarian terms: 'the emotions of the heart and conscience change in proportion as knowledge encreases [sic]; they are different in different persons . . . . It is very well for a man to follow the influence of his heart and conscience, while he knows of no other guides' (1796, pp. 202–3). Nitsch's formulation points to the influence of the Scottish common sense school, perhaps more importantly, however, it reflects his efforts to open up Kant's moral law for people of different classes (excluding women in so far as the treatise only addresses men). Contrary to Nitsch, Coleridge's invocation of the moral law in *The Friend* strengthened social hierarchies by reinforcing the mariners' subordination. In much the same way as Coleridge described Burke's capacity for 'half contradictions', Coleridge presented Kant's moral principle as a means to separate himself from his radical past. Ironically, Coleridge used a Jacobin philosopher to defend himself against the charges of Jacobinism. Still, Coleridge became the most important mediator of Kantian philosophy in the nineteenth century. *The Friend* went through three editions, 1809–10, 1812 and the three-volume one of 1818. Eager to suppress Kant's and his own Jacobinism, Coleridge played a major role in making Kant known as a proponent of conservatism.

A further 'half-contradiction' consisted in Coleridge's use of the same strategy of divorcing metaphysics and morals from politics in *Biographia Literaria*. It has often been commented that Coleridge's narrative structure resembles *Tristram Shandy* (Engell 2002, p. 62); fiction is an essential part of *Biographia Literaria*. What gives us historical insights are the discrepancies between Coleridge's narrative self-construction and historical evidence; his departures and omissions are revealing and help us to understand his intellectual development as well as each of his works. Chapter 10 already begins with such a discrepancy. The most delicate part of this chapter is Coleridge's attempt to establish 'how opposite even then my principles were to those of jacobinism' (*Biographia* I, p. 184). Yet Coleridge understates the significance of the entire chapter by heading it with the note: '*A chapter of digression and anecdotes, as an interlude preceding that on the nature and genesis of the imagination or plastic power*' (*Biographia* I, p. 168). Subsequently, Coleridge set up an opposition between 'fashionable philosophy' (*Biographia* I, p. 199) and 'my thoughts and studies to the foundations of religion and morals' (p. 200). Coleridge used an argument similar to Abbé Barruel's conspiracy theory by criticizing the 'tendency to infidelity or scepticism in the educated classes' (*Biographia* I, p. 199) and by linking it directly to the violent outcome of the French Revolution: 'The same principles dressed in the ostentatious garb of a fashionable philosophy once more rose triumphant and effected the French revolution' (*Biographia* I, p. 199). Like Barruel, Coleridge hinged the blame for the bloodshed on the 'detestable maxims and correspondent measures of the late French despotism' (*Biographia* I, p. 199). In contradistinction to such conspiratorial philosophy, the text makes the repeated claim that Coleridge's settling into a cottage in Nether Stowey in late 1796 amounted to a retirement from politics: 'I retired to a cottage at Stowey' (*Biographia* I, p. 187); 'I retired to a cottage in Somersetshire at the foot of Quantock' (*Biographia* I, p. 200). The retreat from politics consisted in philosophical studies: Coleridge 'devoted [his] thoughts and studies to the foundations of religion and morals' (*Biographia* I, p. 200). This is another instance of Coleridge's use of Kantian philosophy for his defence against the charges of Jacobinism. I agree with Wellek that Coleridge's criticism of the Cartesian evidence 'could not have been written in the form it stands without the knowledge of Kant' (1931, p. 103). The subject of Coleridge's study and his alleged retreat from politics was known in England through Nitsch as a Kantian topic:

> I was pleased with the Cartesian opinion, that the idea of God is distinguished from all other ideas by involving its *reality*; but I was not wholly satisfied. I began then to ask myself, what proof I had of the outward *existence* of any thing? . . . I saw, that in the nature of things such proof is impossible; and that of all modes of being, that are not objects of the senses, the existence is *assumed* by a logical necessity arising from the constitution of the mind itself. (*Biographia* I, p. 200)

The passage paraphrases the results of Kant's refutation of the ontological argument for the existence of God, which I have outlined in Chapter 1 (*KrV* B 627). As discussed in Chapter 1, Kant arrived in England under the auspices of rational theology and English periodicals transmitted the particular focus which Reinhold had developed to make the *Critique of Pure Reason* a pertinent source for the pantheism controversy. As a result, Kant's 'Transcendental Dialectic' lay at the heart of the contemporary discussion on the German philosopher not only in the German states, but also in London; 1796 was the anus mirabilis in the early dissemination of Kantian texts. Coleridge's mentor Beddoes published an article on Kant using Reinhold during this year. Nitsch was the exponent who laid out Kant's theological principles in most detail among the English mediators. This passage in Chapter 10 of *Biographia Literaria* recounts Coleridge's study of the topic of Kant's 'Transcendental Dialectic' in late 1796. Contrary to the persistent view that J. F. A. Hort (1856, p. 317) and John H. Muirhead (1930, p. 56) put forward many years ago, I contend that it is very unlikely that Coleridge merely used these Kantian terms retrospectively. Coleridge must have become acquainted with English versions of them at the time. Coleridge however did not acknowledge Kant as a source. What is suspiciously absent not only from this depiction but also from the rest of Coleridge's work is the fact that Kant was associated with those 'detestable' French 'maxims'. In 1796 the *Gentleman's Magazine* had reported explicitly that all that could be learnt from Kant's philosophy was 'that like the French, all first principles are to be done away, and we are to being with a new set [of principles]' (*Gentleman's Magazine* 66 [1796], p. 137). It is revealing that Coleridge's narrative embraces the counter-revolutionary condemnation of conspiratorial French philosophy spearheaded by Barruel but omits the fact that engaging with Kant, as Chapter 10 suggests that Coleridge did in 1796, was seen as equally Jacobin.

Coleridge's deliberate repression of Kant's political stance emerges from a further discrepancy between his presentation and historical fact. The narrative constructs Kant as intimidated aged man. According to Coleridge,

> He [Kant] had been in imminent danger of persecution during the reign of the late king of Prussia, that strange compound of lawless debauchery, and priest-ridden superstition: and it is probable that he had little inclination, in his old age, to act over again the fortunes, and hair-breath escapes of Wolf [sic]. (*Biographia* I, p. 154)

The passage alludes to the reprimand delivered by Johann Christoph Wöllner under Friedrich Wilhelm II in October 1794 (Stangeth 2003, p. xl; see Chapter 4). 'Priest-ridden superstition' is an allusion to the king's belief in clairvoyance (Stangeth 2003, p. xxxiii). The reprimand threatened Kant with unpleasant measures ('unangenehme Verfügungen') if he continued denigrating Christianity (cited in Stangeth 2003, p. xl), which certainly meant 'dismissal or forced retirement without pension, and could have included banishment' (Kühn 2001, p. 379). Kant responded to the reprimand with a letter to the king in which he objected that he could not have 'negatively evaluated Christianity because he had not evaluated Christianity at all' (Kühn 2001, p. 380). However, Kant promised his majesty Friedrich Wilhelm II to refrain from 'discoursing publicly, in lectures or writings, on religion, whether natural or revealed' (Kühn 2001, p. 380); a promise that Kant respected until the death of Friedrich Wilhelm II in 1797 and not longer as the promise was made to this king and not his successor. Kant was not a victim in this incident. On the contrary, Kant had consciously provoked the censors in Berlin. The royal ministers had been uncertain as to how to respond to Kant's insistence on scepticism. Due to their indecision, the king interfered. Nonetheless, no severe measures against Kant ensued and Kant was able to 'show his true colours' (Kühn 2001, p. 380). So unsatisfactory was the whole affair for Friedrich Wilhelm II that he had Wöllner reprimanded for his leniency and his ineffectiveness in suppressing the forces of rationalism.

Further repressive attempts ensued in Halle. A commission was ordered to investigate the orthodoxy of the professors at the local university in 1794. But students rioted, smashing windows of the hotel where the members of the commission stayed, and thus made them leave the city (Kühn 2001, pp. 380–1). None of the sociopolitically transformative power of Kant is evident in Coleridge's description. On the contrary, Coleridge tellingly omitted the fact that the reprimand did not prevent Kant from publishing his republican pamphlet *Perpetual Peace* in 1795 and that Kant published his response to the king in *Streit der Fakultäten* (*Conflict of the Faculties*). Kant stopped teaching in 1796; his mental powers began to decline that year (Kühn 2001, pp. 386–422). But Coleridge's assumption that Kant's old age entailed retreat is not supported by Kant's actions during the period. Kant rekindled his theological disputes right after the death of Friedrich Wilhelm II in 1797 and maintained that the French Revolution would never be forgotten as a sign that we can progress and improve (Kühn 2001, p. 405). The suggestion in *Biographia Literaria* that the censure by Friedrich Wilhelm II silenced Kant permanently was incorrect and misleading. Considering Coleridge's motive to defend himself against Jacobinism, this inaccuracy seems intentional and further supports the thesis that Coleridge constructed the image of Kant consciously in such a way that it suited his political reorientation. Due to Coleridge's inner conflict with Kant on political grounds, it is all the more remarkable that Coleridge advocated the Jacobin philosopher publicly in *Biographia Literaria*. I propose that his motives for doing so were even stronger than his fading fear of being exposed as a proselyte of German philosophy.

Coleridge's self-construction as a philosopher of genius

To come back to the 'giant hand' moment in Chapter 9, the third and perhaps most important aspect is its relevance for Coleridge's self-construction in general and in particular in *Biographia Literaria*. As such it also accounts largely for the question of why Coleridge publicly endorsed Kant alongside Fichte and Schelling despite his major concerns about the Germano-Jacobin associations. After the Congress of Vienna and the restoration of the powers of monarchies across Europe in 1815, German philosophy gradually lost its threat for British culture. Apart from this change in the cultural climate in Britain, Kant had simply fascinated Coleridge probably from the start. The poet's observation in *Biographia Literaria* that critical philosophy had an immediate impact on him bears witness to this fact (Shaffer 2004, p. 39): critical philosophy 'at once invigorate[d] and discipline[d] my understanding'. Moreover, critical philosophy had become a part of Coleridge's claims to the status of genius. The 'giant-hand' moment has obscured the slow and gradual process that the present study discloses. Coleridge became familiar with Kantian principles through materials that were available in English, learnt German and only then was able to study Kant's work seriously from late 1800 and early 1801 onwards. None of these efforts are mentioned in the giant-hand moment. What Coleridge created in the quotation above was no memory of his study sessions in Keswick or elsewhere but a fully fledged epiphany. It is, as mentioned, a brilliant piece of writing in which Kant features as a philosophical icon – or, as Hazlitt observed disapprovingly, as the 'great German oracle Kant' (Hazlitt 1933 XVI, p. 123). The idolization of Kant and the omission of intellectual efforts as such are not unusual except that they are indicators of Coleridge's systematic self-construction as a philosopher of genius in *Biographia Literaria*.

Hazlitt appears to have understood the implied claim: oracles communicate immediate truths but only to those who are capable of deciphering them. The recipient of these truths has to be chosen. Coleridge's Kantian epiphany is anticipated by the phrase: 'TRUTH takes possession of an uneducated man of genius' (*Biographia* I, p. 150). The parallel use of the phrase 'to take possession' for Coleridge's study of Kant and for a 'man of genius' who encounters 'TRUTH' does not appear accidental. Coleridge's sudden conversion resonates also with Nitsch's view that the person, who 'attempts to read Kant's Works, without being acquainted with the spirit and fundamental principles of his Philosophy, [must be] a Philosopher of a very penetrating genius' (1796, p. 168). The quotation supplements Coleridge's moment of sudden illumination with a central term in this chapter: 'the spirit' of Kant's philosophy. The above-quoted moment of sudden conversion is hence more concerned with Coleridge than Kant in so far as it insinuates that Coleridge was the philosopher of genius capable of grasping Kant's spirit immediately. It is, in other words, an instance of Coleridge's attempt to establish himself as a philosopher of genius.

In her inspiring article, Raimonda Modiano has recently shown the integral connection between Coleridge's Kantian 'Essays on the Principles of Genial Criticism' (first published in *Felix Farley's Bristol Journal* in August and September 1814) and the creation of his own genius in *Biographia Literaria* (2009, p. 224). Modiano observes that 'the subject of the *Biographia* has always been genius and the revelation of Coleridge's greatness as writer, philosopher and critic of genius' (Modiano 2009, p. 231).[3] It is known that Coleridge's main target in the essays was Richard Payne Knight's *Analytical Inquiry into the Principles of Taste* (1805) (*Shorter Works* I, p. 355). To counteract Knight's treatise, Coleridge turned to Kant's *Kritik der Urteilskraft (Critique of the Power of Judgment);* scholars agree that the *third critique* was Coleridge's main source for the series of essays occasioned by Allston Washington's exhibition (Wellek 1931, pp. 111–12; Orsini 1969, pp. 168–9). Modiano notes that 'the most important influence on Coleridge's concept of "genial criticism" was Kant's *Critique of Judgment,* a connection critics have neglected, focusing instead on Kant's predominant role in shaping Coleridge's theory of the beautiful, taste and aesthetic pleasure' (2009, p. 224). Coleridge considered the four essays in *Felix Farley's Bristol Journal* 'the best compositions, *I* have ever written' (*Letters* III, p. 535) and he thought that, as Henry Crabb Robinson recorded, 'the "Kritik der Urtheilskraft" [was] the most astonishing of Kant's works' (1869 I, p. 305). The title 'Essays on the Principles of Genial Criticism' for the series of three essays, though the first was called 'of Sound Criticism' (*Shorter Works* I, p. 356), brings us back to Coleridge's autograph commentary on the margins of 'Destiny of Nations' in *Poems* (1828), discussed in Chapter 3 of this book. Coleridge recalled his philosophical transition to a 'less shallow and more genial System'. The meaning of 'genial', though notoriously slippery (*Shorter Works* I, p. 356), is imbued with Kant's philosophy in Coleridge's writings. 'It is apparent', Modiano observes, 'that the vocabulary and philosophical underpinnings of Coleridge's *Essays*, as well as his statement that his goal was to develop critical principles in congruence with the "spirit in which" the artists "produced" and the "laws and impulses" which "animate and guide" them, come straight out of section 49 of Kant's *Critique of Judgment*' (2009, p. 225). While her brilliant essay has helped to shape my reading of *Biographia Literaria*, this chapter examines a problem behind the analogies with the *Critique of the Power of Judgment*.

Modiano points out perceptively that '[w]ithin the Kantian framework, such a presupposition [of a critic as genius] is preposterous, as it is genius who sets the rules for art and thus, a true genius is beyond critique' (2009, p. 227). She does, however, not address the problem that arises from §46 of the *third critique*. It strictly speaking excludes science in the sense of natural philosophy as spearheaded by Newton (*KdU* p. 308; *CJ* 5:308) from the domain of genius. The status of genius is reserved for artists in the *third critique*. Jochen Schmidt points out the ambivalence that arises from Kant's link of genius and taste, which entails the genial capacity to solicit as well as to make aesthetic judgements. Accordingly, the lines between creation and assessment of art start to blur (Schmidt 1985, p. 355). However, Kant states explicitly that genius cannot account for the rules of his own productions: 'selbst nicht beschreiben, oder wissenschaftlich anzeigen könne . . . selbst nicht weiss, wie sich in ihm die Ideen dazu herbei finden' (*KdU* p. 308) ('That it cannot itself describe or indicate scientifically how it brings its products into being' [*CJ* 5:308]).

Therefore, the view 'that a critic can access the rules that guided an artist in their creation and, like the artist, can even be elevated to the status of genius' (Modiano 2009, p. 224) is not supported by the *third critique* as the capacity for genial criticism alone does not constitute the genius. This point is relevant for Wellek's assessment of Coleridge's significance within the history of literary criticism. Wellek gave Coleridge little credit for his aesthetic theory except for 'his specific theory of poetry', that poetic genius is constituted by a genuine 'attempt of synthesis' between poetry and philosophy: 'the inclusiveness [of his concept of genius] of such philosophic requirements' (1981, p. 161). In contrast to Modiano, Wellek attributed this synthesis of philosophy and poetry to Coleridge alone. I do not agree with either of these two positions and take the discrepancy between Coleridge's genial construction and the *Critique of the Power of Judgment* as a starting point for the following discussion of Coleridge's self-construction as a philosopher of genius.

Kant determined four criteria of genius in §46: genius possesses (1) originality, (2) understanding to distinguish between original non-sense and truly exemplary originality, that is, the ability to create new prototypes ('Muster'), (3) no awareness of or calculation for his creativity. The fourth and last criterion on Kant's list was the condition that genius pertains to art, not science; or to be more precise, genius is the medium through which Nature gives rules to art, but not to science and natural philosophy. This point precludes the possibility of a philosopher of genius; however, it is crucial that Kant had not always defined genius in such narrow terms.

According to *Biographia Literaria* and *The Friend*, philosophy belongs within the domain of genius contrary to the *Critique of the Power of Judgment*: 'There is a philosophic, no less than a poetic genius' (*Biographia* I, p. 299). For both a poet and a philosopher of genius, originality was equally important as in the *third critique*: 'In poems, equally as in philosophic disquisitions, genius produces the strongest impressions of novelty, while it rescues the most admitted truths from the impotence caused by the very circumstance of their universal admission' (*Biographia* I, pp. 81–2). Coleridge did not explicitly rule out non-sense as Kant did, but he stipulated that 'the essential mark of the true philosopher [was] to rest satisfied with no imperfect light' (*Biographia* I, p. 242). Likewise, he aimed at establishing 'an analogy between genius and virtue' (*Biographia* I, p. 224). A recurring theme, and frequent cause for complaint,

..*ographia* is the unqualified criticism by reviewers, be it those of Coleridge's ..n work or, in one instant, of Kant's writings: 'they had been all their lives admiring without judgment, and were now about to censure without reason' (*Biographia* I, p. 72). As James Chandler notes, 'Coleridge's controlling purpose through most of the *Biographia* is to explain what he describes as seventeen years of "persecution" at the hands of critics' (1984, p. 257). Yet not all reviewers were hostile; some reviewers and particularly one critic were also competitors. Among those unqualified commentators, William Wordsworth, who had just published the distinction between fancy and imagination in his Preface to the 1815 edition of his *Poems,* was for Coleridge perhaps the most serious rival. In the attempt to distinguish himself, Coleridge assumed the role of philosophic genius, though tentatively, when he declared that 'the theory of the fine arts, and of poetry in particular [such as *Biographia Literaria* or 'Essays on the Principles of Genial Criticism'], could not, I thought, but derive some additional and important light. It would in its immediate effects furnish the torch of guidance to the philosophical critic; and ultimately to the poet himself' (*Biographia* I, p. 85). His claims to fulfil Kant's criterion that genius cannot be learnt is manifest in Coleridge's Kantian epiphany in so far as the sudden taking possession through the giant hand obviates any form of study. In addition it suggests an almost sublime moment as if a rule of nature, or rather 'the spirit of fundamental principles' (Nitsch 1796, p. 168), overwhelmed Coleridge with their power of insight. Although Coleridge's role as a genius is somewhat passive in the giant-hand moment, Kant's 'taking possessing' is conceptually indispensible for Coleridge's construction as a genius because it demonstrates that the act is not calculable, but unaware. The third criterion in §46 says as quoted that the creator is unable to consciously explain or define the process in which he forms the products he owes to his genius (*KdU* p. 308; *CJ* 5: 308). Kant linked this unconscious dimension with the old Latin use of *genius*:

> Daher vermutlich das Wort Genie von *genius*, dem eigentümlichen, einem Menschen bei der Geburt mitgegebenen schützenden und leitenden Geist, von dessen Eingebung jene originalen Ideen herrührten, ableitet ist. (*KdU* p. 308)
> (For that is also presumably how the word 'genius' is derived from genius, in the sense of the particular spirit given to a person at birth, which protects and guides him, and from whose inspiration those original ideas stem. [*CJ* 5: 308])

The image of the giant hand poeticizes the fourth criterion of section 46 and at the same time visualizes a central aspect of Coleridge's 'genial criticism' in the 1814 essays: 'the specific object of the present attempt is to enable the spectator to judge in the same spirit in which the Artist produced, or ought to have produced' (*Short Works* I, 360). Spirit ('Geist') in §49 of the *Critique of the Power of Judgment* is the invigorating principle of our mind. In chapter 15 of *Biographia Literaria*, Coleridge derived a brilliant explanation of the 'poetic power' and 'promise of genius' in Shakespeare's 'Venus and Adonis' (*Biographia* II, pp. 21, 20):

> It is throughout as if a superior spirit more intuitive, more intimately conscious, even than the characters themselves, not only of every outward look and act, but of

the flux and reflux of the mind in all its subtlest thoughts and feelings, were placing the whole before our view. (*Biographia* II, p. 21)

Coleridge's point is strikingly Kantian: the poetic characters carry the source of their creation and power within them.

Kant's *third critique* developed this concept over time. Spirit is the trademark of genius, the capability of producing aesthetic ideas through imagination.

[Geist] sei nichts anders als das Vermögen der Darstellung *ästhetischer Ideen;* unter einer ästhetischen Idee aber verstehe ich diejenige Vorstellung der Einbildungskraft, die viel zu denken veranlaßt, ohne daß ihr doch irgend ein bestimmter Gedanke, d. i. *Begriff,* adäquat sein kann, die folglich keine Sprache völlig erreicht und verständlich machen kann. - Man sieht leicht, daß sie das Gegenstück (Pendant) von einer *Vernunftidee* sei, welche umgekehrt ein Begriff ist, dem keine *Anschauung* (Vorstellung der Einbildungskraft) adäquat sein kann. (*KdU* pp. 313–14)

([Spirit] is nothing other than the faculty for the presentation of *aesthetic ideas;* by an aesthetic idea, however, I mean that representation of the imagination that occasions much thinking though without it being possible for any determinate thought, i.e. *concept,* to be adequate to it, which, consequently, no language fully attains or can make intelligible. – One can readily see that it is the counterpart (pendant) of an *idea of reason,* which is, conversely, a concept to which no *intuition* (representation of the imagination) can be adequate. [*CJ* 5: 313–14])

Aesthetic ideas are presentations of the imagination for which no single thought (concept) is adequate. The imagination ('Einbildungskraft') is a term that Kant adopted from the aesthetic tradition initiated by Alexander Gottlieb Baumgarten. Baumgarten's aesthetics tried to bridge the gap between rationality and sensibility (Schmidt 1985, p. 371). Aesthetic ideas set the imagination and the faculty of the Understanding ('Verstand'), which constitutes experience and knowledge, into harmony (*KdU* pp. 316–17, *CJ* 5: 316–17). Genius is hence instrumental in the creation of an intellectual balance of the mind. Aesthetic ideas are 'counterparts' – mirror images – to rational ideas. 'By way of aesthetic idea, the genius thus places a hint of the supersensible object of rational ideas into the sensible object' (Burnham 2000, p. 115). Aesthetic ideas are the way in which spirit manifests itself. We use them instead of logical representations ('statt logischer Darstellung', *KdU* p. 315, *CJ* 5: 315). They are superior to logic representations in so far as aesthetic ideas give us an empirical (sensible) hint of rational ideas. 'The notion of aesthetic ideas then is the only hypothesis that can account for the integration of the sensible, aesthetic and intellectual elements in the work of fine arts' (Burnham, p. 115). This spirit (aesthetic ideas) was so important for Kant that he used it to define genius in the *third critique* and separated it from the genius of invention, science and philosophy (Giordanetti 1995, p. 430). Kant distinguished between 'redenden Künste' (*KdU* p. 321) or 'the arts of speech' (*CJ* 5: 312), 'bildende Künste' (*KdU* p. 321) or '*pictorial* arts' (*CJ* 5:321), and 'Kunst des schönen Spiels der Empfindungen' (*KdU* p. 324) or 'arts of the beautiful play of sensations' (*CJ* 5: 324). Among these, poetry (as part of the arts of speech) is the kind of art that sets the imagination most at liberty to produce aesthetic ideas; as such Kant categorizes poetry as the highest form of art (*KdU* p. 326, *CJ* 5: 326). In the first essay on 'genial criticism' Coleridge transformed this statement proclaiming that 'All the fine Arts are different species of Poetry' (*Shorter Works* I, p. 358). In praise of Allston Washington's painting, Coleridge extended the freedom of imagination to painting and sculptures, although he did not do so permanently.

Kant distinguished between science and art and their respective mechanical and aesthetic modes of cognition (*KdU* pp. 304–6, *CJ* 5: 304–6). In analogy, Kant separates the poetic genius sharply from the scientific mind (Schmidt 1985, p. 364). Coleridge endorsed Kant's position fully. Echoing Kant's definition that the purpose of aesthetic art is (intellectual) pleasure (*KdU* p. 306, *CJ* 5: 306), Coleridge announced that 'The common essence of all [art] consists in the excitement of emotion for the immediate purpose of pleasure thro' the medium of beauty; herein contra-distinguishing poetry from science, the immediate object and primary purpose of pleasure of which is truth and possible utility' (*Shorter Works* I, p. 358). The definition is probably a revision of Coleridge's lecture notes, which can be found in the *Notebooks* (III, §4111), dated by Coburn to the time between November 1810 and November 1811. In *Biographia Literaria* Coleridge adhered to the specific link made by Kant in the *Critique of the Power of Judgment* between genius and poetry:

> [Poetry] is a distinction resulting from the poetic genius itself, which sustains and modifies the images, thoughts, and emotions of the poet's own mind. The poet, described in *ideal* perfection, brings the whole soul of man into activity, with the subordination of its faculties to each other, according to their relative worth and dignity. He diffuses a tone, and spirit of unity, that blends, and (as it were) fuses, each into each, by that synthetic and magical power, to which we have exclusively appropriated the name imagination. (*Biographia* II, p. 16)

The 'perfection' that brings the 'soul of man into activity' seems to be the spring inside of the genius at the beginning of section 49: 'Geist'. Coleridge realized the full potential of Kant's concept of poetic genius: aesthetic ideas bring imagination and the Understanding into harmony, they 'blend' and 'fuse' and render 'the spirit of unity' (otherwise inaccessible within the realm of space and time) as if it were empirically manifest. As mentioned before, the concept of aesthetic ideas is the only hypothesis in the *third critique* that provides a hint of integration of the supersensible ideas through art. One might say this possibility was achieved at the expense of other kinds of genius that lay outside of art.

Historically speaking it is important, as John Zammito notes, that Kant's 'theory of genius which asserted the firm conviction that genius had no place in science' was the result of Kant's attempt to 'explain the excesses of the Stürmer, on the one hand, and give adequate recognition to true genius, on the other' (1992, p. 41). His position mediated between the values of the 'Sturm und Drang' and the Enlightenment by taming the theory of genius (Schmidt 1985, p. 360).[4] Kant's separation of aesthetic genius from the scientific mind did not imply any slight of the latter. On the contrary, 'what is important to grasp is that the exclusion of science from genius was not a disparagement of science but rather of genius, and was grounded in Kant's disdain for the *Sturm and Drang'* (Zammito 1992, p. 41). For Coleridge it was important that Kant had not always defined genius in such narrow poetic terms.

The fact that Coleridge tried to establish himself as a philosopher, critic and writer of genius in terms that are so similar to Kant and that yet diverges significantly from the *Critique of the Power of Judgment* might be seen a sign of his superficial engagement with the text. This would potentially confirm Wellek's declaration of the 'bankruptcy of [Coleridge's] thought' on the grounds of 'technical details of Kant [that] have been taken by Coleridge undigested' (1931, p. 69).[5] Modiano argues that Coleridge's inclusive conception of genius can be accounted for with section 49: 'in the process of differentiating between genuine imitation and slavish copying Kant in effect erases the boundary that separates pupil, artist and critic in their relationship to a "genial" predecessor' (2009, p. 225). However, this explanation still leaves open the question of why Coleridge claimed to be not only a genial critic, but also a philosopher of genius. In the *third critique*, Kant's concept of genius was so opposed to learning that he denied Newton the status of a genius because he acquired this knowledge and was able to impart it in such a way that he could explain each step not only of the elements of geometry but also of his profound inventions (*KdU* p. 309, *CJ* 5: 309). This capacity to judge and explain is the very criterion that excludes Newton from genius in the *third critique*. Someone like Coleridge in *Biographia Literaria* who claims to establish such rules of criticism can hardly be a genius according to section 47. Despite this apparent incongruence in Coleridge's reading, I agree with the view that Coleridge did not engage with Kantian terms on a superficial level (Hedley 2000, pp. 18–19; Vigus 2009, p. 49). Indeed, the Kantian affinities lead into Coleridge's past in the late 1790s.

Coleridge's lost copy of a student transcript of Kant's lectures on logic

The impact of the *Critique of the Power of Judgment* on Coleridge's thinking has been discussed widely (for instance by Vigus 2009, p. 50; Brice 2007, p. 83; Kooy 2002, p. 100), but commentators on Coleridge's response have failed to consider that, historically speaking, the *Critique of the Power of Judgment* emerged over the course of decades of Kant's research (Schlapp 1901, p. 115; Giordanetti 1995, p. 410). In the 1770s Kant did not limit genius to the arts (Giordanetti 1995, p. 408). He lectured widely, but never taught a single course on aesthetics only (Schlapp 1901, p. 8). His lectures on art formed part of empirical psychology, anthropology and logic. These connections are apparent, for instance, in Kant's *Anthropologie* (1798), as the book contains a succinct delineation of genius in the section 'Von der Orginalität des Erkenntnisvermögens oder dem Genie' (*Anthropologie*, pp. 224–7) ('On the originality of the cognitive faculty, or genius' [*Anthropology*, pp. 224–7]). According to Schlapp, the documentations of Kant's logic contain the early beginnings of his aesthetics (1901, p. 18). Reinhard Brandt and Werner Stark emphasize that there is clear evidence that Kant was aware of the external interest in his lectures at Königsberg from the 1770s onwards: in fall 1778, he made sure that Marcus Herz, a young friend and auditor who had moved to

Berlin, would receive copies of the lectures from the mid-1770s for distribution (1997, p. lv). The thought of genius became prominent in Kant's lectures in the early 1770s: both Schlapp and Giordanetti date this development to this period (1901, p. 115; 1995, p. 407). Kant mentioned Gerard's *Essay on Genius* (*Reflexionen*, p. 420), which was a source of inspiration for him (Bruno 2010, p. 31). Kant could peruse the essay in German – he did not read English – since the German translation by Christian Garve was published in 1776 (Zammito 1992, p. 41). In the 1770s, Kant shared with Gerard the view that genius pertained to the arts as well as science (Giordanetti 1995, p. 411). A copy of transcripts called Pillau's copy or *Anthropologie-Pillau* discloses that during the time of his lectures in the winter semester 1778 and 1779 Kant regarded philosophy as the only science of genius: 'Wissenschaften des Genis und der Erlernung sind die Philosophie und Mathematic, wovon jenes zum *Genie*, dieses zur Erlernung gehört' (*Anthro Vorlesung* II, p. 784). ('The sciences of genius and of learning are philosophy and mathematics, of which the former belongs to genius, the latter to learning' [my translation]).[6] Such a thing as a philosopher of genius existed for Kant at least in the 1770s.

Despite its relevance, the history of the evolution of Kant's aesthetics, in particular his theory of genius, has been overlooked in Coleridge studies.[7] It is known that Coleridge brought back from Germany, as mentioned in Chapter 5, a pirate copy of Kantian lectures on logic: 'a thin Octavo of two or at most 3 Sheets, under the name of Kant's Logic – doubtless, published by, or from the Notes of, one of his Lecture-pupils' (*Marginalia* III, p. 256). Such transcripts, even though the title page might have born a name, usually gave no clear indication of the author (Young 1992, p. xxiii). Recently, Kant scholars have uncovered evidence for the existence of more than twenty transcripts of Kant's logic lectures, of which eleven are known to have survived (Stark 1987, pp. 123–64). Coleridge's first copy of Kant's logic could have been one of those twenty. Nonetheless, the logic documentation by Blomberg ('Logik-Blomberg'), which recorded Kant's lectures from the early 1770s (Young 1992, p. xxiv), includes statements similar to that of Pillau with regard to Coleridge's extension of the status of genius to philosophers: 'Die Philosophie, und die Kunst zu Philosophieren kann unmöglich erlernet werden, wohl aber die Mathematic' (*Logik Vorlesung* I, p. 53) ('Philosophy, and the art of philosophizing, cannot possibly be learned, but mathematics surely can' [*Logic Lecture*, 53]). Philosophy here is an art that cannot be learnt, but which requires inborn talent.

The following passage in §23 of 'Logik Blomberg' contains Coleridge's aspirations as a philosopher of genius in a nutshell (which is the reason why I give a full quotation):

So können Wißenschaften erworben warden, ja selbst in dem Grad der Vollkommenheit, der ihrer Natur gemäs ist, mitgetheilet werden. Es giebt Wißenschaften der Nachahmung der Erlernung, aber auch andere Wißenschaften des Genies, die nicht erlernet werden können. . . . man lerne nicht im geringsten Philosophieren, wenn man Philosophie anderer abcopiret, und so ganzt genau erlernet. vielmehr könne man weit eher noch etwas profitiren, wenn man sich angewöhnt, und die Wißenschaft erlernet, über die Philosophie anderer Critisiren, und urtheilen zu können. *Meine Philosophie muß in mir selbst, und nicht in dem*

Verstand anderer/ gegründet seyn. es muß mich dieselbige ja an kein Original Muster Binden. die Methode die Philosophieren zu dociren ist also zweifach:

1me Diejenige, welche den philosophischen Geist Cultiviret, und sich nicht erlernen, noch nachahmen läßt.

2me oder die, welche einem gewißen Autori treulich folget, ihn erkläret, und bey der Philosophie das Gedächtniß zu Hilfe nehmen will.

Dieses gehet wohl bey der Mathematic, aber nicht bei der Philosophie an. (*Logik Vorlesung* I, pp. 53–4; my emphasis)

(Thus sciences can be acquired, indeed, even communicated, to the degree of perfection conformable to their nature. There are sciences to be imitated [or] to be learned, but also sciences of genius, which cannot be learned. . . . one does not in the least learn to philosophize when one copies and learns quite exactly the philosophy of others. One can rather profit far more if one accustoms oneself to, and learns the science of, being able to criticize and judge the philosophy of others. *My philosophy must be grounded in myself, and not in the understanding of others.* It must not bind me to any original model. The method of teaching philosophy is thus twofold:

1st the one that cultivates the philosophical spirit, and does not let itself be learned or imitated.

2nd that which follows a certain *autor* [sic] faithfully, comments on him, and which tries to use memory as an aid in philosophy.

This might do in mathematics, but not in philosophy. [*Logic Lecture* 53–4]; my emphasis)

In the early 1770s, philosophy was a science of genius for Kant, which he endeavoured to cultivate in his students. In philosophy, it would not do for Kant to follow certain authors faithfully. On the contrary, he encouraged students to detect the 'philosophical spirit' and tried to cultivate it in them. According to Young, the 'Logik-Blomberg' is not the only transcript that contained such a view: Kant's 'aim throughout, as he often stated, was not to teach his students philosophy, but instead to show them how to philosophize' (1992, p. xxii). Although Kant later limited genius to art, his preliminary views are significant for the history of Coleridge's reception and Coleridge studies as a whole. The fact that Coleridge owned a student transcript of Kant's lectures on logic strongly suggests his familiarity with 'Logik-Blomberg' or another record of Kant's instructions of how to philosophize. Kant's instructions in his logic lectures legitimize Coleridge's free use of his philosophy. We can see the momentous importance of this thought in Coleridge's notebooks. His entries contain traces of these lecture transcripts including a decisive comment.

According to Coburn, a notebook entry dated to September and October 1803 captures for the first time Coleridge's intention to write *Biographia Literaria* (*Notebooks* I, §1515). It is this entry that displays a striking similarity with the above-quoted excerpt from the logic transcript that the philosophy of genius is the philosophy that is grounded in the self. Coleridge decided in 1803 to write his philosophy in the form of his autobiography – a resolution which he jotted down only for his private record: 'Seem to have made up my mind to write my metaphysical works, as *my Life, & in* my Life – intermixed with all the other events/ or history of the mind & fortunes of S. T. Coleridge' (*Notebooks* I, §1515). About fifteen years later, Coleridge's *Biographia Literaria* was published with the introductory explanation:

> I have used the narration [of my life] chiefly for the purpose of giving a continuity to the work, in part for the sake of the miscellaneous reflections suggested to me by particular events, but still more as introductory to the statement of my principles in Politics, Religion, and Philosophy, and the application of the rules, deduced from philosophical principles, to poetry and criticism. (*Biographia* I, p. 5)

It seems as if Coleridge drew the conclusion from Kant's instruction that his work on metaphysics was ideally written in the form of his autobiography. The entry appears as a direct response to the Kantian instruction in the student transcript. The lecture transcripts from the 1770s and the echo in Coleridge's notebook indicate that by 1803 Coleridge was familiar with the concept of the philosopher of genius that the *third critique* excluded (1790). The early terms of Kant's concept of genius suited Coleridge so well that he insisted on it later on in *Biographia Literaria* even though he knew the *Critique of the Power of Judgment* very well, in which Kant had attributed this status and function to artists alone. Besides the lost pirate copy of the transcript, another person appears to have helped to shape Coleridge's understanding of genius.

'Esprit fort'

In March 1796, Beddoes reviewed Kant's *third critique* (1790) for the *Monthly Magazine*. He translated the title *Kritik der Urteilskraft* as 'Examination of the Judgement' and published the article in May of the same year (*Monthly Magazine* 1 [1796], p. 266). This review, written at the time when Coleridge and Beddoes jointly protested against the Gagging Bills (see Chapter 2), suggests that Beddoes exposed Coleridge initially to Kantian aesthetics around the same time. On 20 March 1797, James Losh sent Wordsworth a package including issues of the *Monthly Magazine* from February to December 1796 (Roe 1988, p. 240; Wordsworth 1935 I, p. 186). It included Beddoes's article, which contained, as I propose, the earliest clue for Coleridge's acquaintance with Kant's concept of genius and is also relevant for Coleridge's eagerness to prove his philosophical superiority over Wordsworth. Beddoes's exposition of parts of section 54 included a translation (by Beddoes) from the German of the *Kritik der Urteilskraft* (*KdU* p. 334, *CJ* 5: 334): 'Voltaire says, that providence has given us *hope* and *sleep*, as a compensation for the many cares of life. He might have added *laughter*, if the wit and originality of humour, necessary to excite it among rational people, were not as rare as the talent for *head-breaking, neck-breaking*, and *heart-breaking* fictions, is common among our mystics, *esprits forts*, and sentimental novelists, respectively' (*Monthly Magazine* 1 [1796], p. 267). Beddoes chose a passage with a particularly sarcastic undertone that indicates Kant's reservations towards the cult of genius as professed by Johann Gottfried von Herder (1744–1803) and the movement of *Sturm und Drang* (Zammito 1992, pp. 8–10). What matters with regard to this particular passage is Beddoes's use of '*esprits forts*' for the German word 'Genies' ('geniuses').

In mid-to late eighteenth-century English, 'Esprit fort' was, according to *Oxford English Dictionary*, commonly understood as 'a "strong-minded" person; usually, one who professes superiority to current prejudices, *esp.* a "freethinker" in religion' (*OED*). René Descartes (1596–1650) and Blaise Pascal (1623–62) used the term 'esprit fort' to designate the unbelievers they intended to convert (Weinberg 1983, p. 5). According to the *Dictionnaire de l'Académie Française* (Paris, 1694), 'esprit fort' was: 'On appelle, Esprits forts, ceux qui se mettent au dessus des opinions et des maxims communes. C'est un esprit fort. il fait l'esprit fort, il ne croit rien, il ne tombe d'accord de rien' (cited in Weinberg 1983, p. 18). Beddoes's translation is remarkable because it deviates from the common Latin root.

By the mid-eighteenth century, the English word 'genius' had begun to denote a 'native intellectual power of an exalted type, such as is attributed to those who are esteemed in greatest in any department . . . ; instinctive and extraordinary capacity for imaginative' (*OED*; Bate 1997, p. 136; Bruno 2010, p. 12). Furthermore, the cult of genius among German intellectuals harkened back to British authors such as Robert Wood (*Essay on Original Genius and Writings of Homer*, 1775) and William Duff (*Essay on Original Genius,* 1767) (Bruno 2010, p. 13; Zammito 1992, p. 23). So central was the topic for German intellectuals that the prize essay of 1775 was dedicated to the question of what constitutes genius (Zammito 1992, p. 42). A year later, the *Popularphilosoph* Garve published his translation of Alexander Gerard's *Essay on Genius* (1776) only two years after its first edition in 1774 (Engell 1981, pp. 80, 88). Despite these affinities between 'Genie' and 'genius' and despite Kant's reference to 'ingenium' (*KdU* p. 307; *CJ* 5: 307), Beddoes refrained from the use of the literal translation. This fact indicates that Beddoes regarded the Kantian definition of 'Genie' as a distinctive notion, which differed from, for instance, Hume's or Burke's use of the word 'genius'. For them, it denoted the character, inclination or disposition of a person, period of time or party, such as in 'genius of the age' and 'genius of the faction' (Bruno 2010, p. 12). Beddoes's use of the term 'Esprit fort', suggests that he had direct recourse to section 49:

> *Geist* in ästhetischer Bedeutung heißt das belebende Princip im Gemüthe. Dasjenige aber, wodurch dieses Prinzip die Seele belebt, der Stoff, den es dazu anwendet, ist das, was die Gemütskrafte zweckmäßig in Schwung versetzt, d. i. ein solches Spiel, welches sich von selbst erhält und selbst die Kräfte dazu stärkt. (*KdU* p. 313)
>
> (*Spirit*, in an aesthetic significance, means the animating principle in the mind. That, however, by which, this principle animates the soul, sets the mental powers into motion, i.e. into a play that is self-maintaining and even strengthens the powers to that end. [*CJ* 5: 314])

Beddoes's translation acknowledged the singular nature of the art of genius professed in Kant's *third critique*. Simultaneously, 'Esprit fort' pointed to the notion that 'spirit' as the invigorating principle and the spring of excessive meaning (i.e. aesthetic ideas) constitutes the distinctive trademark of genius according to Kant.

Beddoes's insight into Kantian genius suited the interests of young Coleridge as well as of his co-author of *Lyrical Ballads* very well; indeed the notion of an 'esprit fort' probably appeared to Coleridge and Wordsworth as a suitable way of thinking about themselves as they were busy compiling the collection of poems that aimed to overthrow established forms of poetic diction. *Lyrical Ballads* constitutes a landmark in literary history, indeed a revolution in poetry which is too expansive and multifaceted to cover adequately in the framework of this Chapter.[8] The following section is intended to draw attention to a curious aspect of *Lyrical Ballads* that is rarely mentioned by scholars. A unique copy of *Lyrical Ballades*, though not directly linked with Kantian genius, indicates that Beddoes played a part in Coleridge and Wordsworth's joint project. The Bristol issue of the 1798 *Lyrical Ballads* held by the British Library can be seen as a token of Beddoes's involvement in Coleridge's and Wordsworth's collection of poems,[9] for this singular print of *Lyrical Ballads* contains a poem by Beddoes called 'The Domiciliary Verses'. The publication history of this copy is contested, as is the status of the poem among the famous ballads (Wise 1922–36 [1926] VIII, pp. 3–4).[10] Nonetheless, scholars agree that the copy indicates a strong link between Beddoes and *Lyrical Ballads*. It is true that a major incentive for the temporary inclusion of Beddoes's poem consisted in Coleridge's and Wordsworth's wish to preserve the anonymity of their authorship and thus to protect *Lyrical Ballads* from Anti-Jacobin prejudice. 'Lewti' betrayed Coleridge's identity because it had previously been published in *Morning Post* (Roper 1978, p. 109). Beddoes's poem replaced, according to Thomas James Wise and D. F. Foxon, Coleridge's 'Lewti' before Wordsworth, Coleridge and Cottle opted for the final solution, that is, Coleridge's 'The Nightingale' (Wise 1922–36 [1926] VIII, pp. 3–4). Irrespective of these details, however, the inclusion of Beddoes's 'Domiciliary Verses' in this single print of *Lyrical Ballads* points to a good deal of involvement on Beddoes's part as friend, mentor and possibly as adviser.

Wordsworth was a philosophical thinker in his own right.[11] Moreover, his sensitivity to the fragility of the harmony between man and nature, to inter-human relations and to memory and psychology is borne out in his verse in ways that tend to transcend philosophical explanation. However, Wordsworth's aspiration to match Milton with his own verse epic and his image of himself as a prodigal son are well known (Butler 2003, p. 46). Wordsworth's poetry and prose, particularly when concerned with himself and his vocation as a poet, convey at times striking parallels with Kant's concept of genius as delineated in the *Critique of the Power of Judgment*, the transcript of Kant's lectures on logic and Beddoes's 'esprit fort'. Kant was also a great admirer of Milton.[12] What matters in the context of this chapter is Wordsworth's sophisticated philosophical arguments in relation to Kant because of the pivotal role of Wordsworth for the genesis of *Biographia Literaria*.[13]

After the return from Germany in 1799, Wordsworth was the only person besides Poole with whom Coleridge shared his Kantian studies (see Chapter 5). In 1805, when Wordsworth read out *The Prelude* to Coleridge over the Christmas holidays (Gill 1991, p.17), the younger poet was struck by despondency as he felt that Wordsworth's great philosophic long poem had anticipated his future work. The desire to compete with Wordsworth slowly began to grow in Coleridge. So far the poets had worked together on fairly equal grounds, as Coleridge had been solely able to claim the role as the philosophical thinker and literary critic. Philosophy was the area in which he could shine when he compared himself to Wordsworth. Yet *The Prelude* in addition to the Prefaces to *Lyrical Ballads* (1800 and 1802) began to threaten Coleridge's niche:

Beddoes when discussing *Lyrical Ballads*. What drove others to reject Kant's theory of genius might have found their approval. August Wilhelm von Schlegel criticized the *Critique of the Power of Judgment* by pointing out that Kant transformed genius into a blind medium of nature (Schmidt 1985, p. 362). Indeed, §46 entitled 'Schöne Kunst ist Kunst des Genies' states that '*Genie ist die angeborene Gemütsanlage (ingenium), durch welche die Natur der Kunst die Regel gibt*' (*KdU* p. 307) ('Beautiful art is art of genius . . . *Genius* is the inborn predisposition of the mind [*ingenium*] through which nature gives the rule to art' [*CJ* 5: 307]). Wordsworth's Preface to *Lyrical Ballads* (1800) declared that 'the principle object' of the collection was to 'make the incidents of common life interesting by tracing in them, truly though not ostentatiously, the primary laws of nature' (*Lyrical Ballads*, pp. 244–5). The poems were intended to show that 'passions of men are incorporated with the beautiful and permanent forms of nature' (*Lyrical Ballads*, p. 245). Wordsworth's 1800 Preface declared the primary aim of communicating the laws of nature in a similar way as Kant's aesthetic principle stipulated that nature gives her rules to art through genial capacity. Similar to section 46 in *Critique of the Power of Judgment*, Wordsworth proclaimed that his style of composition could not be taught, 'I do not know how without being culpably particular I can give my Reader a more exact notion of the style', and that it had no precedent, 'the pleasure which I have proposed to myself to impart is of a kind very different from that which is supposed by many persons to be the proper object of poetry' (*Lyrical Ballads*, p. 251). Whereas Schlegel considered being a medium of nature as a kind of blind reduction, Wordsworth endorsed the concept that nature gave rules to poetry through the genial poet: so much so that the poet claimed he could not explain his own inspiration. This claim was strategic. The sense of condescension to knowledge acquired from books, study or other conscious efforts is palpable in Wordsworth's writing and Kantian genius.

Wordsworth repeated this genial claim and made it an important component of *The Prelude*. Book III of *The Prelude* (1805) hinges the poet's construction of his genius on the rejection of book learning and education in general:

> Of College labours, of the lecturer's rooms,
> . . . books . . .
> I make short mention.
> Things they were which then
> I did not love, nor do I love them now:
> Such glory was but little sought by me,
> And little won.
>
> (*Prelude*, p. 106, ll. 60–72)

This reduction of academic study allows the narrator in *The Prelude* to stipulate his utterly innate ability: 'Of genius, power,/ Creation and divinity itself/ I have been speaking, for the theme has been/ What passed within me!' (*Prelude*, p. 112, ll. 171–4). This profession contains an allusion to the Latin 'ingenium', which Kant also used as model for his definition. When Wordsworth revised the Preface for the third edition of *Lyrical Ballads* in 1802, he inserted a section about the identity of the poet. Here Wordsworth contradistinguished the poet from the 'man of science' on similar grounds as Kant: 'personal and individual acquisition' (*Lyrical Ballads*, p. 259). According to section 47, Newton was no genius because his skills were acquired. According to Wordsworth, the knowledge of the man of science, on the one hand, is a 'personal and individual acquisition, slow to come to us, and by no habitual and direct sympathy connecting us with our fellow beings' (*Lyrical Ballads*, p. 259). On the other hand, the poet gives the knowledge that 'cleaves to us as a necessary part of our existence, our natural and unalienable inheritance' (*Lyrical Ballads*, p. 259). For Wordsworth as for Kant in the *third critique* the poet's distinctive character depended on an inborn talent; learning threatened to diminish genius.

Around the time when Coleridge lived with the Wordsworths, immersed in the production of *The Friend*, Wordsworth composed a part of his *Guide through the District of the Lakes*, a fragment on the beautiful and the sublime. Wordsworth's use of the concept of the sublime here has barely anything to do with the stylistic terms of the Longinian sublime. Edmund Burke's *Philosophical Enquiry into the Origin of our Ideas of the Sublime and the Beautiful* (1757) was the first to use the term 'sublime' for an experience of tension followed by relaxation and the final release of the feeling of sublimity (Bode 1992, pp. 38–41). Wordsworth's account of the sublime displays a striking similarity with that of Kant's sublime in Nature in sections 28 and 29 of the *third critique*. Wordsworth sublimates fear and thus creates a positive form of self-respect in much the same way as Kant in §28 (*KdU* p. 260, *CJ* 260): 'Thus has been given an analysis of the attributes or qualities the co-existence of which gives to a Mountain the power of affecting the mind with a sensation of sublimity' (*W Prose* II, p. 353). Wordsworth carefully explained that the sublime experience depended on the perceiving subject, rather than the perceived object (*KdU* pp. 265–6, *CJ* 5: 265–6). If the perceiver was, for instance, familiar with the precipices in the Lake District this situation reduced the sublime effect: 'Familiarity with these objects tends very much to mitigate & to destroy the power which they have to produce the sensation of sublimity as dependent upon personal fear or upon wonder' (*W Prose* II, p. 353). However Wordsworth thought that such familiarity did not entirely prevent the experience of the sublime: 'a comprehensive awe takes the place of the one [unfamiliar], and a religious admiration of the other, & the condition of the mind is exalted accordingly' (*W Prose* II, p. 353). The forms of mental exaltation varied depending on the person; familiarity damped the feeling of awe but added to spiritual appreciation. For Kant, the sublime constitutes one of the rare moments in which our mind can feel ('sich fühlbar machen') its own purpose ('Bestimmung') (*KdU* p. 262, *CJ* 5: 262). Likewise, Wordsworth observed, the sublime 'calls upon the mind to grasp at something towards which it can make approaches but which it is incapable of attaining' (*W Prose* II, p. 354). The mind can approach but not fully reach this higher principle. Wordsworth's prose in the fragment seems at times obscure as if the text was the result of laborious thinking and study; it seems likely that these thoughts included some form in which Kant's sublime had been expounded.

Independent of the question whether Wordsworth occasionally used Kantian concepts consciously or not, Coleridge must have been aware of his friend's grasp on transcendental questions including self-consciousness, the sublime, and above all, genius. In 1815 this thought appears to have transformed into anxiety when Coleridge realized that Wordsworth's philosophical treatises and poetry were a matter of serious competition, possibly of threat, for his philosophic authority.

In the first volume of *Biographia Literaria*, Coleridge declared that Wordsworth had outlined the fruits of the poetic imagination, but that the time had come for Coleridge to 'add the trunk, and even the roots as far as they lift themselves above ground, and are visible to the naked eye of our common consciousness' (*Biographia* I, p. 88). The subsequent Chapters 5–12 sketched Coleridge's philosophic thought as if it had been an evolution from British associationism over native Neo-Platonism and the gospel of St John to German idealism. The end of Chapter 12 returns to Wordsworth, closes the philosophic tour de force and announces the culmination of Coleridge's theory (Chapter 13): 'it will probably appear in the next chapter, that deeming it necessary to go back much further than Mr Wordsworth's subject required and permitted, I have attached meaning to both fancy and imagination, which he had not in view' (*Biographia* I, p. 294). Coleridge knew the epic potential of his philosophical enquires, as his notebook shows: the Latin 'res' sparked in him the idea of 'the Iliad of Spinozo-Kantian, Kanto-Fichtian, Fichto-Schellingian Revival of Plato-Plotino-Proclain Idealism in a Nutshell from a Lilliput Hazel' (*Notebooks* II §2784). Chapters 3 and 4 of the present book contend that, instead of such a strict succession of philosophers, Coleridge harboured a strong interest in various philosophies simultaneously. In *Biographia Literaria*, however, Coleridge used a narrative of linear philosophic progression to convince his readers that his thought was as solid as the 'trunk' and 'roots' of poetry in contrast to Wordsworth's mere 'poetic *fruitage*' (*Biographia* I, p. 88). This endeavour entailed a perceived risk because Coleridge confronted his readers with a complex and challenging treatise. At the same time, Coleridge also intended to affirm his claims to the status of a genius. The interruption of the transcendental deduction of the power of the imagination in Chapter 13 – 'I received the following letter from a friend' (*Biographia* I, p. 300) – offered a solution for both of these objectives at the same time. The letter served to support his claims to philosophic authority and to genius.

In Chapter 13, Coleridge hinged his aspiration to be a genial philosopher on a moment of subconscious awareness in a way that is reminiscent of his earlier poetry. In the 'Ancient Mariner' (1798), death and disaster are reversed in the moment when the speaker 'bless'd them [the water-snakes] unaware' (*Lyrical Ballads*, p. 21, l. 265). Had the visitor of Porlock not interrupted the genial process of composing 'Kubla Khan', it would not have been as easily apparent that the state in which the poem was written was entirely subconscious. The unconscious state of producing works of genius was crucial for Coleridge, too. Coleridge transferred the genial state of the poetic mind to a moment of philosophic insight in the above-mentioned 'giant hand' paragraph in Chapter 9. The 'giant hand' is a rhetorically essential device because it demonstrates that the conversion is neither the result of calculated effort nor prolonged study. Like Kant in section 47 of the *third critique*, and similar to Wordsworth's self-construction as a genial poet, Coleridge invoked the spirit of genius that lies outside of human deliberation; and he did so in Chapter 13 of *Biographia Literaria*, too. Coleridge substituted the deduction of the imagination with the experience of the fictional friend. The fictitious epistolary affirms Coleridge's capacity to solicit a moment of ontological revelation in others: '*that state of mind . . . in your note, p. 72, 73 . . . as if I had been standing on my head*' (*Biographia* I, p. 301). The state of mind presented here hardly appears as anything else than the germ of post-Kantian philosophy, the question of the union of contemplated and contemplating self (see Chapter 7). Instead of demonstrating his intellectual prowess, Coleridge turned to ways in which his thought was to affect his readers. The description of the effect, though hidden in a footnote on a previous page, left no doubt about his genius in so far as Coleridge claimed to produce in his friend

> the psychological condition, or that which constitutes the possibility of . . . the visual image or object by which the mind represents to itself its past condition, or rather, its personal identity under the form in which it imagined itself previously to have existed. (*Biographia* I, p. 72)

As the identities of the narrator of *Biographia Literaria* and the fictional friend blur in the letter, the image that emerges of Coleridge oscillates between the genial critic capable of grasping philosophic spirit and the creator of philosophic spirit himself. What plays a crucial part in this construction is the suspension, not of disbelief, but of philosophic education. Coleridge explained modestly that he only wanted to acquaint his audience with some philosophic insight:

> To me it will be happiness and honor [sic] enough, should I succeed in rendering the [Kantian and post-Kantian] system itself intelligible to my countrymen, and in the application of it to the most awful of subjects for the most important of purposes. (*Biographia* I, pp. 163–4)

Nonetheless, Coleridge's claim to be a genius of philosophy necessarily entailed the suppression of those materials and those persons that had helped him to study critical philosophy. It seemed impossible for Coleridge to build his genius on either studiousness or lessons. The philosophic genius had to enter 'one of our largest Gothic cathedrals in a gusty moonlight night of autumn' alone (*Biographia* I, p. 301).

Thomas Carlyle helped to perpetuate the specific claim of Coleridge's genial self-image in *Biographia*. Echoing Chapter 13, Carlyle used 'moonshine' (Carlyle 1851, p. 83), just like 'moonlight' (*Biographia* I, p. 301), repeatedly to refer to Coleridge's philosophy. Rather sarcastically, Carlyle played into Coleridge's claim of being a singular connoisseur of Kant: Coleridge 'knew the sublime secret of believing "the reason" what "the understanding" had been obliged to fling out as incredible' (Carlyle 1851, p. 69). This sense of secrecy in Kantianism had outraged James Walker (*Anti-Jacobin Review* 5 [1800], p. 568). Walker used secrecy as another word for obscurity. *Blackwood's Magazine* condemned Kantianism in *Biographia Literaria* on the grounds of incomprehensibility, too: 'We do not wish to speak of what we do not understand, and therefore say nothing of Mr Coleridge's Metaphysics' (Jackson 1970, p. 348). Coleridge's *Biographia* managed to transform such alleged obscurity by making it part of Coleridge's narrative of genius. So effective was its construction that the fellow Kantians have remained hidden.

Coleridge, Nitsch and the Distinction between Reason and Understanding

The seventh and last chapter closes this book with a circle. The first chapter has demonstrated that the first English advocates of the *Critique of Pure Reason*, influenced by Reinhold's *Briefe, Beyträge* and *Versuch*, focused their attention on the 'Transcendental Dialectic' and 'Transcendental Method', gave priority to Reason in its constitutive function and shared a progressive Enlightenment perspective in favour of sociopolitical reform. In that chapter, we have also learnt that most of those genuinely interested in Kant's work belonged to the dissenting milieu; the majority of the favourable material on Kant by English writers stems from, or was circulated by, non-conformists or radicals or both, including William Enfield, Joseph Johnson, John Aikin junior, William Taylor, Revd Thomas Morgan, John Thelwall, William Godwin and, above all, Thomas Beddoes. While these people and texts played an important role in shaping Coleridge's view of Kant as a rational theologian, this chapter is concerned with establishing the profound link between Nitsch and Coleridge through an analysis of the evolution of the distinction between Reason and Understanding in Coleridge's unpublished writing and mainly in *The Friend*. On the basis of their conceptual affinities, the chapter then recovers the ideological transformations, deviations and unstable reversal introduced by Coleridge's assimilation.

Coleridge, Kantianism and Unitarianism

Between 1818 and 1826, Coleridge recorded the following observation on the margins of his copy of Kant's *Religion*:[1] Kant's denial of the divinity of Christ 'is, doubtless, the strongest Argument in support of the Socinian Scheme – in truth, the only strong one. But as by a number of yet stronger Arguments, both scriptural & rational, Socinianism stands confuted' (*Marginalia* III, p. 305; see *Religion*, p. 119; *Religion 2*, 6: 116). Pages 78 and 79 in the second edition of *Die Religion innerhalb der Grenzen der blossen [sic] Vernunft* (1794) reminded Coleridge of his former adherence to Unitarianism. In the course of the previous chapters, we have seen how complicated yet pervasive Coleridge's connection with Kant was. The autograph commentary illustrates that an important point has hitherto been overlooked: for Coleridge there existed an underlying link between Kant's philosophy and Unitarianism. The Unitarians had a natural interest in particularly one version of Kantianism, namely Reinhold's 'gospel of Reason'. Coleridge's autograph commentary illustrates that this link can be traced throughout Coleridge's work. It is reflected in Coleridge's selective reading of the *Critique of Pure Reason*, to which I will come later. The passages singled out by Reinhold and inserted into the pantheism controversy in the 1780s include also the ones that influenced Coleridge the most: 'The "Dialectic"', as Boulger notes, 'made the most serious impression on him [Coleridge], influencing his thinking in metaphysics and theology for the remainder of his life' (1961, p. 72). Despite Thomas McFarland's seminal study on pantheism (1969), Coleridge studies have barely paid any attention to these striking similarities between Coleridge on the one hand and Reinhold as mediated by English publications on the other hand; neither have scholars of the effective history of Kant's philosophy investigated the body of works spearheaded by Beddoes, Nitsch and O'Keeffe. One of the crucial philosophical concepts that Coleridge is known to have adopted from the 'Transcendental Dialectic', and to have subsequently transformed, is that speculative Reason has no constitutive power to extend our knowledge beyond any object that has been given by experience; speculative Reason hence operates merely as a regulative principle (*KrV* B 699; *CpR* B 699). Only within the domain of morality does Reason play a constitutive role, that is, only practical Reason has a forming part. Coleridge came to assimilate this distinction by drawing on a number of Kantian texts that go far beyond the 'Transcendental Dialectic'. Like Kant, Coleridge used, with few exceptions, the terms 'Understanding' and 'Reason' to distinguish between two essentially different modi operandi of Reason. It is also known in Coleridge studies that the distinction between Reason and Understanding is of central importance; so much so that McFarland once claimed that 'there is an infallible way to distinguish a true Coleridgean from a dabbler or from those who have encountered him in survey courses, no matter how enthusiastic these dilettantes may seem to be. That shibboleth, that litmus test, is provided by Coleridge's distinction between reason and understanding' (1993, p. 165). It is true that J. H. Muirhead claimed that the distinction was Platonic: 'As a matter of fact it had been before the world since the time of Plato' (1930, p. 65). But the majority of nineteenth- and twentieth-century scholars do not agree with Muirhead. Donald MacKinnon states clearly that the 'distinction between Reason and Understanding, which Coleridge of course found in Kant, was for him of the very greatest significance' (1974, p. 190). Little more than a decade after Coleridge's death, F. J. A. Hort noted without a shadow of a doubt that the 'cardinal distinction of Coleridge's philosophy was obviously derived from Kant' (1856, p. 319). Hort added in a revealing way that Coleridge in conversation, or rather in monologue, 'frequently mentioned Kant's name with gratitude, as he did those of others, especially in this affair of the reason and understanding' (1856, p. 320). From the letters we know that Coleridge explained privately to Joseph Hughes the central importance of the distinction:

> My philosophy (as metaphysics) is built on the distinction between the Reason and the Understanding. He who, after fairly attending to my exposition of this point in the '*Friend*,' (vol. I. pp. 254–77,) and in the Appendix to the *first* Lay-Sermon, can still find no meaning in this distinction . . . for him the perusal of my *philosophical* writings, at least, will be a mere waste of time. (*Letters* VI, pp. 1049–50)

As noted here, Coleridge published essays on the distinction between Reason and Understanding in *The Friend* (1809 and 1818), the Appendix C to the *Statesman's Manual* (1816) and additionally in *Aids to Reflection* (1825).[2] In *Biographia*, he also declared that to 'establish this distinction was one main object of THE FRIEND' (I, p. 175). The distinction between Reason and Understanding carries enormous weight within Coleridge's thought as a whole and in particular within his morality, theology and political philosophy.

Previous scholarship

The topic is especially controversial as it has wide ramifications. W. H. Walsh once called the disagreement on Kant's attitude towards metaphysics a scandal: 'it is scandal to philosophy generally and to Kantian scholarship in particular that commentators are unable to agree about Kant's attitude to metaphysics' (1976, p. 372). Chapter 1 has sketched that there are good reasons for this situation; the ambivalence in the *first critique* has inevitably also affected the study of Coleridge's adaptation. Chapter 3 has shown how the controversy and concomitant disregard for the highest good in the twentieth-century Kant scholarship on ethics contributed to the view that Coleridge did not understand Kant adequately. In regard to the 'Transcendental Dialect' in the *first critique*, Wellek has put forward the now common view that Coleridge's preference for constitutive Reason signifies a philosophical blemish. For Wellek, Reinhold's system represented merely 'confusion' (1931, p. 5). Wellek has criticized Coleridge's interpretation accordingly: 'Reason under Coleridge's hands returned to its old meaning of intellectual intuition, the limits between practical and theoretical reason are erased thereby and the whole flood of traditional metaphysics can again celebrate its triumphant entry' (1931, p. 108). Discussing Coleridge's significance within the history of modern criticism, Wellek notes that 'Coleridge disconcertingly wavers between a psychological and an epistemological foundation for such an analysis [of poetry]' (1981, p. 158). In accordance with Wellek renowned scholars like Orsini (1969, p. 137) and Bode (2009, p. 610) have supported the defendable view that Coleridge was an unqualified Kantian.[3] However, Wellek, for instance, attributes no significance to the fact that Kant's preface to the second edition stated explicitly that the *first critique* limited knowledge to give way to faith. Coleridge's profound engagement with the *Critique of Pure Reason* appears in a completely different light from the point of view of more recent Kant scholarship. What Walsh described as the scandal of indecision in the 1970s has taken on a more definite direction since the mid-1980s. Kühn observes that scholars no longer disagree about the question whether Kant's *first critique* was anti-sceptical, but how it achieved this goal: 'it sometimes appears that the only thing that was clear in the interpretation of Kant during the last twenty years or so was "what Kant was trying to prove". His first *Critique* was meant to "undercut" scepticism' (Kühn 2005, p. 115). This view and the above-quoted passage from Kant have been the natural point of departure for theologically orientated Coleridge scholars like Boulger, Hedley and Vigus. In his study of Coleridge as religious thinker, Boulger clarified his point of view that '[t]his "corruption" of Kant's purpose has of course been deplored by some modern commentators, yet it cannot be doubted that Kant had left the door ajar for a troop of theological speculators' (1961, p. 75). With regard to the 1787 preface, Hedley observes that

> Kant is arguing for the priority of practical over theoretical Reason. Whereas the theoretical intellect has access only to the transcendentally ideal realm, practical reason has access to the intelligible, objective, underlying reality: the intelligible world contains the ground of the sensible world and therefore also of its laws. (2000, p. 165)

Like Vigus's recent essay (2012), this chapter argues that Kant's notion of moral faith gave Coleridge (and his contemporaries) sufficient grounds to further develop the affirmative mode of Reason.

Usually Coleridge's work is seen in opposition to Kant's fidelity to experience and the limits of knowledge. Scholars compare Coleridge with canonical post-Kantian philosophers. Kathleen Wheeler, for instance, has traced the similarities between Coleridge's defiance of Kant's 'barren dualism' to Hegel (1986, pp. 27–8). Mary Anne Perkins has compared Coleridge's deviation from Kant's strict aesthetic formalism to Schelling and Hegel: 'Coleridge aimed, like Hegel, to produce a system which reconciled the truths of empiricism and realism with those of idealism' (1994, p. 94). Paul Hamilton compares Coleridge's attempt to reconcile his desire for metaphysical disclosure with experience to Hegel and Schelling: 'Schelling was the philosopher who came nearest to Coleridge's theoretical positing. Existential where Hegel was rational, Schelling felt able to be as philosophically inclusive as the Jena Romantics while claiming that a special philosophical insight licensed his acceptance of the diversity of the world and our different forms of orientation within it' (2007, p. 26). Vigus points to Jacobi's role in Coleridge's transgressions of the limits of knowledge imposed by Kant (2012). Yet the possibility that Nitsch's exposition alongside those of Beddoes and other early mediators primed Coleridge with the affirmative role of Reason in critical philosophy has not been considered yet.

Coleridge's anticipation of and response to the *first critique*

The possibility of metaphysics was a focal point of Coleridge's philosophical thinking. As Seamus Perry points out, the question whether the existence of absolute oneness cannot be proven in the face of manifold experiences was 'perhaps the central concern of STC's metaphysics' (Coleridge 2002a, p. 157). Coleridge's notebook entry from November 1799 conveys his fervent desire to hold onto the concept of metaphysical oneness: 'I would make a pilgrimage to the burning sands of Arabia, or &c &c to find the Man who could explain to me there can be *oneness*, there being infinite Perceptions – yet there must be *oneness*, not an intense Union but an Absolute Unity, for &c' (*Notebooks* I, §556). Coleridge repeated this wish in October 1803, adding a significant elucidation which points to the central paradox which Hume and Kant exposed: 'the co presence of Feeling & Life, [is] limitless by their very essence, with Form, by its very essence limited – determinate – definite'

(*Notebooks* I, §1561). It seems that by this time Coleridge was more consciously alert to the contradictions of metaphysical oneness. His entry points out the paradox of limiting the limitless, of determining the indeterminate, of defining the infinite or of conditioning the unconditional and indicates his familiarity with and awareness of the criticisms of traditional metaphysics. In 1806, Coleridge responded harshly to Hume in a letter to Thomas Clarkson.[4] He condemned 'the unphilosophical jargon of Hume and his Followers' (*Letters* II, p. 1194) and thus confirmed that he knew how damaging Hume's arguments were for his belief in metaphysics. In 1805, Coleridge wrote in notebooks 'never let the names of Darwin, Johnson, Hume, *furr* it [England] over – If these must be England let them be another England' (*Notebooks* II, §2598; Perry 2007b, pp. 264–6). In the early 1830s, Coleridge wrote on the margins of Pepys's *Memoirs* that 'Hume has . . . been extravagantly overrated' (*Marginalia* IV, p. 75). Coleridge's opinion of Hume was evidently low and indicates his eagerness to refute his scepticism. Coleridge would eventually come to believe, as Hedley notes, 'that the distinction between the understanding as the adaptive power of mankind and reason as the divine light or Logos provides the only possible response to Hume's theological spider' (2000, p. 200). Sara Coleridge also made it very plain:

> The truth was that he never beheld in Kant the foe of Christianity; he kept his eye on the great characteristic parts of Kant's teaching, and these, he maintained, might be brought to the service of Christianity, as far as they went; might strengthen the faith by purifying it and bringing it into co-incidence with reason. (1847, p. cxxix)

This conviction of Coleridge is rooted in the poet's initial exposure to critical philosophy.

Nitsch and Beddoes presented Kant as the perfect ally against Hume (see Chapter 1). What is, in other words, essential about Coleridge's acquaintance with the expositions by Nitsch (1796) and to some degree with Beddoes's *Observations* (1793) and article on Reinhold in the *Monthly Magazine* (1796) is that they introduced critical philosophy to Coleridge from the start as a remedy against scepticism. Nitsch predicted that critical philosophy would aid rational belief:

> The influence which Kant's Philosophy in general, and particularly his arguments concerning the Deity and the immortality of the soul, may have on religion, is that it secures these two important objects against all manner of demonstrations, which have done more mischief in the moral world than even Fatalism . . . by thus destroying improper arguments, which never fail to produce Scepticism, room is made for a rational belief, which, although it be not the highest degree of conviction, yet is perfectly sufficient to make us strive after virtue from disinterested motives. (1796, pp. 232–3)

Nitsch conceded that Kant's theology would not satisfy dogmatists, but declared that critical philosophy silenced sceptics through the moderation of rational belief. Coleridge's annotations to the *Critique of Pure Reason* suggest that Coleridge approached Kant's work exactly with the anticipation of a cure against scepticism and that Nitsch lies behind this expectation.

Coleridge's thorough study of Kant appears to have entailed an element of disappointment. Similar to his frustrated response to the *Groundwork* in 1803 (Chapter 3), Coleridge found the *Critique of Pure Reason* at first unsatisfying because it was unconstructive for his belief. He was reading a copy of the fifth edition published in Leipzig by Johann Friedrich Hartnoch.[5] His autograph commentaries in this thick volume are few and neatly written in the back of the copy. They strongly support the view that Coleridge, like any reader of Nitsch's introduction, expected to find affirmative propositions for his belief in the *Critique of Pure Reason*. Coleridge concluded one of his study sessions by writing on the margins of the book: 'But Kant I do not understand – i.e. I have not discovered what he proposes for my Belief' (*Marginalia* III, p. 249). His doubts were bound up with the notion of intuitions and the emptiness of the categories (the latter mould and filter manifold intuitions, but cannot produce any perceptions by themselves). Coleridge raised the question of 'I apply the Categoric forms to a Tree? – well! but first *what* is this tree? How do I come by this Tree?' (*Marginalia* III, p. 249). Coleridge added in his copy of the *Critique of Pure Reason* that the sections from the 'transcendental deduction of the pure concepts of Understanding' up to the beginning of the 'analytic of principles', that is, pages 'p. 129 to 169 comprehend the most difficult and obscure passages of this Critique – or that the *knot* of the whole System' (*Marginalia* III, p. 242). Kant told his readers that the 'deduction of the pure concepts of the Understanding' was the most difficult part of the composition of the *first critique* for him (*KrV* A XVI). Struggling with these very chapters Coleridge wondered: 'Was ist Erfahrung?' ('What is experience?') (*Marginalia* III, p. 248) and 'What do you mean by a *fact*, an empiric Reality, from which alone can give solidity (inhalt) to our Conceptions?' (*Marginalia* III, p. 248). Coleridge took issue with aspects of the *Critique of Pure Reason* linked with the question of intuitions. Wellek notes, as mentioned, that Coleridge reintroduced the notion of intellectual intuitions in the critical system and thus reduced it to traditional metaphysics (1931, p. 108).

Intellectual intuitions

By the mid-1810s, Coleridge wrote that Kant excluded this notion:

> He [Kant] therefore consistently and rightly denies the possibility of intellectual intuitions. But as I see no adequate reason for this exclusive sense of the term, I have reverted to its wider signification authorized by our elder theologians and metaphysicians, according to whom the term comprehends all truths known to us without a medium. (*Biographia* I, p. 289)

Coleridge was unwilling to limit intuitions ('Anschauungen') to the effects of empirical objects on our receptivity, that is, to sensuous intuitions 'which can be represented in space and time' (*Biographia* I, p. 289). Indeed, Kant explained in the *Critique of Pure Reason* that if 'intellectual intuition' ('intellektuelle Anschauung') were a form of determining the existence of our consciousness, this would preclude our relation to anything outside of us (*KrV* B XL; see B 68). It is commonly thought that Coleridge adopted and expanded the notion of 'intellectual intuitions' not from Kant but from post-Kantian philosophers spearheaded by Friedrich Wilhelm Joseph Schelling (1775–1854) and Johann Gottlieb Fichte (1762–1814) (Harter 2011, pp. 92–101; Orsini 1969, p. 189; Wheeler 1980, pp. 70–80). Manfred Frank notes that the 'intellectual intuition' was a key concept of early German Romantic philosophy. It played a crucial role in works by Kant as well as those by Fichte and his disciples. The concept of 'intellectual intuition' does not merely address any problem of subordinate importance, but pertains to the core of German idealist philosophy (1987, p. 96). Why is that so?

Following the Cartesian tradition, Kant made pure self-consciousness the highest point of his epistemological system. The 'I think' is the pure or original apperception and must as such be able to accompany all representations (*KrV* B 131–2; *CpR* B 131–2). The pure apperception provides us with the unity necessary for the synthesis of concept and intuition in the construction of cognitions ('Erkenntnisse'); it thus links the spontaneity of our intellect with our receptivity; receptivity appears in comparison to the intellect as a passive mental faculty. The act of the synthesis of cognition is spontaneous and intellectual (*KrV* B 130; *CpR* 130); likewise, the pure apperception operates exclusively on an intellectual level. This insight leads to the philosophical impasse that, within the critical system, the existence of self-consciousness cannot be proven. This is so, as we have seen in Chapter 1, because existence is not a predicate and cannot be unpacked from other concepts. In other words, the intellectual nature of pure apperception excludes the possibility of that which is necessary to prove its existence: receptivity and intuitions. In order to prove the existence of self-consciousness, it would be necessary to have an original synthesis 'die ursprüngliche Synthese' (Götze 2001, p. 51). This is the solution that Fichte found.

Fichte built on this impasse and transformed the presupposition of an original synthesis into an original act that he called 'Tathandlung' (Frank 1987, p. 106). Fichte defined 'intellectual intuitions' as Halmi observes, 'as "the immediate consciousness that I act and of my actions [*dass ich handle, und was ich handle*] . . . a faculty whose existence cannot be demonstrated through concepts and whose content [*was es sey*] cannot be developed through concepts"' (Fichte cited in Halmi 2007a, p. 147). This theory gave rise to 'a new mythology' (Halmi 2007a, p. 147). The impasse of Kant's dual system and the post-Kantian transformations of it are well known in British Romanticism, German idealist philosophy and Coleridge studies. However Coleridge's acquaintance with the early mediators and their respective works prior to his acquaintance with Schelling has been overlooked although it sheds a new light on the evolution of the central issue of Coleridge's uses of the concept of 'intuition'.

Nitsch's introduction of 'Intuitions'

Despite the notice in Robert Hall's article (1970, p. 315) and current listings in the *Oxford English Dictionary* (2012), scholars have failed to observe that Nitsch had used the translation 'intuition' for 'Anschauungen' before Coleridge did. Both men knew the common translation practice to revert to Latin roots; accordingly Coleridge quoted 'intueri' as his source (*Biographia* I, p. 289). Nevertheless, the way in which Nitsch introduced intuitions matches Coleridge's 'wider signification' in a striking way. The first chapter explained that Reinhold replaced the validity of cognition with representations ('Vorstellungen'). Frank points out that Kant was surprised to find that his immediate students, for instance Reinhold and Fichte, decided to dedicate themselves to the study of the problem of self-consciousness which arose from Kant's philosophy (1987, p. 97). Nitsch had also studied directly under Kant and he, too, was particularly interested in the spontaneity of our intellect. Nitsch paraphrased the pure apperception: 'The "I am", and the "I think", must accompany all our ideas, or else they will not belong to us nor ever become objects of our attention' (1796, p. 111). In addition, Nitsch's treatise had a particular bias. In Nitsch's view, 'the analytical method [which he applied in his treatise was] better calculated to remove those difficulties of . . . the synthetical method' (1796, p. 111). By 'synthetical method' he appears to have referred to the deduction of the concepts of the Understanding. Nitsch explained that his treatise gave priority to analytic over synthetic judgements: 'I have resolved to treat of the above principles, without which Kant will never be understood, according to the analytical method, which seems to admit of more clearness' (1796, p. 168). In contrast, 'the synthetical method', Nitsch observed, 'is attended with some degree of unavoidable obscurity' (1796, p. 168). In other words, Nitsch's exposition barely treated the crucial part in which Kant established the ways that give objective validity to cognition through the synthesis of concept and intuition. These were the passages in which Kant 'reintroduces', as Guyer notes, 'his claim that we need intuitions as well as concepts in order to have knowledge, so that the categories must be applied to our experience of empirical intuitions with its spatio-temporal form, through the what he calls their "schematism" ' (2006, p. 71). In doing so, Nitsch introduced intuitions in a way that missed this gist of Kant's epistemology (*KrV/CpR* B XVI–XVII, B 119–22). For Nitsch, the 'synthesis of recognition' represented merely the last of three functions of 'Spontaneity' (1796, pp. 76–7). What Nitsch did explain was that 'all our intuitions arise in consequence of such changes or alterations in our Receptivity' (1796, p. 84). He drew on a passage at the beginning of the 'Transcendental Aesthetic' in the *Critique of Pure Reason*:

> Die Fähigkeit, (Rezeptivität), Vorstellungen durch die Art, wie wir von Gegenständen afficirt werden, zu bekommen, heißt *Sinnlichkeit*. Vermittelst der Sinnlichkeit also werden uns Gegenstände gegeben, und sie allein liefert uns Anschauugen. (*KrV* B 33)
>
> (The capacity [receptivity] to acquire representations through the way in which given we are affected by objects is called *sensibility*. Objects are therefore given to us by means of sensibility, it alone affords us intuitions. [*CpR* B 33])

Nitsch made clear that it is our receptivity that provides us with intuitions, but failed to state clearly that one of the main purposes of intuitions is their part (besides concepts) in constituting the objective cognition of objects outside of ourselves. Nitsch's treatise addressed the deduction of the pure intuitions of space and time in the 'Transcendental Aesthetic'. It expounded vaguely that the 'idea of time exhibits to the mind the general form of internal intuitions' (1796, p. 83). Subsequently he distinguished between 'internal', 'pure' and 'a priori' intuitions and those that are 'external', 'empirical', 'a posteriori' (1796, p. 84). But Nitsch did not discuss empirical intuitions any further. Rather, for Nitsch 'to *think* in the widest sense of the word' was to 'apprehend, connect, and reproduce, especially to connect the affections of our external and internal senses into intuitions' (1796, p. 77). Nitsch hardly ever separated the external from the internal sense. Thus he made the lines between different types of intuition (e.g. pure and empirical) blur and opened the possibility for intellectual intuitions. Nitsch's exposition of critical philosophy was geared to support the validity of the existence of self-consciousness at the expense of Kant's dualism. His system did not explicitly exclude nor include the notion of intellectual intuitions; yet his emphasis on spontaneity, inner sense and internal intuitions paved the way for intellectual intuitions.

Coleridge's affinity with Nitsch

Thus Nitsch brought to England an exposition of Kant's philosophy that shared the early German Romantics' fascination with pure apperception and self-consciousness and tried to overcome the concomitant impasse between the self that thinks and the self that simply is. Coleridge would call it '*Ego contemplans*' and '*Ego contemplatus*' in *Biographia* (I, p. 72). He recorded his 'Doubts during a first, perusal – i.e. Struggles felt, not arguments objected' (*Marginalia* III, p. 247). As early as around 1800 he apparently knew that this impasse was the germ for much productive philosophical thought. Coleridge's autograph commentary states: 'At least, the difference between the original Unity of Consciousness, and empirical Consciousness is the great point, the germ' (*Marginalia* III, p. 243).

It is very unlikely Nitsch had no part in this brilliant insight. Coleridge made it unmistakably clear that he had expected a version somewhat closer to intellectual intuitions than that of Kant '– Fichte I understand very well – only I cannot believe his System. But Kant I do not understand' (*Marginalia* III, p. 249). In the 1810s, Coleridge deemed Fichte's system 'truly metaphysical and of a *metaphysique* [sic] truly systematic: (i.e. having its spring and principle within itself.)' (*Biographia* I, p. 158). If Nitsch primed Coleridge for the study of the *first critique*, it would explain a major reason for his affinity to Fichte and his reservation towards the *first critique* during his first perusals. Further traces of Nitsch's treatise elsewhere in Coleridge's handwritten commentary on his copy of the *Critique of Pure Reason* indicate that this was the case indeed.

Coleridge repeated what Nitsch's treatise made sufficiently clear, namely that 'All intuitions, als sinnlich, beruhen auf Affectionen'. Yet pure intuitions puzzled Coleridge: 'If sinnlich here = sensual, empirisch, how does this apply to the pure Intuitions, as the immediate products of the intuitive Act? If not applicable, then *all* intuitions do not rest on *Affections*' (*Marginalia* III, p. 242). Nitsch's treatise had blurred the distinction between pure and empirical intuitions; Coleridge seems to have transferred this conflation onto the *Critique of Pure Reason*.

Another instance suggests that Nitsch gave Coleridge at least a rough idea of the constitution of cognitions of external objects. One of Coleridge's illustrations of human perception echoes an example used by Nitsch. The lecturer observed that

> in viewing a rose, we distinguish two things, first, a variety, and then a connection
> of that variety into a regular and figured whole; which connection makes the thing

to be one and not many thing, gives it unity, and may be called form, which the variety may be called the matter of the rose. (1796, pp. 73–4)

A Coleridge letter dating from 1806 resonates with Nitsch's illustration: 'I have a distinct Thought of a Rose-Tree; but what countless properties and goings-on of that plant are there, not included in my *Thought* of it?' (*Letters* II, p. 1195). Coleridge's observation is remarkable in so far as it includes the two vital elements for the cognition of an empirical object in Kant's epistemology (which does not use the same example): 'countless properties' (intuitions) and 'a distinct Thought' (a concept). If Coleridge remembered Nitsch's example for the constitution of our cognition of an object, he thought certainly of the 1796 treatise, too, when it came to one of Coleridge's most pressing questions about the existence of God. Nitsch introduced Kant as a remedy against Hume, but on his initial perusal of the *first critique* Coleridge was disappointed to find little or none that was satisfying.

Implications of Nitsch's 'Intuition' lessons for Coleridge

Nitsch's treatise, through its emphasis on the spontaneity of intellect and link between inner sense and external intuitions, appears to have primed Coleridge for the adoption of 'intellectual intuitions' at a very early stage in his career. Despite the initial struggle when Coleridge first read the *Critique of Pure Reason*, he understood that the germ of critical philosophy for Kant's immediate students consisted in resolving the impasse of the inexistence of pure apperception. Nitsch thought that it was necessary to familiarize his students with 'the spirit of fundamental principles' of Kant before they could embark on a proper study of critical philosophy (Nitsch 1796, p. 168). The fact that Coleridge grasped the germ of post-Kantian philosophy probably on the occasion of his first perusal of the *first critique* can partly be explained through his stay in Lower Saxony, but it also points to Nitsch's lasting influence. He appears to have primed Coleridge with the spirit of critical philosophy. In the *Essays on the Principles of Genial Criticism* Coleridge established as a trademark of genial criticism the capacity to grasp the spirit in which a work was composed. This principle was largely inspired by various Kantian sources, such as the *third critique*, the transcript of Kant's logic and Nitsch's treatise. At the same time, this engagement with the spirit of a work also captured the essence of Coleridge's experience as a reader, which he described as follows in an unpublished letter:

> there was a period of my Life, when I could read a Volume before almost any other person could have got thro' a chapter and yet be able to give a full and faithful account of Contents – But then no more of them in the order to cite with authority, in what part of the Volume it was. (cited in Walker 1997, p. 325)

Coleridge was an extraordinarily fast, but also chaotic reader. He barely used tedious page marks or notes, but rather devoured the content of books. Despite his rapid perusals, he retained the content although he remembered it no longer in terms of the structure or by the sequence of chapters or headings. Rather, he transformed the content while reading into an accurate, but independent reproduction, be it by way of talking or writing. It was characteristic of Coleridge to grasp the spirit of writings while he had difficulties recording his sources: 'I neglected to make a pencil Mem. on the blank lea[f] of the Book, or put in a bit of paper' (cited in Walker 1997, p. 325). Mr Bernhard Krusve, or 'Kruse' according to Wellek (1981, p. 155), a German, was the first to confront Coleridge with the notion that the contents of his lecture on Romeo and Juliet at the Royal Institution were derived from A. W. Schlegel's lectures delivered at Vienna in 1808. In response to this accusation, Coleridge replied:

> Suppose myself & Schlegel (my argument not my vanity leads to these seeming Self-flatteries) nearly equal in natural powers, of similar pursuits & acquirements, and it is only necessary for both to have mastered the spirit of Kant's Critique of the Judgment to render it morally certain, that writing on the same Subject we should draw the same conclusion by the same trains [of reasoning] from the same principles, write to one purpose & write one spirit. (*Letters* III, p. 360)

In *Biographia Literaria*, Coleridge anticipated charges of plagiarizing Schelling by giving a similar explanation: 'We [Schelling and Coleridge] had studied in the same school; been disciplined by the same preparatory philosophy, namely, the writings of Kant' (*Biographia* I, p. 161). The statement appears genuine in so far as Coleridge recognized early and partly through the help of Nitsch that there was a common 'germ' among the post-Kantians. He probably read in the transcripts of Kant's logic dating from the 1770s that one does not learn how to philosophize by copying and learning by heart the philosophies of others; one should not bind oneself to an original but develop one's own capacity to criticize and assess the philosophy of others (Chapter 6). Coleridge captured a similar idea when he wrote privately: 'There are two Kinds of Heads in the world of Literature. The one I would call, SPRINGS: the other TANKS' (*Letters* III, p. 355). 'TANKS' were a type of critic that considered 'all Thoughts' as 'traditional' (*Letters* III, p. 355). 'If they find a fine passage in Thomson, they refer it to Milton; if in Milton to Euripides or Homer; and if in Homer, they take for granted its pre-existence in the lost works of Linus or Musaeus' (*Letters* III, p. 355). Coleridge described 'TANKS' satirically as critics who presupposed that all ideas should be traced to the invention of scripture, when 'the Alphabet was revealed to Adam' (*Letters* III, p. 355). Coleridge preferred the 'SPRINGS' because of their ability to distinguish 'living production . . . from mechanical formation' (*Letters* III, p. 355).

As the proponent of genial criticism, Coleridge favoured 'Generation' over 'Fabrication' and defined the former as that which evolves from within 'is ab intra, *evolved*' (*Notebooks* II, §2444). Just like the genial critic, the 'SPRING' generates ideas by partaking in the spirit of the literature or philosophical principles. Only 'TANKS' copy and learn the philosophy of others. The line between being a 'SPRING' and a plagiarist seems thin in Coleridge's case. Yet provided that Coleridge knew Kant's 1770s instructions for students, as he most likely did, then his 'SPRING' approach to reading Schelling appears understandable and cannot be easily equated, as scholars have noted before, with plagiarism in the sense of conscious intentional concealments (Coleridge 1847, p. vi; Keanie 2009; Schaffer 2004, p. 42; McFarland 1974).[6] Coleridge transformed the contents he read. Sara Coleridge once defended her father by observing that 'There can be no reasonable doubt, that he was at least in the same line of thought with him

[Schelling] – was in search of what Schelling discovered – before he met with his writings' (1847, p. xxix). Nitsch's case further supports this and Coleridge's argument of having 'studied in the same school' as Schelling: the German expatriate primed him for Schelling's as well as for Fichte's philosophy. Coleridge spoke of 'Generation' as a special kind of the inception of ideas: 'the transmission of a *Life*, according to the kind of the living Transmitter' (*Notebooks* II, §2444). Possibly Nitsch was such a 'living Transmitter' for Coleridge.

Reason and Understanding in October 1806

The gradual development of his distinction between Reason and Understanding includes further marks of Nitsch in Coleridge's thinking. The philosophical distinction occurred for the first time in Coleridge's writings, according to John Beer (1993, p. lxxix), in October 1806. At the time, Coleridge no longer regarded himself as a Unitarian and found himself in a profound speculative crisis (see Chapter 6). Critical philosophy appears to have been part of Coleridge's deepest theological enquiries throughout his life, sometimes as a source of comfort and at other times as a source of frustration. From Nitsch, Coleridge must have gathered that Kant offered no straightforward solutions to the demonstrability of the existence of deity and hence no full satisfaction for his desire for ontological revelation. And yet, the way Nitsch described Kantian 'Reason' in his exposition probably had an enormous appeal for Coleridge.

According to Nitsch, the 'unconditioned unity, though the most abstract idea that can be formed, must necessarily be thought by every man who would make any use of his reason' (1796, p. 126). Here, Reason was said to produce unconditioned unity. Nitsch's exposition offered possible answers for Coleridge's most pressing spiritual question regarding metaphysical oneness (*Notebooks* I, §556). The text included the following gloss, which was based on Reinhold's *Versuch* (1789, p. 519) and Kant's *Critique of Pure Reason* (*KrV* B 280–1; *CpR* B 280–1). It described Understanding and Reason as a kind of double vision of the world:

> All the phenomena in the world make a whole which is supported by mutual action and re-action; but considered by the understanding alone, this whole discovers a determinate co-existence, consequence, and duration; for the understanding reaches not farther than what it has actually comprehended. – Reason views this whole as infinitely determinable in its duration, co-existence, mutual actions, and as a boundless coherence in time, where there is nothing unconnected, and, consequently, nothing absolutely beginning. *In mundo non datur casus purus.* (1796, p. 138)[7]

The Understanding features here as the restrained faculty that is unable to reach beyond the empirical world that is ruled by causality and temporality. Coleridge mentioned a very similar view of the Understanding in his letter to Thomas Clarkson dating from October 1806. Responding to Clarkson's question, Coleridge wrote: 'What is the difference between the Reason, and the Understanding? — I would reply, that

Faculty of the Soul which apprehends and retains the mere notices of Experience . . . we may call the Understanding' (*Letters* II, p. 1198). Here and throughout his future work, Coleridge assumed that the Understanding played an inferior role.

Implications for existing standard view

The assumption has been since Wellek (1931, pp. 115–31) that this definition of Understanding is not directly supported by the *first critique*. Christoph Bode, who shares this opinion and gives a concise overview of the body of literature that supports it, speaks of 'Coleridge's unique use of Reason and Understanding' (2009, p. 602). This chapter shows that Coleridge's use of Reason and Understanding was not unique but largely inspired by a late eighteenth-century interpretation that can be traced via Nitsch and Reinhold to the section on the postulates of empirical thinking in the *Critique of Pure Reason*. Kant had revised this section substantially for the second edition. Edward Caird once declared that

> these alterations are important, not, as has been maintained by Schopenhauer and others, because they show a tendency in Kant to recoil to the point of view of the ordinary common sense Realism from an idealistic position similar to that of Berkeley; but because they indicate his progress towards an Idealism in which the subjectivity of Berkeley's theory is corrected. (1909 I, p. viii; see pp. 543–604)

The fact that one of the founding members of British absolute idealism came to this conclusion is telling. Caird wrote from a perspective within an English philosophical tradition that can be traced back to Nitsch via Coleridge. The English early mediators including Coleridge had in common that they expanded the already existing idealist tendency in the *Critique of Pure Reason*.

Strong believers in the power of Reason

In his explanation for Clarkson, Coleridge contradistinguished Reason by using the same rhetoric of double vision as the above-quoted passage from Nitsch. Coleridge described the simultaneously contingent and non-contingent view of a triangle, which corresponded to the respective points of view of the Understanding and of Reason. The Understanding perceives, according to Coleridge, the accidental size, colour and material of the triangle, 'as for instance that such an object has a triangular figure, that it is of such or such a magnitude, and of such and such a colour, and consistency, with the anticipation of meeting the same under the same circumstances' (*Letters* II, p. 1198). Such anticipation ranks lower than Reason because it mainly depended on empirical data; Coleridge summed up that 'in other words, all the mere φαινόμενα of our nature, we may call the Understanding' (*Letters* II, p. 1198). Coleridge gave pride of place to the non-contingent components of a triangle, that is, to 'all such notices, as are characterized by UNIVERSALITY and NECESSITY' (p. 1198). Reason offered a more advanced point of view for Coleridge because it was able to grasp 'that every Triangle *must* in all places and at all times have it's two sides greater than it's third—and which are evidently not the effect of any Experience' (*Letters* II, p. 1198). The passage points ahead to Coleridge's explanation of a priori truths in geometry and his illustration of a circle in Thesis IV, Chapter 12 of *Biographia Literaria* (I, pp. 269–70). 'We may call Reason', Coleridge notes, 'the condition of all Experience, & that indeed without which Experience itself would be inconceivable' (*Letters* II, p. 1198). Coleridge's presentation of Reason agreed with Nitsch's definition that 'the term reason, taken in a more confined sense, will therefore comprehend, besides what is properly called reason, also the judging faculty or the understanding, and exclude the faculty of sense' (1796, p. 32). Coleridge's example lessens the importance of the faculty of the Understanding compared to Kant's system in so far as the former does not acknowledge the central function of the Understanding for the constitution of experience.

A possible source for Coleridge's example of the triangle is Nitsch's explanation that 'the conception of a triangle in general . . . can only exist in our thoughts, because it comprehends all species of triangles and abstracts from the necessary qualifications of a particular triangle' (1796, p. 103). Nitsch explained Kant's notion of schema (*KrV* B 180) as certain forms or rules of the 'productive imagination' through which the understanding is able to apply its 'categories' to the manifold of sense-perception in the process of realizing knowledge or experience. Coleridge's above-quoted definition that Reason contains the conditions of experience is compatible with Kant's notion of schema, which Nitsch paraphrased as forms of 'pure intellect' (Nitsch 1796, p. 103); but, contrary to Coleridge's explanation, schema also pertained to the Understanding, not only to Reason. Coleridge's double perspective for the triangle mainly captured the priority of Reason and the inferiority of the Understanding on the grounds of contingency; Coleridge reduced the function of the Understanding to the passive receptivity of changeable sense impressions and probably did so on the basis of the hints he gathered from Nitsch.

The pre-eminence of constitutive Reason has been the cause of much debate in Coleridge studies because its various possible sources, particularly Platonic and Christian (Neo-)Platonic doctrines, are difficult to locate. Boulger observed that 'Coleridge wanted constitutive principles, not merely regulative ones, and this introduces into his higher reason an un-Kantian element' (1961, p. 92). As mentioned, I contend that the primacy of Reason in Coleridge's thought was arguably Kantian. What has been overlooked so far is the possibility that Coleridge was acquainted with Nitsch's treatise and by extension with Reinhold's amplifications of the power of Reason before Coleridge had studied the *first critique* by himself.

When Coleridge extolled the distinction between Reason and Understanding for the first time in the letter to Clarkson (October 1806), he declared that 'Reason is therefore most eminently the Revelation of an immortal soul, and it's best Synonime [sic]— it is the forma formans, which contains in itself the law of it's own conceptions' (*Letters* II, p. 1198). Here, Coleridge unleashed Reason to such an extent that he even claimed that it was capable of revelation. At first glance, this might seem incompatible with the *first critique*. However, the claim is close to Nitsch's interpretation of Reason. His treatise provided readers with a table of 'primary Ideas of Reason' (1796, p. 131), which listed 'Unconditioned Totality', 'Unconditioned Limitation', 'Absolute Substance',

'Absolute Cause', 'Unconditioned or absolute Concurrence Absolute Necessity' (1796, p. 131). According to Nitsch, Reason contained the origin of these ideas in itself:

> These ideas of Reason are not derived from experience; for experience can offer no shadow of object to which they can in any manner refer; they are consequently ideas *a priori*; the roots from which they shoot up lie in reason, and reason, which produces them, is pure reason. (1796, p. 131)

Here, Reason is not said to proffer revelation, but it is a self-generating principle that appears to have inspired, at least in part, Coleridge's formulation of Reason as a 'forma formans'. Nitsch's exposition imparted a version of the Kantian system that was certainly better suited to aid Coleridge's urgent quest for metaphysical oneness than the *Critique of Pure Reason* itself. The latter baffled Coleridge in parts and left him wondering what it could do for his belief, whereas Nitsch's introduction had introduced critical philosophy as a relatively straightforward defence of rational belief. Coleridge appears to have followed Nitsch's treatise even after he had read Kant in the original mainly because its idealist tendency was at times more fitting for Coleridge metaphysical quest than the original *first critique*. Yet, apparently in 1806, not even Nitsch's defence of rational belief could fully convince Coleridge any more that rational theology alone 'deserved the name of a religion in any sense' (*Letters* II, p. 1189).

Four years later, Coleridge inserted the notion of divine Trinity into his Kantian thought and regarded the threefold nature of deity as a universal and necessary concept of theoretical Reason:[8] 'The Trinity of Persons in the unity of God would have been a necessary *Idea* of my speculative Reason, deduced from the necessary Postulate of an intelligent Creator' (*Notebooks* III, §4005 [Section 8]). Sara Coleridge once observed, '[m]y Father's vocation, if he had any in this province, was to defend the Holy Faith by developing it, and shewing its accordance and identity with ideas of reason' (1847, p. lxv). Similarly Beer notes, Coleridge 'was to retain for the rest of his life the set of convictions recorded' in his letter to George Fricker dating from 4 October 1806 (1993, p. xliv). The letter included the view that people should 'build the miracle on the faith, not the faith on the miracle' (*Letters* II, pp. 1189–90). Coleridge's statement agrees with the above-quoted passage from Nitsch's exposition that Kant's critique of speculative Reason and the concomitant refutation of demonstrative evidence of the deity were no basis for the 'highest degree of conviction' but for a solid one for the pursuit of 'virtue from disinterested motives' (1796, p. 233). Although the blade of Kant's *critique* was blunted, Coleridge's assimilation of Kant's dialectic in the *first critique* to debates within the liberal Church establishment was reformative: 'Accepting the negative element in Kant, we have seen Coleridge take his place as the first English religious thinker to criticize adequately, in *Philosophical Lectures* and *Aids*, the decayed rationalism which permeated the Established Church' (Boulger 1961, p. 86). Coleridge respected and subscribed to Kant's criticism of divine disclosure and asserted it accordingly: 'It is therefore evident to my Reason, that the existence of God is absolutely & necessarily insusceptible of a scientific Demonstration – and that Scripture has so represented it' (*Notebooks* III, §4005 [Section 2]).

'Sense', 'Understanding' and 'Reason' in *The Friend*, 1809

The clearest sign of Coleridge's knowledge and adaptation of Nitsch's treatise occurs in *The Friend*, specifically in the issue of 28 September 1809. In a footnote to 'Essay IV: ON THE PRINCIPLES OF POLITICAL PHILOSOPHY', Coleridge distinguished between 'Sense', 'Understanding' and 'Reason' (*Friend* II, p. 104). This threefold discrimination corresponds exactly to the first principle in *A General and Introductory View*: Nitsch announced at the outset of his delineation of the *Critique of Pure Reason* that Kant's theoretical principles were the results of an enquiry into the nature of the 'Power of Knowledge, and the faculties of Reason, Understanding, and Sense' (1796, p. 71). Nitsch explained in a footnote partly anxious not to overwhelm his readers with the new terminology, partly motivated by his personal interest, that 'all the Kantean Principles which I have adduced and shall adduce, are of great importance to Practical Philosophy, as will be shewn in the sequel of these pages' (1796, p. 76 n). Coleridge adopted Nitsch's threefold discrimination hence literally. Coleridge expounded that 'we make a threefold distinction in human nature . . . that it is a distinction not a division, and that in very act of mind the *Man* unites the properties of Sense, Understanding and Reason' (*Friend* II, p. 104 n). While sharing Nitsch's emphasis on ethics, Coleridge added that 'it is of great practical importance, that these distinctions should be made and understood' (*Friend* II, p. 104 n). The particulars of Coleridge's threefold discrimination convey an equally exact concurrence with that of Nitsch.

Nitsch placed a Reinholdean distinction at the beginning of his one hundred and one Kantian principles.[9] The threefold character of Nitsch's distinction was based on the second book of the *Versuch*, in which Reinhold propounded that Sense ('Sinnlichkeit'), Understanding ('Verstand') and Reason ('Vernunft') constitute the components of the human capacity for representations ('menschliches Vorstellungsvermögen'): 'das Wort Vorstellungsvermögen fasst in seiner engeren Bedeutung *Sinnlichkeit, Verstand* und *Vernunft* zusammen' (Reinhold 1789, p. 212) ('The term "capacity for representations" comprises in its distinctive meaning Sense, Understanding and Reason' [my translation]). The position of this distinction at the beginning of the theoretical exposition in his treatise allowed Nitsch simultaneously to lay out the Lockean element in critical philosophy and to emphasize the role of spontaneity within the Kantian system in much the same way as Reinhold had done. Principle IX in Nitsch's introduction gave the following explanation of the 'Sense': 'That a given variety can occur in our perception, knowledge, &c. supposes a Receptive Faculty in the mind, or a Receptivity which is totally passive' (1796, p. 74); in Principle XII he added that 'Receptivity' was synonymous with Sense, whereby he distinguished between 'external' and 'internal' Sense' (1796, p. 75). Coleridge defined 'SENSE' in the exact same way, even using the same terms 'passive' and 'outward' and 'inner sense':

> Under the term SENSE, I comprise whatever is passive in our being, without any reference to the questions of Materialism or Immaterialism, all that Man is in common with animals, in kind at least- his sensations, and impressions whether of his outward senses or the inner sense. (*Friend* II, p. 104 n)

Through the third element 'Sense', it was clear at first glance for readers that this system included a passive element of the mind. By contrast, Understanding and Reason emerged as active elements.

Coleridge defined 'Understanding' as follows: 'By the Understanding, I mean that faculty of thinking and forming *judgements* on the notices furnished by the Sense, according to certain rules existing in itself, which rules constitute its distinct nature' (*Friend* II, p. 104 n). This explanation harkened back to Principles XXVIII to XXXIII of Nitsch's treatise: intuition might be called sensations because they are the results of changes in our receptivity (1796, p. 84). Nitsch added in Principle XXX that 'man would be lost in an infinite crowd of particulars if he had no faculty to reduce them into certain order' (1796, p. 85). Principle XXXI consequently spelt out which of the three faculties fulfilled this task:

> There are, for this reason, a certain kind of ideas which immediately formed from intuitions, and which contain their common nature. This kind of ideas may be called Conceptions, and are begotten by the Understanding. Hence the Understanding is a faculty of forming conceptions. (Nitsch 1796, p. 85)

The two excerpts from Coleridge and Nitsch give strikingly similar definitions of the Understanding above; the word 'forming' occurs in both. The Understanding establishes order by imposing rules on manifold sense appearances.

This description in *The Friend* of 1809 attributes higher significance to the Understanding than in 1806 in so far as it gives the Understanding credit for forming cognitions. This enhanced role of the Understanding is critical for the overall argument within the essay on political philosophy in which it is published, as I will explain below. At the same time, however, Coleridge upheld a similar love of Reason in 1809 as he had done in 1806. Nitsch's introduction expounded the notion, based on Reinhold's *Versuch* (1789, p. 498), that the 'action [of Reason] consists like that of the intellect, in connecting a variety' (Nitsch 1796, p. 119). In addition Nitsch emphasized that 'Reason is a faculty of mind which may be called the third and highest degree of mental Spontaneity' (Nitsch 1796, p. 119). Combined with the above-mentioned table of the primary ideas of Reason (1796, p. 131) and with Nitsch's stipulation that 'Reason, by connecting the Categories . . . produces the idea of an unconditioned Limitation . . . absolute Substance . . . absolute Cause . . . the idea of absolute Necessity' (1796, pp. 127–30), the statement attributed a constitutive function not only to practical but also to the speculative mode of Reason. Respectively, Coleridge defined 'pure Reason': 'By the pure Reason, I mean the power by which we become possessed of Principle, (the eternal Verities of Plato and Descartes) and of Ideas, (N. B. not images) as the ideas of a point, a line, a circle, in Mathematics; and of Justice, Holiness, Free-Will, &c. in Morals' (*Friend* II, p. 104 n). For Coleridge, practical and speculative Reason seem inseparable: pure Reason generated the truths of Plato and Descartes in us as well as justice, holiness and free-will. What counted for Coleridge was that Reason possessed constitutive power. Nitsch's one hundred and one principles had introduced Kant's *first critique* in such broad terms.

Coleridge even adopted a similar way of addressing the readers of this philosophical distinction as Nitsch had done. Anticipating the audience's objections, Nitsch presented himself as a unbiased mediator: 'I must further remark, that this view of Kantean principles is not at all intended to convince the reader of their truth' (1796, p. 70). Likewise, Coleridge emphasized that his exposition entailed no obligation to adopt Kantian views: 'I am not asking my Readers to admit the truth of these distinctions at present, but only to understand my words in the same sense in which I use them' (*Friend* II, p. 104 n). It seems that both were equally sensitive to the resistance of a large part of their readers to the complexity of Kant's philosophy, especially of the new terminology often dismissed as jargon. Coleridge maintained this defensive attitude through much of his writings (Chapter 5).

One of Nitsch's legacies

While Nitsch's name appears, as far as I know, nowhere in Coleridges papers, his work left nevertheless an unmistakable mark in Coleridge's thought. Coleridge did not maintain the threefold form of the discrimination (Sense, Understanding and Reason); the use of these Reinholdean terms was temporary. What remained permanent in Coleridge's thought was a conception of Reason that agreed with the following rather beautiful expression in Nitsch's treatise: 'reason forms designs, or discovers means, when it traces the systems of immense worlds, where the eye sees only small luminous spots, when it penetrates into the secrets of invisible regions and climbs up to that first of all beings' (1796, p. 32). To clarify, Nitsch added decidedly that Reason 'must do this by means of conclusions. – This assertion must be granted, provided reason shall remain an active faculty' (1796, p. 32). This assertion was even granted by Kant himself, if we accept the validity of his letter to Nitsch. Following Kant's advice, Nitsch's treatise built on the assumption that Reason's final intention was the ascent from the sensible to the supersensible (Kant cited in Baum and Malter 1991, p. 466). Evidently this explanation did not fail to attract Coleridge's attention.

Later on, in 1818, Coleridge elaborated another aspect of the distinction between Reason and Understanding in strikingly similar terms as Nitsch. The above-quoted passages include the notion that the formative power of Reason depends on making conclusions: 'must do this by means of conclusions' (1796, p. 32). In the essay on 'Landing Places' in *The Friend* (1818) Coleridge made the same point by insisting on the scientific validity of logic inference by way of deduction. For Coleridge deduction was superior to induction because the former adhered more adequately to the universal and necessary laws of Reason. The latter belonged, according to the essay, to the 'truths of science', whereas empirical knowledge was merely an accumulation of 'facts, or things of experience'. Coleridge gave two examples to illustrate his point. In the first he provided a series of inferences:

> in one instance he begins with some one self-evident truth (that the radii of a circle, for instance, are equal,) and in consequence of this being true sees at once, without any actual experience, that some other thing must be true likewise, and that, this being true, some *third* thing must be equally true, and so on. (*Friend* I, p. 158)

Here, an insight is inferred from another as if truth was an inherent quality that could be unpacked. Coleridge contrasted this 'marvellous power' (*Friend* I, p. 158) with the method of induction which he described as the bringing 'together the facts of experience, each of which has its own separate value, neither may have preceded it; and making these several facts bear upon some particular project' (*Friend* I, p. 158). Subsequently he concluded that deduction performed by Reason was the highest '*scientific* Faculty' (*Friend* I, p. 158). This stipulation chimes with Nitsch's delineation of the functions of Reason. The lecturer repeatedly emphasized that 'Reason connects by conclusion' (1796, p. 120), and that 'every analytical judgement is a judgement *a priori*, because we *unfold* what already lies in the conception; for instance, all bodies are extended' (1796, p. 89; my emphasis).[10] It remains a matter of speculation whether Nitsch's and Coleridge's preference for the analytic had any bearing at all on the developments of the twentieth century. In any case, Coleridge and Nitsch shared their reverence for Reason. In this regard, Coleridge's 1809 essay on political philosophy contains a remarkable departure.

Coleridge's 'Essay on the Principles of Political Philosophy', *The Friend* 1809

Coleridge revised his negative view of Understanding slightly but significantly in *The Friend*. In 1806, he had attributed the conditions of experience to Reason; in 1809, he used Nitsch's threefold distinction of 'Sense', 'Understanding' and 'Reason'. This triple version had the advantage for Coleridge that it attributed an active function to the Understanding in the process of forming cognitions (only 'Sense' was utterly passive). This shift might have had several reasons; one of them was certainly political. The analysis of Coleridge's triple distinction of Sense, Reason and Understanding within the context in which it was published shows that Coleridge used it as a part of his attempt to reinvent himself as a proponent of expedience. Indeed it formed part of Coleridge's systematic strategy in *The Friend* of severing critical philosophy not only from the radical Enlightenment discourse of natural and human rights but also from political action in general. Coleridge's political reorientation that resulted in his stipulation of expedience in politics obliged him to attribute more importance to experience as a philosophical concept than he had previously done. The threefold discrimination accommodated this ideological change.

In his 1809 essay on political principles, Coleridge embraced prudence:

> I shall perhaps seem guilty of an inconsistency, in declaring myself an Adherent of this second System, a zealous Advocate for deriving the origin of all Government from human Prudence, and of deeming that to be just which Experience has proved to be expedient. (*Friend* II, p. 104)

He admitted the inconsistency of having previously 'expressed myself . . . with comparative slight of the Understanding considered as the sole Guide of human Conduct' (*Friend* II, p. 104). This means in the context of the essay that he had underrated the importance of experience, not only in the constitution of knowledge but also in the political arena. In essays four and five (28 September and 5 October 1809), Coleridge endorsed the second of three theories on the 'rightful Origin of Government' (*Friend* II, p. 98). This second system corresponded, contrary to Coleridge's preference for Reason, to the 'point of view under which the Human Being may be considered, namely, as an animal gifted with Understanding, or the faculty of suiting Measures to Circumstances' (*Friend* II, p. 103). Coleridge realized that his growing political conservatism was no longer congruent with his adherence to critical philosophy and his favouritism of Reason. His insistence on expedience required a philosophical adjustment. In much the same way as in the 1790s, Coleridge rejected in 1809 the assertors of those political systems that were based on the epistemological assumption that the mind is entirely passive. The theory that 'the mind consists of nothing but manifold modifications of passive sensations, considers Men as the highest sort of Animals' entailed the 'Government of Fear' for Coleridge (*Friend* II, p. 98) and hence a system he condemned: 'This is the System of Hobbes' (*Friend* II, p. 98). However, in stark contrast to his radical lectures in 1795 (Chapter 2), he also denounced those systems of government 'derivable from Principles contained in the REASON of Man' (*Friend* II, p. 105).

In the essay 'On the Principles of Political Philosophy', Coleridge drove a wedge between the moral-theological and the active political function of Reason. He condemned in particular the claims of natural and universal rights:

> Nothing is to be deemed rightful in civil Society, or to be tolerated as such, but what is capable of being demonstrated out of the original Laws of pure Reason. Of course, as there is but one System of Geometry, so according to this Theory there can be but one Constitution and one System of Legislation, and this consists in the freedom, which is the common Right of all Men, under the control of that moral necessity, which is the common Duty of all men. Whatever is not *every where* [sic] necessary, is *no where* right. On this assumption the whole Theory is built. To state it nakedly is to confute it satisfactorily. (*Friend* II, p. 105)

The Jacobin ideology described here could equally be used to delineate Kantian ideas, for instance, the analogy of the geometry and constitutions on the grounds of universal and necessary concepts (*first critique*), or the view that all nations should have the same, namely republican, constitution (*Perpetual Peace*), and the common duty of all men (*Groundwork*). However, Coleridge attributed these views to Rousseau's *Du Contrat Social* and Paine's *Rights of Man* (*Friend* II, p. 105).[11] His relation to Kant's philosophy became increasingly conflicted over the years. In the 1810s, Coleridge was prepared, even eager, to defend himself against charges of Jacobinism; he adopted conservative views and still remained a firm supporter of Kant, who had consistently supported republicanism and the French Revolution (see Chapter 4). The essay shows that Coleridge continued to draw on aspects of Kant's moral and theological philosophy while discounting the elements that had become uncongenial, such as Kant's republicanism, his resistance against oppression and his demand for the freedom to make public use of Reason (Chapter 1).

Commentators have read *The Friend* as an adequate expression of Kantian politics. Coleman has assigned Coleridge's divorce of morality from politics to Kant's

Metaphysik der Sitten (*Metaphysics of Morals*). This attribution disregards one of Kant's most detailed discussions of the relation between morality and politics in *Perpetual Peace*. The text acknowledges tensions, but stipulates the priority of morality after all: 'Der Grenzgott der Moral weicht nicht dem Jupiter (Grenzgott der Gewalt)' (*Ewiger Frieden*, p. 370) ('The tutelary god of morals does not yield to Jupiter [the god of power]' [*Perpetual Peace*, 8: 370]). The moral principle that should ideally underlie politics was, according to Kant, honesty: 'so ist doch der gleichfalls theoretische [Satz]: *Ehrlichkeit ist besser den alle Politik,* über allen Einwurf unendlich erhaben' (*Ewiger Frieden*, p. 370) ('the equally theoretical proposition *honesty is better than all politics* is raised infinitely above all objections' [*Perpetual Peace*, 8: 370]). Accordingly, Kant proclaimed the transcendental formulation of public right and demanded transparency in political affairs (see Chapter 4): 'Alle auf das Recht anderer Menschen bezogene Handlungen, deren Maxime sich nicht mit der Publicität verträgt, sind unrecht' (*Ewiger Frieden*, p. 381) ('All actions relating to the rights of others are wrong if their maxim is incompatible with publicity' [*Perpetual Peace*, 8: 381]). Kant differentiated between moral law and public right, yet, contrary to Coleridge's appropriation of Kantian ethics, he did not 'drive a wedge between morality and politics' (Coleman 1988, p. 157). Kant left no doubt that he regarded the doctrine of prudence as a denial of any form of morals: 'eine allgemeine Klugheitslehre [heißt], d. i. eine Theorie der Maximen verstehen, zu seinen auf Vortheil [sic] berechneten Absichten die tauglichen Mittel zu wählen, d. i. läugnen [sic], daß es überhaupt eine Moral gebe' (*Ewiger Frieden*, p. 370) ('a general doctrine of prudence, that is, a theory of maxims for choosing the most suitable means to one's purposes aimed at advantage, that is, to deny that there is a [doctrine of] morals at all' [*Perpetual Peace*, 8: 370]). It was Coleridge who introduced this separation and thus effectively reversed the sociopolitical force behind critical philosophy.

Coleridge severed morality from the public exertion that Kant demanded in his 'Enlightenment' essay. Instead, he presented the principles of pure ideas of Reason as a lesson of modesty, self-restraint and acceptance for the individual citizen:

> Thus the dignity of Human Nature will be secured, and at the same time a lesson of Humility taught to each Individual, when we are made to see that the universal necessary Laws, and pure IDEAS of Reason, were given us, not for the purpose of flattering our Pride and enabling us to become national Legislators, but that by an energy of continued self-conquest, we might establish a free and yet absolute Government in our own Spirit. (*Friend* II, p. 111)

This passage expresses the opposite of Kant's political philosophy in his essay on *Aufklärung* and *Zum Ewigen Frieden*. It represents Reason as an instrument of self-regulation; indeed it locks Reason into the inner realm of the individual. Kant's rational principles by contrast, his demand of the public use of Reason, the progress of history towards justice, the transcendental formulation of public right, were all directed outwards; indeed Reason largely worked as a driving force to achieve reform. In *The Friend*, Coleridge managed to select aspects of critical philosophy that matched his changing political views and his persistent religious convictions. The discrimination between Sense, Understanding and Reason in the essay on political philosophy served as a means to justify Coleridge's recent transformation into a proponent of expedience in politics. A new rationale had become necessary because expedience required a readjustment of the low status of experience in his distinction between Reason and Understanding (for instance, in 1806). Accordingly, Coleridge resolved the inconsistency by stressing the empirical dimension by virtue of introducing temporarily a third faculty. Some have said that Coleridge's increasing conservatism was driven by his stipulation of German idealism. Ironically, one could also say in this particular case that Coleridge's stipulation of expedience made it necessary for him to redeem the empirical dimension within this system.

So effective was Coleridge's reversal of Kant's Enlightenment principles that Thomas Carlyle, when concerned with Coleridge's teachings, deemed Kantianism utterly incompatible with political reform and internationalism as professed by the young John Sterling, who visited the Sage of Highgate regularly between 1828 and 1830 (Carlyle 1851, pp. 81–2). According to Carlyle's biography *The Life of Sterling*, Coleridge had turned critical philosophy into a 'haze-world' (1851, p. 74) or 'moonshine':

> Hitherto, while said [Coleridgean] moonshine was but taking effect, and colouring the outer surface of things without quite penetrating into the heart, democratic Liberalism, revolt against superstition and oppression, and help to whosoever would revolt, was still the grand element in Sterling's creed. (1851, p. 83)

While Carlyle's opinion gives a good example for the legacy of Coleridge's reversal of Kantian politics in *The Friend*, the question remains open what Coleridge and Sterling talked about, and whether in conversation Coleridge still discounted Kant's radicalism. Via Sterling and Joseph Blanco White there is, for instance, a link between Coleridge and the Spanish Liberals in exile in London: 'The Spanish exile community absorbed, reformulated and took back to Spain their new understanding of British politics and literature' (Shaffer 2007a, p. 7). In progressively inclined circles, Coleridge expressed, as we saw in the lectures at the 'Crown and Anchor', more daring views. Such contradictions do not come as a surprise considering that Coleridge is known for his 'double-mindedness'. Perry has proposed that 'Coleridge's thought is best understood . . . as the experience of a *muddle*' (Perry 1999, p. 7). Coleridge was also in two minds about critical philosophy: he used Kantian philosophy to reinvent himself and Kant as conservative thinkers, while he, at the same time, retained remnants of Kant's progressive principles. Coleridge was a contradictory Kantian, at once sociable and solitary, public and hidden, radical and conservative, genial and copying, and it was in these conflicting terms that Coleridge used critical philosophy consistently, and at times intensively as well as emotionally. Nevertheless, his public mediation had one effect in particular: it contributed profoundly to a conservative image of Kant in England, which remains one of Coleridge's lasting legacies.

Conclusion: Beyond Coleridge

As the gap persists between two philosophic traditions that seem to have been irreversibly separated in the twentieth century by the labels 'analytic' and 'Continental', the primary purpose of this study is to further contribute to the understanding of the historical intersections between 'Anglo-American' and 'Continental' philosophy. While 'Continental philosophy' is often understood to be '(primarily) philosophy after Kant in Germany and France in the nineteenth and twentieth centuries' (Leiter and Rosen 2007, p. 1) or 'any philosophy after 1780 originating on the European continent', Alan D. Schrift defines it in the preface to the *History of Continental Philosophy* as follows:

> Continental philosophy [is] *historically* a tradition that has its roots in several different ways of approaching and responding to Immanuel Kant's critical philosophy, a tradition that takes its definitive form at the beginning of the twentieth century as the phenomenological tradition, with its modern roots in the work of Edmund Husserl. (Nenon 2011, p. vii)

John Stuart Mill was, according to Schrift, one of, if not the first to use the expression 'Continental philosophy' in *On Bentham and Coleridge* (1840) to designate the tradition on the continent initiated by critical philosophy (Nenon 2011, p. xii). In his nuanced essay, Mill identified 'Continental philosophy' completely with Coleridge and ultimately rejected the philosophy on political grounds, although he emphasized its achievements, above all in history, and advocated the study of Coleridge's writings. Mill used the terms 'Coleridge's philosophy', 'Continental philosophy', 'Germano-Coleridgian school' and 'Germano-Coleridgian doctrine' interchangeably. Mill recognized Coleridge's indebtedness to German philosophy while he praised Coleridge's 'original powers'. Bentham founded a system, according to Mill, but

> Coleridge, though he has left on the system he inculcated, such traces of himself as cannot fail to be left by any mind of original powers, was anticipated in all the essentials of his doctrine by the great Germans of the latter half of the last century. (Mill 1967, p. 103)

Alongside German, Mill casually added French philosophy 'accompanied in it by the remarkable series of their French expositors and followers' (1967, p. 103). For Mill, 'Continental philosophy' belonged doubtlessly to the conservative camp: 'the philosophers of the reactionary school – of the school to which Coleridge belongs' (1967, p. 129). He distinguished between 'Conservative thinkers' and 'transcendentalists' on the one hand, and 'Liberals' and 'admirers of Hobbes and

Locke' on the other hand (1967, p. 104). Indeed, Mill contradistinguished 'Continental philosophy' as follows:

> It expresses the revolt of the human mind against the philosophy of the eighteenth century. It is ontological, because that was experimental; conservative, because so much of that was infidel; concrete and historical, because that was abstract and metaphysical; poetical, because that was matter-of-fact and prosaic. In every respect it flies off in the contrary direction to its predecessor. (1967, p. 109)

Mill's essay indicates how successful Coleridge had been in assimilating critical philosophy for his political reorientation as a conservative thinker. For a leading Victorian reformer like Mill, 'Continental philosophy' was merely 'ontological', 'conservative' and 'poetical' (the third opposition 'historical' and 'metaphysical' collapses as Mill's essay praises the 'Continental philosophy' for its contribution to history). The early roots and radicalism of critical philosophy had disappeared completely thanks to Coleridge's repression.

Coleridge made Kant known in the Anglo-Saxon world as a philosopher who deprived Reason of its reformative powers for civil rights and national and international affairs. In *The Friend*, Coleridge influentially purported that the extension of the moral law to politics would amount to a form of Jacobinism and therefore had to be kept strictly separate from political affairs. In *Biographia Literaria*, Coleridge introduced Kant to his readers as a fearful aged man permanently silenced by Friedrich Wilhelm II. In *Aids to Reflection*, he used Kant's critique of metaphysics in such a way that it gave a perceptive reader like Sara Coleridge the impression that '[h]ad he [Kant] been brought up a Churchman he could never have divested himself of dogmatic divinity' (S. Coleridge 1847, p. cxxxvi). The statement gives an example of how distorted a picture of Immanuel Kant was and is derived from Coleridge's eventually very successful works.

Coleridge was the most important mediator of German philosophy in the nineteenth century. This role does, however, not mean that 'in England Coleridge stood quite alone' with 'the adaptation and importation of the Germans' (Wellek 1981, p. 157). On the contrary, in the mid-1790s, a window opened for a relatively short amount of time through which critical philosophy reached England. The series of Kantian publications spearheaded by Nitsch, Beddoes and O'Keeffe during the anus mirabilis of 1796 was a version of critical philosophy that had been filtered through the pantheism controversy mainly thanks to Reinhold's *Briefe, Versuch* and *Beyträge*. English dissenters had a natural interest in the rational theology that Reinhold had extracted from the *Critique of Pure Reason*. Nitsch, a student of Kant, realized that critical philosophy had something to offer that English religious dissenters desired, but which their then-predominant philosophy, Hartley's and Priestley's associationism, ultimately denied: free will. Beddoes, O'Keeffe and, above all, Nitsch succeeded in disseminating critical philosophy until their efforts became doomed when the conspiracy theory largely inspired by Abbé Barruel and spread by the *Anti-Jacobin Review* gained currency from 1799 onwards. While this interval of English interest in critical philosophy was short, it had a highly formative impact on Coleridge before he went to Germany. Because previous investigations have focused on Coleridge's post-1808 works, such as his *Lectures, Biographia Literaria, The Friend* and *Aids to Reflection*, the transformative impact of Kant's philosophy for society and politics (religion excluded) was lost. When Coleridge ceased identifying himself with Unitarians and became an opponent of democracy, he severed Kant's philosophy from its reformative Enlightenment stance as well as from the predominantly radical and dissenting milieu into which critical philosophy had been absorbed when it first reached England. Sara Coleridge observed that her father talked 'of Germany as if its history belonged to that of Kamschatka, by his language respecting Immanuel Kant' (1847, p. cxxviii). It is possible that Coleridge was not aware of Kant's provocations that led to the royal reprimand, nor of the student riots in Halle that were bound up with the Wöllner affair. However, Coleridge's reluctance to acknowledge Kantian principles in public, his repeated publications of his encounter with the anti-Kantian Klopstock rather than with young and rebellious Kantians in Germany as well as Coleridge's silence about the accusations of conspiracy against Kant by Abbé Barruel and about the continued charges against himself in the *Anti-Jacobin Review* are clear indications of his conscious repression of Kant's Jacobinism. At the same time, Coleridge discounted the republican notional contents within the Kantian body of works, even when he had formerly applied them in his writings. Coleridge did not acknowledge, either in public or in private, that he was familiar with the first English translation of Kant's *Perpetual Peace*, although Coleridge's discussion of the 'Law of Nations' in *The Friend* (II, pp. 321–2), in particular his stipulation of non-coerciveness, agrees strikingly with the second definite article of *Perpetual Peace* (De Paolo 1985), not to mention the conceptual affinities between the entire pamphlet and 'France: An Ode'.

To uncover the importance of the early mediators for Coleridge's reception of Kant means to bring scholarly attention to the tensions that have been overlooked by philosophic and cultural historians of the period. Within the history of political dissent, the Romantic period is usually characterized by a turn away from the transformative power of Reason: 'Romanticism was', Roland Bleiker observes,

> amongst other things, a reaction against Enlightenment determinism. It penetrated France towards the end of the eighteenth century and took hold of a disintegrating world characterised by the Napoleonic wars and turmoil. One of the key assumptions of the Enlightenment, the idea that the spread of reason and science would inevitably lead towards progress, towards a better world, had not materialised. With the failure of the French Revolution, the belief in linear progress was shattered. (2000, p. 79)

The study of the early mediators brings to the foreground the support of the French Revolution, of republicanism and constitutional reform in the works of Coleridge and Kant and thus of two thinkers who are commonly seen as the major leading figures in Romanticism's retreat to inwardness. Coleridge obscured the radical dimension of his interest in critical philosophy influentially. Nevertheless, Coleridge demonstrated considerable constancy in maintaining throughout his life a philosophic idol that stipulated the transformative power of Reason. Mill's insights into Coleridge's thought were limited. In 1840, Coleridge was 'a man who produced no systematic work, any of the fragments which may have contributed to an edifice [were] still incomplete'

(Mill 1967, p. 133). In 2002, the final volume of the splendid edition of Coleridge's notebooks was published. The edifice of Coleridge's works stands, and does so impressively, in many volumes.[1] The exclusion of Coleridge and Nitsch from the eight-volume edition of the *History of Continental Philosophy* contributes to perpetuating the gap between the 'Anglo-Saxon' and 'Continental' philosophy.[2] It is time for historians of 'Continental philosophy' to further investigate Coleridge's body of work alongside the works of the less well-known figures, especially of Nitsch, but also O'Keeffe, Thomas Beddoes and others.

It is also time to break down the boundary between critical philosophy and British political and religious dissent that Coleridge's later work established so effectively. Leading English intellectual figures in the 1790s harboured a significant interest in critical philosophy. They included political reformers such as Godwin, whose attendance of Nitsch's lectures coincided with a period in Godwin's life when he revised *Political Justice* substantially. Besides Godwin, John Thelwall, William Blake and women writers, such as Mary Hays, Fanny Holcroft and possibly Mary Wollstonecraft appear to have been exposed to Nitsch's teaching either in person or in print. They also included Wordsworth, whose response to Kant merits further investigation especially with regard to Nitsch's treatise (Wu 1993, pp. 80–1). O'Keeffe is said to have taken political refuge in Priestley's commune in Pennsylvania (Class 2007, p. 214). The circulation of critical philosophy after 1787 went further than is commonly assumed; it certainly went beyond the geographical boundaries of continental Europe and across the Atlantic. Samuel Taylor Coleridge's miscellaneous works built a bridge for German Continental philosophy. Yet Coleridge's construct represents, in many ways, a 'dome of air' isolated and removed as it was from the initial winding paths that led critical philosophy through political and religious dissent to the English-speaking world in the late eighteenth century.

Notes

Introduction

1   The initial correspondence between Coleridge and Thelwall is now lost.

2   The translations of the German reviews were published in a section called 'Foreign Intelligence'. I thank Christian Deuling for his explanation of the Jena periodicals.

3   Distinguished scholars speak of Coleridge's singular knowledge of Kant. 'He was alone in his time, in the dimension of his knowledge of Kant and the quality of his interest in him' (Ashton 1980, p. 48). Ashton's view agrees, for instance, with that of James Engell (1981, pp. 172–83) and Elisabeth Winkelmann (1933, p. 31).

4   Coleridge's relation to Kant is overshadowed by the highly charged stigma of plagiarism since J. F. Ferrier's notorious review (1840, pp. 287–99). Plagiarism is still perceived as such a major problem that a commentator has recently called it '[p]erhaps the chief cause of the complexity' to study Coleridge's afterlife (Wilson 2008, p. 171). This study disagrees with this view.

5   Criticism itself is subject to history. In the direct aftermath of the Second World War, National Socialism and the Holocaust, Wellek's and Warren's call to overcome national boundaries appears in part as a reaction against the devastating consequences, particularly of German nationalism.

6   By 'hermeneutic' I mean the theoretical position that significance of texts is subject to a process of interpretation, as discussed by Michael N. Forster (2007, p. 30).

7   Sandra M. den Otter's account of Kant's early reception misattributes the date of Nitsch's publication to 1797 (1996, p. 20) as well as Coleridge's annotation to Willich's *Elements* (1996, p. 20). The annotations were not by Coleridge but by Joseph Henry Green (*Marginalia* VI, p. 335). Moreover, den Otter makes the assumption that Nitsch was the translator of *Perpetual Peace* (1996, p. 20). The source named by den Otter, that is, William Taylor's review in the *Monthly Review* 25 (1798), pp. 584–5, does not provide sufficient evidence for this conjecture; it merely mentions two Kantian publications, that of Nitsch and *Perpetual Peace*.

8   Fredrick Burwick gives a subtle and sensitive discussion of De Quincey's complicated relationship with Coleridge, including accusations of plagiarism (2008, pp. 36–53).

9   Hamilton makes a similar point about New Historicist criticism of Wordsworth (2003b, p. 220).

10 William Taylor published 'Kant: Project on Perpetual Peace' (*Monthly Review* 22 [1797], pp. 114–15); 'Kant: Observation sur le Sentiment du Beau and [et] du Sublime' (*Monthly Review* 25 [1798], pp. 584–5); 'Elements of Critical Philosophy' (*Monthly Review* 28 [1799], pp. 62–9).

11 Thomas Beddoes published, for instance, 'Kant: Zum Ewigen Frieden' (*Monthly Review* 20 [1796], pp. 486–90); 'Goethe: Wilhelm Meisters Lehrjahre' (*Monthly Review* 27 [1798], pp. 543–55); 'Schiller: Die Horen' (*Monthly Review* 21 [1796], pp. 574–6).

12 Bodley: Shelf mark: Per. 3977 d. 190.

Chapter 1

1   The first reaction to Kant's *Critique of Pure Reason* (1781) was reserved (Sassen 2000; Kühn 2006).

2   Norbert Hinske delineates the dissemination of Kant's philosophy by the Jena theologians (1995, pp. 231–43). A renaissance in Reinhold studies began with Lauth's collection of essays *Philosophie aus einem Prinzip: Karl Leonhard Reinhold* (1974), which was followed by a number of important studies including Henrich's *Konstellationen* (1991) and *Grundlegung aus dem Ich* (2004), Frank's *Unendliche Annäherung* (1997), Bondeli's *Anfangsproblem* (1995) and Lazzari's *Das Eine, was der Menschheit Noth ist* (2004). In Anglophone countries, studies by Beiser (1987), by di Giovanni (2005, 2010) and by Ameriks, that is, his introduction to the English translation of Reinhold's *Letters* (2005) as well as his essay on Reinhold reprinted in *Kant and the Historical Turn* (2006), pp. 185–206, have done a great deal for Reinhold scholarship.

3   Only in the German translation of his biography does Kühn explain the different spellings of this name (2007, p. 14).

4   German Enlightenment philosophers assimilated Scottish common sense philosophy widely (Oz-Salzberger 1995). It was David Hume's work that changed Kant's thought profoundly. Hume's major essays had been translated into German in a four-volume collection in the late 1750s; his subsequent essays followed swiftly. 'The consistency and brilliance of Hume's skeptical distinction of matters of fact and relations of ideas, of empirical from necessary connections, made an impression on all serious philosophers in Europe in the 1750s and 1760s' (Zammito 1993, p. 30).

5   According to Henrich, Kant was aware that the argument of the radical difference between a concept and existence had been used before (1960, pp. 137–8).

6   As the cosmological and the physico-theological argument also run into the contradiction of absolute necessity, they are not treated separately in this brief sketch (Guyer 2006, p. 147).

7   Jonathan Bennett takes a critical stance: 'The Dialectic is full of mistakes and inadequacies . . . and *of course* this is consistent with its being a valuable contribution to philosophy' (1974, p. viii). Allen Wood criticizes Kant for his stipulation of synthetic judgements that 'the theistic hypothesis should not be treated as an object of empirical confirmation or disconfirmation' (1978, p. 145). Michelle Grier argues that 'the *Critique* clearly reflects the desire to return to the attempt made in the *Dreams [of a Spirit Seer]* to curb the theoretical pretensions of reason, while at the same time securing the "subjective" function of reason as the "highest" faculty of knowledge' (2001, p. 305).

8   The full title of Jacobi's work was 'Über die Lehre des Spinoza in den Briefen an den Herrn Moses Mendelssohn' (Scholz 1916, pp. 45–218).

9   Because the *first critique* only contains a limited answer to Hume's scepticism, Kühn rightly criticizes scholars for not having discussed sufficiently Kant's answer in the *second critique* (1983, p. 192).

10 The current edition of the *Oxford English Dictionary* (2012) lists Nitsch's *A General and Introductory View* as the second publication to use the term 'necessitarian' after Dawson (1783) and as the first to use it as a designation for a philosophical party (see Hall 1970, p. 315). However, William Cockin, for instance, used the term to designate the opposite of liberty (1791, p. v).

11 Chapter 3 includes an overview of the twentieth-century debate on the highest good.

12 Reid advanced arguments against necessitarianism (Harris 2005; Vigus 2010, p. 2).

13 Felicity James and Ian Inkster give an excellent account of the Aikin-Barbauld circle (2012).

14 Jachmann has been completely neglected by Wellek's study of Kant's effective history in England (Wellek, 1931).

15 Thomas Cogan's article 'Prize Dissertation relative Natural and Revealed Religion' was published in *Monthly Review* 3 [1790], pp. 481–95. The next important article is by Benjamin Sowden, 'Verhandelingen uitgegeeven door de Hollandsche Maatschappye: Memoirs published by the Philosophical Society of Haarlem' (*Monthly Review* 10 [1793], pp. 523–31). The title is misleading as Sowden used the occasion of the Dutch philosophy competition to write an essay about critical philosophy.

16 Carolyn D. Williams gives some biographical information about Sowden in her *DNB* article 'Cogan, Thomas (1736–1818)' (Williams 2012).

17 Beddoes discusses Kant on pp. 89–103 (1793).

18 A summary of O'Keeffe's life and work is available (Duddy 2004, p. 267); Wellek mentions and Micheli discusses his work and its review (Wellek 1931, p. 7; Micheli 1990, pp. 236–40). I have uncovered O'Keeffe's friendship with Nitsch and his emigration to Priestley's colony elsewhere (Class 2007). Nitsch's life and work will be discussed below.

19 Beddoes might also have used an article from the *Allgemeine Literatur-Zeitung*, or from Reinhold *Versuch einer neuen Theorie des menschlichen Vorstellungsvermögens* (1789) (Micheli 1990, p. 251).

20 O'Keeffe translated excerpts from the *first critique* (Wellek 1931, p. 7; Class 2007, p. 211).

21 Wellek regarded the absence of fragmented translations in Nitsch's treatise as his main achievement and spoke of a 'very decent introduction' (1931, p. 9).

22 Kant's motives would require further investigation. In part his instruction served to find a common ground with the English audience; in part it reflects an opinion similar to that of beauty as the symbol of goodness in the *Critique of the Power of Judgment*.

23 Halmi points out that the Kantian sublime and the concept of aesthetic ideas 'bear witness to [Kant's own] disquiet with the fundamental dualisms of his critical project' (2007, p. 49). Nitsch's treatise merits an investigation in how far his work as a student of Kant further attests to this disquiet.

24 The entry is signed with the initial 'M', which identifies the author of the article as one of the three editors of the sixth volume of *General Biography*. Morgan composed the 1807 volume together with John Aikin (junior) and William Johnston. Each entry in the volume is signed by either 'A' for Aikin, 'J' for Johnston or 'M' for Morgan.

25 According to Timothey Whelan, Thomas Hood was most likely a dissenter and took over the London-based publishing house after the death of Thomas Vernor, a Baptist, in 1793 (2008, p. 225n).

26 Nitsch was born around 1767 (Micheli 2010, p. 858).

27 Kraus was 'perhaps Kant's most talented student during the seventies. Kraus became his colleague in 1780 and taught moral philosophy. Today he is best known as one of the people who introduced Adam Smith's ideas into Germany. Even though Kraus and Kant were good friends, even sharing a common household at one time, they had a falling out sometime before the third *Critique* was published' (Kühn 2001, p. xiii; see pp. 329–31).

28 By October 1796, Nitsch lived in No 34 Wimpole Street (*Monthly Magazine* 2 [1796], p. 705).
29 Count Wedel-Jarlsberg was 'Envoy Extraordinary and Minister Plenipotentiary from the King of Denmark' and involved in negotiations with Grenville in 1800 (Scott 1918, p. 478).
30 Ernest Belfort Bax translated an excerpt from Voigt's biography of Kraus (1819, pp. 355–6) as part of his introductory biography of Kant (1883, pp. xi–lxxi).
31 It was the denial of free will that led Henry Crabb Robinson to doubt and ultimately abandon his necessitarianism (Vigus 2010, pp. 2–4).
32 Nitsch was possibly the author of this article as he published three anonymous articles about his work in the *English Review* according to Micheli (1990, p. 240–8).
33 The list of scholars who have contributed significant research on this topic includes Ameriks (2006), Beiser (1987), Frank (1997), Henrich (2004) and Bondeli (1995). Ameriks explains the centrality of history to Reinhold's thought and gives an overview of the scholarly discussion (2010, pp. 113–23).
34 'Henry James Richter . . . took a radical position in politics' (Micheli 1990 p. 255). John Richter, the brother of Henry James Richter, was arrested for high treason and acquitted together with Thomas Hardy, John Horne Took and John Thelwall (Prochaska 2012).
35 http://godwindiary.bodleian.ox.ac.uk/diary/1795-03-23.html.
36 http://godwindiary.bodleian.ox.ac.uk/people/unidentified/wirgman.html.
37 Violet Stockoe claimed that on 13 August 1812 Godwin might have met with Coleridge and Wirgman and discussed critical philosophy (1926, p. 25). I have been unable to confirm this claim. Crabb Robinson's diary contains an entry for 12 August 1812, which records his meeting with Coleridge alone (Robinson 1869 I, p. 395).
38 http://godwindiary.bodleian.ox.ac.uk/diary/1812-05-05.html. The name appears over the period of time between 1794 and 1830.
39 Godwin might have been attracted to Kant by virtue of similar aspirations. Both experienced the tension between their desire for widespread recognition and their reservations against popular taste.
40 'Daß nämlich der Begriff des Guten und Bösen nicht vor dem moralischen Gesetze (dem es dem Anschein nach sogar zum Grunde gelegt werden müßte), sondern nur (wie hier auch geschieht) nach demselben und durch dasselbe bestimmt werden müsse' (*KpV* p. 63).
41 In his article 'Letters to a Young Man whose Education has been Neglected', De Quincey did much to derogate these attempts, (*The London Magazine* 7 [1823], pp. 84–90).

Chapter 2

1 The suspension of habeas corpus, which had started in May 1794, ended a few months before the Guildhall meeting, in July 1795; Thompson (1963, pp. 102–88) and Barrell (2000, pp. 571–7; 2005, pp. 85–112) give detailed accounts of the period between 1794–6.
2 This is a standard account. The events were more complicated, as Mike Jay points out. He gives a detailed description of the scientific and political situation that led Beddoes to resign his post as a reader in chemistry at the University of Oxford (Jay 2009, pp. 50–72).

3   I agree with Jay that exact date of their first encounter is uncertain, yet it is safe to say that the two men started supporting each other publicly by 20 November 1795 (Jay 2009, p. 115).

4   Coleridge in 'Religious Musings' called Benjamin Franklin 'the Patriot Sage' (Brice 2007, p. 125; Wylie 1989, pp. 49–50).

5   Coleridge published 'Effusion IV' condemning the attack on Priestley's house on December 11, 1794, in the *Morning Chronicle* (Coleridge 2004, p. 14).

6   In 'An Answer to "A Letter to Edward Long Fox, M. D."', Coleridge defended Edward Long Fox publicly against accusations of an unidentified Bristol counter-revolutionary.

7   Dorothy Stansfield suggests that Beddoes attended Coleridge's Bristol lectures in spring 1795 (1984, pp. 128–44).

8   'In the 1770s and 1780s, many dissenters and reformists were associated with Jesus College: among them were William Frend, Gilbert Wakefield, Robert Robinson, Felix Vaughan, George Dyer, and – a little later – Coleridge' (Roe 1988, p. 85).

9   William Frend was charged for having published the pamphlet *Peace and Union Recommended by the Associated Parties of Republicans and Anti-Republicans* (1793), which argued against the declaration of war against France (Watson 2003, p. 48).

10 To John Thelwall, 13 March 1796. Coleridge called the abolition of property 'Aspheterism'. To Robert Southey, 13 July 1794 (*Letters* I, p. 88).

11 To Robert Southey, 21 October 1794. In the 1810s, Coleridge denied, however, universal male suffrage for property reasons in *The Friend* (I, p. 202). John Morrow's study of Coleridge's political theory focuses on the relation of property and power. Morrow compares Coleridge to Godwin, Priestley and Price and points out that it was Coleridge alone who linked the end of oppression with the abolition of property rights – a conclusion that Coleridge drew from Harrington's theory of the relationship between property and political power (1990, p. 31; see also Kitson 1993 and 2002, p. 158).

12 Peter Mann and Lewis Patton compare 'glorious band' to the character of the 'Elect' in 'Religious Musings' (*Lectures 1795*, p. 12n). However, it is 'not clear', as Ben Brice points out, 'how it is possible to argue that the moral character of an Elect individual is predestined from eternity, while maintaining that this same virtuous character is the product of an active and "long cultivation of that moral taste which derives our most exquisite pleasures from the contemplation of possible perfection"' (2007, p. 122).

13 To John Thelwall, 17 December 1796. Roe traces Coleridge's friendship with John Thelwall and its political implications (1990, pp. 60–80; see also Thompson 1997, pp. 427–56). Coleridge moved to the cottage in Nether Stowey at the end of 1796.

14 Building on Nicola Trott's important article (1990), I suggest that Coleridge's 'religion for democrats' is also an answer to Thelwall.

15 To John Thelwall, 17 December 1796.

16 In the second and third editions published in 1796 and 1798, respectively, Godwin revised *Political Justice* substantially regarding the role of pleasure and pain, the principle of feeling and the condemnation of private affections (Philp 1986, p. 142).

17 Godwin uses the terms 'mechanism of the human mind' or 'intellectual mechanism' (1793 I, p. 341).

18 In 1794, Coleridge subscribed partly to the principles of *Political Justice* and wrote a poem in Godwin's praise, but by 1796, he regretted his 'foolish verses' (*Letters* I, p. 221). This fact complicates Marilyn Butler's assumption that Coleridge rejected

Godwin on the basis of atheism 'the most innovative radical books to appear in England during his formative years. Once radicalism denoted atheism he could not be radical' (1981, p. 80).

19   'Religious Musings' was completed in 1796. In 1794, Coleridge wrote 'I am a compleat necessitarian', Letter to Robert Southey, December 11 (*Letters* I, p. 137).

20   Beddoes's obituary: 'His philosophical speculations had a direct tendency to Atheism . . . . He was a man of very lively parts, of highly respectable talents; but he was of that school, the doctrines of which have operated, with poisonous influence, on the great of society' (*Gentlemen's Magazine* 79 [1809], p. 120).

21   Coleridge borrowed the second volume of Berkeley's works in March 1796 according to George Whalley (1949, p. 122).

22   'Balguy had long been interested in the subject of Hume's attack; as an undergraduate he published a Latin poem entitled "Divina bonitas demonstrari potest a posteriori" ("The divine goodness is capable of proof from its effects")' (Rivers 2012).

23   The sermon is extant evidence for Coleridge's first public reference to Hobbes. Further indications are contained in Coleridge's letter to Thelwall in December 1796 (*Letters* I, p. 295).

24   The Enlightenment tradition of disinterestedness in England is long. Rivers distinguishes six main positions in her monumental study of the foundation of British ethics between 1660 and 1780; she classifies the Stoics, Cicero, Whichcote, Shaftesbury, Hutchinson, Butler, Fordyce, Wishart, Turnbull, Hume and Adam Smith as the main proponents of disinterested benevolence, as well as 'moral sense, natural, kind, and social affections, instinct, sentiment, the constitution and dignity of our nature, implanted determinations and dispositions of our nature' (Rivers 2000, p. 204). Rivers teases out the rhetorical manoeuvres, for instance, between Hutchinson and his disciple, Butler, in their respective attempts to claim the higher moral ground and the authority over the question what it means to be utterly selfless (Rivers 2000, pp. 216–22).

25   In an entry (*Notebooks* I, §243), Coleridge transcribed a passage from Hutton in late 1795 and early 1796.

26   James Engell discusses Hobbes, albeit in a different context, as the forefather of the Romantic imagination (1981, pp. 11–21).

27   According to H. W. Piper, the corporeality of thought suggests that Coleridge had been reading Hartley in Priestley's edition, or at least that he knew and accepted Priestley's interpretation (1962, p. 32).

28   I discuss Coleridge's gradual but incomplete abandonment of Unitarian principles in Chapter 6.

29   Coleridge published *The Vision of the Maid of Orleans: A Fragment* in the *Morning Post* on 26 December 1797. The fragment excludes the philosophical enquiry into the foundation of freedom in Coleridge's contributions to Book II of Robert Southey, *Joan of Arc* (Bristol, London, 1796) (Coleridge 2004, p. 125).

30   According to Morton Paley, Joan of Arc is a ' "Prenatural Agency", a libertarian heroine under the direction of a divinely appointed Tutelary Spirit' (1999, p. 93; see pp. 91–103).

31   Piper traces the footnote back to Baxter's *Immateriality of the Soul*, which Coleridge read by 1795 (1962, pp. 33, 38).

32   In his philosophical *Lectures 1818–19*, Coleridge elaborated his critique of Locke in Lecture 13 (II, pp. 564–5).

Chapter 3

1 Quoted from the original manuscript (see also *PW* I.1, p. 280). According to Mays, the marginalia were written in ca. 1832. The annotated copy is kept as part of the Marlay Bequest 1912 at the Fitzwilliam Museum, Cambridge; the annotations are at the foot of the page between lines 462–3 (see also *PW* I.1, p. 280; *PW* II.1, p. 383).

2 Coleridge used Kantian ideas prior to this date, but he did so surreptitiously without acknowledging his source. For further explanation, see Chapter 6.

3 STC wrote a letter to Joseph Hughes, 24 November 1819: 'My philosophy (as metaphysics) is built on the distinction between Reason and Understanding' (*Letters* VI, p. 1049). The genealogy of Coleridge's distinction of Reason and Understanding is discussed in Chapter 7.

4 The publication of the *Opus Maximum* shows that Coleridge did not succeed in establishing his own transcendental system, as Nicholas Halmi notes (2007b, p. 49).

5 Kathleen Coburn suspected that Coleridge started to learn about Kant in the mid-1790s: 'Hutton may have been a factor in Coleridge's movement away from Hartley, and from Priestley and Berkeley, towards Kant' (Coburn, *Notebooks [Notes]* I, §243). 'I cannot help wondering if both entries are related to some early and garbled attempt to grasp someone's summary of Kant' (Coburn, *Notebooks [Notes]* I, §248). Coburn saw a connection between entries §248 and §249.

6 Wellek dates the letter to 'Jan. 14, 1824'.

7 The importance of print-runs, sales figures and prices in reading and reception studies in the Romantic period has been emphasized lately by William St. Clair (2004).

8 By idealism, I mean the concept that the mind plays a constitutive part in empirical sensations.

9 The 'Göttingen Review' is known as the 'first' and 'most notorious' review of the *first critique* (Beiser 1987, p. 172, see pp. 172–7; Sassen 2000, pp. 1, 6–7, 270–1). Kühn points out two earlier reviews (2006, pp. 633–4; see Kühn 1987, pp. 70–85); as do G. Schulz (1960, pp. 123–88) and Klemme and Kühn (2010 I, pp. 372–81).

10 I quote the English translation by Sassen of: [Anonymous], *Zugabe zu den Göttingischen Anzeigen von gelehrten Sachen* (19 January 1782), pp. 40–8. Kühn explains the importance of this periodical (1987, pp. 49–50).

11 For instance, Nitsch (1796, p. 150); Gleig (1801 II, p. 359); this issue would become a standard empiricist objection against critical philosophy in the years to come according to Sassen (2000, p. 7).

12 Nonetheless, Coleridge retained the term 'outness' from Berkeley (see *Notebooks* III, §1) 'within the much more nuanced idealism learnt from Kant and others' (Perry in Coleridge 2002a, p. 236).

13 The quotation from Hutton: 'To give (says he) the common people philosophic or metaphysical notions, whether of Religion, or of [Principles of Government, is evidently to unfit them for their proper station in the commonwealth or state]' (*Lectures 1795*, pp. 353–4). In the sermon, Coleridge advocated the education of the poor in Sunday schools. Touching upon the alleged 'infidel' notion of philosophy as 'the only true friend of civil freedom', Coleridge reclaimed the emancipating power of miracles.

14 Ian Wylie has pointed out the striking similarities between Cudworth's and Coleridge's prose and poetry: Coleridge's 'Remarks, &c. on Atheism' echoed Cudworth's view that Moses was 'the first inventor of this atomical philosophy' and

thus endorsed notions 'which were, even two generations before, anachronistic and unsubstantiated'. In addition, Wylie has traced Coleridge's monotheist idea in 'Religious Musings' – the notion that the elect can understand the truth of the one God even though others 'have split the deity into a trinity of God' – back to Cudworth's *True intellectual System* (1989, pp. 18–19; 24).

15 Cudworth renounced materiality and stipulated moral formalism in a similar way as Kant in the *Groundwork*. In the *Treatise concerning Eternal and Immutable Morality*, Cudworth stated that 'all moral Goodness, Justice and Virtue that is exercised in obeying positive commands, and doing such things as are positive only, and to be done for no other Cause but because they are Commanded, or in respect to Political Order, consisteth not in the Materiality of the Action themselves, but in that Formality of yielding obedience to the Commands of Lawful Authority in them' (1731, p. 25).

16 Coburn's commentary (*Notebooks [Notes]* I, §249) remains important. The entry has been part of Wheeler's study (1981, p. 10) and Stansfield's article (1986, p. 131).

17 More recently, Beiser explains that Kant's emphasis on motivation has 'existential' reasons (Beiser 2006, p. 616).

18 The translation of *Groundwork of the Metaphysics of Morals* did not appear until 1798 (Boswell 1991, p. 247). Werner Beyer traces Coleridge's German language skills (1955, pp. 192–200).

19 'Handle so, dass Du wollen kannst, deine Maxime solle ein allgemeines Gesetz werden (der Zweck mag sein, welcher er wolle)' (*Ewiger Frieden,* p. 377) ('So act that you can will that your maxim should become a universal law [whatever the end may be].' [*Perpetual Peace,* 8: 377]).

20 There are exceptions; for instance, Jacqueline Mariña criticizes the concept of the highest good (2000, pp. 329–55).

21 The article was continued (*English Review* 27 [1796], pp. 354–7); Wellek mentions the article (1931, p. 6).

22 Nitsch's article was four pages long (*Monthly Magazine* 9 [1796], pp. 702–5); as was Enfield's article on Nitsch (*Monthly Review* 22 [1797], pp. 15–18).

23 Earlier reviews, such as the *Monthly Review* 10 [1793], pp. 523–31, placed Kant among freethinkers and rational faith independent of Nitsch.

24 Rivers points out, 'that the movement known as freethinking or deism has been the subject of a great deal of confusion' (2000, p. 7). She prefers the term 'freethinking' because it is 'more inclusive . . . than deism' (p. 9). In the late seventeenth century, the terms 'Arian, Socinian, and Unitarian . . . were gaining ground' (p. 9).

25 According to Schneewind, this explanation is correct (1992, pp. 309–10).

26 I thank Anthony Harding for his insightful and detailed comments on Coleridge's relation with British freethinkers.

27 The reviewer commented: 'What do we have here? A flat and spiritless disfigurement of the fundamental moral precept of the Gospel?' (*British Critic* 8 [1796], p. 146).

28 Patton and Mann have suggested Coleridge's awareness of Nitsch's lectures, too (1971, p. xxvi).

29 Anonymous, 'A Sketch of the Philosophy of Dr Kant, Professor of Philosophy at the University of Konigsberg [sic] in Prussia. By a Disciple of Kant's I' (*English Review* 27 [1796], pp. 106–11); Anonymous, 'A Sketch of the Philosophy of Dr Kant, Professor of Philosophy at the University of Konigsberg [sic] in Prussia. By a Disciple of Kant's II' (*English Review* 27 [1796], pp. 354–7).

30 Hamilton's following observation indicates that this early acquaintance with Nitsch had a profound and lasting effect on Coleridge: 'Coleridge's difference with Stoicism is here [in *Aids to Reflections*] described not doctrinally but as a disagreement over affect. Stoicism denies feelings in order to be moral' (2007, p. 76).

31 The idea of Coleridge's reading by way of anticipation was first formulated by James Vigus (2007, pp. 65–73; 2009, pp. 96–8).

32 It was the following edition: Immanuel Kant, *Grundlegung zur Metaphysik der Sitten*, 4th edition (Riga: Johann Friedrich Hartnoch, 1797), (BL C 126 e 9).

33 Vigus's study investigates Coleridge's Platonism in his writings before *Aids* (1825) (2009, p. 9). Claud Howard claimed incorrectly that the Cambridge Platonists anticipated all essential point of Kant's philosophy (1924, p. 98), a claim that has been repeated by Christina Flores's *Plastic Intellectual Breeze* (2008).

34 Coburn suggests as a possible source Schiller's *Über Anmut und Würde* (*Notebooks* I, §1705), but in my opinion, Coleridge's allusion is closer to Schiller's invocation of the naïve quoted above (Curran 2005, pp. 21–54).

Chapter 4

1 Holmes notes that 'the shift of interest from France to Germany also marks a move away from political radicalism to more purely intellectual interests' (1989, p. 117).

2 Kant's stance on politics and its place within his philosophy has been a subject of scholarly debate over decades. Leonard Krieger spoke 'a subordinate place [of politics] in [Kant's] philosophical interests' and of Kant as a 'devotee of enlightened absolutism' (1957, p. 89) whereas Beiser has done much to revise this position by highlighting that the 'apolitical conception of Kant's philosophy fails to consider the importance of politics in his intellectual development . . . Kant's new concept of autonomy was formulated primarily in a political rather than in a metaphysical context' (1992, pp. 27, 30).

3 Marilyn Butler reads the last stanza of 'France: An Ode' as a 'retreat from ideas themselves', that is, from liberty (1981, p. 80). Similarly, Richard Cronin remarks that the last lines of the poem are 'emphatically not Jacobin' in (2000, p. 73). Morrow sees 'France: An Ode' as the 'determination to "disengage" . . . from oppositional and reformist politics in England' (1990, p. 44). Mark Rawlinson argues that 'France: An Ode' is 'a document of alarm, signifying patriotism and anxiety, bellicosity and revulsion' (2000, p. 118). Rosemary Ashton holds that Coleridge 'dissociates himself from his earlier support' of the French Revolution(1996, p. 133) and that 'Coleridge settled down to marriage, parenthood, and more orthodox political views' in 1798 (1980, p. 30). In contrast to her, Roe has carefully pointed out Coleridge's ambivalences towards his revolutionary ideals but also sees *Fears in Solitude* as a 'memorial' and the departure to Germany as the effective conclusion of Coleridge's radical years (1988, pp. 262–8). De Paolo holds that 'France: An Ode' recants Coleridge's 'revolutionary enthusiasm' and converts 'political concepts into metaphors of the mind in relationship with nature' (1992, p. 27).

4 According to his letter to Joseph Cottle, 10 February 1797 (*Letters* I, p. 309), Coleridge did not have the 'heart to finish the poem' after Charles Lamb had expressed his dislike. For an analysis of the political implications of the publication

of 'The Destiny of Nations' in *Sibylline Leaves* under the group of poems 'Odes and Miscellaneous Poems' (Paley 1999, p. 102).

5   This tradition includes: Hugo Grotius (1583–1645) *De jure belli et pacis* (1625), Cornelius Bykenshoek (1673–1743) *De dominiomaris* (1702), Freiherr Samuel von Pufendorf (1632–94) *De habitu religionis Christianae advitam civilam* (tr. 1719 *Of the Relation of State and Church),* Christian von Wolff (1679–1754) *Jus naturae and Jus Gentium* (1740–9) to Emmerich de Vattel (1714–67) *Du Driots de Gens* (1758). Coleridge referred to these international-law authors in a footnote in *The Friend* (1809) (*Friend* II, p. 322). De Paolo points out the overlap with *Perpetual Peace* in the choice of these authors (1985, p. 5).

6   Taylor, 'Perpetual Peace', *Monthly Review,* 22 (1798), pp. 114–15; Anonymous, 'Zum Ewigen Frieden', *Analytical Review,* 23 (1796), pp. 558–9; Anonymous, 'Project for Perpetual Peace', *Analytical Review,* 25 (1797), pp. 211–13; Anonymous, 'Perpetual Peace', *Critical Review,* 20 (1797), 89–91; Anonymous, 'Perpetual Peace', *Gentleman's Magazine,* 67 (1797), p. 136; Anonymous, 'Perpetual Peace', *Monthly Mirror,* 3 (1797), p. 166.

7   'Alle auf das Recht anderer Menschen bezogene Handlungen, deren Maxime sich nicht mit der Publizität verträgt, sind unrecht.' (*Ewiger Frieden* p. 381) ('All actions relating to the rights of others are wrong if their maxim is incompatible with publicity.' [*Perpetual Peace* 8: 381]).

8   'Kant . . . counted on the existence of a transparent and surveyable public sphere formed by literary means and open to arguments, the membership of which would be borne by a small class of educated citizens' (Habermas 1997, p. 124).

9   According to Höffe, Kant's conception to confine his discussion of peace to the protection of life and freedom in legal terms is one of the characteristics of *Perpetual Peace* (2004, p. 140). For epistemological connections between 'Friede' and 'frei', see (Höffe 2004, p. 18). 'The pacifying effects of law [Recht] is its [*Perpetual Peace's*] basic theme' (Bohmann and Lutz-Bachmann 1997, p. 2).

10 Guyer emphasizes that for Kant 'there must be a deeper problem here, namely that his own analysis of radical evil, published just two years before *Perpetual Peace* in his book on *Religion,* implies that human beings can subvert any natural means toward a beneficial outcome if that is how they choose to use their freedom' (2006, p. 297).

11 The following remark suggests Beddoes's awareness of the complexity of Kant's *Natura dædala rerum:* 'he [Kant] manifests no inconsiderable share of ingenuity' (*Monthly Review* 20 [1796], p. 488). The word 'ingenuity' and Beddoes's sarcastic use of it point to the important ambivalence in Kant's first supplement.

12 This passage from Beddoes's review refers to the following German passage: 'Aber die Natur will es anders. – Sie bedient sich zweier Mittel, um Völker von der Vermischung abzuhalten und sie abzusondern, der Verschiedenheit der Sprachen und der Religionen, die zwar den Hang zum wechselseitigen Hasse und Vorward zum Kriege bei sich führt'(*Ewiger Frieden* p. 367). The current translation is very similar to that of Beddoes: 'But *nature wills* otherwise. It makes use of two means to prevent people from intermingling and to separate them: difference of language and of religion, which do bring with them the propensity to mutual hatred and pretexts for war' (*Perpetual Peace* 8: 367).

13 Beddoes wrote: 'We regret, however, that it should require an indefinite time, and the continuance of so dreadful a process as war. We add that, according to our foresight, a sense of justice, and not the spirit of commerce, is to tranquillize the dissentions of mankind. In the middle classes of society, there already prevails a suspicion that,

even in affairs of state, honesty is the best policy; and that powerful nations finally become the victims of the wrongs which they perpetrate' (*Monthly Review* 20 [1796], p. 489).

14 Like *Religion within the Boundaries of Mere Reason*, *Perpetual Peace* analyses the nature of human evil. Chapter 3 explains Kant's 'Copernican Revolution' in ethics. Pablo Muchnik's *Kant's Theory of Evil* discusses the problem in great detail by separating a priori and empirical strands in Kant's complex analysis of human action (2009, pp. xiii–xiv). Hans Ebeling notes that the evil nature of Kant's devils in *Perpetual Peace* is limited to selfishness and hence too angelic 'vielzuengelhaft' (1996, p. 88).

15 To George Coleridge, 10 March 1798 (*Letters* I, pp. 394–8). Brice sees the letter as Coleridge's 'personal recantation of his support of the French Revolution' (2007, p. 132; see pp. 128–46). This reading draws on the Calvinist notion of the 'Elect' arguing that *Fears in Solitude*, and in particular 'Frost at Midnight', conveys Coleridge's resignation to ever be able to read the divine message of history in Nature.

16 Harding refers to Coleridge's letter to George Coleridge of 6 November 1794 (*Letters* I, p. 126).

17 'The fourth stanza of the original manuscript [of 'France: An Ode'] has been lost since Coleridge, Stuart, or some inconceivable sub-editor of the Post took the precaution of excluding it and informing readers that it "alluded to the African Slave Trade as conducted by this Country, and to the present Ministry and their supporters"' (Woodring 1961, p. 183). According to E. H. Coleridge, it was not the fourth stanza but the fifth stanza that was omitted. As a consequence of this removal, the beginning of the last stanza changed (i.e. Stanza Six in the original) (Coleridge 1962 I, p. 247).

18 These lines were probably replaced by new beginning to Stanza Five (formerly Stanza Six): 'The sensual and the Dark rebel in vain . . . graven on a heavier chain!'.

19 This ballad, entitled 'Recantation: Illustrated in the Story of the Mad Ox', is an allegory of Revolutionary France in which a frightened beast tries to escape its captivity. The poem was published in the same paper as and only a few months after 'France: An Ode'. I agree with Magnuson that 'the picture of the ox liberated in gladness and goaded into madness displays . . . a greater sympathy with France' (1998, p. 80). The image of the ox is innocent and thus morally unquestionable. But I do not share his opinion that Coleridge's allegorical figure of wrath precludes the poet's 'liberal attitude that Whigs and Friends of Freedom had held for some time' (1998, p. 80). Wrath can also convey the speaker's empathy with the experience of injustice.

20 Gurion Taussig links this kind of excessive patriotism with the Burkean sublime (2002, p. 173).

21 Catriona McKinnon uses the same image to illustrate that Kant's argument in *Perpetual Peace* that local commitments should be extended to justice on the global level requires a leap of faith (2005, pp. 246–7).

22 Saint-Pierre wrote his *Projet* for 'the occasion of the Congress of Utrecht, which successfully resolved several dynastic and religious disputes among ruling families in England, France and Spain' (Wood 1998, p. 60).

23 At the same time, *Perpetual Peace* was not designed as a specific peace treaty between any numbers of countries and was in so far 'purely *philosophical*' (Wood 1998, p. 62). As John Pizer points out, *Perpetual Peace* is 'not instrumentalized into

direct state service, [as a treatment of] philosophy [it] can operate in the realm of
ideals and analyze these ideals as they progressively develop' (2007, pp. 343 ff.).
Albeit theoretical, Kant's engagement with peace politics is interested in social
reality.

24   The question continues to preoccupy scholars: John N. Kim reads the passage as part
of Kant's 'critique of the political censorship of philosophical texts on the one hand,
and of Prussian imperial expansion into republican Poland on the other' (2007,
p. 203). Contrary to these views, Shell holds that Kant's satirical introduction equates
the prospect of peace with death, and that the overall project is 'self-cancelling' and
peace 'invisible' (1997, p. 151–2).

25   Curren (1986, p. 66), Duff (2009, pp. 204–5) and Fairer (2009, p. 293) discuss the
evolution of the ode in the Romantic period.

26   In the second edition of *Zum Ewigen Frieden*, Kant included, in a subtly ironic
fashion, a secret article according to which any secrecy was forbidden (Höffe
2004, p. 7).

27   According to Bobbio, the transition from the state of nature to the state of society
begins 'once the state of war has begun' (1993, p. 4).

28   'Rousseau does not reproach Hobbes for having described the state of nature as a
state of war, but instead for having located it at the beginning of human history,
rather than at a subsequent moment' (Bobbio 1993, p. 5).

29   *Social Contract* (Book I, Chapter VIII). However, Rousseau excluded moral freedom
from his disquisition in order to avoid contradictions: 'I have already said more than
enough on this point, and the philosophical sense of the word *freedom* is not my
subject' (Rousseau 1994, p. 60).

30   Pizer notes that 'Kant, in the anthropology essay and *Zum ewigen Frieden*,
established bellicosity as an innate human condition driven largely by a consistently
inequitable distribution of wealth, a condition that will be ameliorated by the spirit
of international commerce' (2007, pp. 343 ff.). Wilhelm A. Schulze speaks of war as
the state of nature in Kant's religious thinking in *Perpetual Peace* (1958/59, p. 500).

31   According to Knud Haakensson, 'natural rights were understood as part of a morally
well-ordered universe structured and lent certainty by the law of nature' (1991,
p. 20); see White (2005, pp. 1–3). Daniel N. Robinson gives a lucid exposition of
the connections between American civil rights and Scottish moral and mental
philosophy (2007, pp. 170–81).

32   'Wer einmal die Gewalt in Händen hat, wird sich vom Volk nicht Gesetze
vorschreiben lassen', (*Ewiger Frieden* 371) ('He who once has power in his hands will
not let the people prescribe laws for him,' [*Perpetual Peace* 8: 371]).

33   Johnson was one of the victims of the recent sedition laws. He was convicted on the
basis of having sold (not published) a pamphlet by Gilbert Wakefield (1756–1801).
Zall notes that Rev. Gilbert Wakefield's pamphlet violated the sedition laws when it
described 'how the constitution had been corrupted by "a set of apostates and thieves
in the present ministry"' (1972, p. 28); see also Mark Crosby (2009, pp. 29–47).

34   Holmes neglects Johnson's German connections, too (1989, p. 201).

35   The third issue of *Wordsworth Circle*, 33 (2002), is dedicated to Joseph Johnson.
Leslie F. Chard (2002, pp. 95–100) and Angela Esterhammer (2002b, pp. 101–4) have
done much to establish the international dimension of Johnson's publishing projects.

36   'Shelley encountered the poem by the period 1815 to early 1816, as both "Fire,
Famine, and Slaughter" and Coleridge's "France: An Ode" were transcribed by Mary
Shelley during this period' (West 2007, p. 28). According to West, 'France: An Ode'

exemplifies 'the kind of symbolic language that [Shelley's] Prometheus must break through if he is to free mankind' (2007, p. 170).

37   This copy of *Fears in Solitude* with Coleridge's annotations – once in the possession of Sir George Beaumont – can be consulted in the J. Pierpont Morgan Library in New York (Coleridge 2004, p. 109–10). The annotations were published by B. Ifor Evans in *Times Literary Supplement* on 18 April (1935, p. 255).

38   In the essay about the idea of a universal history, 'Idee zu einer allgemeinen Geschichte in weltbürgerlicher Absicht', Kant similarly contends that Nature uses antagonism as a means to solicit human progress that is geared towards establishing a just civil society (*Idee*, pp. 20–2).

Chapter 5

1   Kooy mentions that there is compelling circumstantial evidence that along with other books Coleridge 'was buying at the time – by Kant, Jacobi, Bürger, Lessing and others – he acquired several volumes of Schiller' (2002, p. 34).

2   According to the preface of Kant's *Logic* (Kant 1800), Jäsche prepared the manual on logic at Kant's request. It is particularly interesting in the context of Coleridge's marginalia that Jäsche wrote the manual with the aid of Kant's personal copy of Georg Friedrich Meier's book, on which Kant lectured during his entire career, and in which he had written extensive notes. Jäsche's *Logic*, like all other texts stemming from Kant's logic notes, cannot be taken as 'a definite statement of Kant's view' (Young 1992, p. xvii–xix). Coleridge's marginalia to Kant's *Logic* thus represent a kind of meta-marginalia: Coleridge's autograph commentary on Kant's marginalia.

3   The final three chapters in Scott Masson's monograph (2004) and Richard Berkeley's article (2004) discuss the meaning that Romantic poets attributed to the word 'silence'.

4   The satire 'New Morality' first appeared in *The Anti-Jacobin, or Weekly Examiner* 2.36 (1798), pp. 623–40.

5   The impact of the *Anti-Jacobin Review* on British culture was strong as a number of studies show (Micheli 1990, p. 286; Roper 1978, pp. 181–3; Tyson 1979, pp. 166–70; Sullivan 1983 II, pp. 12–21; Mortensen 2005).

6   The satire presented the universal freedom of man as a meaningless hyperbole and sneered at the young idealists' internationalist aspirations:

> Fram'd for thy Freedom, universal man?
> No- through the extended globe his feelings run
> As broad and general as th' unbounded sun!
> No narrow bigot he; - his reason'd view
> Thy interests, England, ranks with thine Peru-
> France at our doors, he sees no danger nigh,
> But heaves for Turkey's woes th' impartial sigh;
> A steady patriot of the world alone,
> The friend of every country – but his own.   (Anonymous 1799, p. 297, ll. 106–14).

7   Prussia made the Peace of Basel for the strategic reason to expand in the east. According to Christopher Clark, the Prussian King Fredrick Wilhelm II (1786–97) withdrew his troops because he intended to expand Prussian territory in the

east, that is, in Poland (2006, pp. 292–311). Bohmann and Lutz-Bachmann note, 'Prussia ceded to France all territory west of the Rhine, in exchange for which Prussia expected to be allowed to join Russia and Austria in partitioning Poland' (1997, p. 1).

8   Weber cited an entry omitted by Snyder (Weber 1935, p. 165) and van Woudenberg recently published an updated list (2003, pp. 66–80).

9   Richard Berkeley merely mentions Coleridge's plan to write a biography of Lessing in passing without further reference to Coleridge's studies at Göttingen (2007, p. 63); Coleridge's entries on Lessing in the context of the function of his notebooks are discussed by John Worthen (2010, p. 45).

10 The pantheism controversy 'quickly became intertwined with the reception of Kant's critical philosophy' (di Giovanni 1998, p. 44). Karl Leonhard Reinhold recognized that the heated debate would aid his efforts of proselyting critical philosophy. His *Letters on Kantian Philosophy (Briefe über die Kantische Philosophie)* appeared at first as a serial publication in the *German Mercury (Teutscher Merkur)* between August 1786 and September 1786 and then in two volumes in Leipzig in 1790 and 1792 (Desmond 2004, p. xvii). Reinhold recognized the controversy could be used to attract readers. He emphasized the relevance of Kant's antimonies in the *Critique of Pure Reason* for the question concerning the possibility of a rational proof for the existence of God which lay at the heart of the controversy. And so it was that Reinhold managed to popularize Kant's philosophy greatly (see Sassen 2000, p. 2; Beiser 1987, p. 235; di Giovanni 1998, p. 44; Desmond 2005, p. xvii). Reinhold's assimilation played an important part in Coleridge's initial encounter with Kant's *first critique*, too, as I will explain in more detail in Chapter 7.

11 By 1794, the career of Reinhold's *Elementarphilosophie* was doomed (Beiser 1987, p. 26).

12 Weimar was also a particularly popular destination for Englishmen in 1797 according to Karl S. Guthke (2002, p. 113).

13 Kooy points out several local journals in Göttingen (2002, p. 34).

14 Forster and Forster give an account of the history of the Georg-August University (1969, pp. 312–20).

15 Franziska Hirschmann discusses Münchhausen as part of her study of eighteenth-century aristocracy (2009, p. 24); Hans Erich Bödeker, Philippe Büttgen and Michel Espagne unfold the history of the human sciences in Göttingen around 1800 (2010).

16 Kühn distinguishes groups in late German Enlightenment: 'the Berliners, the Göttingers, the sensationists, and the critical empiricists' (1987, p. 49).

17 Di Giovanni criticizes the *Popularphilosophens'* misrepresentation of Kant (2005, p. 62). Bronislawa Rosenthal examines Lessing in the context of the *Popularphilosophen* (1967).

18 According to Beiser, Feder belonged to the *Popularphilosophen* who 'themselves unwitting allies of Jacobi and Wizenmann, whom they otherwise bitterly opposed' (1987, p. 167). That is, Feder indirectly supported through his attack on Kant Jacobi's polemic that Reason led to 'nihilism' – the philosophical position of doubting everything, 'the external world, other minds, God, and even the permanent reality of his own self' (Beiser 1987, p. 4) with the result that nothingness is all that can be affirmed.

19 Feder lost his post in 1796 according to Kurt Röttgers (1984, p. 431; Brandt 1989, pp. 249–64).

20 'Schulz' might also refer to Johann Ernst Schulz (1739–1805), a friend of Kant who defended critical philosophy and eventually was appointed full professor (Kühn 2001, p. xiii).

21 Coleridge might have learnt from Blumenbach about Kant. Based on Timothey Lenoir's article on the exchange of knowledge between Kant and Blumenbach (Lenior 1980, pp. 77–108), Philipp Hunnekuhl emphasizes the significance of this link for Coleridge's turn towards the notion of the independence of the human mind (2007).

22 Guyer clarifies that Kant's theory goes beyond his analogy with Copernicus. In contrast to Copernicus, Kant's theory proposes that 'we are supposed to downgrade our experience of objects to mere appearances without knowing anything about the real character of those objects at all' (2006, p. 51).

23 It remains subject to further investigation what the public responses were like to Johann Gottfried Herder, August Wilhelm von Schlegel and Jean Paul Richter and in how far this might have impacted on Coleridge's use of their writings. Foakes explains Coleridge's reading and use of German sources in his lectures (1987, pp. liii–lxiv).

24 The next two chapters contain a detailed analysis of Coleridge's assimilation.

25 My analysis draws on Jackson's excellent introduction including an overview of various phases in Coleridge's life in which he worked intensively on the history of philosophy (Jackson 2000, pp. xlvi–lvi).

Chapter 6

1 The English translation of Mme de Staël *De l'Allemagne* (1813) marked the end of the long moratorium on significant Continental books in Britain (Butler 1981, p. 120). Mme de Staël's book was, according to Beiser, instrumental for creation of the 'myth of the apolitical German' (1992, p. 10). With an introduction from Southey, Coleridge visited Mme de Staël in London in October 1813. Coleridge reported nothing of the encounter except that Mme de Staël made a disparaging remark about Goethe's *Faust* (Whalley 1972, p. 202), whereas Mme de Staël famously remarked 'Think of him? Why, that he is very great in monologue, but that he has no idea of dialogue?' (quoted in Whalley 1972, p. 202). The English response to Mme Staël's publication must have encouraged Coleridge to openly advocate Kant in *Biographia*.

2 William Hazlitt made a similar point about Coleridge's apostasy in 'The Spirit of the Age' (1933 XI, p. 34); the edition of Coleridge's Letters includes a summary of Hazlitt's attacks on Coleridge (*Letters* IV, p. 668).

3 Modiano's 2009 essay on *Biographia Literaria* and its link with Coleridge's *Essays on the Principles of Genial Criticism* has been a major source of insight for this chapter.

4 Genius for the *Sturm und Drang* included chaos and to some extent madness. The English equivalent of this tradition has been discussed by Monroe (1992) and Burwick (1996).

5 Wellek criticized the 'clash of styles' in Coleridge's philosophical architecture, 'here a storey from Kant, there a part of a room from Schelling, there a roof from Anglican theology' (1931, p. 67).

6 Giordanetti discusses Kant's nuanced view on the relation of genius and mathematics in detail (1995, pp. 411–13).

7 The lecture transcripts in Volume 24 of the Academy edition appeared in 1966. The edition was not available when Wellek formulated his harsh judgement of Coleridge.

8 Seamus Perry and Nicola Trott's collection of essays (2001) explores different aspects especially with regard to Wordsworth's poetic manifesto published in the preface to the 1800 (second) edition.

9 *Lyrical Ballads with a Few Other Poems* (Bristol: Printed by Biggs and Cottle, For T. N. Longman, Paternoster-Row, London, 1798), pp. 62–3*. British Library shelf mark Ashley 2250.

10 'Cottle or Coleridge may at first have asked Beddoes for permission to use [the verses] as a possible substitute' (Foxon 1954, p. 233); Duncan Wu's investigation has revived the discussion recently, arguing that the poem is 'Beddoes's "literary imposture"' (1993, pp. 332–5).

11 Jonathan Wordsworth (1982), James Chandler (1984), Stephen Gill (1989; 2003), David Bromwich (2000), Simon Jarvis (2007) and David Simpson (2009) give profound studies of Wordsworth's life, poetry, philosophy and his relation to politics.

12 The impact of Wordsworth's and Kant's mutual admiration for Milton on their respective poetics and the parallels, differences and possible historical interconnections between them merit further investigation. A recent study has shown the profound impact of Milton on Kant's aesthetics (Budick 2010).

13 The analogies between Kant and Wordsworth have been examined with regard to the concept of originality, however without considering the historical context of Anglo-German relations at the time (Gould 1982, pp. 179–94). This chapter examines different conceptual analogies than the essay by Gould.

14 In 1815, in his early forties, Coleridge found a new, sympathetic home in the Morgan family, consisting of John, his wife and sister-in-law. Their help, especially that of John as Coleridge's amanuensis, was indispensible for the completion of the *Biographia* (Engell and Bate 1983, p. xiv).

15 For Coleridge, Milton and Shakespeare came to personify two competing principles of poetry. Perry notes, 'In *Biographia* the subject to be illuminated by these principles is Wordsworth, and the mythology is showily established at this point because Milton and Shakespeare symbolize the dual elements which compose the provocative muddle of Wordsworth' (Perry 1999, p. 210).

16 It has been pointed out (Miall 2000) that the poem has been criticized because of Wordsworth's neglect for the poverty and industrialization in the Wye Valley, notably by Jerome McGann (1983), Marjorie Levinson (1986) and Kenneth R. Johnston (1983).

Chapter 7

1 The great importance of Kant's *Religion innerhalb der Grenzen der bloßen Vernunft (Religion Within the Limits of Reason Alone)* for Coleridge's religious thought is known (Loades 1978; Welch 1985; Shaffer 2004). Mary Warnock (1986) and David Jasper (1983) have contributed important research to Coleridge's theology, too.

2 The respective passages include *Friend* (1818) I, pp. 154–61; *Lay Sermons*, pp. 59–93; *Aids*, pp. 216–36. The passages in *The Friend* of 1809 are discussed in the chapter.

3   Orsini argues that 'Coleridge does not seem to have grasped firmly and continuously the fact that categories of the understanding' (1969, p. 137). Bode notes that '[O]ne major reason can be given for these faultlines: Coleridge's religious views and needs . . . these religious convictions are basically, that is to say, *systematically*, incompatible with the philosophical materials Coleridge assembled' (2009, p. 610).

4   Coleridge's relationship to Hume has been discussed, among others, by Hedley (2000, pp. 162–3, 194–200), Taylor (1986, pp. 40 ff.) and Harding (1974, pp. 171–4).

5   Coleridge's copy of the *Critique of Pure Reason* is at the British Library under the shelf mark C 43 b 8.

6   The accusation was first brought forward by Thomas de Quincey after Coleridge's death in 1834. Following Wellek (1981, pp. 151–6), Norman Fruman's *Coleridge, the: Damaged Archangel* launched a fierce attack on Coleridge (1971).

7   'nichts geschieht durch ein blindes Ohngefähr (in mundo non datur casus)' (*KrV* B 280) ('Nothing happens through a mere accident [in mundo non datur casus]' [*CpR* B 280]). A similar passage can be found in Reinhold's *Versuch* (1789, p. 518) and is translated by Mehigan and Empson (Reinhold 2011, p. 253).

8   Halmi discusses Coleridge's resistance to the orthodox Christian Trinity (1995, pp. 26–31).

9   Reinhold's *Versuch* contained 88 principles (1789, p. 578).

10 Nitsch translated Kant's 'analytisch' as 'analytical' (1796).

11 Coleridge attacked Rousseau for reasons that *Du Contrat Social* does not support; he presented Rousseau as the originator of the idea that 'a perfect Constitution of Government' (*Friend* II, p. 126) should be derived from the autonomy of Reason possessed by each member of the common wealth. According to *The Friend*, Rousseau allegedly tried 'to find a form of Society according to which each one uniting with the whole shall yet obey himself only and remains as free as before' (*Friend* II, p. 126). Coleridge omitted Rousseau's distinction between legislative power and executive power and indirectly accused Rousseau on the basis of this assumption of supporting military despotism.

Conclusion

1   The Bollingen Series alone consists of thirty volumes (fifteen different titles).

2   Similarly, Boucher and Vincent attribute little importance to Coleridge's studies with regard to the British Idealists at the end of nineteenth century: 'Direct contact with the text elevated the level of scholarship far beyond that which could be found in the paraphrases of Coleridge and Carlyle' (2012, p. 15).

Bibliography

Periodicals and newspapers

English periodicals

The Analytical Review; or, History of Literature . . . , (1788–98), T. Christie and J. Johnson (eds), Vols 1–28. London.

The Annual Biography, and Obituary, for the Year, (1817–37), Vols 1–21. London: A. Strahan.

The Anti-Jacobin, or Weekly Examiner, (1797–8), W. Gifford (ed.), No. 1–36. London.

The Anti-Jacobin Review and Magazine, (1798–1810), J. Gifford (John R. Greene) (ed.), Vols 1–35. London.

The Britannic Magazine; or Entertaining Repository of Heroic Adventures, (1793–1807), Vols 1–12. London.

The British Critic, (1793–1813), R. Nares and W. Below (eds), Vols 1–42. London.

The Critical Review; or Annals of Literature, Series 2, (1791–1803), Vols 1–39; Series 3, (1804–11), G. Gregory and J. M. Good (eds), Vols 1–24. London.

The English Review; or An Abstract of English and Foreign Literature, (1783–96), Vols 1–28. London.

The Gentleman's Magazine, (1731–1833), J. Nichols (ed.), Vols 1–103. London.

The London Magazine, Series 1, (1820–4), Vols 1–10. London: Baldwin.

The Monthly Magazine and British Register, (1796–1826), Vols 1–16. Richard Phillips (proprietor). London.

The Monthly Mirror; Reflecting Men and Manners, (1795–1806), Vols 1–22. London.

The Monthly Review, Series 2, (1790–1825), R. Griffiths and E. Griffiths (eds), Vols 1–108. London.

The Morning Chronicle, (1770–1862). London.

Oracle and Public Advertiser, (1794–1802). Peter Stuart (proprietor). London.

The Political Magazine, (1780–91), Vols 1–21. London.

The Quarterly Review, (1809–24), W. Gifford (ed.), Vols 1–61. London.

The Star, (1788–1831). William Lane (proprietor). London.

Telegraph, (1794–7), David Evans Macdonnel (ed.). London.

True Briton, (1793–1804), J. Heriot (ed.). London.

German periodicals

Allgemeine Literatur-Zeitung, (1785–1803). Jena und Leipzig.

Berlinische Monatschrift, (1783–1811), J. E. Biester and F. Gedike (eds). Berlin.

Neuer Teutscher Merkur, (1790–1810), C. M. Wieland (ed.). Weimar.

Teutscher Merkur, (1775–89), C. M. Wieland (ed.). Weimar.

Primary literature

Aikin, J. and Enfield, W. (eds) (1799–1815). *General Biography; or Lives, Critical and Historical*, 10 vols. London: G. G. and J. Robinson.

Anonymous. (1799). *The Beauties of the Anti-Jacobin; or Weekly Examiner; Containing Every Article of Permanent Utility in That Valuable and Highly Esteemed Paper, Literary and Political; the Whole of the Excellent Poetry; Together with Explanatory Notes, Biographical Anecdotes, and a Prefatory Advertisement by the Editor*. London: Plymsell, Anti-Jacobin Press, C. Chapple.

Balguy, T. (1781). *Divine Benevolence Asserted; and Vindicated from the Objections of Ancient and Modern Sceptics*. London: Lockyer Davis.

Barruel, A. (1799). *Memoirs: Illustrating the History of Jacobinism, Written in the French by Abbe Barruél and Translated by Hon. Robert Clifford*. 4 vols. Hartford: Hudson and Goodwin for Cornelius Davis.

Beddoes, T. (1793). *Observations on the Nature of Demonstrative Evidence; with an Explanation of Certain Difficulties Occuring in the Elements of Geometry: And Reflections on Language*. London: Josheph Johnson.

—. (1795). *A Word in Defence of the Bill of Rights, against Gagging Bills*. Bristol: N. Biggs and J. Johnson.

Berkeley, G. (1784). *The Works of George Berkeley. D. D. Late Bishop of Cloyne in Ireland. To Which Is Added, an Account of His Life, and Several of His Letters to Thomas Prior, Esq. Dean Gervais, and Mr. Pope*. Dublin: John Exshaw.

Bürger, G. A. (1796). *Leonora, a Poem from the German of Mr. Bürger*. Norwich: John March, Joseph Johnson.

Burke, E. (1790). *Reflections on the Revolution in France, and on the Proceedings in Certain Societies in London Relative to That Event. In a Letter Intended to Have Been Sent to a Gentleman in Paris*. London: J. Dodsley.

—. (1990). *Philosophical Enquiry into the Origin of Our Ideas of the Sublime and the Beautiful*, A. Phillips (ed.). Oxford: Oxford University Press.

Carlyle, T. (1851). *The Life of Sterling*. London: Chapman and Hall.

Cockin, W. (1791). *The Freedom of Human Action Explained and Vindicated: In Which the Opinions of Dr. Priestley on the Subject Are Particularly Considered*. London: G. Nicol.

Coleridge, H. N. and Coleridge, J. T. (1990). *Table Talk*, C. Woodring (ed.), 2 vols. London: Routledge.

Coleridge, S. T. (1798). *Fears in Solitude*. London: J. Johnson.

—. (1828). *The Poetical Works of Samuel Taylor Coleridge, Including the Dramas of Wallenstein, Remorse and Zapolya*. London: William Pickering.

—. (1956–71). *The Collected Letters of Samuel Taylor Coleridge*, E. L. Griggs (ed.), 6 vols. Oxford: Clarendon Press.

—. (1957–2001). *The Notebooks of Samuel Taylor Coleridge*, K. Coburn, M. Christensen and A. Harding (eds), 5 vols. London: Routledge.

—. (1962 [first published 1912]). *The Complete Poetical Works of Samuel Taylor Coleridge*, E. H. Coleridge (ed.), 2 vols. Oxford: Clarendon Press.

—. (1969). *The Friend*, B. E. Rooke (ed.), 2 vols. London: Routledge & Kegan Paul.

—. (1970). *The Watchman*, L. Patton (ed.). London: Routledge & Kegan Paul.

—. (1971). *Lectures 1795: On Politics and Religion*, L. Patton and P. Mann (eds). London: Routlegde & Kegan Paul.

—. (1972). *Lay Sermons*, R. J. White (ed.). London: Routledge & Kegan Paul.

—. (1976). *On the Constitution of Church and State*, J. Colmer (ed.). London: Routledge & Kegan Paul.

—. (1978). *Essays on His Times in the Morning Post and the Courier*, D. V. Erdman (ed.), 3 vols. London: Routledge & Kegan Paul.

—. (1980–92). *Marginalia*, G. Whalley and J. R. de J. Jackson (eds), 6 vols. London: Routledge & Kegan Paul.

—. (1981). *Logic*, Jackson J. R. de J. (ed.). London, Princeton: Routledge & Kegan Paul.

—. (1983). *Biographia Literaria or Biographical Sketches of My Literary Life and Opinions*, J. Engell and W. Jackson Bate (eds), 2 vols. London: Routledge & Kegan Paul.

—. (1987). *Lectures 1808–1819 on Literature*, R. A. Foakes (ed.), 2 vols. London: Routledge & Paul Kegan.

—. (1993). *Aids to Reflection*, J. Beer (ed.). London: Routledge.

—. (1995). *Shorter Works and Fragments*, H. J. Jackson and J. R. de J. Jackson (eds), 2 vols. London: Routledge.

—. (2000). *Lectures 1818–1819 on the History of Philosophy*, J. R. de J. Jackson (ed.), 2 vols. Princeton, New Jersey: Princeton University Press.

—. (2001). *Poetical Works*, J. C. C. Mays (ed.), 3 vols. Princeton, New Jersey: Princeton University Press.

—. (2002a). *Coleridge's Notebooks: A Selection*, S. Perry (ed.). Oxford: Oxford University Press.

—. (2002b). *Opus Maximum*, T. Mcfarland and N. Halmi (eds). Princeton: Princeton University Press.

—. (2004). *Coleridge's Poetry and Prose*, N. Halmi, P. Magnuson and R. Modiano (eds). New York, London: Norton.

Cudworth, R. (1731). *A Treatise Concerning Eternal and Immutable Morality*. London: James and John Knapton.

—. (1743). *The True Intellectual System of the Universe: The First Part; Wherein All the Reason and Philosophy of Atheism Is Confuted, . . . With a Discourse Concerning the True Notion of the Lord's Supper*. London: J. Walthoe.

De Quincey, T. (1863). *Last Days of Immanuel Kant and Other Writings*. Edinburgh: Adam and Charles Black.

De Staël, Madame A. L. G. (1813). *Germany,* 3 vols. London: John Murray.

Di Giovanni, G. and Harris, H. S. (eds and trans.) (1985). *Between Kant and Hegel: Texts in the Development of Post-Kantian Idealism Translated and Annotated by George Di Giovanni and H. S. Harris*. Albany: State University of New York Press.

Duff, W. (1767). *An Essay on Original Genius; and Its Various Modes of Exertion in Philosophy and the Fine Arts, Particularly in Poetry*. London: Edward and Charles Dilly.

Fairer, D. and Gerrard, C. (eds) (2004). *Eighteenth-Century Poetry: An Annotated Anthology*. Oxford: Oxford University Press.

Fichte, J. G. (1964–2011). *J. G. Fichte-Gesamtausgabe der Bayerischen Akademie der Wissenschaften*, R. Lauth, H. Jacob, E. Fuchs and P. K. Schneider (eds), 42 vols. Stuttgart-Bad Cannstatt: Friedrich Frommann Verlag (Günther Holzboog).

Frend, W. (1793). *Extracted from the Appendix of a Pamphlet. Entitled Peace and Union, Recommended to the Associated Bodies of Republicans and Anti-Republicans; by William Frend, M. A. Fellow of Jesus College Cambridge*. London.

Gerard, A. (1774). *En Essay on Genius*. London: W. Strahan.

Gleig, G. (ed.) (1801). *Supplement to the Encyclopaedia Britannica*, Vol. 2. Edinburgh: Bell and Macfarquhar.

Godwin, W. (1793). *An Enquiry Concerning Political Justice, and Its Influence on General Virtue and Happiness*. 2 vols. Dublin: printed for Luke White.

—. (1993). *Political and Philosophical Writings of William Godwin*, M. Philp (ed.), 7 vols. London: Pickering.

216   *Bibliography*

Goethe, J. W. v. (1985). *Die Leiden des Jungen Werther*, S. Blessin (ed.). Frankfurt am Main: Diesterweg.

Grotius, H. (1913–25). *De Jure Belli Ac Pacis Libri Tres : In Quibus Jus Naturae & Gentium, Item Juris Publici Præcipua Explicantur*, 2 vols. Washington, District of Columbia: Carnegie Institution of Washington.

Hartley, D. (1749). *Observations on Man, His Frame, His Duty, and His Expectations*. 2 vols. London: S. Richardson.

—. (1775). *Hartley's Theory of the Mind, on the Principle of the Association of Ideas; with Essays Relating to the Subject of It*, J. Priestley (ed.). London: J. Johnson.

Hays, M. (2004). *The Correspondence (1779–1843) of Mary Hays, British Novelist*, M. Brooks (ed.). Lewiston: Edwin Mellen.

Hazlitt, W. (1933). *The Complete Works of William Hazlitt*, P. P. Howe (ed.), 21 vols. London, Toronto: J. M. Dent and Sons, LTD.

Hobbes, T. (1839). *Leviathan, or the Matter, Form, and Power of a Commonwealth Eccleciastical and Civil*, Sir W. M. Bart (ed.), 11 vols. Vol. 3. London: John Bohn.

Hume, D. (1935). *Dialogues Concerning Natural Religion*, N. K. Smith (ed.). Oxford: Clarendon Press.

—. (2000). *An Enquiry Concerning Human Understanding: A Critical Edition*, T. L. Beauchamp (ed.). Oxford: Clarendon Press.

—. (2007). *A Treatise of Human Nature*, D. F. Norton and M. J. Norton (eds), 2 vols. Oxford: Clarendon Press.

Hutton, T. (1794). *An Investigation of the Principles of Knowledge, and of the Progress of Reason, from Sense to Science and Philosophy*. Edinburgh, London: A. Strahan, T. Cadell.

Jacobi, F. H. (1916). 'Über die Lehre des Spinoza in Briefen an den Herrn Moses Mendelssohn', in H. Scholz (ed.), *Die Hauptschriften zum Pantheismusstreit*. Berlin: Renther and Reichard, pp. 45–281.

Kant, I. (1796). *Project for a Pertual Peace: A Philosophical Essay*. London: printed by Stephen Couchman for Vernor & Hood.

—. (1797). *The Principles of Critical Philosophy, Selected from the Works of Emmanuel Kant Member of the Royal Academy of Sciences in Berlin; and Professor of Philosophy in the University of Koenigsberg; and Expounded by James Sigismund Beck Extraordinary Professor in the University of Halle: Translated from the German by an Auditor of the Latter*, trans. J. Richardson. Escher, London: J. Johnson, W. Richardson.

—. (1798–9). *Essays and Treatises on Moral, Political, and Various Philosophical Subjects, by E. Kant. From the German by the Translator [John Richardson] of the Principles of Critical Philosophy*, trans. J. Richardson, 2 vols. London: William Richardson.

—. (1799). *The Metaphysic of Morals, Divided into Metaphysical Elements of Law and of Ethics, by Emanuel Kant . . . From the German by the Translator of Kant's Essays and Treatises. In Two Volumes*, trans. J. Richardson. Hamburg, London: William Richardson.

—. (1800). *Logik ein Handbuch zu Vorlesungen*, G. B. Jäsche (ed.). Königsberg: Friedrich Nicolovius.

—. (1819a). *Logic from the German of Emmanuel Kant*, trans. J. Richardson. London: printed for Simpkin & Marshall.

—. (1819b). *Prolegomena to Every Future Metaphysic, Which Can Appear as a Science; from the German by J Richardson*, trans. J. Richardson. London: printed for Simpkin & Marshall.

—. (1836a). *Metaphysics of Ethics*, trans. with an introduction and appendix by W. J. Semple. Edinburgh: Thomas Clark; London: Hamilton, Adams & Co, pp. 85–161.

—. (1836b). *Metaphysical Works of Emanuel Kant, Translated from the German, with a Sketch of His Life and Writings, by J Richardson, Containing, 1 Logic 2 Prolegomena to Future Metaphysics 3 Enquiry into the Proofs for the Existence of God, and into the Theodicy.* London: Printed for Simpkin and Marshall.

—. (1838). *Critick of Pure Reason*, trans. Ananymous. London: William Pickering.

—. (1845). *Critique of Pure Reason*, trans. J. M. D. Meiklejohn. London: Bohn.

—. (1848). *Critick of Pure Reason*, trans. F. Haywood. London: William Pickering.

—. (1883). *Prolegomena and Metaphysical Foundations of Natural Science*, trans. with a biography and introduction Ernest Belfort Bax. London: George Bell.

—. (1892). *Kritik of Judgment*, trans. J. H. Bernard. London: Macmillan.

—. (1900–25). *Kant's gesammelte Schriften*, Königlich Preussische Akademie der Wissenschaften (ed.). Berlin: G. Reimer.

—. (1926–54). *Kant's gesammelte Schriften*, Preussische Akademie der Wissenschaften (ed.). Berlin: W. de Gruyter.

—. (1955–73). *Kant's gesammelte Schriften*, Deutsche Akademie der Wissenschaften (ed.). Berlin: de Gruyter.

—. (1974–96). *Kant's gesammelte Schriften*, Akademie der Wissenschaften der Deutschen Demokratischen Republik (ed.). Berlin: de Gruyter.

—. (1996a). *Practical Philosophy*, trans. M. J. Gregor. Cambridge: Cambridge University Press.

—. (1996b). *Religion and Rational Theology*, trans. A. W. Wood and G. di Giovanni. Cambridge: Cambridge University Press.

—. (1997). *Kant's gesammelte Werke.* Berlin-Brandenburgische Akademie der Wissenschaften (ed.). Berlin: de Gruyter.

—. (2000a). *Critique of Pure Reason*, trans. P. Guyer and A. W. Wood. Cambridge: Cambridge University Press.

—. (2000b). *Critique of the Power of Judgment*, trans. P. Guyer and E. Matthews. Cambridge: Cambridge University Press.

—. (2006). *Anthrolopology from a Pragmatic Point of View*, trans. R. B. Louden. Cambridge: Cambridge University Press.

Knight, R. P. (1805). *An Analytical Enquiry into the Principles of Taste.* London: Printed for T. Payne and J. White.

Locke, J. (1975). *Essay Concerning Human Understanding*, P. H. Nidditch (ed.). Oxford: Clarendon Press.

—. (1988). *Two Treatises of Government*, P. Laslett (ed.), Cambridge: Cambridge University Press.

—. (2005). *The Selected Political Writings of John Locke*, P. E. Sigmund (ed.). New York: Norton.

Mendelssohn, M. (1785). *Morgenstunden oder Vorlesungen über das Daseyn Gottes.* Berlin: Christian Friedrich Voß und Sohn.

Mill, J. S. (1967). 'Coleridge', in F. R. Leavis (ed.), *Mill on Bentham and Coleridge.* London: Chatto & Windus, pp. 99–168.

Morgan, T. (1807). 'Kant', in J. Aikin and W. Enfield (eds), *General Biography; or Lives, Critical and Historical,* 10 vols. Vol. 6. London: G. G. and J. Robinson, pp. 3–11.

Nitsch, F. A. (1796). *A General and Introductory View of Professor Kant Concerning Man, the World and the Deity.* London: J. Downes.

— (1993). *A General and Introductory View of Professor Kant's Principles Concerning Man, the World and the Deity.* London: Routledge, Thoemmes.

O'Keeffe, J. A. (1795). *An Essay on the Progress of Human Understanding.* London: V. Griffiths.

Pater, W. (1922). *Appreciations, with an Essay on Style*. London: Macmillan and Co.

Priestley, J. (1777). *The Doctrine of Philosophical Necessity Illustrated: Being an Appendix to the Disquisition Relating to Matter and Spirit. To Which Is Added, an Answer to the Letters on Materialism, and on Hartley's Theory of the Mind*. London: J. Johnson.

Pufendorf, S. F. v. (1719). *Of the Relation between Church and State: Or, How Far Christian and Civil Life Affect Each Other; Being a Translation of a Book of Baron Puffendorf's, Upon This Important Subject. With a Preface, Giving Some Account of This Book, and Its Use, with Regard to the Present Controversies*. London: J. Wyat.

Reinhold, K. L. (1789). *Versuch einer neuen Theorie des menschlichen Vorstellungsmögens*, Prag und Jena: C. Widtman und I. M. Mauke.

—. (1790). *Beyträge zur Berichtigung bisheriger Missverständnisse der Philosophen*, Jena: Johann Michael Mauke.

—. (1791). *Über das Fundament des Philosophischen Wissens*, Jena: Johann Michael Mauke.

—. (1794). *Beyträge zur Berichtigung bisheriger Missverständnisse der Philosophen (Zweiter Band)*. Jena: Johann Michael Mauke.

—. (1923 [first published in book form 1790–2]). *Briefe über die Kantische Philosophie*, R. Schmidt (ed.). Leipzig: P. Reclam.

—. (2003 [first published 1790]). *Beiträge zur Berichtigung bisheriger Mißverständnisse der Philosophen (Erster Band)*, F. Fabbianelli (ed.). Hamburg: Felix Meiner.

—. (2005). *Letters on the Kantian Philosophy*, trans. K. Ameriks and J. Hebbeler. Cambridge: Cambridge University Press.

—. (2011). *Essay on a New Theory of the Human Capacity for Representation*, trans. T. Mehigan and B. Empson. Berlin, New York: de Gruyter.

Richardson, J. (1797). *The Principles of Critical Philosophy*. Escher, London: 1797.

Robinson, H. C. (1869). *Diary, Reminiscences, and Correspondence of Henry Crabb Robinson, Barrister-at-Law*, T. Sadler (ed.), 3 vols. London: Macmillan.

Robison, J. (1797). *Proofs of a Conspiracy against all the Religions and Governments of Europe*. Edinburgh: William Creech.

Roehr, S. (1995). *A Primer on German Enlightenment: With a Translation of Karl Reinhold Leonhard's the Fundamental Concepts and Principles of Ethics*. Columbia, London: University of Missouri Press.

Rousseau, J.-J. (1994). *The Social Contract*, trans. C. Betts. Oxford: Oxford University Press.

—. (2003). *Emile, or, Treatise on Education*, trans. W. H. Payne. Armherst: Prometheus Books.

Schiller, F. (1792). *The Robbers*, trans. A. F. Tytler. London: G. G. H. & J. Robinsons.

—. (1940–2003). *Schillers Werke Nationalausgabe*, Julius Petersen, Lieselotte Blumenthal, B. von Wiese and S. Seidel (eds), 42 vols. Weimar: Hermann Böhluas Nachfolger.

—. (1988). 'From "On Naïve and Sentimental Poetry"', in D. Simpson (ed.), *The Origin of Modern Critical Thought: German Aesthetic and Literary Criticism from Lessing to Hegel*, trans. D. Simpson. Cambridge: Cambridge University Press, pp. 148–76.

Schulze, E. G. (1792). *Aenesidemus oder über die Fundamente der von dem Herrn Prof. Reinhold in Jena gelieferten Elementar-Philopsophie*. Helmstadt: Fleckeisen.

Scott, W. (1902). 'Essay on the Imitations of Ancient Ballads', in T. F. Henderson (ed.), *Minstrelsy of the Scottish Border: Consisting of Historical and Romantic Ballads*, Vol. 4. Edinburgh: Robert Cadell, pp. 1–78.

Southey, R. (1796). *Joan of Arc, an Epic Poem*. Bristol, London: Joseph Cottle, Cadell and Davies.

—. (1800). *Annual Anthology: Volume Ii*. Bristol: Biggs, Cottle, T. N. Longman and O. Rees.

Steffens, H. (1822). *Anthropologie*, Breslau: Max.

Sterne, L. (1983). *The Life and Opinions of Tristram Shandy*, I. C. Ross (ed.). Oxford: Oxford University Press.

Stones, G. (ed.) (1999). *Parodies of the Romantic Age*, Vol. 1. London: Pickering & Chatto.

Vattel, E. D. (1758). *Le Droit des Gens. Ou Principes de la Loi Naturelle, Appliqués à la Conduite & aux Affaires des Nations & des Souverains.* London [Neuchâtel].

Wilkes, J. and Jones, G. (eds) (1810–29). *Encyclopædia Londinensis; or, Universal Dictionary of Arts, Sciences, and Literature*, 24 vols. London: James Adlard, John White, Champante and Whitrow.

Willich, A. F. M. (1798). *Elements of Critical Philosophy.* London: T. N. Longman.

Wirgman, T. (1817). 'Moral Philosophy', in J. Wilkes (ed.), *Encyclopædia Londinensis; or, Universal Dictionary of Arts, Science, and Literature. Comprehending, under One General Alphabetical Arrangement, All the Words and Substance of Every Kind of Dictionary Extant in the English Language*, Vol. 15. London: The Proprietor, at the Encyclopaedia Office, Ave-Marie-Lane, St. Paul's, pp. 763–83.

Wood, R. (1775). *An Essay on the Original Genius and Writings of Homer: With a Comparative View of the Ancient and Present State of the Troade.* London: H. Hughs, T. Payne, P. Elmsly.

Wordsworth, W. (1935). *The Early Letters of William and Dorothy Wordsworth (1787–1805)*, E. de Selincourt (ed.), Vol. 1. Oxford: Clarendon Press.

—. (1969–93). *The Letters of William and Dorothy Wordsworth*, E. de Selincourt and A. G. Hill (eds), Vols 2–8. Oxford: Clarendon Press.

—. (1974). *The Prose Works of William Wordsworth*, W. J. B. Owen and J. W. Symser (eds), 3 vols. Oxford: Clarendon Press.

—. (1995). *The Prelude: The Four Texts (1798, 1799, 1805, 1850)*, J. Wordsworth (ed.). London: Penguin.

Wordsworth, W. and Coleridge, S. T. (1991). *Lyrical Ballads*, R. L. Brett and A. R. Jones (eds). London, New York: Routledge.

Secondary literature

Adams, N. (2010). 'Kant', in D. Fergusson (ed.), *The Blackwell Companion to Nineteenth-Century Theology.* Chichester: Blackwell, pp. 3–30.

Altmann, A. (1973). *Moses Mendelssohn: A Biographical Study.* Alabama: University of Alabama Press.

Ameriks, K. (2000 [first published 1982]). *Kant's Theory of Mind: An Analysis of the Paralogisms of Pure Reason.* Oxford: Clarendon Press.

—. (2005). 'Introduction', in K. Ameriks and J. Hebbeler (eds), *Reinhold Letters on the Kantian Philosophy.* Cambridge: Cambridge University Press, pp. ix–xxxvi.

—. (2006). *Kant and the Historical Turn: Philosophy as Critical Interpretation.* Oxford: Oxford University Press.

—. (2010). 'Reinhold, History and the Foundation of Philosophy', in G. di Giovanni (ed.), *Karl Leonhard Reinhold and the Enlightenment*, Vol. 9. Dordrecht, Heidelberg, New York, London: Springer, pp. 113–32.

Andrews, S. (2003). *Unitarian Radicalism: Political Rhethoric, 1770–1814.* Basingstoke: Palgrave Macmillan.

Ashton, R. (1980). *The German Idea: Four English Writers and the Reception of German Thought.* London, New York: Cambridge University Press.

—. (1996). *The Life of Samuel Taylor Coleridge.* Oxford: Blackwell.

Barrell, J. (2000). *Imagining the King's Death: Figurative Treason, Fantasies of Regicide 1793-96.* Oxford: Clarendon Press.

—. (2005). 'London and the London Corresponding Society', in K. Gilmartin and J. Chandler (eds), *Romantic Metropolism: The Urban Scene of British Culture.* Cambridge, New York: Cambridge University Press, pp. 85–112.

Bate, J. (1997). *The Genius of Shakespeare*. London: Picador.

Baulch, D. M. (2004). 'The "Perpetual Exercise of an Interminable Quest": The *Biographia Literaria* and the Kantian Revolution'. *Studies in Romanticism*, 43, 557–81.

Baum, G. and Malter, R. (1991). 'Kant in England: Ein Neuer Brief: Kant and Friedrich August Nitsch'. *Kant-Studien*, 82, 456–68.

Bax, E. B. (1883). 'Biography of Kant', in E. B. Bax (ed.), *Kant's Prolegomena and Metaphysical Foundations of Natural Science*. London: George Bell, pp. xi–lxxi.

Beck, L. W. (1957). 'Introduction', in L. W. Beck (ed.), *Immanuel Kant Perpetual Peace*. New York: Liberal Arts Press, pp. i–xiv.

—. (1971). 'Kant and the Right of Revolution'. *Journal of the History of Ideas*, 32, 411–22.

—. (1984 [first published 1960]). *A Commentary on Kant's Critique of Practical Reason*. Chicago, London: University of Chicago Press.

Beer, J. (1977). *Coleridge's Poetic Intelligence*. London: Macmillan.

—. (1993). 'Editor's Introduction', in J. Beer (ed.), *Aids to Reflection*. London: Routledge, pp. xli–cxlix.

Beers, H. (1899). *A History of English Romanticism in the Eighteenth Century*. London: Paul Kegan.

Beiser, F. C. (1987). *The Fate of Reason: German Philosophy from Kant to Fichte*. Cambridge, Massachusetts: Harvard University Press.

—. (1992). *Enlightenment, Revolution, & Romanticism*. Cambridge, Massachusetts; London: Harvard University Press.

—. (2002). *German Idealism: Struggle against Subjectivism, 1781–1801*. Cambridge, Massachusetts; London: Harvard University Press.

—. (2006). 'Moral Faith and the Highest Good', in Paul Guyer (ed.), *The Cambridge Companion to Kant and Modern Philosophy*. Cambridge, New York, Melbourne: Cambridge University Press, pp. 588–629.

Bennett, J. (1974). *Kant's Dialectic*. Cambridge: Cambridge University Press.

Berkeley, R. (2004). 'Silence and the Pantheistic Sublime in Coleridge's Early Poetry'. *Coleridge Bulletin*, 24, 59–67.

—. (2007). *Coleridge and the Crisis of Reason*. Basinstoke: Palgrave Macmillan.

Beyer, W. (1955). 'Coleridge's Early Knowledge of German'. *Modern Philology*, 52, 192–200.

Bleiker, R. (2000). *Popular Dissent, Human Agency and Global Politics*. Cambridge: Cambridge University Press.

Bloom, H. (1971). *The Visionary Company: A Reading of English Romantic Poetry*. New York: Cornell University Press.

Bobbio, N. (1993). *Hobbes and the Natural Law Tradition*. Chicago: Chicago University Press.

Bode, C. (1992). *"And What Were Thou ...?": Essay über Shelley und das Erhabene*. Essen: Die Blaue Eule.

—. (2009). 'Coleridge and Philosophy', in F. Burwick (ed.), *The Oxford Handbook of Samuel Taylor Coleridge*. Oxford: Oxford University Press, pp. 588–619.

Bödecker, H. E., Büttgen, P. and Espagne, M. (eds). (2010). *Göttingen Vers 1800: L'Europe des sciences de l'homme*. Paris: Edition de Cerf.

Boening, J. (1982). 'Pioneers and Precedents: The "Importation of German" and the Emergence of the Periodical Criticism in England'. *Internationales Archiv für Sozialgeschichte der deutschen Literatur*, 7, 65–87.

Bohmann, J. and Lutz-Bachmann, M. (1997). 'Introduction', in J. Bohmann and L.-B. Matthias (eds), *Perpetual Peace: Essays on Kant's Cosmopolitan Ideal*. Cambridge, Massachusetts: The MIT Press, pp. 1–22.

Bondeli, M. (1995). *Das Anfangsproblem bei Karl Leonhard Reinhold: Eine Systematische und Entwicklungsgeschichtliche Untersuchung zur Philosophie Reinholds in der Zeit von 1789 bis 1803*. Frankfurt a. M.: Klostermann.

—. (2010). 'The Conception of Enlightenment in Reinhold's "Letters on the Kantian Philosophy"', in G. di Giovanni (ed.), *Karl Leonhard Reinhold*. Dordrecht, Heidelberg, New York, London: Springer, pp. 43–64.

Boswell, T. (1991). 'A Bibliography of English Translations of Kant'. *Kant-Studien*, 82, 228–47.

Boucher, D. (2001). 'British Idealism and the Human Rights Culture'. *History of European Ideas*, 27, 61–78.

Boucher, D. and Vincent, A. (2012). *British Idealism: A Guide for the Perplexed*. London, New York: Continuum.

Boulger, J. D. (1961). *Coleridge as Religious Thinker*. New Haven: Yale University Press.

Brandt, R. (1989). 'Feder Und Kant'. *Kant-Studien*, 80, 249–64.

Brandt, R. and Stark, W. (1997). 'Einleitung', in Akademie der Wissenschaften zu Göttingen (ed.), *Kant's Vorlesungen*, Vol. 2.1. Berlin: Walter de Gruyter & Co., pp. vii–cli.

Breazeale, D. (2010). 'Reason's Changing Needs: From Kant to Reinhold', in G. di Goivanni (ed.), *Karl Leonhard Reinhold and the Enlightenment*. Dordrecht, Heidelberg, New York, London: Springer, pp. 89–112.

Breitkreuz, H. (1973). 'Coleridge at Göttingen'. *American Notes and Queries*, 12, 56–59.

Brett, R. L. and Jones, A. R. (1991). 'Introduction', in R. L. Brett and A. R. Jones (eds), *Wordsworth and Coleridge: Lyrical Ballads*. London: Methuen, pp. xix–liv.

Brice, B. (2007). *Coleridge and Scepticism*. Oxford: Oxford University Press.

Bromwich, D. (2000). *Disowned by Memory: Wordsworth's Poetry of the 1790s*. London, Chicago: Chicago University Press.

Brown, C. (2011). *The Art of Comparison: How Novels and Critics Compare*. Leeds: Legenda.

Bruno, P. W. (2010). *Kant's Concept of Genius: Its Origin and Function in the Third Critique*. London, New York: Continuum.

Budick, S. (2010). *Kant and Milton*. Cambridge, Massachusetts; London: Harvard University Press.

Burnham, D. (2000). *An Introduction to Kant's Critique of Judgement*. Edinburgh: Edinburgh University Press.

Burwick, F. (1989). 'Introduction', in F. Burwick (ed.), *Coleridge's Biographia Literaria: Text and Meaning*. Columbus: Ohio State University Press, pp. vii–xix.

—. (1996). *Poetic Madness and the Romantic Imagination*. University Park, Pennsylvania: Pennsylvania State University Press.

—. (2008). 'De Quincey and Coleridge', in J. Vigus and J. Wright (eds), *Coleridge's Afterlives*. Houndsmills, Basingstoke: Palgrave Macmillan, pp. 36–53.

Butler, J. (2003). 'Poetry 1798–1807: Lyrical Ballads and Poems, in Two Volumes', in S. Gill (ed.), *The Cambridge Companion to Wordsworth*. Cambridge: Cambridge University Press, pp. 38–54.

Butler, M. (1981). *Romantics, Rebels and Reactionaries: English Literature and Its Background*. Oxford: Oxford University Press.

Caird, E. (1892). *Essays on Literature and Philosophy*. Glasgow: James Maclehose and Sons.

—. (1909). *The Critical Philosophy of Immanuel Kant*. Glasgow: James Maclehose and Sons.

Carlson, J. (1994). *In the Theatre of Romanticism: Coleridge, Nationalism and Women*. Cambridge: Cambridge University Press.

Chandler, D. (1995). 'Coleridge's "Address to a Young Jack-Ass": A Note on the Poetic and Political Context'. *Notes and Queries*, 42, 179–80.

—. (1997a). 'The Foundation of "Philosophical Criticism": William Taylor's Connection with the Monthly Review, 1792–93'. *Studies in Bibliography,* 50, 359–71.

—. (1997b). *Norwich Literature, 1788–1797: A Critical Survey,* Doctoral Dissertation, University of Oxford.

Chandler, J. (1984). *Wordsworth's Second Nature: A Study of the Poetry and Politics.* Chicago: Chicago University Press.

Chard, L. F. (2002). 'Joseph Johnson in the 1790s'. *The Wordsworth Circle,* 33, 95–100.

Clark, C. (2006). *The Iron Kingdom: The Rise and Downfall of Prussia, 1600–1947.* London: Penguin.

Class, M. (2007). 'Dr J. A. O'Keeffe: Kantian Philosophy – Life, Work and Legacy'. *Eighteenth-Century Ireland,* 22, 206–14.

—. (2009a). 'Coleridge and the Radical Roots of Critical Philosophy'. *The Wordsworth Circle,* 40, 51–5.

—. (2009b). 'Coleridge, the Early Mediators of Kant and the Sensuous Departure from the Categorical Imperative', in R. Gravil (ed.), *Grasmere 2008: Selected Papers from the Wordsworth Summer Conference.* Penrith: Humanities-Ebooks, pp. 22–37.

Coburn, K. (1962). 'Foreword to Third Edition', in I. A. Richards (ed.), *Coleridge on Imagination.* London: Routledge and Kegan Paul, pp. xvii–xxiv.

Colclasure, D. (2011). 'Just War and Perpetual Peace: Kant on the Legitimate Use of Political Violence', in E. Krimmer and P. A. Simpson (eds), *Enlightened War: German Theories and Cultures of Warfare from Frederick the Great to Clausewitz.* Columbia, South Carolina: Camden House, pp. 241–57.

Coleman, D. (1988). *Coleridge and the Friend (1809–10).* Oxford: Clarendon Press.

Coleridge, S. (1847). 'Introduction', in S. Coleridge and H. N. Coleridge (eds), *Biographia Literaria, or Biographical Sketches of My Literary Life and Opinions,* Vol. 1. London William Pickering, pp. v–clxxxvii.

Colmer, J. (1959). *Coleridge, Critic of Society.* Oxford: Oxford University Press.

Craig, C. (2007). *Associationism and the Literary Imagination: From the Phantasmal Chaos.* Edinburgh: Edinburgh University Press.

Crisman, W. (1991). '"Thus Far Had the Work Been Transcribed": Coleridge's Use of Kant's Pre-Critical Writing and the Rhetoric of "on the Imagination"'. *Modern Language Quarterly,* 52, 404–22.

Cronin, R. (2000). *The Politics of Romantic Poetry: In the Search of the Pure Commonwealth.* Basingstoke: Macmillan.

Crosby, M. (2009). '"A Fabricated Perjury": The [Mis]Trial of William Blake'. *Huntington Library Quarterly: Studies in English and American History and Literature,* 72, 29–47.

Curran, J. V. (2005). 'Schiller's Essay "Über Anmut Und Würde" as Rhetorical Philosophy', in J. V. Curran and C. Fricker (eds), *Schiller's "on Grace and Dignity" in Its Cultural Context.* Woodbridge: Camden House, pp. 21–54.

Curran, S. (1986). *Poetic Form and British Romanticism.* Oxford: Oxford University Press.

De Paolo, C. (1992). *Coleridge: Historian of Ideas,* Victoria, B. C., English Literary Studies.

Den Otter, S. (1996). *British Idealism and Social Explanation.* Oxford: Clarendon Press.

Desmond, W. (2004). 'Introduction', in W. Desmond, E.-O. Onnasch and P. Cruysberghs (eds), *Philosophy and Religion in German Idealism.* Dordrecht, London: Kluwer Academic.

Dilthey, W. (1976). 'Entwürfe zur Kritik der Historischen Vernunft', in H.-G. Gadamer and G. Boehm (eds), *Seminar: Philosophische Hermeneutik.* Frankfurt a. M.: Suhrkamp, pp. 189–220.

Di Giovanni, G. (1998). 'Hume, Jacobi and Common Sense: An Episode in the Reception of Hume in Germany at the Time of Kant'. *Kant-Studien,* 89, 44–57.

—. (2005). *Freedom and Religion in Kant and His Immediate Successors: Vocation of Humankind 1774-1800.* Cambridge: Cambridge University Press.

—. (2010). 'Karl Leohard Reinhold and the Enlightenment: Editor's Presentation', in G. di Giovanni (ed.), *Karl Leonhard Reinhold and the Enlightenment.* Dordrecht, Heidelberg, London, New York: Springer.

Duddy, T. (2002). *A History of Irish Thought.* London: Routledge.

—. (2004). 'J. A. O' Keeffe' (Fl 1795), in T. Duddy (ed.) *Dictionary of Irish Philosophers.* Padstow: Thoemmes Continuum.

Duff, D. (2009). *Romanticism and the Uses of Genre.* Oxford: Oxford University Press.

Dwyer, P. G. (1994). 'The Politics of Prussian Neutrality 1795-1806'. *German History,* 12, 351-73.

Ebeling, H. (1996). 'Kant's "Volk von Teufeln", der Mechanismus der Nature und die Zukunft des Unfriedens: Über den Mythos der Kommunikativen Vernunft', in K.-M. Kodalle (ed.), *der Vernunft-Frieden: Kants Entwurf Im Widerstreit.* Würzburg: Könighausen & Neumann, pp. 87–94.

Ellison, D. (2001). *Ethics and Aesthetics in European Modernist Literature: From the Sublime to the Uncanny.* Cambridge, New York: Cambridge University Press.

Engell, J. (1981). *The Creative Imagination: Enlightenment to Romanticism.* Cambridge, Massachusetts: Harvard University Press.

—. (2002). 'Biographia Literaria', in L. Newlyn (ed.), *The Cambridge Companion to Coleridge.* Cambridge: Cambridge University Press, pp. 59–74.

Engell, J. and Bate, W. J. (1983). 'Introduction', in J. Engell and W. J. Bate (eds), *Literaria: Or Biographical Sketches of My Literary Life and Opinions: Coleridge Collected Works,* Vol. 1. Princeton: Princeton University Press, pp. xli–cxxxvi.

Erdman, D. V. (1978). 'Editor's Introduction', in D. V. Erdman (ed.), *Essays on His Times,* Vol. 1. London: Routledge and Paul Kegan, pp. lix–clxxix.

Esterhammer, A. (2000). *The Romantic Performative: Language and Action in British and German Romanticism.* Stanford: Stanford University Press.

—. (2002a). 'Continental Literature, Translation, and the Johnson Circle'. *The Wordsworth Circle,* 33, 101–4.

—. (2002b). 'The Romantic Ode: History, Language, Performance', in A. Esterhammer (ed.), *Romantic Poetry.* Amsterdam: Benjamins, pp. 143–62.

Evans, B. I. (1935). 'Coleridge's Copy of "Fears in Solitude"'. *Times Literary Supplement,* 18 April, 255.

Fairbanks, A. H. (1975). 'Coleridge's Opinion of "France: An Ode"'. *Review of English Studies: A Quarterly Journal of English Literature and the English Language,* 26, 181–2.

Fairer, D. (2009). *Organising Poetry: The Coleridge Circle, 1790-1798.* Oxford: Oxford University Press.

Flores, C. (2008). *Plastic Intellectual Breeze: The Contribution of Ralph Cudworth to S. T. Coleridge's Early Poetics of the Symbol.* Bern: Peter Lang.

Foakes, R. A. (1987). 'Introduction', in R. A. Foakes (ed.), *Lectures 1808-1819 on Literature: Coleridge Collected Works,* Vol. 1. London. Princeton: Princeton University Press.

Fogle, R. H. (1962). *The Idea of Coleridge's Criticism.* Berkeley, Los Angeles: University of California Press.

Forster, A. (2003). 'Review Journals and the Reading Public', in I. Rivers (ed.), *Books and Their Readers in Eighteenth-Century England: New Essays.* London, New York: Continuum, pp. 171–90.

Forster, M. N. (2007). 'Hermeneutics', in B. Leiter and M. Rosen (eds), *The Oxford Handbook of Continental Philosophy.* Oxford: Oxford University Press, pp. 30–74.

Forster, R. and Forster, E. (eds). (1969). *European Society in the Eighteenth Century.* New York, Evanston, London: Harper and Row.

Foxon, D. F. (1954). 'The Printing of Lyrical Ballads'. *The Library: The Transactions of the Bibliographical Society,* 9, 221–41.

Frank, M. (1987). 'Intellektuelle Anschauung: Drei Stellungnahmen zu einem Deutungsversuch von Selbstbewusstsein: Kant, Fichte, Hölderlin/Novalis', in E. Behler and J. Hörisch (eds), *Die Aktualität der Frühromantik.* Paderborn, München, Wien, Zürich: Ferdinand Schöningh, pp. 96–126.

—. (1989). *Einführung in die Frühromantische Ästhetik: Vorlesungen.* Frankfurt a. M.: Suhrkamp.

—. (1997). *Unendliche Annäherung: Die Anfänge der Philosophischen Frühromantik.* Frankfurt a. M.: Suhrkamp.

—. (2004). *The Philosophical Foundations of Early German Romanticism.* Albany, New York: State University of New York Press.

Fruman, N. (1971). *Coleridge the Damaged Archangel.* London: George Allen & Unwin.

—. (1985). 'Review Essay: Aids to Reflection on the New Biographia'. *Studies in Romanticism,* 24, 141–73.

—. (1989). 'Editing and Annotating the *Biographia Literaria*', in F. Burwick (ed.), *Coleridge's Biographia Literaria: Text and Meaning.* Columbus, Ohio: Ohia State University Press, pp. 1–19.

—. (1992). 'Coleridge and the Retreat from Democracy'. *The Review,* 14, 115–33.

Gailus, A. (2006). *Signs of Passion: Revolution and Language in Goethe, Kant, and Kleist,* Baltimore: John Hopkin's University Press.

Garber, F. (1993). 'Genre', in A. Preminger and T. V. F. Brogan (eds), *The New Princeton Encyclopedia of Poetry and Poetics.* Princeton: Princeton University Press, pp. 456–9.

Gibbs, W. (1930). 'An Unpublished Letter from John Thelwall to S. T. Coleridge'. *Modern Language Review,* 25, 85–90.

Gill, S. (1989). *William Wordsworth: A Life.* Oxford: Oxford University Press.

—. (1991). *William Wordsworth: The Prelude.* Cambridge, New York: Cambridge University Press.

—. (2003). 'The Philosophic Poet', in S. Gill (ed.), *The Cambridge Companion to Wordsworth.* Cambridge: Cambridge University Press, pp. 142–60.

Gilmartin, K. (1996). *Print Politics: The Press and Radical Opposition in Early Nineteenth Century England.* Cambridge: Cambridge University Press.

Giordanetti, P. (1995). 'Das Verhältnis von Genie, Künstler, und Wissenschaftler in der Kantischen Philosophie'. *Kant-Studien,* 86, 406–30.

Goodman, D. (1994). *The Republic of Letters: A Cultural History of the French Enlightenment.* London, Ithaca: Cornell University Press.

Götze, M. (2001). *Ironie und Absolute Darstellung: Philosophie und Poetik in der Frühromantik.* Paderborn, München, Wien, Zürich: Ferdinand Schöningh.

Gould, T. (1982). 'The Audience of Originality: Kant and Wordsworth', in T. Cohen and P. Guyer (eds), *Essays in Kant's Aesthetics.* Chicago, London: University of Chicago Press, pp. 179–94.

Grier, M. (2001). *Kant's Doctrine of Transcendental Illusion.* Cambridge: Cambridge University Press.

Groos, K. (1901). 'Hat Kant Hume's Treatise Gelesen?'. *Kant-Studien,* 5, 177–81.

Guthke, K. S. (2002). 'Destination Goethe: Travelling Englishmen in Weimar', in N. Boyle (ed.), *Goethe and the English-Speaking World.* Cambridge: Camden House, pp. 111–32.

Gutting, G. (2005). *Foucault: A Very Short Introduction.* Oxford: Oxford University Press.

Guyer, P. (2005). *Kant's System of Nature and Freedom: Selected Essays.* Oxford: Clarendon Press.

—. (2006). *Kant.* London: Routledge.

Haakensson, K. (1991). 'From Natural Law to the Rights of Man: A European Perspective on American Debates', in M. J. Lacey and K. Haakensson (eds), *A Culture of Rights: The Bill of Rights in Philosophy, Politics and Law.* Cambridge: Cambridge University Press, pp. 19–61.

Habermas, J. (1997). 'Kant's Idea of Perpetual Peace, with the Benefit of Two Hundred Years's Hindsight', in J. Bohmann and L.-B. Matthias (eds), *Perpetual Peace: Essays on Kant's Cosmopolitan Ideal.* Cambridge, Massachussets; London: The MIT Press, pp. 113–54.

Hall, R. (1970). 'Some Antedatings in Kantian Philosophy'. *Notes and Queries,* 17, 315–16.

Halmi, N. (1995). 'How Christian Is the Coleridgean Symbol?'. *The Wordsworth Circle,* 26, 26–31.

—. (2007a). *The Genealogy of the Romantic Symbol.* Oxford: Oxford University Press.

—. (2007b). 'Nicholas Halmi Reads: Coleridge's Assertion of Religion: Essays on the "Opus Maximum"'. *Coleridge Bulletin,* 30, 48–50.

Hamilton, P. (1983). *Coleridge's Poetics.* Oxford: Basil Blackwell.

—. (2003). 'Wordsworth and Romanticism', in S. Gill (ed.), *The Cambridge Companion to Wordsworth.* Cambridge: Cambridge University Press, pp. 213–29.

—. (2007). *Coleridge and German Philosophy: The Poet in the Land of Logic.* London, New York: Continuum.

Hampton, J. (1986). *Hobbes and the Social Contract Theory.* Cambridge: Cambridge University Press.

Harding, A. J. (1974). *Coleridge and the Idea of Love: Aspects of Relationship in Coleridge's Thought and Writing.* London: Cambridge University Press.

—. (2000). 'Coleridge, Natural History, and the "Analogy of Being"'. *History of European Ideas,* 26, 143–58.

—. (2007). 'Introduction', in A. J. Harding (ed.), *Coleridge's Responses: Coleridge on the Bible,* Vol. 2. London, New York: Continuum, pp. 1–38.

—. (2010). 'Radical Bible: Coleridge's 1790s West Country Politics', in N. Roe (ed.), *English Romantic Writers and the West Country.* Houndsmill, Basingstoke: Palgrave Macmillan, pp. 129–54.

Harris, J. A. (2005). *Of Liberty and Necessity: The Free Will Debate in Eighteenth-Century British Philosophy.* Oxford: Clarendon Press.

Harter, J. (2011). *Coleridge's Philosophy of Faith: Symbol, Allegory, and Hermeneutics.* Tübingen: Mohr Siebeck.

Hay, D. (2010). *Young Romantics: The Shelleys, Byron and Other Tangled Lives.* London: Bloomsbury.

Hedley, D. (2000). *Coleridge, Philosophy and Religion.* Cambridge: Cambridge University Press.

Henrich, D. (1960). *der Ontologische Gottesbeweis: Sein Problem und seine Geschichte in der Neuzeit.* Tübingen: Mohr.

—. (1991). *Konstellationen: Probleme und Debatten am Ursprung der Idealistischen Philosophie 1789–1795.* Stuttgart: Klett-Cotta.

—. (2004). *Grundlegung aus dem Ich: Untersuchungen zur Vorgeschichte des Idealismus.* Darmstadt: Wissenschaftlicher Verlag.

Hinske, N. (1995). 'Ausblick: der Jenaer Frühkantianismus als Forschungsausgabe', in N. Hinske, L. Erhard and H. Schröpfer (eds), *der Aufbruch in den Kantianismus: der Frühkantianismus an der Universität Jena von 1785-1800 und seine Vorgeschichte.* Stuttgart, Bad-Cannstatt: Frommann-Holzboog, pp. 231-43.

Hirschmann, F. (2009). *Formen Adeliger Existenz im 18. Jahrhundert: Adel Zwischen Kritik und Reformen.* München: AVM.

Höffe, O. (1994 [first published 1992]). *Immanuel Kant.* Albany, New York: State University of New York Press.

—. (2004 [first published 1995]). 'Einleitung: der Friede – Ein Vernachlässigtes Ideal', in O. Höffe (ed.), *Immanuel Kant: Zum Ewigen Frieden,* 2nd edn. Berlin: Akademie Verlag, pp. 5-31.

—. (2010 [first published 2007]). *Can Virtue Make Us Happy: The Art of Living and Morality,* trans. D. R. McGaughey. Evanston: Northwestern University Press.

Holmes, R. (1989). *Coleridge: Early Visions.* London: Hodder & Stoughton.

—. (1998). *Coleridge Darker Reflections, 1804-1834,* New York: Pantheon Books.

Hort, F. J. A. (1856). 'Coleridge', in *Cambridge Essays Contributed by the Members of the University.* London: John W. Parker and Son, pp. 292-351.

Howard, C. (1924). *Coleridge's Idealism: A Study of Its Relationship to Kant and to Neo-Platonism.* Boston: Gorham Press.

Hunnekuhl, P. (2007). *Imagination and Growth: Coleridge and Wordsworth in Germany,* MSc dissertation, University of Edinburgh.

Isaacs, J. (1935). 'Coleridge's Criticial Terminology'. *Essays and Studies by Members of the English Association,* 21, 101.

Jackson, J. R. De J. (ed.) (1970). *Samuel Taylor Coleridge: The Critical Heritage Volume I.* The Critical Heritage Series. London: Routledge & Kegan Paul.

—. (1981). 'Editor's Introduction', in J. R. de J. Jackson (ed.), *Samuel Taylor Coleridge: Logic.* London, Princeton: Routledge & Kegan Paul, pp. xxxiii-lxvii.

—. (2000). 'Introduction', in J. R. de J. Jackson (ed.), *Lectures 1818-1819 on the History of Philosophy: The Collected Words of Samuel Taylor Coleridge,* Vol. 1. Princeton: Princeton University Press, pp. xxxv-cxlv.

Jacob, M. C. (1981). *Radical Enlightenment: Pantheists, Freemasons and Republicans.* London: George Allan & Unwin.

James, F. (2008). *Charles Lamb, Coleridge and Wordsworth: Reading Friendship in the 1790s.* Basingstoke: Palgrave Macmillian.

James, F. and Inkster, I. (eds). (2012). *Religious Dissent and the Aikin-Barbauld Circle, 1740-1860.* Cambridge: Cambridge University Press.

Jarvis, S. (2007). *Wordsworth's Philosophic Song.* Cambridge: Cambridge University Press.

Jasper, D. (1983). 'The Two Worlds of Coleridge's "the Ancient Mariner"', in J. R. Watson (ed.), *An Infinite Complexity: Essays in Romanticism.* Edinburgh: Edinburgh University Press, pp. 125-44.

Jay, M. (2009). *The Atmosphere of Heaven: The Unnatural Experiments of Dr Beddoes and His Sons of Genius.* Yale: Yale University Press.

Johnston, K. R. (1983). 'The Politics of "Tintern Abbey"'. *The Wordsworth Circle,* 14, 6-14.

Keanie, A. (2009). 'Coleridge and Plagiarism', in F. Burwick (ed.), *The Oxford Handbook of Samuel Taylor Coleridge.* Oxford: Oxford University Press, pp. 435-54.

Kersting, W. (2004). *Kant über Recht.* Paderborn: Mentis.

Kim, J. N. (2007). 'Kant's Secret Article: Irony, Performativity, and History in Zum Ewigen Friede'. *Germanic Review,* 82, 203-26.

Kitson, P. (1993). '"Our Prophetic Harrington": Coleridge, Pantisocracy, and Puritan Utopians'. *The Wordsworth Circle,* 24, 97-102.

—. (2002). 'Political Thinker', in L. Newlyn (ed.), *The Cambridge Companion to Coleridge*. Cambridge: Cambridge University Press, pp. 156–69.

Klancher, J. P. (1987). *The Making of the English Reading Audiences, 1790–1832*. London: Wisconsin University Press.

Klemme, H. F. (1992). 'Einleitung', in H. F. Klemme (ed.), *Immanuel Kant: Über den Gemeinspruch: Das Mag ich in der Theorie Richtig sein, Taugt aber nicht für die Praxis; Zum Ewigen Frieden: Ein Philosophischer Entwurf*. Hamburg: Felix Meiner, pp. vii–liii.

Klemme, H. F. and Kühn, M. (eds). (2010). *The Dictionary of Eighteenth-Century German Philosophers*, 3 vols. London, New York: Continuum.

Kooy, M. J. (2000). 'Coleridge's Francophobia'. *Modern Language Review*, 95, 924–41.

—. (2002). *Coleridge, Schiller and Aesthetic Education*. Basingstoke: Palgrave Macmillan.

Kühn, M. (1983). 'Kant's Conception of "Hume's Problem"'. *Journal of the History of Philosophy*, 21, 175–93.

—. (1985). 'Kant's Transcendental Deduction of God's Existence as a Postulate of Pure Reason'. *Kant-Studien*, 76, 152–69.

—. (1987). *Scottish Common Sense in Germany, 1768–1800*. Kingston, Montreal: McGill's University Press.

—. (2001). *Kant: A Biography*. Cambridge: Cambridge University Press.

—. (2005). 'The Reception of Hume in Germany', in P. Jones (ed.), *The Reception of David Hume in Europe*. London: Thoemmes Continuum, pp. 98–138.

—. (2006). 'Kant's Critical Philosophy and Its Reception – the First Five Years (1781–6)', in P. Guyer (ed.), *The Cambridge Companion to Kant and Modern Philosophy*. Cambridge: Cambridge University Press, pp. 630–64.

—. (2007). *Kant: Eine Biographie*, trans. Martin Pfeiffer. München: Beck.

Lauth, R. (ed.) (1974). *Philosophie aus einem Prinzip: Sieben Beiträge nebst einem Briefekatalog aus Anlaß seines 150. Todestages*. Bonn: Bouvier.

Lawler, J. (2005). *The Battle of Metaphysics in Modern Western Philosophy before Kant*. Woodbridge: Rochester University Press.

Lazzari, A. (2004). *Das Eine, Was der Menschheit Noth ist: Einheit und Freiheit in der Philosophie Karl Leonhard Reinholds (1789–1792)*. Stuttgart, Bad-Cannstatt: Frommann-Holzboog.

Leask, N. (1988). *The Politics of Imagination in Coleridge's Critical Thought*. Basingstoke: Macmillan.

Leiter, B. and Rosen, M. (eds). (2007). *The Oxford Handbook of Continental Philosophy*. Oxford: Oxford University Press.

Lenoir, T. (1980). 'Kant, Blumenbach, and Vital Materialism in German Biology'. *Isis*, 71.1, 77–108.

Levere, T. H. (1981). *Poetry Realized in Nature:Samuel Taylor Coleridge and Early Nineteenth-Century Science*. Cambridge: Cambridge University Press.

Levinson, M. (1986). 'Insight and Oversight: Reading "Tintern Abbey"', in M. Levinson (ed.), *Wordsworth's Great Period Poems: Four Essays*. Cambridge: Cambridge University Press.

Loades, A. (1978). 'Coleridge as Theologian: Some Comments on His Reading of Kant'. *Journal of Theological Studies* 29, 410–26.

Lockridge, L. S. (1977). *Coleridge the Moralist*. Ithaca, London: Cornell University Press.

Lovejoy, A. O. (1924). 'On the Discrimination of Romanticisms'. *Modern Language Association*, 39, 229–53.

—. (1940). 'Coleridge and Kant's Two World'. *Essays in the History of Ideas*, 7, 341–62.

Lowes, J. L. (1955 [first published 1927]). *The Road to Xanadu: A Study in the Ways of the Imagination*. Bungay: Picador.

MacKinnon, D. (1974). 'Coleridge and Kant', in J. Beer (ed.), *Coleridge's Variety: Bicentenary Studies*. Basingstoke: Macmillan, pp. 183–203.

—. (1990). 'Aspects of Kant's Influence on British Theology', in G. MacDonald Roos and T. McWalter (eds.), *Kant and His Influence*. Bristol: Thoemmes, pp. 348–66.

Maertz, G. (1998). 'Reviewing Kant's Early Reception in Britain: The Leading Role of Henry Crabb Robinson', in G. Maertz (ed.), *Cultural Interactions in the Romantic Age*. Albany, New York: State University of New York Press, pp. 209–26.

Magnuson, P. (1998). *Reading Public Romanticism*. Princeton: Princeton University Press.

Malter, R. (1984). 'Nachwort', in R. Malter (ed.), *Immanuel Kant. Zum Ewigen Frieden*. Stuttgart: Reclam, pp. 69–85.

—. (1995). 'Kant-Bibliographie 1993'. *Kant-Studien*, 86, 487–511.

Manning, S. (1997). 'Literature and Philosophy', in H. B. Nisbet (ed.), *The Cambridge History of Literary Criticism: Eighteenth Century*, Vol. 4. Cambridge: Cambridge University Press, pp. 587–613.

Mariña, J. (2000). 'Making Sense of Kant's Highest Good'. *Kant-Studien*, 91, 329–55.

Masson, S. (2004). *Romanticism, Hermeneutics and the Crisis of the Human Sciences*. Aldershot, Burlington: Ashgate.

McFarland, T. (1974). 'Coleridge's Plagiarism Once More: A Review Essay'. *Yale Review*, 63, 254–86.

—. (1989). 'Coleridge and the Charge of Political Apostasy', in F. B. (ed.), *Coleridge's Biographia Literaria: Text and Meaning*. Columbus, Ohio: Ohio State University Press, pp. 191–232.

—. (1993). 'Aspects of Coleridge's Distinction between Reason and Understanding', in T. Fulford and M. D. Paley (eds), *Coleridge's Visionary Language*. Woodbridge: D. S. Brewer, pp. 165–80.

—. (1995). *Romanticism and the Heritage of Rousseau*. Oxford: Clarendon Press.

McGann, J. (1983). *The Romantic Ideology: A Critical Investigation*. Chicago: Chicago University Press.

McKinnon, C. (2005). 'Cosmopolitan Hope', in G. Brock and H. Brighouse (eds), *The Political Philosophy of Cosmopolitanism*. Cambridge: Cambridge University Press, pp. 234–49.

McLoughlin, K. (2011). *Authoring War: The Literary Representation of War from the "Iliad" to Iraq*. Cambridge: Cambridge University Press.

Mee, J. (1992). *Dangerous Enthusiasm: William Blake and the Culture of Radicalism in the 1790s*. Oxford: Clarendon Press.

—. (2003). *Romanticism, Enthusiasm, and Regulation: Poetics and the Policing of Culture in the Romantic Period*. Oxford: Oxford University Press.

Miall, D. (2000). 'Locating Wordsworth: "Tintern Abbey" and the Community with Nature'. *Romanticism on Net*, 20, (no pagination).

Micheli, G. (1990). 'The Early Reception of Kant's Thought in England 1785–1805', in G. M. Ross and T. Mcwalter (eds), *Kant and His Influence*. Bristol: Thoemmes, pp. 202–314.

—. (1993). 'New Introduction', in G. Micheli (ed.), *Immanuel Kant: Essays and Treatises*, Vol. 1. Bristol: Thoemmes, pp. v–lii.

—. (2010). 'Nitsch, Friedrich August', in H. F. Klemme and M. Kühn (eds), *The Dictionary of Eighteenth-Century German Philosophers*, Vol. 2. London: Continuum, pp. 858–9.

Miller, R. D. (1970). *Schiller and the Ideal of Freedom: A Study of Schiller's Philosophical Works*. Oxford: Clarendon Press.

Milnes, T. (1999). 'Eclipsing Art: Method and Metaphysics in Coleridge's *Biographia Literaria*'. *Journal of the History of Ideas*, 60, 125–47.

—. (2003). *Knowledge and Indifference in English Romantic Prose*. Cambridge: Cambridge University Press.

Modiano, R. (1985). *Coleridge and the Concept of Nature*. London, Basingstoke: Macmillan.

—. (2009). 'Coleridge as Literary Critic: Biographia Literaria and Essays', in F. Burwick (ed.), *The Oxford Handbook of Samuel Taylor Coleridge*. Oxford: Oxford University Press, pp. 204–34.

Monroe, R. R. (1992). *Creative Brainstroms: The Relationship between Madness and Genius*. New York: Irvington.

Montluzin, E. L. (1988). *The Anti-Jacobins 1798–1800*. Basingstoke: Macmillan.

Morgan, B. Q. and Hohlfeld, A. R. (1949). *German Literature in British Magazines, 1750–1860*. Madison: University of Wisconsin Press.

Morrison, R. (1995). ' "Reviewers and Frenchman" in Coleridge's *Biographia Literaria*'. *Notes and Queries,* 42, 180–1.

Morrow, J. (1990). *Coleridge's Political Thought: Property, Morality and Limits of Traditional Discourse*. Basingstoke: Macmillan.

Mortensen, P. (2005). *British Romanticism and Continental Influences: Writing in an Age of Europhobia*. Houndsmill: Palgrave Macmillan.

Muchnik, P. (2009). *Kant's Theory of Evil: An Essay on the Dangers of Self-Love and the Apriroicity of History*. Lanham: Rowman & Littlefield Publishers.

Muirhead, J. H. (1930). *Coleridge as Philosopher*. London: George Allen & Unwin LTD.

Murphy, J. (1966). 'The Highest Good as Content for Kant's Ethical Formalism'. *Kant-Studien,* 56, 102–10.

Myers, V., O'Shaughnessy, D. and Philp, M. (eds). (2010). *The Diary of William Godwin*. Oxford: Oxford Digital Library http://godwindiary.bodleian.ox.ac.uk.

Nangle, B. C. (1955). *The Monthly Review Second Series 1790–1815: Indexes of Contributors and Articles*. Oxford: Clarendon Press.

Nenon, T. (ed.) (2011). *The History of Continental Philosophy - Kant, Kantism, and Idealism: The Origins of Continental Philosophy*, 8 vols. Vol. 1. Durham: Acumen.

Norton, R. E. (1995). *The Beautiful Soul: Aesthetic Morality in the Eighteenth Century*. Ithaca, London: Cornell University Press.

Nussbaum, M. (1997). 'Kant and Cosmopolitanism', in J. Bohmann and M. Lutz-Bachmann (eds), *Perpetual Peace: Essays on Kant's Cosmopolitan Ideal*. Cambridge, Massachusetts: The MIT Press, pp. 25–58.

O'Neill, M. (1997). Romanticism and the Self-Conscious Poem. Oxford: Clarendon Press.

—. (2009). 'Coleridge's Genres', in F. Burwick (ed.), *The Oxford Handbook of Samuel Taylor Coleridge*. Oxford: Oxford University Press, pp. 375–91.

Orsini, G. N. (1969). *Coleridge and German Idealism: A Study in the History of Philosophy*. London, Amsterdam, Illinois: Southern Illinois University Press.

Oz-Salzberger, F. (1995). *Translating the Enlightenment: Scottish Civic Discourse in Eighteenth-Century Germany*. Oxford: Clarendon Press.

Paley, M. D. (1999). *Apocalypse and Millennium in English Romantic Poetry*. Oxford: Clarendon Press.

Palmquist, S. (1996). 'P. Guyer (ed.): The Cambridge Companion to Kant (Book Review)'. *Kant-Studien,* 87, 1996, 369–74.

Park, R. (1968). 'Coleridge and Kant: Poetic Imagination and Practical Reason'. *British Journal of Aesthetics,* 8, 335–46.

Paton, H. J. (1956 [first edition 1948]). *The Moral Law or Kant's Groundwork of the Metaphysics of Morals*. London, Melbourne, Sydney: Hutchinson.

Patton, L. and Mann, P. (1971). 'Editor's Introduction', in L. Patton and P. Mann (eds), *Lectures 1795: On Politics and Religion.* Princeton: Princeton University Press, pp. xxiii–lxxx.

Perkins, M. A. (1994). *Coleridge's Philosophy: The Logos as Unifying Principle.* Oxford: Clarendon Press.

Perry, S. (1999). *Coleridge and the Uses of Division.* Oxford: Oxford University Press.

—. (2001). 'Coleridge and Wordsworth: Imagination, Accidence and Inevitability', in S. Perry and N. Trott (eds), *1800: The New Lyrical Ballads.* Basingstoke: Palgrave, pp. 169–95.

—. (2007a). 'Coleridge's English Afterlife', in E. Shaffer and E. Zuccato (eds), *The Reception of S. T. Coleridge in Europe.* London, New York: Continuum, pp. 14–26.

—. (ed.) (2007b). *Coleridge's Responses: Coleridge on Writings and Writers,* Vol. 1. London: Continuum.

Perry, S. and Trott, N. (eds) (2001). *1800: The NewLyrical Ballads.* Basingstoke: Palgrave.

Philp, M. (1986). *Godwin's Political Justice.* London: Duckworth.

Piper, H. W. (1962). *The Active Universe: Pantheism and the Concept of the Imagination in English Romantic Poets.* London: Athlone Press.

Pizer, J. (2007). 'The German Response to Kant's Essay on Perpetual Peace: Herder Contra the Romantics'. *Germanic Review,* 82, 343–68.

Pollin, B. R. (1970). 'John Thelwall's Marginalia in a Copy of Coleridge's *Biographia Literaria'. Bulletin of the New York Public Library,* 74, 81–94.

Poschmann, A. (1963). 'Die Ersten Kantianer in England: Friedrich August Nitsch aus Gumbinnen und Dr. Anton Willich aus Rößel', in E. Bahr (ed.), *Studien zur Geschichte des Preussenlands.* Marburg: N. G. Elwert, pp. 470–82.

Preminger, A. and Brogan, T. V. F. (eds). (1993). *The New Princeton Encyclopaedia of Poetry and Poetics.* Princeton: Princeton University Press.

Prochaska, A. (2012 accessed online). 'Richter, John (1769?–1830)', in Oxford University Press (ed.), *Oxford Dictionary of National Biography.* Oxford: Oxford University. Press. http://www.oxforddnb.com.

Procházka, M. (2007). 'A Spectre or an Unacknowledged Visionary? Coleridge in Czech Culture', in E. Shaffer and E. Zuccato (eds), *The Reception of S. T. Coleridge in Europe.* London, New York: Continuum, pp. 254–74.

Rawlinson, M. (2000). ' "Invasion!" Coleridge, the Defence of Britain and the Cultivation of the Public's Fear', in P. Shaw (ed.), *Romantic Wars.* Aldershot: Ashgate, pp. 110–37.

Reid, N. (1994). 'Coleridge and Schelling: The Missing Transcendental Deduction'. *Studies in Romanticism,* 33, 451–79.

Reinman, D. H. (ed.) (1972). *The Romantic Reviewed: Contemporary Reviews of British Romantic Writers,* 2 vols. London: Garland.

Reiss, H. S. (1956). 'Kant and the Right of Rebellion'. *Journal of the History of Ideas,* 17, 179–92.

Richards, I. A. (1962 [first published 1934]). *Coleridge on Imagination.* London, Routledge and Kegan Paul.

Rivers, I. (2000). *Reason, Grace and Sentiment: Shaftesbury to Hume,* Vol. 2. Cambridge: Cambridge University Press.

—. (2012 accessed online). 'Balguy, Thomas (1716–95)', in Oxford University Press (ed.), *Oxford Dictionary of National Biography.* Oxford: Oxford University Press. http://www. oxforddnb.com.

Rivers, I. and Wykes, D. L. (eds). (2008). *Joseph Priestley: Scientist, Philosopher and Theologian.* Oxford: Oxford University Press.

—. (eds). (2011). *Dissenting Praise: Religious Dissent and the Hymn in England and Wales.* Oxford: Oxford University Press.

Roberts, D. S. (2000). *Revisionary Gleam: De Quincey, Coleridge and the High Romantic Argument.* Liverpool: Liverpool University Press.

Robinson, D. N. (2007). 'The Scottish Enlightenment and the American Founding'. *The Monist,* 90, 170–81.

Roe, N. (1988). *Wordsworth and Coleridge: The Radical Years.* Oxford: Oxford University Press.

—. (1990). 'Coleridge and John Thelwall: The Road to Nether Stowey', in M. Lefebure and R. Gravil (eds), *The Coleridge Connection.* London: Macmillan, pp. 60–80.

—. (2002 [first published 1992]). *The Politics of Nature: William Wordsworth and Some Contemporaries.* Basingstoke: Macmillan.

Roper, D. (1978). *Reviewing before the Edinburgh 1788–1802.* London: Methuen.

Rosenthal, B. (1967). *Der Geniebegriff des Aufklärungszeitalters (Lessing und die Popularphilosophen).* Nendeln, Liechtenstein: Kraus Reprint.

Rothenberg, M. A. (1993). *Rethinking Blake's Textuality.* Columbia: Missouri University Press.

Röttgers, K. (1984). 'J. G. H. Feder Beitrag zur Verhinderungsgeschichte eines deutschen Empirismus'. *Kant-Studien,* 75, 420–40.

Ruffing, M. (1997). 'Kant-Bibliographie 1995'. *Kant-Studien,* 88, 473–511.

Russell, G. (2002). 'Spouters or Washerwomen: The Sociability of Romantic Lecturing', in G. Russell and C. Tuite (eds), *Romantic Sociability: Social Networks and Literary Culture in Britain, 1770–1840.* Cambridge: Cambridge University Press, pp. 123–41.

Russell, G. and Tuite, C. (2002). 'Introducing Romantic Sociability', in G. Russell and C. Tuite (eds), *Romantic Sociability: Social Networks and Literary Culture in Britain, 1770–1840.* Cambridge: Cambridge University Press, pp. 1–23.

Sassen, B. (2000). *Kant's Early Critics: The Empiricist Critique of the Theoretical Philosophy.* Cambridge: Cambridge University Press.

Schlapp, O. (1901). *Kants Lehre vom Genie und der Enstehung der "Kritik der Urteilskraft".* Göttingen: Vandenhoeck & Ruprecht.

Schmidt, J. (1985). *Geschichte des Geniegedankens in der deutschen Literatur, Philosophie und Politik, 1750–1945: von der Aufklärung bis zum Idealismus.* Heidelberg: Universitätverlag Winter.

Schneewind, J. B. (1992). 'Autonomy, Obligation, and Virtue: An Overview of Kant's Moral Philosophy', in P. Guyer (ed.), *The Cambridge Companion to Kant.* Cambridge: Cambridge University Press, pp. 309–41.

—. (1997). 'Introduction', in P. Heath and J. B. Schneewind (eds.), *Immanuel Kant. Lectures on Ethics.* Cambridge: Cambridge University Press, pp. xiii–xxvii.

Schneider, J. H. (2000). 'Nature', in M. Brown (ed.), *Romanticism,* Vol. 5. The Cambridge History of Literary Criticism, Cambridge: Cambridge University Press, pp. 92–115.

Schofield, R. E. (1963). *The Lunar Society of Birmingham: A Social History of Provincial Science and Industry in Eighteenth-Century England.* Oxford: Clarendon Press.

Scholz, H. (ed.) (1916). *Die Hauptschriften des Pantheismusstreit.* Berlin: Renther und Reichard.

Schulz, G. (1960).'Christian Garve und Immanuel Kant: Gelehrten-Tugenden im 18. Jahrhundert'. *Jahrbuch der Schlesischen Friedrich-Wilhelm Universität zu Breslau,* 5, 123–88.

Schulz, M. F. (1985). 'Samuel Taylor Coleridge', in F. Jordon (ed.), *English Romantic Poets: A Review of Research.* New York: Modern Language Association of America, pp. 427–47.

Schulze, A. (1958/59). 'Die Religiösen Gedanken in Kants "Zum Ewigen Frieden"'. *Kant-Studien*, 50, 500–4.

Scott, J. B. (ed.) (1918). *The Armed Neutralities of 1780 and 1800: A Collection of Official Documents Preceded by the Views of Representative Publicists*. London, Toronto, Melbourne, and Bombay: Oxford University Press.

Scrivener, M. (1978). 'Godwin's Philosophy: A Revaluation'. *Journal of the History of Ideas*, 39, 615–26.

—. (2001). *Seditious Allegories: John Thelwall & Jacobin Writing*. University Park: Pennsylvania State University.

Shaffer, E. (1970). 'Kant and Coleridge's Aids to Reflection'. *Journal of the History of Ideas*, 31, 199–218.

—. (1975). *'Kubla Khan' and the Fall of Jerusalem*. Cambridge: Cambridge University Press.

—. (2004). 'Coleridge and Kant's "Giant Hand"', in R. Görner (ed.), *Anglo-German Affinities and Antipathies*. Munich: Iudicium, pp. 39–56.

—. (2007a). 'Introduction', in E. Shaffer and E. Zuccato (eds), *The Reception of S. T. Coleridge in Europe*. London, New York: Continuum, pp. 1–13.

—. (2007b). 'Series Editor's Preface', in E. Shaffer and E. Zuccato (eds), *The Reception of S. T. Coleridge in Europe*. London, New York: Continuum, pp. vii–xi.

—. (2009). 'Coleridge's Dialogues with German Thought', in F. Burwick (ed.), *The Oxford Handbook of Samuel Taylor Coleridge*. Oxford: Oxford University Press, pp. 555–87.

—. (2010). 'Review: Coleridge and the Crisis of Reason, by Richard Berkeley'. *Coleridge Bulletin*, 35, 115–18.

Shell, S. M. (1997). 'Cannibals All: The Grave Wit of Kant's Perpetual Peace', in H. de Vries and S. Weber (eds), *Violence, Identity, and Self-Determination*. Stanford, California: Stanford University Press, pp. 150–61.

Sigmund, P. E. (2005). 'Introduction to an *Essay Concerning Human Understanding*', in P. E. Sigmund (ed.), *The Selected Political Writings of John Locke: Texts, Background Selections, Sources, Interpretations*. New York: Norton, pp. 182–4.

Silber, J. (1963). 'The Importance of the Highest Good in Kant's Ethics'. *Ethics*, 73, 179–95.

—. (1966). 'The Copernican Revolution in Ethics: The Good Re-Examined'. *Kant-Studien*, 51, 85–101.

Simpson, D. (1993). *Romanticism, Nationalism, and the Revolt against Theory*. Chicago: Chicago University Press.

—. (2009). *Wordsworth, Commodification and Social Concern*. Cambridge: Cambridge University Press.

Sisman, A. (2007). *Wordsworth and Coleridge: The Friendship*. London: Harper Perennial.

Snyder, A. D. (1928). 'Books Borrowed by Coleridge from the Library of the University of Göttingen, 1799'. *Modern Philology*, 25, 377–80.

Speck, W. A. (2006). *Robert Southey: Entire Man of Letters*. London: Yale University Press.

St Clair, W. (2004). *The Reading Nation in the Romantic Period*. Cambridge: Cambridge University Press.

Stafford, F. (2010). *Local Attachments: The Province of Poetry*. Oxford: Oxford University Press.

Stangeth, B. (2003). 'Kants Schädliche Schriften: Eine Einleitung', in B. Stangeth (ed.), *Die Religion innerhalb der Grenzen der bloßen Vernunft*. Hamburg: Felix Meiner Verlag, pp. IX–LXXIII.

Stansfield, D. A. (1984). *Thomas Beddoes M. D. 1760–1808: Chemist, Physician, Democrat*. Dordrecht: D. Riedel Publishing Company.

—. (1986). 'A Note on the Genesis of Coleridge's Thinking on War and Peace'. *The Wordsworth Circle*, 17, 130–4.

Stark, W. (1987). 'Neue Kant-Logiken', in R. Brandt and W. Stark (eds), *Kant-Forschungen: Neue Autographen und Dokumente zu Kants Leben, Schriften und Vorlesungen*. Kant-Forschungen, Hamburg: Felix Meiner pp. 123–64.

Stephen, L. (1910). *Studies of a Biographier*. London: Duckworth & Co.

Stockley, V. (1929). *German Literature as Known in England*. London: Routledge.

Stockoe, F. W. (1926). *German Influence in the English Romantic Period 1788–1818, with Special Reference to Scott, Coleridge, Shelley and Byron*. London: Cambridge University Press.

Stokes, C. (2011). *Coleridge, Language, and the Sublime: From Transcendance to Finitude*. Basingstoke: Palgrave Macmillian.

Sullivan, A. (1983a). *British Literary Magazines: The Augustan Age and the Age of Johnson, 1698–1788*, Vol. 1. London, Westport: Greenwood Press.

—. (1983b). *British Literary Magazines: The Romantic Ages, 1789–1836*, Vol. 2. London, Westport: Greenwood Press.

Sweet, W. (ed.) (2010). *Biographical Encyclopaedia of British Idealism*. London, New York: Continuum.

Taussig, G. (2002). *Coleridge and the Idea of Friendship*. Newark, Delaware: University of Delaware Press.

Taylor, A. (1986). *Coleridge's Defense of the Human*. Columbus, Ohio: Ohio University Press.

Tee, V.-Y. (2009). *Coleridge, Revision and Romanticism: After the Revolution, 1793–1818*. London, New York: Continuum.

Thompson, E. P. (1963). *The Making of the English Working Class*. London: Gollanzc.

—. (1969). 'Disenchantment or Default: A Lay Sermon', in C. C. O' Brien and D. Vanch (eds), *Power and Consciousness*. London: London University Press, pp. 149–81.

—. (1971). 'Bliss was it in that Dawn: The Matter of Coleridge's Revolutionary Youth and How It Became Obscured'. *Times Literary Supplement*. 6 August, 929.

Thompson, J. (1997). 'An Autumnal Blast, a Killing Frost: Coleridge's Poetic Conversation with John Thelwall'. *Studies in Romanticism, 36*, 427–56.

Thorslev, P. (1993). 'German Romantic Idealism', in S. Curran (ed.), *The Cambridge Companion to British Romanticism*. Cambridge: Cambridge University Press, pp. 74–94.

Tonelli, G. (1966). 'Die Anfänge von Kants Kritik der Kausalbeziehungen und Ihre Voraussetzungen im 18. Jahrhundert'. *Kant-Studien, 57*, 417–60.

Trott, N. (1990). 'The Coleridge Circle and the "Answer to Godwin" '. *Review of English Studies: A Quarterly Journal of English Literature and the English Language, 41*, 212–29.

Tyler, C. (2012 accessed online). 'British Idealists (Act. 1850s–1920s)', in Oxford University Press (ed.), *Oxford Dictionary of National Biography*. Oxford: Oxford University Press. http://www.oxforddnb.com.

Tyson, G. (1979). *Joseph Johnson: A Liberal Publisher*. Iowa City: Iowa University Press.

Uglow, J. (2002). *The Lunar Men: The Friends Who Made the Future, 1730–1810*. London: Faber and Faber.

Ulmer, W. A. (2006). 'The Alienation from the Elect in Coleridge's Unitarian Prophecies'. *Review of English Studies, 57*, 526–44.

Vardy, A. D. (2010). *Constructing Coleridge: The Posthumous Life of the Author*. Houndsmill, Basingstoke: Palgrave Macmillan.

Vickers, N. (1997). 'Coleridge, Thomas Beddoes, and Brunian Medicine'. *European Romantic Review, 8*, 47–94.

—. (2004). *Coleridge and the Doctors 1795–1806*. Oxford: Clarendon Press.

—. (2009). 'Coleridge's Marriage and Family', in F. Burwick (ed.), *The Oxford Handbook of Samuel Taylor Coleridge*. Oxford: Oxford University Press, pp. 68–106.

Vigus, J. (2007). 'Did Coleridge Read Plato by Anticipation'. *Coleridge Bulletin*, 29, 65–73.
—. (2009). *Platonic Coleridge*. London: Legenda.
—. (2010). 'Introduction', in J. Vigus (ed.), *Henry Crabb Robinson: Essays on Kant, Schelling, and German Aesthetics*. London: Modern Humanities Research Association, pp. 1–25.
—. (2012 [in press]). 'The Philosophy of Samuel Taylor Coleridge', in W. Mander (ed.), *The Oxford Handbook of British Philosophy in the Nineteenth Century*. Oxford: Oxford University Press.
Voigt, J. (1819). *Das Leben des Professors Christian Jacok Kraus aus Mittheilungen seiner Freunde und seinen Briefen*. Königsberg: Universität Buchhandlung.
Walker, E. C. (1997). 'Reading Proof, Aids to Reflection, and Phrenology'. *European Romantic Review*, 8, 323–40.
Walsh, W. H. (1976). 'Kant and Metaphysics'. *Kant-Studien*, 67, 372–84.
Warnock, M. (1986). 'Religious Imagination', in J. P. Machey (ed.), *Religious Imagination*. Edinburgh, pp. 142–57.
Watson, J. R. (2003). *Romanticism and War: A Study of British Romantic Period Writers and the Napoleonic Wars*. Houndsmill: Palgrave Macmillan.
Webb, R. K. (1996). 'The Emergence of Rational Dissent', in K. Haakensson (ed.), *Enlightenment and Religion*. Cambridge: Cambridge University Press, pp. 12–41.
Weber, C. A. (1935). *Bristols Bedeutung für die Englische Romantik und die Deutsch-Englischen Beziehungen*. Halle: Max Niemeyer Verlag.
Weinberg, F. M. (1983). 'The Idea of Soul in Descartes and Pascal'. *French Forum*, 8, 5–19.
Welch, C. (1985). 'Samuel Taylor Coleridge', in N. Smart (ed.), *Nineteenth Century Religious Thought in the West*, Vol. 2. Cambridge: Cambridge University Press, pp. 1–26.
Wellek, R. (1931). *Immanuel Kant in England 1793-1838*. Princeton: Princeton University Press.
—. (1981 [first published 1955]). *A History of Modern Criticism, 1750-1950: The Romantic Age*, Vol. 2. Cambridge: Cambridge University Press.
Wellek, R. and Warren, A. (1949). *Theory of Literature*. London: Jonathan Cape.
West, S. (2007). *Coleridge and Shelley: Textual Engagements*. Hampshire, Burlington: Ashgate.
Whalley, G. (1949). 'The Bristol Library Borrowings of Southey and Coleridge, 1793–98'. *The Library: The Transactions of the Bibliographical Society*, 4, 114–31.
—. (1972). 'England: Romantic – Romanticism', in H. Eichner (ed.), *'Romantic' and Its Cognates: The European History of a Word*. Toronto: Toronto University Press, pp. 157–262.
Wheeler, K. (1980). *Sources, Processes and Methods in Coleridge's Biographia Literaria*. Cambridge: Cambridge University Press.
— (1981). *The Creative Mind in Coleridge's Poetry*. London, Heinemann.
—. (1986). 'Coleridge's Theory of the Imagination: A Hegelian Solution to Kant?', in J. David (ed.), *The Interpretation of Belief: Coleridge, Schleichermacher, and Romanticism*. Basingstoke: Macmillan, pp. 1–40.
Whelan, T. (2008). *Politics, Religion, and Romance: The Letters of Benjamin Flower and Eliza Gloud Flower*. Aberystwyth: Llyfrgell Genedlaethol Cymru.
White, R. S. (2005). *Natural Rights the Birth of Romanticism in the 1790s*. Basingstoke: Palgrave Macmillan.
Willey, B. (1972). *Samuel Taylor Coleridge*. London: Chatto and Windus.

Williams, C. D. (2012 accessed online). 'Cogan, Thomas (1736–1818)', in Oxford University Press (ed.), *Oxford Dictionary of National Biography.* Oxford: Oxford University Press. http://www.oxforddnb.com.

Wilson, R. (2008). 'Coleridge's German "Absolutism" ', in J. Vigus and J. Wright (eds), *Coleridge's Afterlives.* Houndsmills, Basingstoke: Palgrave Macmillan, pp. 171–87.

Winkelmann, E. (1933). *Coleridge und die Kantische Philosophie: erste Einwirkungen des Deutschen Idealismus in England.* Leipzig: Mayer & Mueller.

Wise, T. J. (1922–36). *The Ashley Library: A Catalogue of Printed Books, Manuscripts and Autographed Letters Collected by T. J. Wise.* London: Printed for Private Circulation.

Wood, A. W. (1978). *Kant's Rational Theology.* Ithaca: Cornell University Press.

—. (1998). 'Kant's Project for Perpetual Peace', in P. Cheah and B. Robbins (eds), *Cosmopolitics: Thinking and Feeling Beyond the Nation.* Minneapolis, Minnesota: University of Minnesota Press, pp. 59–76.

Woodring, C. (1961). *Politics in the Poetry of Coleridge.* Madison: Wisconsin University Press.

Wordsworth, J. (1982). *William Wordsworth: The Borders of Vision.* Oxford: Clarendon Press.

—. (1995). 'Introduction', in J. Wordsworth (ed.), *William Wordsworth. The Prelude: The four texts (1798, 1799, 1805, 1850).* London: Penguin Books, pp. xxv–xlvii.

Worthen, J. (2010). *The Cambridge Introduction to Samuel Taylor Coleridge.* Cambridge: Cambridge University Press.

Woudenberg, M. v. (2003). 'Coleridge's Literary Studies in Göttingen in 1799: Reconsidering the Library Borrowings from the University of Göttingen'. *Coleridge Bulletin,* 21, 66–80.

Wright, L. S. H. (2010). *Samuel Taylor Coleridge and the Anglican Church.* Notre Dame, Indiana: University of Notre Dame Press.

Wu, D. (1993). 'Lyrical Ballads (1798): The Beddoes Copy'. *The Library: The Transactions of the Bibliographical Society,* 15, 332–5.

Wykes, D. L. (1996). 'The Contribution of the Dissenting Academy to the Emergence of Rational Dissent', in K. Haakensson (ed.), *Enlightenment and Religion.* Cambridge: Cambridge University Press, pp. 99–139.

Wylie, I. (1989). *Young Coleridge and the Philosophers of Nature.* Oxford: Clarendon Press.

Young, J. M. (1992). 'Translator's Introduction', in J. M. Young (ed.), *Immanuel Kant: Lectures on Logic.* Cambridge: Cambridge University Press, pp. xv–xxxii.

Zall, P. M. (1972). 'The Cool World of Samuel Taylor Coleridge: Joseph Johnson, or the Perils of Publishing'. *The Wordsworth Circle,* 3, 25–30.

Zammito, J. H. (1992). *The Genesis of Kant's Critique of Judgement.* Chicago, London: Chicago University Press.

Index

Lightning Source UK Ltd.
Milton Keynes UK
UKOW030102060513

210180UK00007B/23/P